Towns and Commerce in Viking-Age Scandinavia

The Viking Age, from c.750 to 1050 CE, was an era of major social change in Scandinavia. By the end of this period of sweeping transformation, Scandinavia, once a pagan periphery, had been firmly integrated into occidental Europe. Archaeological remains offer evidence of this process, which included and intertwined with Christianisation, state formation and the dawn of urbanisation in Scandinavia. In this volume, Sven Kalmring offers an interdisciplinary and geographically wide-ranging approach to understanding the emergence of towns and commerce in Viking-age Scandinavia and their eventual demise by the end of the period. Using the towns of Hedeby, Birka, Kaupang and Ribe as case studies, he also tracks the diverging characteristics of these urban communities against the background of traditional social structures in the Viking world. Instead of tracing the results of Viking-age urbanisation, or mapping that process by establishing economic networks, Kalmring focusses on the very reasons behind the emergence of towns and their eventual decline.

SVEN KALMRING is a scholar of Viking-age archaeology who specialises in maritime archaeology and early medieval urbanisation. A former researcher at the Centre for Baltic and Scandinavian Archaeology in Schleswig, Germany, and docent at Stockholm University, Sweden, he serves on the board of the Medieval Europe Research Community and is a delegate to the Viking Congress. Today, he works as a senior curator of Late Iron Age and Viking Age collections at the Swedish National Historical Museums.

Cover image: Hedeby, present-day northern Germany. Hoard from Hedeby harbour 1980, dated to *c.* 825 (inventory no. KSD 652.1–8; © Museum für Archäologie, Stiftung Schleswig-Holsteinische Landesmuseen Schloss Gottorf, Schleswig). The hoard comprised 598 blue and while monochrome beads, six KG 3 Hedeby coins and one Carolingian Christiana-Religio-denarius of Louis the Pious from 822/23–840.

Towns and Commerce in Viking-Age Scandinavia

SVEN KALMRING
Centre for Baltic and Scandinavian Archaeology, Schleswig

Shaftesbury Road, Cambridge CB2 8EA, United Kingdom

One Liberty Plaza, 20th Floor, New York, NY 10006, USA

477 Williamstown Road, Port Melbourne, VIC 3207, Australia

314–321, 3rd Floor, Plot 3, Splendor Forum, Jasola District Centre, New Delhi – 110025, India

103 Penang Road, #05–06/07, Visioncrest Commercial, Singapore 238467

Cambridge University Press is part of Cambridge University Press & Assessment, a department of the University of Cambridge.

We share the University's mission to contribute to society through the pursuit of education, learning and research at the highest international levels of excellence.

www.cambridge.org
Information on this title: www.cambridge.org/9781009298056

DOI: 10.1017/9781009298070

© Sven Kalmring 2024

This publication is in copyright. Subject to statutory exception and to the provisions of relevant collective licensing agreements, no reproduction of any part may take place without the written permission of Cambridge University Press & Assessment.

First published 2024

Printed in the United Kingdom by TJ Books Limited, Padstow Cornwall

A catalogue record for this publication is available from the British Library.

A Cataloging-in-Publication data record for this book is available from the Library of Congress.

ISBN 978-1-009-29805-6 Hardback
ISBN 978-1-009-29809-4 Paperback

Cambridge University Press & Assessment has no responsibility for the persistence or accuracy of URLs for external or third-party internet websites referred to in this publication and does not guarantee that any content on such websites is, or will remain, accurate or appropriate.

Publication of this book has been aided by a subvention from the Centre for Baltic and Scandinavian Archaeology (ZBSA), Stiftung Schleswig-Holsteinische Landesmuseen Schloss Gottorf, Schleswig, Germany.

Harbour, n. A place where ships taking shelter from storms are exposed to the fury of the customs.

Ambrose Bierce (1842–1914), The Devil's Dictionary.

Contents

List of Plates	*page* x
List of Figures	xi
List of Maps	xiv
Acknowledgements	xv
List of Abbreviations	xviii

1 Introduction   1

2 The Viking-Age Town: Context and Academic Debate   7
   2.1 'Seehandelsplätze', Proto-towns, *Emporia* and Viking-Age Towns   9
   2.2 Central Place and Network Theories   17

3 The Viking World   21
   3.1 A Rural Agrarian Society   21
   3.2 One Viking World or Local Groups?   25

4 Cult, Jurisdiction and Markets: *Things* and Regional Fairs at Traditional Centres of Power   29
   4.1 Traditional Centres of Power and Cult   29
   4.2 Assemblies and Fairs   34
   4.3 Palaces of an Itinerant Kingship?   43

5 Local Society and Viking-Age Towns   50
   5.1 Duality of Early Towns and Royal Estates   50
   5.2 Exterritorial Sites: Early Towns in No Man's Land   56

6	An Urbanisation Based on Harbours	62
	6.1 Landing Sites and Beach Markets	63
	6.2 Transformation from Landing Sites to Early Towns: Impetus of Royal Power	74
7	Jurisdiction and Taxes	84
	7.1 Defensive Fortifications and Customs Borders	84
	7.2 Shipping Duties and Port Administration in the Post-Roman World	90
	7.3 An Own Jurisdiction in Viking-Age Maritime Trading Towns?	95
	7.4 The King's Representative On-Site: Royal Administration	98
8	Free Trade within Narrow Boundaries	105
	8.1 An Active Scandinavian Trade Policy	105
	8.2 Protection of Foreign Merchants during Trading Voyages	110
	8.3 Cosmopolitan Trading Centres with Rigid Boundaries	114
9	Special Economic Zones of Their Time	123
	9.1 The Hinterland Question	123
	9.2 Special Economic Zones	130
	9.3 Desirables in 'Underdeveloped' Scandinavia	138
10	Development after the Inception Phase	147
	10.1 Impact of the 850s Crisis and a Shattered Balance of Power	148
	10.2 Birka's Fall and Hedeby's Transformation	154

11 Discussion: Hedeby's Abandonment and the Foundation
    of Slesvig   187

12 Summary and Conclusions   196

    References   212
    Index   266

    Color plates are to be found between pages 110 and 111.

Plates

I   Viking-age town of Hedeby, present-day northern Germany.
II   Viking-age town of Ribe, western Denmark.
III   Viking-age town of Kaupang, Oslofjord, Norway.
IV   Viking-age town of Birka, eastern middle Sweden.

Figures

1 What describes a Viking-age town? Conceptual denominations borrowed from contemporary written sources and/or within the academic debate *page* 16
2 Viking towns as nodal points with interrelated local markets in complex network theory, based on the distribution of various artefact types across southern Scandinavia 18
3 Klinta, Öland, Sweden. Contemporary three-dimensional representation of a longhouse depicted on top of the Klinta iron staff 22
4 'Decolonizing the Viking Age.' Different death rituals concerning treatment of the dead from various limited settlement districts in south-eastern Scandinavia 27
5 Gamla Uppsala, Uppland, Sweden. Monumental royal mound *Östhögen*, burial ground at vicarage, assembly mound *Tingshögen* and Vendel-period manorial complex 32
6 *De nundinis glacialibus (On Ice Fairs)*. Disting winter fair on the frozen river Fyriså near Uppsala. Copper engraving from Olaus Magnus' *Historia de gentibus septentrionalibus (Description of the Northern* Peoples) from 1555 40
7 Tissø, Zeeland, Denmark. Reconstruction of the manorial complex at Tissø-Fugledegård 47
8 Hovgården and Birka, Uppland, Sweden. In the foreground is the church of Adelsö with the monumental mounds as well as the royal manor Alsnö hus; in the background, across the strait, is the island of Björkö with the Viking-age town of Birka 51

9 Viking-age towns in no man's land: (a) language areas of medieval Schleswig-Holstein, Germany, reflecting the four main ethnicities: (1) Frisian, (2) Danish, (3) Saxon/German and (4) Slavonic; (b) Lake Mälaren with the medieval administrative provinces of Uppland (inclusive of coastal Roden), eastern central Sweden   58

10 Lynæs, Roskilde fjord, Denmark. Seasonal beach market at landing site   65

11 *Royal Frankish Annals (Annales Laurissenses)*. Entry for the year 808 on the destruction of Reric and the transferral of its merchants to 'Sliesthorp' (Hedeby)   81

12 Ribe, western Denmark. The shallow boundary ditch *bygrøft A* demarking the marketplace and indicating 'the peace of the town' within   86

13 Portus, Ostia Antica, Italy. Third-century relief with Roman harbour administration   91

14 Hedeby, present-day northern Germany. Miniature lead anchor as a 'customs stamp' for paid harbour fees?   97

15 Hovgården, Uppland, Sweden. Rune stone U 11 from Adelsö, mentioning the royal representative Tolir as King Håkan's bailiff   99

16 Berezan, Dnieper-Bug Estuary, Ukraine. Ukraine's sole rune stone, raised in the eleventh century by Grani for his deceased trading partner Karl on the island of Berezan   109

17 Viking-age long-distance merchant from the Baltic, with folding scales and precious furs as merchandise   112

18 Theodosian Land Walls, Istanbul, Turkey. Xylokerkos/Belgrade Gate within the late antique walls of Constantinople, leading to the Rus' commercial hostels at the St Mamas quarter   116

19	'Early Nordic coins' in Hedeby and its hinterland. Distribution of Hedeby coins KG 3 and KG 7–9 in Hedeby and its 'local numismatic region'	127
20	Hedeby, present-day northern Germany. The harbour and its jetties as the marketplace and arena for major economic activities	135
21	Hedeby, present-day northern Germany. Technical innovations pointing to an active knowledge transfer via Viking-age towns: (a) pulley of a treadle loom; (b) blade of a water wheel	144
22	*The Normans at Dorestad* (Dut. *De Noormannen voor Dorestad*). History wall chart by J. H. Isings Jr (1927)	149
23	Birka, Uppland, Sweden. Graves with sets of beads assigned to J. Callmer's (1977) bead periods	161
24	Danevirke and Hedeby, present-day northern Germany. Phases of development with new or reinforced sections highlighted in bold	170
25	Hedeby, present-day northern Germany. Bronze bell and wooden frame found in Hedeby harbour. A bell from a church inside an Ottonian-Christian *civitas*?	179
26	Slesvig, present-day northern Germany. Urnes-style rune stone DR6 from c.1050 found within the foundations of the Cathedral of St Peter at Slesvig	190

Maps

1 Places in Anglo-Saxon England and Continental Europe mentioned in the text. *page* xx
2 Places in present-day northern Germany, Denmark and Norway mentioned in the text. 210
3 Places in Denmark and Sweden mentioned in the text. 211

Acknowledgements

This volume is an attempt to synthesise my many years of scholarly work on Viking-age towns in a pan-European perspective, endeavouring to gather comprehensive insights from Scandinavia to the Caliphate and from Anglo-Saxon England to the Byzantine Empire. Although the specialist literature on the individual sites literally fills entire libraries on almost all aspects, as a student only a few comparable syntheses were available. Also, despite all the scholarly discussion on this particular topic, the central question of the causes and reasons for the emergence of this urban phenomenon in northern Europe precisely during the Viking Age remained largely unanswered. The book at hand is an attempt to fill that gap.

My personal interest in the topic began when I was primary-school age, when I visited the Viking-age town of Hedeby for the first time with my parents and my younger brother. At a time when there were no reconstructed 'Wikinger Häuser Haithabu' at the monument, I still had to walk the entire semicircle rampart, to the astonishment of my parents. Many years later, after a term abroad in Lund and as a doctoral student in pre- and proto-history at Kiel University, I found myself at the portal of Gottorf Castle, the seat of the Archaeological State Museum, studying the harbour of Hedeby. For the support of my academic teacher Michael Müller-Wille (†) and my doctoral supervisor Claus von Carnap-Bornheim, as well as for the trust placed in me by the excavator Kurt Schietzel when assigning the topic, I am very grateful.

Almost immediately after completing my doctorate, and thanks to my director Claus von Carnap-Bornheim, I was given the unique opportunity to join the newly founded Centre for Baltic and Scandinavian Archaeology (ZBSA). The doctoral thesis led not only to the successful application of the priority programme Harbours from the Roman Period to the Middle Ages (von Carnap-Bornheim and Kalmring 2011) of the German Research Foundation (DFG) but also to the insight that harbours can only be understood as part of a system: for every port of departure, there must also be a port of destination that offered ships comparable mooring possibilities. A Feodor Lynen fellowship for postdoctoral researchers of the Alexander von Humboldt Foundation (AvH) allowed me to stay for two years at the Archaeological Research Laboratory at Stockholm University; this highly rewarding endeavour would not have been possible without the support of my host Kerstin Lidén and my AvH-supervisor Per Ramqvist. On-site, thanks to the generous and unconditional support of my close colleague Lena Holmquist, I was able to study Hedeby's twin town Birka comparatively and in depth. Also, with the background of the insights from Hedeby and a systemic understanding of harbours, we eventually could jointly conduct a re-excavation in Birka's harbour. In the academic exchange, it was even possible to carry out a limited excavation on the hillfort 'Hochburg' of Hedeby with a Swedish excavation team. After initial reflections on the modalities of maritime long-distance trade conducted through the ports, which were some sort of early by-product of my doctoral thesis, this close scholarly exchange at the same time led to an increased interest in the phenomenon of Viking-age urbanisation as such and resulted in the organisation of the international conference 'New Aspects of Viking-Age Urbanism, c.750–1100' at the Swedish History Museum in Stockholm in 2013.

Even after returning to the Centre for Baltic and Scandinavian Archaeology in Schleswig, I remained a visiting researcher at Stockholm University. During my year as a lecturer at Aarhus University in 2016, I had the pleasure, among other things, of giving a joint seminar with Søren Sindbæk entitled 'Urbanisation and Networks', deepening the discussions on this topic and adding a Danish perspective. The subsequent heading of the excavation in the inhumation burial ground of Hedeby, carried out with German and Danish students, brought me back to my intellectual starting point once again. At the same time, I also had the privilege of continuing to accompany various training excavations of the Archaeological Research Laboratory in Birka. Thanks to the support of Kerstin Lidén and the benevolent reviews of Birgitta Hårdh and Anders Andrén, I became an associate professor at Stockholm University and, most recently, senior curator for the Late Iron Age and Viking Age collection at the National Historical Museums in Stockholm.

A great source of inspiration for me in writing this book was the work of Adriaan Verhulst (†) (2002) on *The Carolingian Economy* and Richard Hodges' (1982, 2012) *Dark Age Economics*. The latter I had the pleasure of meeting personally during a visit to Schleswig in 2022. Without the intensive exchange of ideas with my German, Scandinavian and British colleagues, the present work would hardly have been possible; naming all the contributors would go beyond the scope of this Acknowledgement. To name but a few, I would like to thank Volker Hilberg, Thorsten Lemm and Joachim Schultze in Schleswig; Lena Holmquist, Charlotte Hedenstierna-Jonson, Torun Zachrisson and Johan Runer in Stockholm; Ny Björn Gustafsson in Visby; Søren Sindbæk and Sarah Croix in Aarhus; Morten Søvsø in Ribe; Unn Pedersen in Oslo; and Steve Ashby in York. The discussions I had with my colleagues both at the 'Viking Congress' conferences and in the context of my work in the Medieval Europe Research Community (MERC) were equally and immensely stimulating.

During the final phase of work on this book, I have received great support and encouragement from Berit Eriksen (the scientific director) and from Doris Rohwäder (the administrative director) at the Centre for Baltic and Scandinavian Archaeology in Schleswig. I would also like to thank the two anonymous reviewers for their diligent evaluation and always justified comments, which have led to important additions to the book and rounded it off for the sake of my readers. For the language revision of the manuscript, I am indebted to Fredrik Sundman. Lastly, I would like to express my gratitude to Cambridge University Press for the realisation of this publication project, especially to my editor Beatrice Rehl, my content manager Nicola Maclean and her entire production team, and my diligent copy-editor Linsey Hague. Thank you very much indeed.

Finally, the last and most important thanks go to my wife Antje Wendt, who not only has endured a long-lasting academic commuter life with me but has always supported me in my work as a researcher over the past years and encouraged me to explore new avenues. Thank you for always believing in me.

Abbreviations

Dan.	Danish
Dut.	Dutch
Fre.	French
Ger.	German
Nrw.	Norwegian
OEng.	Old English
OI	Old Irish
OldWN	Old West Norse
ON	Old Norse
OSwd.	Old Swedish
Swd.	Swedish

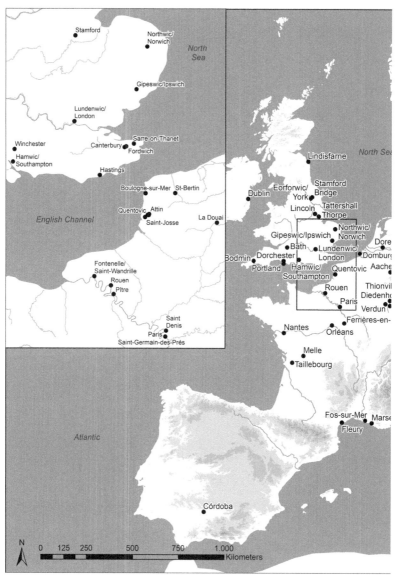

MAP 1 Places in Anglo-Saxon England and Continental Europe mentioned in the text. (S. Kalmring).

MAP 1 (cont.)

1 Introduction

The Viking Age – traditionally framed by the historic raid on the monastery at Lindisfarne in Northumbria in 793 and the battles of Stamford Bridge and Hastings in 1066, and nowadays archaeologically set to c.750–1050 – was an era of major societal changes in Scandinavia that has fascinated generations of scholars and laypeople. This sweepingly transformative period led to the integration of this formerly pagan periphery of the European North into occidental Europe, as these societies became unified Christian kingdoms. One of the most central fields to Viking-age archaeology – alongside research problems relating to the Christianisation of Scandinavia and the intertwined processes of state formation, or more specifically the development 'From Tribe to State' (Mortensen & Rasmussen 1991) – is the initial and unprecedented dawn of urbanisation in Scandinavia, which was distinctly different from the archetypes of ancient towns of the former Roman Empire. As novel centres of trade and crafts, these emerging Viking-age towns were inseparably linked to the spheres of economy, maritime connectivity, and patronage. However, despite some significant scholarly attention in Scandinavia itself, only four such sites have been recognised as proper Viking-age towns, namely Hedeby in northern Germany, Ribe in Denmark, Kaupang in Norway and Birka in Sweden (see Plates I–IV). Since the end of the nineteenth century, these four sites, however, have attracted continuous scholarly attention, due to their extraordinary archaeological records. It is noteworthy that two of them, Birka (in 1993) and Hedeby (in 2018), have become UNESCO World Heritage Sites. Nowadays, academic publications dealing with these urban sites – describing artefact groups and building features from various excavations – fill metres of shelf space, which makes the subject matter increasingly hard to grasp. Consequently, there are but a few comprehensive publications on the Viking-age urban phenomenon (e.g. Hodges 1982; Clarke & Ambrosiani 1991).

In the past, and indeed for decades, significant effort has gone into defining the nature of the Viking-age urban phenomenon as observed by archaeologists, since it did not quite fit any historical definition corresponding to the origins of medieval towns. Basically, the question was *what* constituted the Viking-age towns and how to describe them appropriately, as well as the need to differentiate them from the historically defined 'proper' European medieval towns. The growing understanding of Viking-age towns, as a chronologically and/or spatially discontinuous phenomenon, underlined the importance of this discussion even further. It is in the nature of things that this approach remained mostly descriptive. Defining what made these towns distinct from others depended on the ability to recognise these first Scandinavian expressions of urbanism as towns in their own right, typical of their era and setting (cf. Reynolds 1992). The resolution of this long debate – leading to the recognition of the phenomenon – can be linked to a growing self-esteem in archaeology as a discipline. Another important part of archaeological research has always been distribution maps for individual artefact groups, which can visualise how products and goods spread, thus establishing patterns of artefact provenance and ultimately providing clues for trade networks and communication. More recently, the digital revolution and models borrowed from network theory have made it easier to identify multiple artefact groups that have been found in more than one place, thus expressing previously hard to establish affiliations as scale-free networks in the shape of nodal points (or hubs) and ties (or links) within trading arenas such as the Baltic Sea. While this approach certainly allows for a deeper understanding of the interconnectivity of Viking-age towns as 'Network Cities' (Hohenberg & Lees 1996) – or rather network towns – that is, as the primary hubs in a web of hierarchically interrelated sites (serving as stepping stones for long-distance trade), it also clearly addresses the problem of *how* these Viking-age centres for trade and craft operated economically. Another recent and important trend in Viking-age urban studies – made possible by an ever-growing body of data – is to abandon the presumptions that these Viking-age towns were stable and almost 'monolithic' entities, whose 'town maps' needed to be explored and subsequently described meticulously. By recognising the chronological depth of their lifespans – up to two and a half centuries – the focus has instead shifted to urban dynamics and to the study of their presumably changing nature in specific, highly resolved time slices.

Only a holistic approach to an enormous, ever-increasing body of data – diligently gathered since the beginnings of archaeology as a scientific discipline – would allow for a deeper understanding of the research subject. Such an approach would involve not only Viking-age towns themselves but the entire Viking world – that is, the Scandinavian homelands and the so-called Viking diaspora (the results of Scandinavian expansion through *landnám* (ON; 'settlement of unoccupied land') and conquest), as well as contemporary conditions in early medieval Europe from Anglo-Saxon England through the Carolingian Empire and on to Byzantium. However, it would enable us to finally approach the inner core of the research problem, which almost resembles the concentric circles of some reversed golden circle model: instead of trying to define the *result* of Viking-age urbanisation (*the what*) as in previous efforts, or else by mapping the *process* of interconnectivity and economic networks of 'network towns' (*the how*) as elaborate follow-up studies, today we might – almost without recognising it – have reached the point to finally address the central question of *why* Viking-age towns emerged. In fact, instead of a mere 'trade and production' as some commonplace answer, we must truly start to ask about the very *purpose* of an unprecedented and suddenly emerging urbanisation in the Scandinavian periphery during the transformation period we call the Viking Age. Through *Towns and Commerce in Viking-Age Scandinavia*, the author attempts such an approach to this core question of *why* Viking-age towns and hence the very *purpose* of Viking-age urbanisation.

Naturally, the focus of any study on Viking-age towns in the Scandinavian heartlands must revolve around Hedeby, Ribe, Kaupang and Birka. Out of these four, Hedeby, on the border between Scandinavia and Continental Europe, by far developed into the largest urban entity. Protected by semi-circular ramparts, Hedeby's settlement area covered 27 ha, while the second largest, Birka, only covered 13 ha. Both sites are briefly mentioned in written sources, mainly in Rimbert's *Life of Ansgar* and Adam of Bremen's *History of the Archbishops of Hamburg-Bremen*. While Hedeby, Kaupang and Birka do not display any noteworthy signs of settlement after the Viking Age, Ribe is still an existing picturesque town. Later activity, or the lack thereof, is visible in how well artefacts have survived and in how accessible the sites are for archaeological investigations. At Ribe, for a long time only the pre- and early Viking-age 'marketplace' from c.700–850 was archaeologically known, yet not 'Ansgar's Ribe' from the middle Viking Age as suggested by the written sources. Meanwhile, recent excavations have managed to fill this knowledge gap. However, by that time Ribe's influence seems to have been surpassed by Hedeby. Kaupang, which is rarely mentioned in the written sources at all, has been exposed to severe bioturbation, heavily affecting the site's preservation conditions. In Birka, the preservation of organic materials has suffered due to dramatic post-Viking-age regression and isostatic rebound of about 5 metres. However, here it is particularly about 1,100 burials, excavated in the late nineteenth century – out of around 3,000 interments altogether on the whole island of Björkö – that contribute to its fame in the scientific community. Modern excavations in the fortified settlement area only started in the 1990s. In Hedeby, in contrast to Birka, a gentle marine transgression of the water level of some 0.8 metres ensured superb preservation conditions for waterlogged wood, allowing for archaeological excavations where some 30 centimetres of wooden walls were still preserved. Finally, while both Birka and Kaupang ceased to exist in the third quarter of the tenth century, Hedeby seems to have persisted until 1066. Even though the processes of transformation are still under debate, in the late Viking Age Birka seems to have been replaced by Sigtuna and Hedeby eventually by medieval Slesvig. Lastly, modern history has also played its part in the understanding of these sites: as a result of the Second Schleswig War in 1864, the duchy of Slesvig – previously a Danish fiefdom – was initially completely integrated into Prussia and eventually split so that its southern part, including Hedeby, became German. Prior to the Second World War, Hedeby researchers had willingly been an important part of the SS *Ahnenerbe* ('ancestral heritage') research. For decades after the war, this meant that research that had dealt with Hedeby, as well as the scholars who were involved with it, was ignored, in both Scandinavian and Anglo-Saxon contexts. It was not until 2005 that Hedeby gained official recognition and representation at the Viking Congress, initially as part of the Danish delegation and later as representatives of the federal state of Schleswig-Holstein. This study will take into account these very different points of departure, and although all four Viking-age towns will be examined, the emphasis will be placed on Hedeby and Birka. To understand the otherness of Viking-age towns, and eventually explain their purpose, as well as the reasons for their sudden emergence in the North, it would be too short-sighted to focus solely on the early urban centres themselves in order to capture the very core of this discontinuous phenomenon that preceded later expressions of high medieval towns. Instead, it needs nothing less than a truly holistic approach. Ideally, this would involve a thorough examination of the societal framework of the circumjacent traditional rural world, mirrored in a supra-regional comparison with Anglo-Saxon England, Continental Europe and Byzantium. It would also require an inclusion of the sparse but no less important information from chronicles and legal texts describing either the conditions in Scandinavia itself or procedures from elsewhere, manifesting similar frameworks that, due to intensified contacts, might have served as models for the Scandinavian conditions. Although this may sound like a vast research undertaking, it is indeed achievable. Actually, most of the pieces required for solving this scientific jigsaw puzzle have been at least partly known and debated for quite some time. With this revision, it is anticipated that their renewed composition will create a comprehensive picture of the earliest stage of urbanisation in Northern Europe. The suggested implementation of the concept of 'special economic zones' to this debate (Kalmring 2016a) may contribute to a more profound understanding of the societal value of these very distinct sites and ultimately answer the pivotal question why and for what purpose did Viking-age towns emerge at this specific point in time.

2 The Viking-Age Town
Context and Academic Debate

One of the primary proto-urban centres of the early medieval world in Northern Europe was without a doubt Hedeby. Hedeby was situated on the border between Scandinavia and Continental Europe, connecting the North Sea with the Baltic Sea by a portage. Its success as a trading hub is inseparably connected to the destruction of the *emporium* Reric – situated in an area controlled by the West Slavic Obotrites – by the Danish king Godfred in 808 (Tummuscheit 2003). In order to control and tax the ongoing trade, Reric's merchants were relocated to Hedeby. However, while in the contemporary historical sources Reric was addressed as an *emporium*, Hedeby was rather referred to as a *portus* (Kalmring 2010a: 42–7). Hedeby's continental denomination *Sliaswīk*, though, includes the element -wic, derived from the Latin *vicus* (Laur 1992: 575). It is not until the report of its destruction in 1066 (Adam of Bremen book 3, chap. 50, scholium 81) and in later sources (cf. Helmold of Bosau, c.1167) that Hedeby is referred to as a *civitas*. Hedeby's counterpart Birka was situated on Björkö in Lake Mälaren, a small island situated not only in the border area between Uppland and Södermanland but also at the southern point of the borders between the provinces (OSwd. *Hundari*; cf. OEng. *Hundred*) Attundaland, Tiundaland and Fjärdhundraland of Uppland. In terms of transport geography, it was favourably situated along the waterway *Fyrisleden* (Ambrosiani 1957), leading from the Baltic Sea via Södertälje and Birka to Gamla Uppsala and Vendel. Birka is referred to as both a *portus* and a *vicus* in contemporary written sources but also as a *civitas*, an *urbs* and even an *oppidum* (Mohr 2005: 98–101; for discussion, see Kalmring 2014/15: 283). The descriptions of both of the sites characterised by these terms are indeed quite similar: Hedeby is described as a Danish port where 'merchants from all parts [of the world] congregated' and the attendance of Frisians and Saxons from Dorestad, Hamburg and Bremen guaranteed that 'an abundance of goods converged there' (Rimbert chap. 24).[1] According to Rimbert (chap. 20), Birka was also frequented by Frisians, complementing Adam of Bremen's (book 1, chap. 60) description of visits by Danes, Norwegians, Slavs, Sambians and 'Scythians' (see Chapter 8, Note 2). Rimbert (chap. 19) also stated that it 'contained many rich merchants and a large amount of goods and money'. What constituted these two almost similarly ascribed Viking-age towns, and what were their roles in the vast communication and trade network sometimes described as the 'Northern Arc' (McCormick 2001: 562–4, 606–12, map 20.4), which stretched from Western Europe to Central Asia? What made it possible for these towns to be able to rise above their regional settings and attract foreign merchants from afar, resulting in abundance and significant wealth? What was the spark that led to the first urban entities emerging so far beyond the borders of the Roman world? Why does the late Iron Age in Scandinavia witness the emergence of Viking-age towns at this specific point in time?

Both sites, Hedeby and Birka, possessed comparable geographically accessible and advantageous locations near borders – that is, where it was easy for people and goods to converge – making them attractive sites for visiting merchants and resulting in considerable economic prosperity. As described in the previous paragraph, there were even similarities in the way they were denoted in contemporary written sources. But can the latter provide further insights into the closer nature of these sites? The labels used in the continental sources for describing such trade sites have been the subject of considerable academic discussion, closely linked to the vast research field that deals with 'early stages of the European town' and urbanisation in Central and Northern Europe in general. Apart from perhaps the Scandinavian Christianisation process, there is hardly any other field of early medieval archaeology and Viking-age studies that has been debated as intensely and with so much controversy. Hence, it is

[1] ... *et hac occasione facultas totius boni inibi exuberaret.* The English translation by Robinson is misleading here.

no coincidence that there is still no generally accepted and straightforward interpretation. This chapter offers a general orientation of the bewildering discussion about the terminology and associated concepts that have been put forward in order to capture – in distinction to the definitions formulated by historians – the specific nature of this Viking-age urbanisation on the eve of the classical medieval town: on the one hand, through the initial attempt to find a suitable definition along with a corresponding conceptual denomination (*the what*; the focus on the result) and, on the other hand, through the application of central place and network theories that focus on the interconnectivity of Viking-age towns as ports for maritime trade and urban production (*the how?*; the focus on the process). By describing and defining these theoretical processes and concepts, as well as their association to a number of specific features of Viking urbanisation, urbanism and urbanity,[2] as a point of departure this compilation at the same time makes it possible for readers to identify the most prominent features of the Viking-age town.

2.1 'SEEHANDELSPLÄTZE', PROTO-TOWNS, EMPORIA AND VIKING-AGE TOWNS

The concept of *Seehandelsplätze* ('maritime trading places') was developed by Jankuhn (1958) as a way of recognising maritime trading sites along the coasts of the North and Baltic Seas as a separate group and different from the early medieval *vici*, which occurred inland. He characterised the *Seehandelsplätze* through their connection to maritime trade and their roles in long-distance trade networks, as well as by their appearance in contemporary written sources and their abandonment during the tenth century, when most of them were replaced by new towns (cf. Steuer 2005). Following the ideas of Polanyi (1963), these types of sites are also subsumed under what is today the somewhat outdated term 'ports of trade', which once more stresses their

---

[2] For a discussion of the interrelated concepts of urbanisation (process), urbanism (urban lifestyle) and urbanity (urban practices), see Kjellberg (2021: 36–8, 60–1, 252–3 figs. 2.11, 12.1).

maritime component. His concept describes trading sites that already had some sort of administrative organisation of trade by an authority in societies that had not yet developed markets. Moreover, these sites were usually located on borders between different political and economic entities, where they could exist without belonging directly to a specific territory. Thus they were able to work as gateways in between various political or economic forms of organisation as well as hubs for the exchange of goods between their respective hinterlands and those of foreign traders (cf. Steuer 1999: 567-74 fig. 78; Steuer 2003).

In her influential historical study on *Die europäische Stadt des Mittelalters* (*The European Town of the Middle Ages*), Ennen (1972) suggested an application of a flexible *Kriterienbündel* ('bundle of criteria') instead of defining one single, and thus quite inflexible, criterion for a town. Without defining exactly which criteria would be indispensable, or how many verifiable criteria were needed for defining a town, she instead addressed the appearance, inner structure and function of medieval towns (Ennen 1972: 11-12 and references therein). In archaeology, this pragmatic approach has later been applied by Biddle (1976: 100) for discussing the various stages of urban development in Anglo-Saxon towns, emphasising aspects of defence, street planning, markets, mints, legislative autonomy, their role as central places, the presence of relatively large and dense populations, diversified economies, 'urban' plots and houses, social differentiation, complex religious organisation and, finally, their role as judicial centres. These concepts were also discussed at the international conference 'Vor- und Frühformen der europäischen Stadt im Mittelalter' ('Proto- and Early Stages of the Medieval European Town') in 1972 at Göttingen, where some of the aims were to clarify conceptual problems, finding a common definition for medieval towns that were subject to research and developing a terminology for earlier sites where such definitions were not yet appropriate (Jankuhn et al. 1973: 8-9). In this context, G. Dilcher (1973) elaborated on the historical aspects of judicial matters in high medieval towns, particularly through four main elements: municipal peace, municipal freedom, town law and civic constitution. Based on these judicial indicators, he concluded that there was no obvious constitutional distinction between the town and its inhabitants and the surrounding countryside in the early towns of the ninth through eleventh centuries (Dilcher 1973: 24–7). In the same volume, Schlesinger (1973: 262) introduced the terms *Vorform* ('proto stage') and *Frühform* ('early stage') of towns. However, he also clarified that such stages should not be understood in any evolutionary sense and were not essential for a town to become 'fully developed' later in the late or High Middle Ages. At the same time, even abandoned urban proto- or early-stage settlements should be considered towns. Despite the pluralistic theoretical approach seen in the Swedish *medeltidsstaden* project ('The Medieval Town' project), its inability to break free of the historical definitions is obvious. This is exemplified by Andersson's (1979) contribution, which suggested that the nature and location of a town are defined either by its function within a spatial network, the topography of the settlement's internal layout or its specific judicial and administrative structure, that is, its town privileges, municipal law, town council, mayor and coat of arms. Depending on the specific emphasis of the approach, his definition would allow for testing whether a site was a 'central site', a 'population centre' or indeed 'a town *in a formal sense*' (Andersson 1979: 6–7; my emphasis).

The term most frequently used for this type of site is *emporium*, initially defined by Hodges (1982: 50–2; cf. Hodges 2000: 76–92; Hodges 2006: 63–71), who distinguished between three types of 'gateway communities' and was the first to classify phases of their development processes. A common feature of these gateway communities is their location on or near territorial borders and coasts. Type-A emporia constitute the earliest category and refer to fairs, used for short periods or only seasonally. The 'classical' type-B emporia may have evolved from type-A emporia and these sites emerge from 725 onwards. They were deeply involved in long-distance trade, featured centralised planning in terms of streets and dwellings and had mercantile communities of foreign traders as well as native crafters. In the cases where type-B emporia were not abandoned due to declining trade, such trading places could develop into type-C emporia, where their roles became more associated with the regional economies. Hodges characterises them by their administrative functions, their fortifications and their partially commercialised level of production. Since its introduction, this classification has certainly been challenged (cf. Scull 2002: 315; Loveluck & Tys 2006: 153) – particularly the evolutionary succession from seasonal type-A to permanent type-B emporia – but with minor revisions this classification as an 'instrument for explaining the rise and fall of the emporia, as well as their differences' (Hodges 2012: 99) is still valid and a very useful tool (Hodges 2012: 97–9; cf. Hodges 2015: 276–7). On a more general level, contemporary publications (Verhaeghe 2005: 260–1; cf. Hodges 2012: 94) rather try to avoid the documented yet ambiguous Latin terms found in written contemporary sources, as they

> are not used consistently by present scholars. Furthermore, their application tends to 'create' specific categories of towns; these then become the focus of attempts to characterise *emporia, civitates, portus* or *wiks* as specific and different types of urban settlement. However, this modern typology of town-types was not necessarily the same as early medieval perceptions of towns, and the differences between the many types of settlements with these urban features or functions are not clear-cut in the contemporary evidence.
> (Verhaeghe 2005: 260–1)

Unfortunately, despite this assessment, occasionally there are still some elaborate scientific attempts to work with this body of historically documented terms (cf. Kleingärtner 2014: 177–91, tab. 10, fig. 30; Malbos 2017: 11–16).

In 1994, Johan Callmer suggested that too much of the discussion dealing with the early urbanisation in Northern Europe was still left to historians and that – based on the constantly growing body of archaeological source material – archaeologists should try to formulate arguments and models of their own. In a comparison from around the Baltic Sea, he was able to develop an elaborate model for the different phases of 'trading sites' and 'early urban sites'. Callmer started off with the emergence of a 'non-permanent trading-site phase', which developed through a North Sea impetus (700–50), after an indistinct break with late Roman Iron Age/Migration period conditions. It was followed by a 'consolidating phase', which led to an increase in size and a growing number of permanent or semi-permanent sites (750–800). This resulted in a 'heyday phase' for early urbanisation, when a hierarchy between sites was developed, as well as closer control and standardisation of the craft production (800–50). Callmer then envisaged impending collapse when second-level trading sites lost their importance or were abandoned due to 'political instability' (850–900), which in turn led to an engagement of local elites at the remaining major sites and a reorganisation of trade in terms of strong regulation and control (900–50). Nonetheless, most of this old system seems to have collapsed (950–1000), leading to a 'complete breakdown in specialised production' (Callmer 1994: 72), which is recognisable in considerable parts of the Baltic Sea area. At the very end of the tenth century, the system was being replaced by royally founded towns based on Western European models. Callmer chose to end his reflections with a phase of continued reorganisation and separate development that occurred on the southern Baltic Sea coast (1000–50), which he describes as 'a different branch of European urbanisation' (Callmer 1994: 80), and led to denser populations and the introduction of brick buildings (1050–1100).

Näsman's (2000) contribution to the debate is not so much in a clear terminology – he applies 'central places of rural character' in opposition to 'central places/trading sites' and 'proto-towns or early towns' (Näsman 2000: 42) as well as 'new economic centres, the emporia' (Näsman 2000: 62) – but rather in his discussion, which deals with the premises for the initial urbanisation. The point of origin for his reflections is the end of the Saxon wars, which led to the first direct border between the Carolingian and Danish realms and to a 'rapidly growing political and economic impact' (Näsman 2000: 37) of the Carolingians and Ottonians on southern Scandinavia. While he alluded to the increasing number of central places and landing sites emerging in the fifth century as 'non-urban centres' (Näsman 2000: 53), he also suggested that the first proto-towns, established in the eighth century, were shaped after Western European prototypes (e.g. Quentovic, Dorestad or Hamwic/Southampton). In addition, he differentiated between proto-towns developing into early towns (Ribe, Hedeby) and coastal markets attached to manors or central places, which were rooted in the Migration/Merovingian period (i.e. Åhus with Vä). According to Näsman (2000: 64-8), the early towns were developed to be both royal strongholds and gateways to the advanced monetary economies of Western Europe, while the lingering central place system would have remained deeply rooted in non-monetary barter markets. Näsman also suggested that the establishment of Ribe and Hedeby in the south-western parts of Denmark resulted in the first urbanised economy in the realm, subsequently turning the region into the main province of Viking-age Denmark. He argued that the kings actively supported these towns as alternative royal power bases in order to finance military and political expenses. However, it was not until the tenth century, through the conversion to Christianity and a more direct royal rule, that a new phase of urbanisation took place.

In his book *Towns and Trade in the Age of Charlemagne*, Hodges (2000) introduced to this debate the term 'non-places', coined by the French anthropologist Marc Augé (1995). Augé argued that 'places' were 'relational, historical and concerned with identity', while 'non-places' did not qualify for such anthropological definitions but were rather products of 'supermodernity', which had no relationship to earlier places (Augé 1995: 77-8). To Hodges, the 'Dark Age emporia' of the post-classical period, which predated the pre-capitalist marketplaces of the later Middle Ages, represented the 'embryonic state' of a developing European post-classical economy. They differed from 'places' as central places (see Section 2.2) that had well-established cosmological roots, while the novel *emporia* instead depended on their links to maritime commerce, which introduced new economic practices, and could only develop in marginal locations outside the bounds of the traditional society. Moreover – and despite their large populations and major public installations, such as harbour facilities – they lacked ritual components and monumental architecture and were hence unable to impart any sense of 'the sacred or history and memory' (cf. Kalmring 2020a). Consequently, as such 'non-places' these *emporia* barely appear in the contemporary historical sources at all (Hodges 2000: 69–71; Hodges 2012: 93–4, 110). Bearing this in mind, and with reference to a discussion article by Theuws (2004: 134, 137), Hodges (2012: 93–5, 115) introduced yet another term, the so called mushroom towns, which refers to the distinctly transitory nature of *emporia* as 'non-places'.[3] To him, they were 'Like mushrooms, these experiments in urbanism grew quickly, some faltered, some were re-configured, and being without monuments, most then vanished or were transformed. In vanishing, most entered "history"' (Hodges 2012: 115).

With reference to the works of Reynolds (1977, 1987, 1992), current research attempts to break away from this bewildering discussion on terminology (Figure 1) and instead tends to refer to these early medieval urban settlements simply as 'towns of their time' or as 'Viking-age towns' (Clarke & Ambrosiani 1991: 3–4; Verhulst 2002: 91; Verhaeghe 2005: 261; Skre 2007: 45–6). In the particular context of the study, however, it is most remarkable that the latter definition becomes quite restrictive when applied. D. Skre (2007: 453–5 fig. 1.4), for instance, argued that:

---

[3] While the term 'mushroom towns' is not used in the quoted paper by Theuws (2004), it had already been used two decades earlier by Hodges himself (Hodges & Whitehouse 1983: 164): 'First of all we have to note the absence of deep roots in the case of these Merovingian mushroom towns. They do not seem solidly anchored to the soil. These *emporia* constituted alien enclaves within the Carolingian world rather than organically belonging to it.' Theuws, however, seems to have picked up on the expression elsewhere (cf. Theuws 2007: 161).

FIGURE 1 What describes a Viking-age town? Conceptual denominations borrowed from contemporary written sources and/or within the academic debate (S. Kalmring).

there are only a few sites in Scandinavia – Hedeby, Birka, Ribe and Kaupang – that show a significant connection with long-distance trade systems before the 11th century. This connection is represented by their large quantities of goods imported from outside Scandinavia. Furthermore, the quantity of balances, weights and coins, and evidence of the use of silver as a currency, is much higher at these four sites than at smaller sites. Similarly, these four sites have a broad range of craftwork that made use of imported raw materials, mainly metal casting and glass-bead production. (Skre 2007: 453)

Later, he concluded: 'With what is known now about the specialised sites for trade and craft production in Scandinavia at the beginning of the Viking Period therefore, only Ribe, Birka, Hedeby and Kaupang can be classified as towns' (Skre 2007: 455).

2.2 CENTRAL PLACE AND NETWORK THEORIES

Another approach to the problem is borrowed from human geography and deals with the geographical concept of a town through a spatial/functional perspective. Its use of the term 'central places' is rooted in the old model of central place theory developed by the German geographer Walter Christaller (1933; cf. Denecke 1973; Schenk 2010), which is identifiable through its characteristic Thiessen polygons. Less sophisticated attempts to reconstruct the catchment areas of major Viking-age towns are based on site-catchment analysis (Randsborg 1980: 77 fig. 20). However, 'central places' or 'central place areas' are settlement agglomerations influenced by many factors, such as power and protection, resources and craft and trade and cult, that are contained within hierarchically structured spaces. The concept of 'central places' is primarily applied to sites dating from the Roman Iron Age to the Migration period (e.g. Fabech 1999; Larsson & Hårdh 2002; Ludowici et al. 2010) that are often characterised by a remarkable chronological continuity. In turn, these 'central places' impact surrounding settlements that have fewer functions and are of lesser – supra-regional, regional or local – significance. However, if all functional criteria are fulfilled, Steuer (2007: 882) argued that it may be valid to recognise 'central places' as correlating to 'early towns', while Søvsø (2020: 16) suggested that it would be more appropriate to compare them to later manorial or estate centres rather than towns.

On the basis of a slowly but constantly increasing number of previously unknown trading sites around the Baltic Sea, Sindbæk (2007a, 2007b) has tried to discern between local markets and trading places of an urban character engaged in long-distance trade by applying complex network theory. Relating to Hohenberg and Lees' (1996: 165) network urbanism as a point of origin, he recognises trading places as traffic junctions within a network. Through quantitative analyses of the amount of imported goods and crafts in relation to the size of miscellaneous excavations, he argued that with Ribe, Kaupang, Birka, Åhus, Truso, Reric and Hedeby only a few sites, or 'nodal points', were primarily and predominantly involved in long-distance trade (Sindbæk 2007a). In such a small-world trading network with a scale-free architecture, the few nodal points possessed a multitude of external connections to dependent local markets along the major sea routes. The local markets, in turn, were closely connected to the hubs but had only a few connections themselves (Figure 2). Sindbæk (2007b) consequently argued that this dependency on a few 'nodal points', or indispensable hubs, would have made the entire long-distance network very fragile in times of crisis or when under threat.

Sindbæk's initial ideas underwent further development and were used to investigate 'maritime network urbanism' in the 'Entrepôt' project, which analysed global maritime exchange patterns

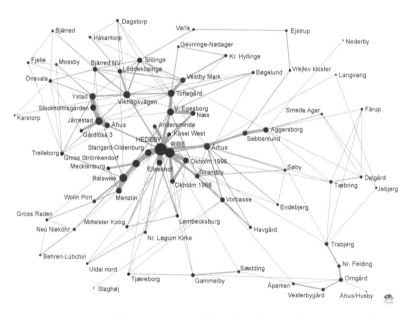

FIGURE 2 Viking towns as nodal points with interrelated local markets in complex network theory, based on the distribution of various artefact types across southern Scandinavia (adapted from Sindbæk 2007a: fig. 5; with kind permission) (S. Kalmring).

in the early Middle Ages, comparing contemporary developments in Northern Europe, the Mediterranean, Eastern Africa, India and Southeast Asia (Sindbæk & Trakadas 2014; cf. Hodges 2012: 108–9). In the context of urbanity, however, 'entrepôt' is a rather vague term, generally describing 'a port, city, or other centre to which goods are brought for import and export and for collection and distribution' (OED 2010: 586). Consequently, in the exhibition catalogue, which presented the project's output, the editors chose to use the term *emporium* instead (Sindbæk & Trakadas 2014). A comparable project in Lund has also investigated the causes behind early urbanisation, focussing on contemporary places in Northern Europe, East Africa and Southeast Asia, in order to gain new insights for this bewildering and paradigmatic subject (Mogren 2013). As a result, Mogren (2013) argued for a deconstruction of the 'central place' concept and for the use of a method that highlighted function, agency and communication instead of morphology and structure as essential parameters for 'urban' and further emphasised aspects relating to the initial self-organisation of trading and craft communities. Most importantly, however, he used a model with orthogenetic and heterogenetic sites as a conceptual pair (cf. Miksic 2000). Here, the orthogenetic sites were associated with stability, whereas heterogenetic sites were related to change and entrepreneurship. While the first type of site would characteristically have been 'placed in areas of surplus agricultural production, are always in some respect central, are populated by a civil, religious and military bureaucracy, might have an aristocratic/royal presence, and are distinguished by some form of monumentality' (Mogren 2013: 80), the latter is often, as in the case of Hedeby and Birka, 'liminally placed, between ecological zones, ethnic or political regions, or different transport zones ... and often lack[s] monumentality' but has 'production and trade of commodities ... [as its] most distinguishing feature' (Mogren 2013: 80). Independent of Mogren's approach, Søvsø (2020) recently came to a similar conclusion and argued for a differentiation between the two quite dissimilar strands that have shaped classical medieval towns: towns that grew out of *civitates* and those that grew out of *emporia* (Søvsø 2020: 12, 16–18, 253–5). In this case, the *civitas* category refers to settlements evolving from Iron Age central places, which functioned as religious (pagan) and political centres and were the homesteads of chieftain dynasties. Such places developed into an idealised version of the 'Heavenly Jerusalem' at the turn of the first millennium. These *civitas* sites correspond well to Mogren's description of heterogenetic sites. Søvsø's *emporium* sites were based on the nodal, later royal trading places within the maritime trade networks and thus resemble Mogren's orthogenetic sites. In the eleventh century, however, even the *emporia* – if they survived their transformation – were likewise remodelled into Christian towns.

Regardless of how these sites are defined academically, the question of the specific purpose of Viking-age towns remains elementary to the problem. What is at the core of this discontinuous phenomenon at the dawn of the high medieval town – beyond a mere 'trade and production' as a commonplace – that these particular places represent? This contribution does not want to introduce yet more new terminology into this already perplexing debate. Instead of posing questions about the *what?* (definitions, focussing on result) or the *how?* (network theory, focussing on process), the aim here is to approach the core problem and to ask about the *why?*, which is at the heart of the golden circle model. The debate on orthogenetic and heterogenetic sites suggests that there is some fundamental difference between traditional centres of power (central places) and the suddenly emerging Viking-age towns. Thus, in order to ultimately define the *purpose* of these novel Viking-age towns and to draw further conclusions about their societal benefits at this specific point in time, it is first necessary to examine how the surrounding traditional, rural Viking world was structured.

3 The Viking World

When envisioning the Viking world in the Scandinavian homelands, enigmatic sites such as Ribe, Kaupang, Hedeby and Birka come to mind. The research about these sites fills monographs, essay collections and exhibition catalogues. Yet none of these places was truly representative of a society that in most ways still remained very traditional, rural and agrarian. Traces of everyday society emerge in the mundane, routinely made rescue excavations performed by heritage services and contract archaeology, which seldom make the headlines or attract scholarly attention. Another limiting factor for a more profound understanding of this society is the often poor preservation conditions at such sites: the remains of building features are often reduced to a series of post-holes situated immediately below the modern plough layer, and often such features are merely accompanied by an ever-repeating canon of household artefacts. Unfortunately, in most cases such insights disappear in technical reports filed in archives, and only rarely are comprehensive publications available, such as on rural West Jutland (Eriksen et al. 2009) or in a more representative and diachronic overview of Swedish conditions, found in Göthberg et al. (1995). However, these are precisely the sites we should look at if we ultimately want to define the exception to the rule, namely the emergence of Viking-age towns against the background of a traditional, rural agrarian society.

3.1 A RURAL AGRARIAN SOCIETY

In large parts of Denmark, Scania and the Mälar Valley, which have favourable agricultural conditions (Gammeltoft et al. 2012: 8–11 fig. 1), the settlement patterns were dominated by intermediate- and large-sized villages. In many parts of Norway, however, where the landscape is dominated by mountain ranges and suitable areas for cultivation are

FIGURE 3 Klinta, Öland, Sweden. Contemporary three-dimensional representation of a longhouse depicted on top of the Klinta iron staff (object no. 107776_HST; The Swedish History Museum/SHM [CC BY 4.0]).

limited (Øye 2009), smaller hamlets – of two to four farmsteads – and single farms were more common. Fundamental to every Viking-age farmstead was the multifunctional three-aisled longhouse (Figure 3). As its main element, it contained two long benches along a central fireplace but also housed a kitchen and various storerooms and represented the central dwelling of the farmers with their extended households. These main buildings, or farms, would have been complemented by a number of minor outbuildings or pit houses – providing additional storage and workshops – as well as wells. The farmsteads would have been surrounded by pastures for hay production and arable land for cultivating grain. Depending on the local topography, these infields would have been surrounded either by fences or by irregular stone walls. From the infields, cattle paths led to the outfields, with common grazing areas (Fallgren 2008; for a more differentiated approach, see Magnus 2002). On the margins of the outfield areas, burial grounds and/or rune stones signalled gateways into the actual farms but also claims to hereditary ownership (ON *óðal*) (Zachrisson 1994, 1998, 2017). Such legal claims depended on the ability to prove five ancestral generations on a property (Brink 2002: 103–5; Zachrisson 2017).

Remarkably, the infield–outfield system of the farmsteads also seems to be reflected in the religious concept of the universe, with Midgard as the cultivated world of the humans contrasted against the wild Utgard, where giants and trolls dwelled (Gurevich 1985: 47; for a more nuanced approach, see Schjødt 1990: 43, 51–4; Steinsland 2005: 139, 143–5). The rural economy was based on pasture farming, with cattle as the most important livestock but also including pigs (wood pasture), sheep and goats, alongside the cultivation of barley, wheat, millet, oat, rye and flax. Another major resource was fishing, in which herring and Atlantic cod were especially important. Even game hunting, for deer, reindeer and elk, was a significant source of meat, furs and antlers. Finally, the exploitation of nearby forests would have been important for the acquisition of timber, firewood, charcoal and wood tar (Bender Jørgensen 2002).[1]

It was only Jutland that had farmsteads and yards with rectangular enclosures (Dan. *tofte*), as displayed by the iconic example of the village of Vorbasse. Chronologically, the entire Vorbasse complex was occupied continually from the first to the eleventh century. In the eighth century, the settlement was moved 500 metres southward, where two villages were merged into one, covering an area of 60,000 square metres. This new complex comprised six farmsteads, which were surrounded by six large rectangular enclosures attached to respective farms, three on each side of a main road ('the earlier settlement'). Additionally, there was one common infield, subdivided into long and narrow strips of land. As a rule, however, each farmstead still consisted of only one central longhouse with storerooms only, accompanied by some outbuildings, pit houses and a well. From the second half of the tenth century onwards, six further and even larger enclosed farmsteads were built, extending the entire village ('the later settlement') westwards to a size of c.180,000 square metres. This latter

---

[1] Recently, a pre-Viking-age 'intensified outland resource colonisation' of the boreal forests (e.g. hunting pits, tar production) has been suggested, which started with seasonal production sites already in the period 300–650 (Hennius 2021; any possible disruptions due to the Late Antique Little Ice Age (LALIA) remain unmentioned).

phase also included one vast farm complex, which covered an area of 25,800 square metres (Hvass 1979, 2006; Ethelberg 2003: 353–6, 365–71). But even for these Jutland villages, Kähler Holst (2014: 184–7) concludes that the hereditary rights to land, although certainly subject to gradual change, would still be reflected in their layouts and actually date back to the early Roman Iron Age. For Viking-age farms in general, Fallgren (2008: 67) suggested that 'the general character of the Viking Age settlement in Scandinavia in most aspects was a continuation of how the settlement was formed and organised earlier ... Any larger structural changes of settlement do not occur during the Viking Age.' Later, he even went a step further: 'The fact that we can find approximately the same classes of farm sizes during the Viking Age as earlier ... indicates that the social structure ... was the same during the Viking Age, at least in its main features' (Fallgren 2008: 70).

The strong rural roots of Viking-age society are also reflected by a completely different facet than just farmsteads and villages, when considering the rune-stone evidence: the famous 'Ingvar stones' comprise at least twenty-six rune stones, commemorating individual crew members who died during the expedition of Ingvar Emundsson (1016–41), described in the Icelandic *Saga of Ingvar the* (Far-) *Traveller* (trans. Tunstall 2013; cf. Pálsson 2013). This quest for fortune took place in around 1040 and was headed east towards *Serkland*. However, as witnessed by the rune stones, the journey ended in disaster, most likely by the Caspian Sea, and it seems very few of the expedition members made it back home (M. G. Larsson 1983, 1986; Jesch 2001: 102–4; G. Larsson 2013). These rune stones are distributed over sites in Södermanland (15), Uppland (8), Östergötland (2) and Västmanland (1) and provide an exceptional opportunity to mirror the catchment area of one single Viking voyage. The so-called Ingvar stones not only are found in the Mälar Valley but, with the examples from Västmanland and Östergötland, cover almost all of eastern central Sweden (cf. Varenius 2002: 250–1 fig. 4). Irrespective of the rather improbable suggestion of the crew members' background being part of the *ledung* system (cf. Larsson 1986) for territorial naval defence, these stones clearly demonstrate that, even as late as in the eleventh century, there were Viking expeditions, which is closely connected to our perception of the Viking Age. More importantly, however, they also demonstrate that most of the expedition members did not come from urban milieus but were recruited from the rural countryside. The same pattern also seems to apply for the raiding parties from the early Viking Age: Androshchuk (2009: 102; 2014: 240–1) has studied the distribution of sword types, prior to the appearance of equestrian and weapon graves of the tenth century (cf. Pedersen 2014), and ties them to the countryside rather than the Viking-age towns. He thus argues that urban sites such as Birka were not 'Viking towns' in the sense of hometowns of Viking raiders but indeed towns of merchants and crafters.

3.2 ONE VIKING WORLD OR LOCAL GROUPS?

As seen, the Viking world in Northern Europe was still a traditional rural society deeply rooted in the Iron Age (cf. Brather 2003; Søvsø 2020: 15). Yet some post-processual scholars have raised the almost heretical question whether it was a coherent culture area at all. One obvious contradictory argument would be that the Old Norse shared one common language. However, a closer look at the *Dǫnsk tunga* ('Danish tongue') reveals that it was in fact subdivided into an Old West Norse, spoken in Norway and around the North Atlantic, as well as an Old East Norse dialect spoken in Old Denmark and Sweden (cf. Byock 2013: 20–3 fig. 5). This suggests some local variation, which is also indicated by differences in the material culture. And even though these differences probably suggest variations on a single theme, some distinct local groups can be defined: Schulte (2008: 181–2), for instance, based such arguments on runic evidence and argued that Viking-age runic inscriptions indicate a significant degree of dissimilarity both through 'regional-dialectic variation[s]' and in 'socio-stylistic patterns' throughout the whole period between 700 and 1050.

In order to track differences in regional identity and territorial organisation, Burström (1988) made a comparison between the medieval *folkland* (OSwd; 'province') division of inner Southern Sweden, with its large burial mounds, burial grounds, Husby sites and rune stones, and the very local distribution of Iron Age boulder tombs (Swd; *järnåldersdösar*). Based on settlement distribution and funerary customs, four years later Callmer (1992: fig. 1) published a map of 'ethnically distinctive areas', demonstrating that there was significant variations between local groups in south-eastern Sweden (and the eastern Baltic coast) at the beginning of the ninth century: although he mainly focussed on the late Iron Age interaction between these ethnic groups across the Baltic Sea, he started off by pointing to cultural differences that defined minor or medium-sized territories within distinct regions. He emphasised that 'for the period of interest, like for earlier periods, ... most people's lives were spent within the region they had been born' (Callmer 1992: 99). He also suggested that such displays of 'social seclusion and relative isolation' were even still reflected in many of the high medieval Swedish provincial laws (Swd.; *landskapslagar*). These laws not only hindered the interaction between different judicial systems but also meant that foreigners, who were not part of the local population, effectively were excluded from legal protection.

In his published doctoral thesis with the provocative title *Decolonizing the Viking Age*, F. Svanberg (2003a, 2003b) studied different death rituals in south-eastern Scandinavia. In his catalogue volume, he concludes that there was no straight-line development from cremation burials to inhumations as an expression of some increasing Christianisation. On the contrary, he argued that none of these customs was exclusive to any specific ritual systems and suggested that a social dimension involving supra-regional aristocratic traditions should be considered as an alternative explanation (Svanberg 2003b: 140). In his analysis, he managed to distinguish ten rather small 'settlement districts' (Figure 4) separated by extensive uninhabited areas, which displayed distinctive collective cultural

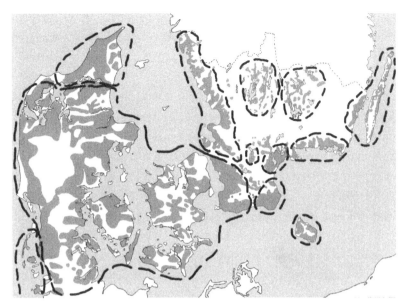

FIGURE 4 'Decolonizing the Viking Age.' Different death rituals concerning treatment of the dead from various limited settlement districts in south-eastern Scandinavia (after Svanberg 2003b: fig. 61; with kind permission).

norms regarding death rituals (treatment of the deceased) and the appearance of burial grounds (grave monuments). These settlement districts were namely Halland and north-western Scania; Finnveden; Värend; Öland and Möre; south-western Scania (with links to present-day Denmark); south-eastern Scania; north-eastern Scania; inner northern Scania; Blekinge and Lister; and finally Bornholm (Svanberg 2003b: 142–7 figs. 59, 61). It is only for the period around 1000 that Svanberg (2003b: 147–50) recognises Christian traditions replacing the old ritual systems, which in turn also displayed local variation.

Sindbæk (2009) reflected over local variations based on the travel accounts of Ohthere and Wulfstan and argued that, in spite of close cultural ties even within entities such as Denmark or Sweden, they still contained many relatively autonomous provinces ('lands') that contributed to cultural differences and regionalism, which were upheld through close social networks. As a basis for his associated study, he shifts the focus from burials to settlement sites by reviewing 522 recorded settlements in Denmark, northern Germany and southern Sweden from the period 700–1100. Even though the identified 'regional clusters of cultural practice' are not separated by sharply demarcated zones, clear cultural boundaries can in fact be identified through different building customs (halls of 'Vorbasse' vs 'Toftegård' types), pottery traditions (round-based vs flat-based vessels), spindle whorls (fired clay vs sandstone) and other artefact types appearing either on one or the other side of the Great Belt, marking a clear division between western and eastern Denmark.[2] Another, less obvious boundary identified by Sindbæk (2009: 182–9 fig. 6) is the one between western Jutland, orientated towards the North Sea – with imports from Frisia and the Carolingian Empire (Muschelgrus and Badorf ware, basalt quern stones) – and eastern Jutland, orientated towards the Baltic Sea. There is also evidence of similar differences between Zealand and Scania, separated by the natural border of Öresund, which is visible through cooking pots ('swallow's nest' vessels vs vessels with upstanding lugs). Additionally, there is an internal regional differentiation between the previously mentioned agrarian village communities of Jutland, which display a normative conformity, and the military-aristocratic organisation of the Danish Isles, which is characterised by central places with great halls as architectural demonstrations of power (Kähler Holst 2014: 189–91). Finally, Sindbæk (2009: 197–8; 2010: 284), similar to Callmer (1992), alluded to the importance of legal customs when researching cultural differences between regions, claiming that 'in a society with few or no urban centres', it was the Viking-age *things* (assemblies), where people of a district met on a regular basis, that contributed to common regional cultural norms, including norms of material culture.

---

[2] This clear division between western and eastern Denmark also seems to coincide with the legal province of Jutland, including Funen and Langeland, and the ones for Zealand and Scania (cf. Semple et al. 2020: 95–6).

4 Cult, Jurisdiction and Markets
Things *and Regional Fairs at Traditional Centres of Power*

In their article *Assembly Sites for Cult, Markets, Jurisdiction and Social Relations*, Nørgård Jørgensen et al. (2010) argued for similarities between the large pit house sites of the Viking Age and the early modern period's so-called church towns (Swd. *kyrkstäder*) in northern Sweden. Church towns are large agglomerations of occasionally inhabited cabins gathered around churches that were used for gatherings during major religious festivals in otherwise sparsely populated areas. In addition to baptisms, weddings and funerals, these gatherings simultaneously provided one of the few opportunities during the year for parliament meetings, tax collection, jurisdiction, market trade at fairs and even social events (Nørgård Jørgensen et al. 2010: 99). Based on these activities, the authors argued for a reinterpretation of larger Viking-age pit house agglomerations as possible temporary accommodation for family groups attending seasonal assemblies (*things*). Even more important in this context is that religious and judicial assemblies in sparsely populated societies were important social events, where a large gathered crowed likewise engaged in trade and exchange.

4.1 TRADITIONAL CENTRES OF POWER AND CULT

The most prominent religious and political centre of the Viking world – apart perhaps from Gammel Lejre on Zealand as the seat of the Danish dynasty of the *Skjǫldungar* (Christensen 2015; cf. Thietmar of Merseburg book 1, chap. 17) – was undoubtedly Gamla Uppsala in Uppland. As a site, Gamla Uppsala was deeply rooted in the Late Roman Iron Age, with a significant development in the early Vendel period (Vendel period c.550–750; cf. Merovingian period). The complex is very much embedded in traditional rural society and – frequently addressed as a central place – had very little to do with the emerging Viking-age towns. Gamla Uppsala was situated in the historic region of Tíundaland in the very heart of Uppland, surrounded by Fjärdhundraland in the west and Attundaland in the east. Not only was it the religious and political centre of the kings of *Svealand*, but it also had – as reflected by the Icelandic sagas – a supra-regional religious role for the entire Viking world as such. Although the accounts of Adam of Bremen (book 4, chaps. 26–7, scholia 134–6) from the 1070s have certainly been coloured by his chronological timeline for Christianisation, they provide a description of a gold-covered temple for *Þórr*, *Óðinn* and *Freyr*, as well as the sacred grove with an evergreen tree, where seventy-two men, horses, dogs and other creatures were sacrificed in a nine-year cycle at the religious festival *dísablót* (cf. Sundqvist 2002, 2013; Nordberg 2006: 86–96). A list of the half-mythological kings of Svealand (and later Norway) and their divine descent is provided in the *Ynglinga* saga, the first part to Snorri Sturluson's *Heimskringla* from c.1230, but actually goes back to the now lost *Ynglingatal*, recorded by Þjóðólfr of Hvinir around 900. According to the saga, (Yngvi-) *Freyr* himself founded the royal house of the Ynglings, named after him, at Gamla Uppsala (cf. Sundqvist 2016: 63–80). It was not until the 1130s that Gamla Uppsala became a diocese, replacing the one in Sigtuna. In 1164, it was elevated to an archdiocese, which in turn was transferred to Östra Aros (present-day Uppsala) in 1273 (Kjellberg 2021: 95–9).

Today, the most prominent features of Gamla Uppsala are the three monumental, 70–80 metres in diameter and 10-metre-high royal mounds raised on its moraine esker (Swd. *Högåsen*; 'the High Ridge'). Traditionally, they are attributed to the graves of the legendary Ynglinga kings Aun, Egill and Aðils. These monumental mounds are connected to a southern burial complex of c.270 medium- and small-sized mounds on the same ridge, probably dating from the Late Roman Iron Age and Migration period through to the Viking Age. North of the royal mounds, at the vicarage (Swd. *prästgården*), a few cremation burials and six smaller Viking-age boat burials have also been found, two of which are recent discoveries (Nordahl 2001; Seiler 2019). The monumental mounds are called the *Östhögen* ('the East Mound'), *Mitthögen* ('the Middle Mound') and *Västhögen* ('the West Mound'). *Mitthögen* has only been partially excavated, and the contents of its main burial are still unknown. *Östhögen* and *Västhögen* both contained cremation graves redated to the late sixth and early seventh centuries, that is, the early Vendel period (Duczko 1996a; Ljungkvist 2008). While *Östhögen* seems to have been erected during one single event occasion, *Mitthögen* and *Västhögen* both feature younger soil deposits that have been interpreted as attempts to enhance the monumentality of the site, in connection with the ancestor worship of the ruling dynasty. Previously, a fourth contemporary mound on Högåsen – *Gullhögen* ('the Gold Mound') – was also examined but its exact location can no longer be established. The so-called *Tingshögen* ('the Assembly Mound') north-east of the royal mounds is characterised by a flat top, and it is debated whether it reflects a secondary usage of an original burial mound (cf. Christiansson & Nordahl 1989: 245–8); its (later?) role as a *thing* site and use for judicial and political purposes, however, are indicated by its name (Lindqvist 1936; Ljungkvist 2013).

The actual pagan temple at Gamla Uppsala, described by Adam of Bremen, was believed to have been situated on the site of the present-day church to the north of the moraine ridge – which is in fact the remains (chancel and central tower) of a larger Romanesque cathedral destroyed in a fire in the 1240s. Sune Lindqvist was the first to actually survey the church floor in 1926. Based on the postholes that he found inside the chancel and in the former northern transept, he presented a blueprint for a wooden temple building measuring approximately 25 by 22 metres, supposedly consisting of an inner and outer quadrangle with a raised central section, which he identified as the 'gold-covered temple' described by Adam of Bremen (Lindqvist 1951, 1967). A thorough review of Lindquist's excavation results, however, could not confirm such a building but instead suggested that it was a house platform for a regular hall building, which would have been replaced by a wooden church built on a raised clay layer (Nordahl 1996). This earlier church would have been situated in the northern transept of the later Romanesque church. Further evidence of the choir to the wooden church and parts of the hall were identified

FIGURE 5 Gamla Uppsala, Uppland, Sweden. Monumental royal mound *Östhögen*, burial ground at vicarage, assembly mound *Tingshögen* and Vendel-period manorial complex (graphics: D. Westergren; © Disir Productions AB).

following geophysical radar surveys in 2003/4 (Alkarp & Price 2005). Outside the present-day cemetery wall, these surveys even revealed another Iron Age house as well as additional outbuildings. To the north of the church, on *Kungsgårdsplatån* ('the Royal Manor Plateau'), there is evidence of a Vendel-period manor complex, consisting of two further house platforms (Figure 5): surveys of the southern platform revealed a building sequence terminated by the remains of an exceptional, 50 by 12 metres large hall building with curved walls from around 600, which burned down in the early ninth century (Hedlund 1993; Nordahl 1993; Duczko 1996b: 41–4; Ljungkvist 2013: 54; Ljungkvist & Frölund 2015: 14–20). The northern platform revealed remnants of two Vendel-period specialised workshops that included traces of garnet processing (Ljungkvist 2013: 54–7; Ljungkvist & Frölund 2015: 21–3). More recent investigations have shown that an eastern platform actually consisted of the remnants of yet another monumental mound, *Norrhögen* ('the Northern Mound'), which was flattened in the twelfth century to create a house terrace (Ljungkvist & Frölund 2015: 24).

Modern large-scale excavations performed east of the manor and the monumental mounds, during the redirection of the Ostkustbanan railway, revealed a permanent settlement occupation with farmsteads consisting of both post buildings and pit houses (Beronius Jörpeland et al. 2017). The most remarkable feature found during these excavations, however, is two rows of monumental posts from the late fifth to early sixth century, which appear to be central to the understanding of the sacred dimensions of Gamla Uppsala. The northern row seems to follow an ancient road to a ford across the Samnan brook, a tributary to the river Fyrisån, and was made up of 144 posts spread over 862 metres. The southern row seems to originate from the southern tip of the Högåsen burial ground and consisted of at least 126 posts spread over 725 metres (Wikborg 2017). Sundqvist has suggested that they formed a symbolic boundary demarking the cultic enclosure of a consecrated area, that is, the sanctuary and assembly site of Gamla Uppsala, and that the northern row seems to have accompanied a ceremonial and processional road leading towards it. Further, since the orientation of the northern row corresponded with the midwinter and midsummer solstices, and the southern row to the spring and autumn equinoxes, Sundqvist argued that their intersection might have symbolically marked the centre of the universe, an *axis mundi*, that acted as an interface with the mythical world. In this respect, the surroundings of Gamla Uppsala may have reflected features of Ásgarðr, which was likewise symbolically enclosed (Sundqvist 2016: 262–3, 301; 2017; cf. Sanmark 2015: 99–101, map 2).

Regarding the positive identification of the pagan temple referred to in the accounts of Adam of Bremen, the question remains whether a cult house comparable to the one of Uppåkra (cf. Larsson & Lenntorp 2004) could be expected or whether it was more of a large hall, such as the one from the southern platform of Kungsgården, which was also used for ceremonial contexts. Sundqvist (2013: 97–100) suggested that the cult of the three gods *Þórr*, *Óðinn* and *Freyr* in Gamla Uppsala was part of a political strategy to establish political control over the entire Mälar region. Through ceremonial practices at the cult site, the *Svea* kings would have demonstrated their close relationship to these mythical powers in order to establish legitimacy for their exercise of power. Apart from the ability to amass large quantities of people from many different regions and with different cultic preferences, these religious events also provided an opportunity to collect taxes – including, inter alia, the *thing* dues (ON *þingfarakaup*; cf. Sanmark 2017: 46). In the context of customs, it seems particularly important to also re-evaluate the fairs associated with the *thing* gatherings (Sanmark 2017: 138–9, 149–50; Semple et al. 2020: 95, 232–47) and to examine what distinguished them from the trade activities in the novel Viking-age towns such as Birka or Hedeby.

4.2 ASSEMBLIES AND FAIRS

As previously mentioned, for a society with few or no urban centres, assemblies (ON *þing*) were of particular importance for the population of the various administrative districts. The *things* were administrative and legal institutions with specific laws based on legal customs and traditions, for example as attested by the 'law of the people' (ON *at liuþriti*), which is quoted on the tenth-century Forsa rune ring (Hs 7) as Scandinavia's oldest textual document of prevailing legal traditions. Before this time, these laws would have been exclusively orally transmitted by high-ranking lawmen (ON *lǫgmaðr*) (Brink 2008: 28–9; cf. Källström 2010; Sundqvist 2013: 377–86). Local legal traditions – older than the Forsa rune ring – have, however, left traceable echoes in high medieval provincial laws, such as the Norwegian *Law of the Gulathing* and *Law of the Frostathing*, the Swedish *Older Law of Västergötland*, and the *Law of Gotland*, as well as in the Icelandic *Grágás* (Sanmark 2017: 9–10; Semple et al. 2020: 10–11, 58–9, 72–4). The administrative levels for assemblies, based on land divisions (local: ON *fjóðungr, þriðjungr*; regional: ON *herað, hundari, skipreiða*; top-level: ON *land, folkland, lǫgsǫgn*), were almost as manifold as their seasons (ON *várþing*, 'spring assembly'; ON *haustþing/leiðir*, 'autumn assembly') and occasions (e.g. ON *almannaþing*, 'public assembly'; ON *skattþing*, 'assembly to claim tax'; ON *vápnaþing*, 'weapon-inspecting assembly'; ON *manndrápsþing*, 'manslaughter assembly') (cf. Sanmark 2017: 37–43; Semple et al. 2020: 20–2, 60, 74–84 figs. 1.8–9, 3.1). Crucial for the legitimacy of these assemblies was the concept of *thing* peace (ON *friðr/griðr*), guaranteeing safety for their participants. Geographically, *thing* sites were often related to specific hills (ON *lǫgberg*), natural slopes (ON *þingbrekka*) or monumental mounds and occasionally were connected to royal manors or farms, too. For obvious reasons, assembly sites depended on accessibility and therefore were located on or near to major communication routes, particularly where land routes, waterways and portages intersected. Moreover, *thing* sites often made use of areas that were enclosed by natural streams, rivers and wetlands, which also became symbolic boundaries (Brink 2002: 101; Sanmark 2017: 20–3, 56–8, 89–103, 122–31; Semple et al. 2020: 84–116). According to written sources, the actual *thing* site (ON *þingstaðr, þingstǫð*), where the assembly was held, was called ON *lǫgrétta*, a circular enclosure surrounded by a rope (ON *vébǫnd*), which was tied to hazel poles. This area was where the judges deliberated, separate from the assembled free landholding participants. Verdicts were apparently confirmed by weapon rattling (ON *vápnatak*) by attendees, which also suggests that the confirmation took place outside the actual consecrated *thing* site, since weapons were banned from that area. Place-name evidence from the immediate vicinity of *thing* names indicates that specific structures such as booths (ON *búðir*; North Atlantic only) for attendees were associated with the sites, while an affiliation with execution sites (e.g. gallows; ON *galgi*) stresses the judicial nature of the *things*. Moreover, *thing* names compounded with ON *skeið* indicate ritual horse fighting or racing (Sanmark 2017: 137–8; Semple et al. 2020: 60).

It is generally assumed that, prior to the emergence of towns and churches in late Viking-age Scandinavia, *things* were exclusively linked to rural local, regional and supra-regional communities (cf. Sanmark 2017: 143–61; Semple et al. 2020: 72).[1] And, in fact, no *thing* site is known for Hedeby, nor are any special assemblies

---

[1] Elsewhere in the same publication, and, by contrast, it is stated that 'Towns had their own set of laws and also their own *thing* sites. This seems to have been the case from the early Viking Age' (Semple et al. 2020: 131).

documented. It is only in its immediate hinterland that there is evidence for local *things*, as a part of the medieval *hundred* organisation (ON *herað*), recorded in the Danish Census Book *Kong Valdemars Jordebog* (Kuhlmann 1958, map 20; cf. Wendt 2012). Recently, though, it has been suggested that the pit houses quarter in the north-western district of Hedeby should have served as temporary accommodation for visitors from a wider area, which might indicate that Hedeby – alongside its acknowledged role for trade and craft – may have had 'administrative, political and religious functions as at other classic assembly sites' (Jørgensen et al. 2019: 170). Near Kaupang, at Tjølling (ON *Þjóðalyng*), the toponymical evidence suggests a sacred lake, Vittersen, devoted to the deities of the *vítr*, in the vicinity of *Helgefjell* ('the Holy Mountain'). The place name *Þjóðalyng* itself can be translated as 'the (assembly) heath of the peoples', which alludes to a *thing* site (Brink 2007). Here, at Tjølling, a small cluster of cooking pits for seasonal sacred feasts from c.600 suggests that an assembly site was already established in the early Iron Age. This site links directly to a still existing twelfth-century *thing*-site basilica, and its postulated tenth- or eleventh-century predecessor, indicating that this assembly site was in use up to the mid-twelfth century. Yet, as in the case of the aforementioned Hedeby, neither does *Þjóðalyng* seem to have been connected to the trading town of Kaupang, indicating some urban assembly. It is more likely to have been the regional (ON *fylki*) *thing* for the Vestfold law province or possibly for the entire historic district of Viken – and as such it rather would have been connected to the 'central-site complex' at Skiringssal (Skre 2007: 385–406 fig. 17.4). Somewhat differently, Semple et al. (2020: 150–3) argued that the actual level of the *thing* at Tjølling remains uncertain, although it is clear that it became the law-*thing* site for the northern law district of Borgarthing in 1223. Additionally, more recent discoveries of early cooking-pit sites at nearby Lunde (cf. Ødegaard 2019) and at Bommestad (ON *Bóndþingstaðir*) contribute to a more complex picture regarding the discussion of possible precursors for the *thing* at Skiringssal (cf. Sanmark 2017: 134–7).

In the case of Birka, however, Rimbert's *Vita Ansgarii* even confirms two *thing* meetings. During Ansgar's first visit in c.830, he and his companion Witmar were given permission for their missionary work directly by King Björn at *Haugi*, although only after he consulted his confidants (*fideles*) (Rimbert, chap. 11). The first assembly actually described in *Vita Ansgarii*, however, took place in 845, after Bishop Gauzbert was expelled from the island of Björkö (Rimbert, chap. 16) and Birka was left without a priest. During this *thing* meeting, the royal agent (*praefectus loci*) Herigar – as the sole remaining Christian – sought proof of God's existence after having been taunted by the attending local pagans. The source does not mention where this *thing* meeting (*colloquium*) was held, apart from a reference to a *scena in campo*, a 'stage ... on an open plain' (Rimbert, chap. 11), most likely on Björkö itself. Arbman (1937: 24; 1939: 78; 1943: xvi, xxiii) associated the isolated Birka burial ground Ormknös – with its three monumental mounds and a ship setting – with a possible assembly site. With the field name Lunden ('the Grove'), and associated place names, such as Lundswyken, Lundsskiär and Lundsängen nearby, there may even have been a sacred *lund*(*a*) name in the immediate vicinity of this postulated *thing* site at Ormknös (cf. Vikstrand 2001: 278–91). In addition, Hallström (1913: 5 n. 5) mentions a possible *domarring* (ON *dómhringa*; cf. Friðriksson & Vésteinsson 1992), that is, a Migration period 'judge' circle or stone circle, north of Ormknös. Another assembly took place in 852, when Ansgar returned a second time to Birka. At a preceding meeting between the missionary and King Olof, remarkably, the king admitted that, as the former priest had been driven off by 'a rising of the people' and not by royal command, he was unable to reconfirm Ansgar's mission without consulting the 'will of the people' at the *thing* (*platicum*) (Rimbert, chap. 26). In fact, before the assembly King Olof even consulted his nobles (*principus*) one more time, and lots were casted to probe the will of the pagan gods. In connection with the following events, when the *thing* meeting finally approved the mission, it is explicitly stated that the meeting took place in the *vicus* Birka. The passage in question reads: *placiti ..., quod in ... vico Byrca habitum est* ('the assembly which was held in the town [vicus] of Birka') (Rimbert, chap. 27). However, this was not the end of the story, since the king could not give his full consent without the approval of another assembly *in altera parte regni* ('in another part of his kingdom'), where the same matter had to be decided separately (Rimbert, chap. 27; cf. Sundqvist 2016: 40–1). This addendum is particularly revealing as it clearly shows that Birka had its own *thing*, separate from that in the countryside – unfortunately, without revealing the location of the latter (cf. Arbman 1939: 39; 1943: xvi).

Distinctly different from regional, local or provincial – and in Birka's case even urban – *things*, the one at Gamla Uppsala, as the traditional centre of power and cult, was the highest ranking one and as such also the gathering of Uppland's three *folkländer* at 'the assembly of all Swedes', that is, the people of Svealand proper (Sanmark 2017: 60–1, 229; Semple et al. 2020: 81–2, 89 fig. 4.2). This is corroborated by the *Ynglingasaga* (*Heimskringla*, chap. 34), which states that: 'There were at that time district kings [*heraðskonungar*] all over Sweden [*Svíþjóð*]. Road-Anund ruled the district of Tíundaland. Uppsala is located there, and there is the place of assembly for all Swedes [*allra Svía þing*]. Great sacrifices were held there, and many kings came to attend them.' The *thing* in Gamla Uppsala was also called OSwd *Disaþing*, indicating a cult aspect relating to the fertility deities *dísir*. This *thing* was held in the third lunar month after the midwinter solstice, around the time of the spring equinox (Nordberg 2006: 107–9). The fact that a major religious event – for example, *dísablót* – was connected to a legal assembly – as the *Disting* – displays a common phenomenon observable in other parts of Scandinavia, and the same applies to the markets that were held at these assemblies, where crowds from all parts of the realm gathered.[2] In Sweden and Norway, seemingly in contrast to Iceland, there seems to

[2] Carver (2015:2) pointedly portrayed the academic discussion on the origins of the market economy in sixth- to ninth-century Europe as one camp arguing for an elite impulse and another as a merchant enterprise. He also stressed the role of 'ideology' as an essential part of a princely right to rule, to hold authority over other worlds and the logic of the market. However, his general premise that 'material wealth is largely the

have been a particular link between the market trade and the highest ranked assembly sites (Sanmark 2017: 52). In Gamla Uppsala, the Saga of Olaf Haraldsson (chap. 77), included in Snorri Sturluson's *Heimskringla*, states that:

> In Svíþjóð [Sweden] it was the old custom, as long as heathenism prevailed, that the chief sacrifice took place in Góe month at Uppsala. Then sacrifice was offered for peace, and victory to the king; and thither came people from all parts of Svíþjóð. All the Things of the Swedes, also, were held there, and markets, and meetings for buying, which continued for a week: and after Christianity was introduced into Svíþjóð, the Things and fairs were held there as before.

Sources suggest that since the plural form of *Disting* – *Distingen* – was used, it is likely that the week of the Disting market (with an accordant market peace, ON *disaþings friþer*) began and ended with two separate assemblies. This would have made it the nine-day event mentioned by Rimbert, with the sacrifice of nine different species on eight subsequent nights, resulting in seventy-two sacrifices in total (Nordberg 2006: 86–96).

The Disting fair was held at the end of February or in early March, which was particularly beneficial for travel and the transport of commodities on ice-covered winter routes over lakes and rivers (cf. Matz 1990). As late as the mid-sixteenth century, the Catholic ecclesiastic and geographer Olaus Magnus, who penned *A Description of the Northern Peoples*, dedicated a separate chapter to such fairs: 'the very ancient custom of setting up markets on the ice, held on flat, open surfaces in many province and attended by very wealthy merchants'. He mentions ice fairs in Strängnäs on Lake Mälaren, in Oviken on Storsjön in Jämtland and that the market in Uppsala was still the most important one (Figure 6): He reports:

> detritus of an ideological program rather than a sign of economic development' cannot be regarded as universally valid, as shown in Chapter 9.

FIGURE 6 *De nundinis glacialibus* (*On Ice Fairs*). Disting winter fair on the frozen river Fyriså near Uppsala. Copper engraving from Olaus Magnus' *Historia de gentibus septentrionalibus* (*Description of the Northern Peoples*) from 1555 (Wikimedia Commons).

[T]he archiepiscopal city of Uppsala in Sweden, through the middle of which a great river [Fyrisån] flows, where, about the beginning of February, the water quite often freezes to such a thickness that it supports the weight of a countless throng of people, draught animals, and merchandise of all kinds. From very early times such a market has been called, and still is called, disting.

(Olaus Magnus, book 4, chap. 6)

This underlines that the market activities from Gamla Uppsala were of such an importance that they were moved to present-day Uppsala, interestingly maintaining not only its date but also its heathen designation (cf. Kjellberg 2021: 93, 127–8). A recent archaeological survey provided material evidence for a similar combination of assemblies and fairs: at the *Gutnal thing*, by Roma on central Gotland, the island's main judicial and political assemblies were held in a 'confined space'; this is also where metal detectorists have found the striking amount of 429 scale weights. While the number otherwise corresponds well with the amount of weights known from most *emporia*, the example of Roma clearly illustrates how *thing* meetings coincided with trade and exchange (Gustafsson & Östergren 2017: 97, 102 tab. II).

The Disting market and similar ones, however, were only singular events held over the course of a year and connected to religious festivals (cf. Sawyer 1979: 145; 1986: 67) and/or legal assemblies. Even from continental charters on toll privileges we are well informed about elaborate contemporary systems of market trade. Generally, these charters distinguish between daily and weekly markets (*mercatum* or *forum*) and seasonal fairs (*nundinae*), which could be further specified as annual fairs (*annuum mercatum* or *nundinae annuale*). The latter were of supra-regional importance and attracted long-distance traders. As a rule, seasonal fairs were connected to religious festivals, for example for local saints (*anniversarium*), where the assembled local population could stimulate an accordant market demand (Endemann 1964: 192–208; van Houtte 1993). Without a doubt, some of the most important supra-regional agricultural fairs in the Carolingian period were the ones at the abbey of Saint Denis, north of Paris (Verlinden 1963; Bur 1995): a prosperous October fair – the St Dionysius' fair – commemorates the martyrdom of Saint Denis and dates back to the Merovingian period, established in 634/5 by Dagobert I. Another example is the Carolingian St Mathias fair, which originated around 775 and was founded by Charlemagne. The initial annual fairs developed west of the river Rhine, within the boundaries of the former Roman Empire. It is noteworthy that from the tenth century they even developed at dioceses and larger abbeys, as well as at palaces and former Roman *castra*, where the surplus from the feudal, manorial system (Ger. *Grundherrschaft*) could be sold and exchanged for luxurious consumables. In the twelfth century, fairs were to develop into regular regional market cycles, where associated fairs succeeded one another throughout the year. Examples are the famous Champagne fairs but also the Flemish fairs, as well as English and Lower Rhine fairs. By identifying so-called productive sites, British metal-detectorist archaeology has unveiled another – somewhat ambiguous – category of inland markets. This category is often found in conjunction with smaller rural centres, where there is evidence of periodical markets. Although these

Middle Saxon 'productive sites' rarely have undergone archaeological excavation, there is a possibility that they could balance the bias between weekly markets and seasonal fairs in this area, as suggested through historical sources (cf. Hodges 2012: 112). However, as in the case of *wics*, these 'productive sites' did not endure beyond the mid-ninth century (Richards 1999; Ulmschneider 2000, 2002; Brookes 2001; Naylor 2004; cf. Pestell & Ulmschneider 2003).[3] It was not until the fourteenth century that urban life in north-western Europe reached a scale that would justify permanent sedentary trade and made annual market cycles of associated fairs obsolete (Verlinden 1963: 137; Irsigler 1989, 1996).

For both early medieval England and Scandinavia, P. H. Sawyer argued that 'local exchanges at markets, [e.g.] fairs ... should be distinguished from long-distance commerce in goods ... offered for sale not by producers, but by middle men or merchants' (Sawyer 1979: 146). He also suggested that local markets and fairs were not by-products of international trade, nor were they attended by long-distance merchants, but that they were normal parts of societal life and provided a means of exchanging surpluses and local produce from the local or neighbouring communities (Sawyer 1986: 59–60, 74). Based on the English evidence, Sawyer (1986: 67) proposed that 'buying and selling took place wherever there were regular assemblies, *congregationes*, for whatever purpose. Churches provided good opportunities, for they attracted people every Sunday and especially on festivals. There were other places at which regular gatherings occurred, such as royal *villas* and the meeting places of shire and hundred courts.' In these settings, important annual fairs that were able to attract foreign merchants would already have constituted

---

[3] In this context, reference should be made to the rural inland site of Henne Kirkeby Vest in central Jutland: situated some 4–5 kilometres from the North Sea coast, it was laid out around a central road, where a great number of pit houses were surrounded by a palisade. The artefact spectrum suggested local textile production, amber processing and an involvement in long-distance trade (cf. Frandsen 2018, 2020). Many of the features found at Henne Kirkeby are otherwise associated with specialised landing sites (Ulriksen 2018: 418–21, 425–6).

exceptions. However, they would still have differed considerably from the market activities in Viking-age towns, where daily and supra-regional market trade was the main purpose throughout the sailing season, between April and October (cf. Falk 1912: 27). When – as in the case of Birka – winter markets on the ice are considered (Arbman 1939: 52; 1943: xiv; 1955: 17), it is possible that market trading may even have been a year-round activity.

4.3 PALACES OF AN ITINERANT KINGSHIP?

The wielding of power in the Viking realms was presumably not too dissimilar from that in north-western Europe, which – from the Frankish up until the high medieval period – was characterised by an itinerant kingship (Ger. *Reisekönigtum*). Itinerant or travelling kingdoms are considered as typical for societies that only possessed rudimentary state structures, which had neither permanent seats or residences for their royal courts nor central administrations. On the other hand, this system allowed the control of the local chieftains, the provision of the royal suite and the collection of regal dues from the yield of the royal demesnes (Peyer 1964: 13–15; Andrén 1983: 36–7; Strömberg 2004: 167–8). Unless it is a high medieval element added by Snorri, evidence of an early Norse itinerant kingship is found in a passage of *The Ynglingasaga* (chap. 33), where it is stated that Anund 'the Land Clearer' 'has roads built throughout Sweden, both through forests and over bogs and mountains … King Anund established estates [*bú*] for himself in every large district [*stórherað*] in Sweden and made his royal progress throughout the land' (cf. Arbman 1943: xiv). It is tempting to see his efforts as the origin of the Swedish *via regia*, the so-called *Eriksgata*, literally the 'journey/road of the absolute ruler' (MSwd. *einríkr*) – which is otherwise only possible to trace back to the late thirteenth century (Sundqvist 2001: 622–3, 633–7; Sanmark 2017: 51–2, 104–6 fig. 4.15; Semple et al. 2020: 120 fig. 4.28). In this context, the *visthus*, that is, 'a building or possibly a group of buildings in which provisions (*vist*) for the king, his retinue, or his agents were stored' (Line 2007: 289 n. 76), recorded already for the eleventh century, is of particular interest since it supports the idea of itinerant royal stopovers (Line 2007: 274). The Norwegian equivalent to the Swedish *visthus* is *veizla*, a network of peasant farms from which the OldWN *lendir menn* gathered provisions (Gurevich 1993: 373). Comparable evidence seems to be found in the archaeological record, which gives us a somewhat more secure basis. A corresponding interpretation has been presented, for example, for the magnate's estate at Tissø on western Zealand (Jørgensen 2003: 204–7), which will be discussed later in this section.

The royal estate par excellence is without a doubt Jelling in Jutland, with its two monumental mounds framing the church and two Jelling stones, which commemorate the founders of the Jelling dynasty King Gorm the Old, his wife Thyra and their son King Harald Bluetooth (Roesdahl 2008: 657–60). The northern mound probably dates back to a Bronze Age predecessor and is 65 metres in diameter and 8 metres high. The southern mound has a diameter of 70 metres and a height of 11 metres. While the southern mound does not contain a burial, excavations of the northern mound revealed an almost empty burial chamber, dated to 958/9, which is generally ascribed to Gorm the Old. After the baptism of King Harald in c.965, he supposedly took his father, King Gorm, from this pagan interment to be reburied in a Christian context inside the church (cf. Roesdahl 1997; differently Gelting 2010). Staecker (2005) argued that the Christian character of grave goods, which remained in the northern mound, instead suggested that the mound was the grave of queen Thyra and that Gorm had never been reburied. Originally, it was thought that the mounds were built on top of the remains of the bow and stern of an older ship setting and that Harald's rune stone (DR 42) was positioned amidships in-between the mounds. More recent data, however, have revealed that one of the stems of the ship setting is indeed buried under the (later) southern mound but also that the ship's centre is in fact situated under the northern mound, which suggests that it is twice as large as previously assumed (Kähler Holst et al. 2012: 483). The Jelling Project of the National Museum of Denmark, which centred on the surroundings of the hitherto known monuments, recently provided a considerable amount of new evidence, contributing to the evolving understanding of the setting for this display of power expressed by the Jelling dynasty. Among many other finds, not only did the project identify traces of three wooden predecessors to the present Romanesque church but the review of the original excavation documentation even revealed clues to a preceding hall building with a deviating orientation (Kähler Holst et al. 2012: 481 fig. 6). Other finds indicated that the entire complex had been surrounded by an enormous rhombic vertical palisade built of rectangular planks supported by slightly irregularly placed pairs of post on either side. The layout seems to have adhered to strict geometric principles, where the 360-metre-long ship setting defines the main axis as well as the maximum extent of the rhombic enclosure and the northern mound was its centre point. In this way, the palisade enclosed a total area of approximately 125,000 square metres. Dendrochronology established that the palisade was built between 958 and 985 (sapwood statistics), most likely around 968 or shortly thereafter (Dengsø Jessen et al. 2014). A large-scale excavation focussing on the north-eastern part of the rhombic palisade uncovered three contemporary Trelleborg-type longhouses, which followed the inner course of the enclosure at regular intervals (Kähler Holst et al. 2012).

Yet what – apart from its sheer size, the monumental mounds and an enormous ship setting as a display of power from an emerging dynasty – makes Jelling so special as an estate? As for the particular geometrically standardised architectural style, obvious links to the contemporary Trelleborg-ring fortresses have been demonstrated, as well as architectural resemblance with royal/aristocratic sites such as Lejre and Tissø in terms of its central hall buildings and their enclosures. Even fenced agricultural settlements like Vorbasse are referred to as having been 'influenced by some of the aristocratic architectural trends' (Kähler Holst et al. 2012: 499, 493–501 fig. 19). The most striking parallel, however, is certainly Lisbjerg, north of Aarhus, from around 1000, which features traces of a central hall building underneath a wooden church which is the predecessor of the present-day church (Jeppesen & Madsen 1995/6). Moreover, additional longhouses of a developed Trelleborg-type face the central hall building and line the inside of a 19,000 square metre enclosure. The gradually growing understanding of the Lisbjerg site has changed the way it has been perceived from a 'farm-estate' (Dan. *storgård*) (Jeppesen & Madsen 1991) to a 'magnate's residence' (Dan. *stormandsgård*) (Jeppesen 2004), suggesting that it was a royal estate and as such also a local administrative centre. Other features, such as a separate special fenced-in area or 'sheltered yard' directly associated to the central hall building, indicate clear links to the magnate estate at Tissø (Jeppesen 2004: 164–8 fig. 6). Overall, this shows how even an extraordinary complex, such as Jelling, displays obvious architectural similarities to other aristocratic and royal manor sites from all over southern Scandinavia (Kähler Holst et al. 2012: 501–2), besides the suggested parallels to Continental European royal sites and fortified aristocratic settlements (Dengsø Jessen et al. 2014: 62).

While places like Lejre, Jelling and Gamla Uppsala can undoubtedly be associated with the main residences of corresponding dynasties, Tissø offers another facet, which may complete the overall picture: the site of Tissø, situated on the western shore of the eponymous lake, has roots in the Vendel/Merovingian period, with an initial manor from the sixth or seventh century ('first manor' at Bulbrogård). Already this enclosed farm complex was of a considerable size and consisted of a large hall building and two additional major buildings, where the smallest had an additional inner fence (Jørgensen 2008: 77; Franck Bican 2010). After a fire in the late seventh century, the manor was relocated some 600 metres south ('second manor' at Fugledegård), which lasted through four different development phases until the eleventh century. This likewise enclosed manor complex grew gradually, with an area of about 10,000 square metres in the initial phase to more than 25,000 square metres in its final phase. A main complex in its centre consisted of a large residential hall with a small extra building enclosed by a fence (Figure 7). In its first two phases, the

FIGURE 7 Tissø, Zeeland, Denmark. Reconstruction of the manorial complex at Tissø-Fugledegård (illustration: R. L. Børsheim; © Arkikon AS).

main hall building was directly connected to this 'special fenced[-in] area', but in phase three, when an even more monumental main building had replaced the initial one, the fenced-in area was separated from the residential hall; at the same time, additional buildings were erected along the western inner side of the enclosure, with their gables facing its main complex. It was not until the fourth phase, from the late tenth century onwards, that the building pattern changed and the formerly special fenced area was completely abandoned (Jørgensen 2003, 2008, 2009: fig. 14)[4]. The special fenced area at Tissø displays similarities not only to the 'sheltered yard' in Lisbjerg but also to Järrestad in Scania, where such features have been interpreted as parts of fenced-in cult buildings. According to Sundqvist (2016: 100–2), these large manorial residences with small cultic houses are further developments of the hall as a pre-Christian ceremonial building, which housed both profane and sacred rooms, and were part of the

[4] Note that an earlier suggested 'small cross-shaped building' from phase 4 (cf. Jørgensen 2003: 199 fig. 15.20–21) has been reinterpreted as a square structure belonging to the fenced-in area of phase 3.

religious strategies for rulership.[5] The ritual components of life at Tissø have been corroborated by weapon sacrifices in the adjacent 'Tyr's lake', as well as a row of cooking pits for ritual meals and a presumed sacrificial site on a nearby hilltop (Jørgensen 2009: 338–44).[6] Based on excavations of a vast number of pit houses at Tissø, which only seem to have been used seasonally, its role as a possible assembly site has also been discussed (Nørgard Jørgensen et al. 2010: 104; Jørgensen et al. 2019: 167, 172–3). As demonstrated in Section 4.2, as in the case of Gamla Uppsala, these centres of power tended to be associated with cultic, legal and even market activities. This also seems to apply to Tissø, where more than eighty pit houses, as well as traces of smaller houses or market booths, have been documented around the manor enclosure. Moreover, towards its south, an extensive workshop area with traces of iron forging and bronze casting have also been found. In the northern part of the Tissø complex, where the river Halleby Å runs by Kalmargården, an additional market area – with an associated landing place by the river mouth facing the Great Belt/Storebælt – has been identified. However, based on the quantity of artefacts, the excavator Jørgensen (2008: 81–2) suggested that 'Compared with the find frequency at *emporia* such as Ribe, Haithabu [Hedeby], Kaupang and Birka, the quantity of finds is smaller at Tissø' and concluded: 'This does not suggest long-lasting occupation in the market and production areas. There seem to have been short, but intense periods of activity.' This suggests that markets activities even took place at the manors and that they were closely linked to the royal estates. However, it also implies that these were limited to seasonal fairs that only benefitted the assembled public from a larger rural catchment area.

The archaeological evidence from the manor complex at Tissø seems contradictory: although there is an obvious lack of auxiliary

---

[5] Whether the fenced-in ceremonial buildings can be linked to ON *blóthús*, mentioned in the Saga literature as pre-Christian farm temples, remains hypothetical (Sundqvist 2016: 156).

[6] These outdoor ritual structures/sacred places, along with the ceremonial building, would qualify as sanctuaries (cf. Sundqvist 2016: 5, 259).

buildings within the limits of the enclosure, large quantities of bone refuse attest to the presence of many people; the abundance of high-status and prestige objects confirm affiliations to an elite. Hence Jørgensen (2003: 204–7 tab. 15.1) convincingly compares Tissø with Carolingian imperial palaces, such as those at Aachen or Tilleda, and links its monumental hall, its adjacent cult area and its temple with the *aula regia*, *atrium* and palatine chapel. Moreover, just as at the Carolingian *Pfalzen*, the elements of representation, cult area, cult activities, retinue, jurisdiction/trials and markets are archaeologically traceable. In conclusion, Jørgensen (2008: 82) argues that it is obvious that Tissø – similarly to the imperial palaces – was not a permanent residence but rather part of a 'royal estate system of a mobile monarchy', where vast amounts of people assembled occasionally.

5 Local Society and Viking-Age Towns

As outlined in previous chapters, the emerging urban communities in Viking-age Scandinavia would not have been an integral part of the rural agrarian society that surrounded them. Instead, they coexisted only on the fringes of these otherwise traditional societies. This was not only true in Scandinavia but also in the Carolingian Empire, as described by Verhaeghe (2005: 283): 'But on the whole, the urban world was still very much a sideline in an essentially rural- and land-based economy and power structure.' As indicated in the Introduction, Viking-age towns were not characterised by local populations but by their vast multi-ethnic ones. This is evident in the town of Birka, which seems to have had its own assembly site, a clear indication that it was separated from the surrounding rural communities. Another important dissimilarity is the continuous engagement in market trade and involvement in long-distance trade as a primary purpose, instead of seasonal fairs. How these emerging towns – as expressions of 'super-modernity' (Augé 1995) – were embedded in this environment and managed to coexist with a traditional society will be demonstrated by discussing the duality of early towns and royal estates, as well as their geographical position in relation to the existing power structures.

5.1 DUALITY OF EARLY TOWNS AND ROYAL ESTATES

One feature that the Viking-age towns have in common is their lack of royal manors within the boundaries of the towns – a feature that is central to medieval descendants, such as at Sigtuna (*äldsta kungsgårdstomten*, see Tesch 2001a: 19–20; Runer 2014) or Slesvig (*Graukloster*, cf. Radtke 1977, 2003), as is the presence of corresponding cathedrals. Therefore, the emerging urban centres must rather be regarded as 'religiously and politically neutral zones' (Søvsø 2020: 254).

FIGURE 8 Hovgården and Birka, Uppland, Sweden. In the foreground is the church of Adelsö with the monumental mounds, as well as the royal manor Alsnö hus; in the background, across the strait, is the island of Björkö with the Viking-age town of Birka (photo ID: KMB_16001000167644_PNN02691; Swedish National Heritage Board/ RAÄ [Riksantikvarieämbetet], Photo: J. Norman 1990 [CC BY]).

However, although the royal presence in these Viking-age towns seems to have been upheld solely by royal representatives (see Section 7.4), it is also clear that royal manors/palaces were placed – or already existed – within eyesight of these towns.

One such example is Hovgården, situated on the island of Adelsö, only 2.7 kilometres north-west of the island of Björkö, across the strait of Björkösundet and Hovgårdsfjärden (Figure 8). This site is defined by three unexcavated monumental or 'royal' mounds, situated on a ridge north of the present-day Adelsö church, dating to the late twelfth century. They have been allotted to Erik (Refilsson), Björn 'at Haugi' and Olof (I of Sweden) – both of the latter are mentioned as kings in the context of Ansgar's visits to Birka in 830 and in 852 (see Section 4.2). Another flat-topped mound – the so-called assembly mound (Swd: *tingshögen*) – is located west of the three previously mentioned; to their north lies the monumental mound *Skopinntull* (the 'shoe-pain customs [toll]', according to Svensson 1958: 290–1) (Rydh 1936: 206–13; Arbman 1973). The latter was excavated by Hanna Rydh in 1917, who found an extraordinarily equipped cremation burial with the burnt remnants of a mature male individual, who had been incinerated with a ship, riding horse and a large variety of sacrificial animals. The burial is dated to the late eighth or early ninth century (Rydh 1936: 104–28). The rune stone *Hovgårdstenen* (U 11) mentions a King Håkan, who is probably to be identified as Håkan the Red, who succeeded King Stenkil and ruled in the last quarter of the eleventh century (Wessén 1940: 11–20). It reads: 'You read the runes! Right let cut them Tolir, bailiff [*bryti*] in Roden, to the king [*kunuki*]. Tolir and Gylla let carve (these runes), this pair after themselves as a memorial ... Håkon bade carve' (Wessén 1940: 12).[1] Until recently, information on the available time frame for a royal presence on Adelsö has been scant: the royal manor does not appear in written sources until 1200 in a deed of donation as *mansionem regiam Alsnu* ('the royal mansion on Adelsö'). In 1917, Thordeman (1920) examined the ruins of 'Alsnö hus', which formed the centre of the medieval royal estate and has been linked to both King Magnus Ladulås and King Birger Magnusson. Thordeman found a two-storied palace made of brick, dating to the second half of the thirteenth century. It was not until the 1990s, when surveys focussing on the actual Viking-age phase of Adelsö were undertaken, that archaeologists were able to find traces of building platforms with possible links to a royal manor from the mid-eighth century. The remains of the Viking-age royal manor itself are thought to lie beneath the ruins of the medieval Alsnö hus (Brundstedt 1996). These investigations were

[1] Källström (2015) offered a convincing reinterpretation of *Hovgårdstenen*, particularly the section on 'Tólir, bailiff in Roden' (toliR : bry[t]i : i roþ). It suggested that the previous interpretation of Roden, as Roslagen, should instead be understood as *rōðr* in the sense of a *rodd* (oar route) and thus reads as 'Interpret the runes! Tólir the bailiff at the fairway had them rightly carved for the King' (Källström 2015: 82–4; my translation). This rereading would have a huge impact on our general understanding of Hovgården on Adelsö, the authority of the bailiff and the significance of royal control on major waterways (see Chapter 7).

supplemented by a study of the former harbour in the bay between Adelsö church and the royal estate, as well as two medieval boat houses of the *naust*-type. But, even on the island of Björkö itself, at the bay of Korshamn, a Viking-age magnate residence with Vendel-period origins was recently identified (Kalmring et al. 2017; Kalmring 2020b). This was located on the north-eastern side of the island, outside the fortified settlement area of the Black Earth (Swd. *Svarta Jorden*). A complete assessment of its relationship to *Hovgården* on Adelsö will require archaeological fieldwork. At this early stage, knowledge is based solely on topographical observations backed by geophysical surveys, as well as on historical accounts, place-names studies and Scandinavian analogies. Finally, it should be noted that there is another royal manor with a monumental mound – ascribed to the ninth-century King Björn Ironside – in Husby, located on the former island of Munsö, approximately 5.8 km north-east of Björkö (Lindqvist 1936: 9; Wessén 1940: 20–1).

The site of Kaupang in Vestfold is located west of the mouth of the Oslofjord. It is considered to be associated with the 'central-place complex' at Skiringssal, which comprised several burial grounds, a Huseby site, the assembly site *Þjóðalyng* and the sacred sites at lake *Vítrir/Vettrir* (Vittersen) and the Helgefjell mountain (Skre 2007: 13–24, 48–50).[2] What in the case of Kaupang and Skiringssal is understood as several functional elements relating to one coherent central place, however, could also be seen as a sphere where a traditional society collides with the novelty of an early town, with only a minimum of mutual influence. And while mere landing places/ beach markets were regular parts of a rural society and as such even appeared in combination with traditional central places like Skiringssal, early (harbour) towns as Kaupang clearly signal something completely different. Hence, if Kaupang is an example of an emerging Viking-age town, it would be more appropriate to focus on what

---

[2] Skre (2008: 86–7) has revised and modified the view on central places and suggested that they were 'old rural places of power, commonly called central places', that 'neither in organization nor in their permanent activities ... [had] an urban character'.

separates it from – rather than on what links it to – the surrounding rural society. One such separating element seems to be the royal administrative farm of Huseby, situated in the vicinity of the urban settlement of Kaupang, which clearly demonstrates such a detached, although slightly adjoined position. Unusually for Norway, it was built on a platform, and only two other examples have been found in all of Norway (cf. Weinmann 1994: 108), otherwise this technique is only known from the Mälar Valley. Huseby, which was not discovered until 1999, was placed on a rocky knoll approximately 2 kilometres north of the early town. Its house platform was built of soil and boulders on top of an early Iron Age burial mound and measured 36 by 13 metres. Erosion and anthropogenic disturbances leading to an absence of stratified layers made the observation conditions during the excavations difficult. Even construction elements such as posthole stone packings were hard to differentiate from the boulders that constituted the house platform. However, after all due consideration, a 35 by 11.7 metres hall building was identified, which is comparable in size to the hall buildings at Tissø and Gamla Uppsala. It was built in the second half of the eighth century and remained in place until around 900 when it was destroyed by fire (Skre 2007: 223–47 fig. 11.8). There is reason to believe that the hall at Huseby was originally called *Skíringssalr* – that is, 'the bright, shining hall' – a name that later applied to the wider Tjølling region (Brink 2007: 60–2). In the eleventh century, or possibly later, a *stofa*-type log cabin, presumably part of a royal administrative farmstead (Huseby), was erected upon the remains of the Viking-age hall building.

Applying similar parameters to Hedeby, across the inner Schlei fjord, the site of Füsing is situated only 6 kilometres away. It was identified in 2003 through metal-detecting and subsequent geophysical surveys (Dobat 2010). Füsing not only is within eyesight of Hedeby but also holds a very strategical position, controlling the mouth of the Füsing river, which, leading to the heart of Anglia, provided access to the settlement cluster around Lake Langsee as well as to the Wellspang and Mühlen brook (Dobat 2022: 2–4, 12 figs. 1–2; cf. Willroth 1992: map

70). Ensuing excavations at Füsing revealed twenty-four longhouses and fifty-two pit houses, as well as vast numbers of cooking pits and fire-cracked stones. The pit houses of the settlement had a round or oval shape and seem to have been occupied only seasonally. They predominately seem to belong to an early settlement phase in the seventh and eighth centuries, while a later settlement phase is characterised by two slightly separate longhouse complexes, both situated in elevated positions: in the Southern Settlement area, two three-aisled longhouses (features OA2-2010 and OA18-2010) from the tenth century were uncovered, aligned at right angles to each other. However, most of the Viking-age activities seem to have taken place on a plateau to the northeast, near the meandering Füsing river. There, another longhouse complex was revealed, consisting of six partly overlapping longhouses, and a section of a palisade. Overlooking the rest of the site, on top of the plateau, was a two-phase longhouse situated, measuring 27 by 9 metres (feature OA123-2011). This longhouse has been dated to around 900, or the first half of the tenth century, and was destroyed by fire shortly thereafter, perhaps due to an enemy attack on the manor (Dobat 2022: 5–8 figs. 4–5). Certain artefacts might indicate that this was an aristocratic elite settlement, possibly even related to the Jelling dynasty. Hence it has been compared to Adelsö and Skiringssal, and as such it was analogously interpreted as a temporary royal residence, too (Dobat 2010: 201–3; 2022: 13–14, 17)[3]. From this, the author rightly concludes that 'Füsing appears to have been deeply rooted in a traditional Scandinavian context and focused on its regional hinterland' (Dobat 2022: 13). The settlement activities at Füsing seem to have started around 700 at the latest – or possibly as early as the late seventh century – and continued until the end of the tenth century (Dobat 2010: 179; 2022: 11). It has even been suggested that the place name *Sliesthorp* – that is, a *thorp* ('hamlet/small village') name instead of the later *Slieaswich*, and its use in the *Royal Frankish Annals* for events

[3] In contrast, Arents and Eisenschmidt (2010: 270) suggested that the royal residence at Hedeby was located in the present village of Busdorf, immediately to the west of the Viking-age town (cf. Müller-Wille 1973).

that took place in 804 and 808 – would refer to Füsing rather than, as generally assumed, to Hedeby. A royal manor at Füsing would supply Hedeby with the early roots that previously have been illusive, and where the earliest recorded activities were not confirmed before 811 and to any major extent only since the 830s (Skre 2007: 459; Dobat 2022: 15–16). It is possible, however, that Hedeby's roots may be older than previously thought, as indicated by the burial ground at Selk (Arents & Eisenschmidt 2010: 62–3) and a local concentration of five gold bracteates, which could point to a Migration-period central place in its immediate vicinity (Dobat 2003; 2006: 89–91). Further support for these early activities can be found in new evidence from the hillfort *Hochburg* with its modest late Merovingian/Vendel-period burial ground (Kalmring 2014/15: 269–78), early metal-detectorist finds from Hedeby's southern limits – from within its semi-circular rampart as well as the Southern Settlement – dating to the Merovingian period (Hilberg 2014: 159; 2018: 135–9 figs. 8–9), the recent re-identification of a likely ninth-century manorial complex at the Southern Settlement (Hilberg 2018: 140–2 fig. 11) and the suggestion that it may have been preceded by a manorial complex from the late Merovingian period (Hilberg 2018: 142),[4] and not least by its prime natural harbour by the Haddeby Noor (Kalmring 2010a: 61–2). Collectively, these indicators support theories suggesting that Hedeby is the actual site mentioned in the annals. Where else would Godfred have transferred the Obotrite merchants from Reric to?

5.2 EXTERRITORIAL SITES: EARLY TOWNS IN NO MAN'S LAND

Sites such as Adelsö, Skiringssal and possibly even Füsing seem to represent manors/palaces of itinerant kingship not dissimilar from sites such as Tissø. Based on the assumption that itinerant kingship

---

[4] If the suggested preceding late Merovingian-period manor in the Southern Settlement of Hedeby can be confirmed, the location would be very similar to the late Vendel-period situation with the raised plateau house at *Erik Steffanssons hemland* in Birka-Korshamn (Kalmring et al. 2017: 125–7) located immediately outside the later town ramparts.

is a trait typical of realms that lack fixed political centres, the Viking-age towns – at least in their initial phase – should not be regarded as centres of political power either. This is supported by the fact that, although royal manors are indeed located in the immediate vicinity of these towns, they are at same time distinctly spatially separate. Regarding the terminological debate on designating early towns, it seems worthwhile to once again refer to the concept of orthogenetic and heterogenetic sites (cf. Mogren 2013). By accepting royal manors such as Adelsö, Skiringssal and perhaps Füsing as orthogenetic sites of some central character, associated with stability and expressions of monumentality, regularly visited by their kings but otherwise administrated by royal, religious and military bureaucracies, the heterogenic sites have to be considered as well, since they are part of this conceptual pair. The heterogenetic sites are not only characterised by their lack of monumentality, or simply by societal change and entrepreneurship associated to trade and bulk commodity production; above all, it is their characteristic placement in border zones between natural landscape units, transport zones or ethnic and political entities (Kalmring 2020a).

For Hedeby, the borderland location is quite obvious. Not only does the site have a remarkably beneficial location from a topographical transport perspective, at the crossroads of the overland route between *Hærvejen* ('the Army Road'; Ger. Ochsenweg), leading from Viborg to Hamburg, and a sea route between the North Sea and Baltic Sea with a portage at Hollingstedt, but it is also immediately on the actual border between Scandinavia and Continental Europe (Kalmring 2010a: 29–34). The latter is indicated not least by the rune stones Haddeby DR 1–4 and Slesvig DR 6 (cf. Jacobsen & Moltke 1941-2), which are the southernmost stones of their kind. Moreover, Hedeby was situated where the areas of four different ethnicities intersected, who all gathered in town and engaged in commerce (Figure 9(a)). The northern Danish sphere stretched as far as the Danevirke/Danewerk and at times even to the river Eider. To the south, the Nordalbingian Saxons lived in what today is the central and western parts of Holstein, between the river Eider and

FIGURE 9 Viking-age towns in no man's land. Maps by David McCutcheon FBCart.S www.dvdmaps.co.uk.: (a) language areas of medieval Schleswig-Holstein, Germany, reflecting the four main ethnicities: (1) Frisian, (2) Danish, (3) Saxon/German and (4) Slavonic (adapted from Müller-Wille 2002a: fig. 646, with additions);
In Figure 9(a), note Hedeby's strategic borderland position at the intersections of these areas.

the lower Elbe. After Charlemagne's Saxon Wars in 772–804, the Nordalbingian Saxons were incorporated into the Carolingian Empire. The *limes Saxoniae*, roughly running from the Kiel fjord to the river Elbe, marked the border between the Saxons and Obotrites (cf. Lemm 2013a: 339–56), a Slavic tribe belonging to the Wends inhabiting eastern Holstein and western Mecklenburg. Lastly, the coast of the Wadden Sea, north of the river Eider, including the North Frisian Islands, was settled by the Frisians (Müller-Wille 2002a: 368–9 fig. 646). The

EXTERRITORIAL SITES: EARLY TOWNS IN NO MAN'S LAND 59

FIGURE 9 (b) Lake Mälaren with the medieval administrative provinces of Uppland (inclusive of coastal Roden), eastern central Sweden (adapted from Andersson 2004: fig. 1, with additions).
In Figure 9(b), note the pie-piece-shaped layout with Birka at the southern tip of the three regions.

border next to Hedeby was marked by the multiphase fortifications of Danevirke/Danewerk (Andersen 1998), which controlled the 16-kilometer-wide land bridge between the Schlei fjord and the boggy river marshes of the west coast, constituting the Schleswig isthmus. In his article on the Danevirke, Dobat (2008: 59; cf. 2022: 15–16) described Hedeby's marginal position as an 'urban island' clearly separated from the older settlement landscapes. He also distinguishes between an initial phase (c.700–950) and a liminal phase (c.950–1000) in the development of the Danevirke fortifications. During the initial phase, the fortifications consisted of Crooked Wall, Main Wall, Northern Wall, the sea defence at Reesholm and the Eastern Wall. It seems obvious that Hedeby's position in front of the Danevirke meant that it was deliberately placed in a no man's land. Even during the liminal phase of the fortifications – which included Hedeby's mid-tenth-century semi-circular ramparts and the Connection Wall from around 965–8, connecting it to Danevirke – as the town was integrated into Danevirke itself, it still remained marginal in relation to its northern hinterland. With its new context as part of the Danevirke, it merely 'moved' onto the border itself, instead of being secured behind it as a true part of the Danish realm.

Birka, too, had an advantageous accessible topographical position, situated as a hub between two of the most important transport routes in eastern central Sweden (Ambrosiani 1989). On the one hand, it was located on the east–westerly transport axis between the Svealand interior and the Baltic Sea. On this route, Birka became an important location for trans-shipping and the stacking of trade goods such as iron, wood and furs, which were transported in winter on sleds from central Sweden (Lindquist 1926: 30; Arbman 1943: xiv). On the other hand, it was situated on the northern–southern axis called *Fyrisleden* (Ambrosiani 1957: fig. 1), which connected Lake Mälaren and Birka to the Baltic Sea via an open strait at (Söder-) Tälje. To the north, it proceeded past the royal manor *Fornsigtuna* ('Old Sigtuna'; cf. Damell 1991) through the eponymous river Fyrisån to Gamla Uppsala and finally on to Vendel, in the very north of the Mälar Valley (and, by land, further towards Bergslagen). Moreover, the relatively small island of Björkö was located in the middle of Lake Mälaren between the provinces of Uppland to the north and Södermanland to the south. Uppland itself was divided into three *folklands* or historical provinces: Fjärdrundaland, Tiundaland and Attundaland, which formed the core of ON *Svíþjóð* – consisting of the provinces of Uppland, Västmanland and Södermanland – with the capital Gamla Uppsala (cf. Sanmark 2017: 58–62 fig. 3.2). The folkland names of Uppland translate as 'land of four', 'land of ten' and 'land of eight', whereas *hund* and *hundare* (OSwd) refer to a group of a hundred, capable of bearing arms and commonly connected with the *ledung* system (ON *leiðangr*) for territorial naval defence (cf. Lund 1996). In Uppland, the term *hundare* is attested as from the eleventh century but without doubt dates back to the Viking Age or even earlier. At some stage, the folkland may all have been self-ruling entities, but in the Viking Age it is likely that a central authority – the king of the *Svear* – controlled all three (Andersson 2000; 2004: 13). Usually Adelsö and Björkö are attributed as parts of Fjärdrundaland. Here, however, the assumption is made that Viking-age Birka, in contrast to the island of Adelsö, did not actually belong to any historical province but – situated near the tip of three almost pie-piece-shaped folklands (Figure 9(b))– had a different, much more autonomous status (cf. Hildebrand 1879: 324; Kalmring 2016a: 15–16 fig. 2b). This assumption is based not only on Björkö's topographical location but also on the fact that written sources suggest that Birka had its own *thing*, detaching it judicially from the surrounding country.

Ribe, too, was situated in the borderland, namely between the Frisian and Danish zones of influence at the northern fringes of the North Sea trading network (Jensen 1991: 69). Furthermore, it was even – separated by the Farris forest – located at the border between the later duchies of Slesvig and Northern Jutland (Søvsø 2020: 79 fig. 44; cf. Pilgaard 2013). A location by a boundary is also true for Kaupang, which developed by the former border of the Danish kingdom, whose sphere of influence at that time included Vestfold (Skre 2007: 445, 461). However, borderland locations are not only a common feature of the Viking-age towns; the trading site of Truso/Janów Pomorski at the Vistula Lagoon, for example, was situated on the border between the West Slavs and the Balts (Brather & Jagodziński 2012: fig 7.12) or – in the words of the Anglo-Saxon merchant Wulfstan, who travelled there from Hedeby – between *Weonodland* and *Witland* (Wulfstan's Report: 15).

6 An Urbanisation Based on Harbours

Mogren (2013: 81–3) emphasised the distinctly maritime character of these trading sites and the importance of an advanced nautical technology, enabling the transport of certain volumes of commodities. Interestingly, it seems increasingly apparent that the tentative introduction of the sail coincides with the establishment of seasonal trading sites (Mogren 2013; Zagal-Mach Wolfe 2013: 272–3; Kastholm 2014). Hence, a closer study of the anatomy of harbours is central to the discussion of urbanisation.[1]

The harbour excavation of Hedeby from 1979/80 (Kalmring 2010a, 2011) up until today must be regarded as one of the very few examples of large-scale harbour surveys in Northern Europe. Its significance for the understanding of the strongly maritime Viking world, as well as its impact on the scientific community at the time, can be best compared to the significance of the recent excavations in the Theodosian harbour of Constantinople (Kocabaş 2012). The analysis of Hedeby harbour shows, among other things, that no harbour can be interpreted solely through presentations of the remains of their facilities. On the contrary, seeing such features as mere responses to needs resulting from developments in shipbuilding and an increased turnover of bulk cargo has to be complemented by factors such as contemporary water depth, the draught of the cargo vessels and ultimately the provided mooring capabilities (Kalmring 2010a). When the

---

[1] In the late 1980s, Westerdahl (1986, 1992) revolutionised ship- and boat-focussed maritime archaeology by defining the elements of the maritime cultural landscape, combining land and sea features. That approach could be applied for a more holistic research approach to harbours, which above all have to be understood as hubs between two very distinct traffic systems on land and on sea: the harbour facilities themselves – although indispensable logistic installations for every *emporium* – depended on a whole bundle of prerequisites both on land and on sea to function properly. Hence, even the latter must be taken into account.

range of excavated finds from a harbour basin is set in relation to its facilities, it may provide crucial and vivid insights into harbour operations, revealing factors such as long-distance trade connections. At a major port such as Hedeby, these finds do not merely reflect an engagement in 'long-distance trade in prestige goods' or an 'early medieval gift-exchange economy' (Verhaeghe 2005: 270), which would rather relate to Hodges' seasonal type-A emporia. Instead, although prestigious objects are present, it is apparent that bulk commodities dominate the range of artefacts (Kalmring 2010a: 390–442), and the same applies for Ribe (Søvsø 2020: 171–2).[2]

For any successful maritime trading site and early town, the development of harbour facilities and their maintenance was a way of safeguarding their economic basis and continued vital participation in long-distance trade. Failure to do so would simply have meant that ships chose another site. Since such a scenario would have immediately deprived any site of its commercial basis, the entire economic success of the emporia was directly tied to the usability of the harbour facilities (Kalmring 2007). This implies that, without a deeper understanding of the harbours, virtually none of the Viking-age towns can be properly understood.

6.1 LANDING SITES AND BEACH MARKETS

In the most basic sense, harbours are facilities for stationary shipping traffic, including both seaward zones for mooring ships and landward ones for loading and unloading cargo. According to this broad definition, the term actually includes both natural harbours (landing sites

---

[2] New evidence has revealed even earlier examples of long-distance trade with bulk cargoes, for example the existence of seventh-century oak barrels from the Rhine-Main area at Dorestad (Jansma & van Lanen 2016: 4–5 fig. 5, tab. 5–7; Jansma et al. 2017: 38) or the import of very fine-grained purple and dark grey schist from Mostadmarka in Trøndelag from c.760 onwards (Baug et al. 2019: 50–64) as well as reindeer antler from Arctic and subarctic outlands from 780 onwards (Ashby et al. 2015) to Ribe. For a discussion on some pre-Viking-age supra-regional trade in Scandinavia exceeding mere ritualised gift exchange, see Skre (2020: 222–4) and Hennius (2021: 114–19).

for beaching) and those with artificial facilities ('wharf constructions' offering floating berths) (Kalmring 2010a: 23–6).

Usually, however, a distinction is made between the categories 'landing sites' and 'harbours' as conceptual counterparts, the latter denoting the respective facilities of major harbour towns or ports. Landing sites are simple landing places at natural harbours without substantial man-made constructions. Generally, landing sites do not face the open sea but use well-protected locations, such as bays or river mouths. Their main characteristic is that boats and ships did not moor afloat but were beached on a soft shore. The only requirement for the use of such a landing place was a moderate displacement and a correspondingly shallow draught of the vessels.

In contrast to the relatively low number of well-studied major harbours (cf. Bill & Clausen 1999), where surveys are often unavoidably connected to large-scale excavations and massive costs, landing sites are well known from both the Baltic Sea and the North Sea regions. The latter formed a dense pattern of sites scattered along the coasts and major waterways, which were often only separated by a day's boat journey. The archaeological traces of landing sites suggest that most appeared during the course of the sixth and seventh centuries and onwards, although the phenomenon seems to have developed since the late Roman period (Ulriksen 1998: 13–14). Important regional studies on landing sites have been performed around the shores of Funen (Crumlin-Pedersen et al. 1996), in the Roskilde fjord (Ulriksen 1998), Gotland (Carlsson 1998) and in the Schlei fjord (Dobat 2004), more recently complemented by a study on their archaeological concepts (Ilves 2012) or on accompanying phenomena such as beacon systems along the sea routes (Lemm 2016a, 2019). As in the case of any harbour, landing sites can serve a whole range of purposes: replenishing food supplies, exporting goods, sites for harbour or border markets, transit harbours, guest harbours, places to shelter from storms, shipyards, fishing harbours, ferry harbours and naval ports. It is particularly noteworthy that the landing sites were often synonymous with trading sites or beach markets (Crumlin-Pedersen 1991: fig. 8). In the maritime

FIGURE 10 Lynæs, Roskilde fjord, Denmark. Seasonal beach market at landing site (illustration © F. Bau).

societies of the Scandinavian late Iron Age, beach markets were the most common arenas for trade and exchange. Markets could be set up wherever a ship landed (Figure 10). Such a beach market is illustrated in an episode in *Egil's Saga* (chap. 79), describing how one summer a ship came to the Hvitá river at Borgarfjörður and a large market (ON *mikil kaupstefna*) was set up, where Egill Skallagrímsson was able to buy a lot of timber for his farm. For this context, it would be useful to recapitulate the close integration and spatial arrangements that existed between long-distance trade and various types of assemblies described in Chapter 4 – since it was certainly not a coincidence that the start of the shipping season in early May corresponded roughly to the period of the local spring *things*. The Icelandic example in particular illustrates that 'Trading seems to have been consciously channelled and managed through the assembly process and sites' (Semple et al. 2020: 246; on the Icelandic conditions, see also 237–8, 241, 246). It is even likely that the classic event of the first Viking attack on Wessex in 789 – predating the attack on Lindisfarne by four years – surprised the local Anglo-Saxon authorities completely, since they were probably expecting to greet visitors to a regular beach market: when the three Danish ships beached at Portland, King Beorhtric's reeve (*exactor regis*) Beaduheard and a few men from nearby Dorchester rode to the beach to redirect the arrivals to the royal villa, expecting 'merchants rather than plunderers' (*putans eos magis negotiators esse quam hostes*), as the source notes (*The Chronicle of Æthelweard*, entry 789 CE; cf. Sawyer 1979: 151). In that case, it may be assumed that the reeve's mission, as an *exactor*, was to exact toll and that the *ripaticum* that he probably expected to collect was due not only for harbour use but also for beaching on unrestricted shores if the visiting mariners intended to hold a market (Adam 1996: 61, 127). Their misjudgement turned out to be fatal, as Beaduheard and his companions were slain on the spot by the Vikings (cf. Sawyer 1973: 82). A later reflection of the rules that governed landing-site operations is found in the town law of Visby (*Visby stadslag*) – which is available in a manuscript from the mid-fourteenth century, although it probably already at that time was more than 150 years older, since it still contained a preamble referring to earlier regulations – granting every visitor peace for themselves and their possessions when landing on the shores of Gotland (Gustafsson 2013: 91; 2020). This makes it likely that the preamble refers to earlier uses of beaches both as landing sites and as beach markets. The passage in question reads:

> In the name of God. Amen. Be it known that when the people in Gotland of various tongues assembled together, they swore peace, that there should be forever all round the land eight fathoms [approx. 14 metres] inland of free foreshore, whether it was cultivated land or meadows, so that everyone might be able thereon the better to land his goods, likewise that those who should come to anchor under the shelter of the island should be under the sworn peace.
> (Wisby Town-Law on Shipping: *preamble*)

Beach markets were an integral part of everyday life in Northern Europe, and recently it has become more and more obvious that every one of the Viking-age towns – Ribe, Kaupang, Birka and Hedeby – was originally an ordinary seasonal beach market.

Similar propositions have been put forward for the *emporia* on the Frisian coast as having their origins as seasonal beach markets.

Verhaeghe (2005: 268) suggested, in spite of a lack of conclusive evidence, that 'major sites [such] as Quentovic and Dorestad may have originated as [Hodges' seasonal] type-A emporia' (cf. Hodges 2012: 101–2). They even went one step further, suggesting that 'some of these settlements may have emerged first as seasonal trading-places, only to attract the attention of rulers at a subsequent stage in their development, as seems to have been the case at Dorestad' (Verhaeghe 2005: 270). More recent research has been able to differentiate this general assessment somewhat and paints a more complex picture. In this context, Malbos emphasised that, in particular, the Frankish *wics* developed in a pre-existing, economically developed hinterland owned by ecclesiastical or secular large landowners (Malbos 2017: 240–3, 356–9, 362–3, esp. 358; cf. Loveluck 2013: 18). For a long time, the emporium Quentovic at the river Canche in Neustria remained known only through historical records and its coinage. More recent evidence, however, suggests that it was actually situated at La Calotterie-Visemarest (Hill et al. 1990; Lebecq 1991, 1993; Leroy & Verslype 2015; Cense-Bacquet 2016; Routier et al. 2016). It appears as though Gesoriacum/Boulogne-sur-Mer, the former headquarters of the Roman *Classis Britannica*, had lost its leading role in the area, which led to an overall reduction in activity during the fifth and sixth centuries (Seillier 2010). The emporium at Quentovic existed between the late seventh and the second half of the ninth century. Among other roles, it seems to have served as the main port for pilgrimages between the continent and Britain – for example, Theodoros of Tarsos (in 668; Bede, book 4, chap. 1) and Wilfrid of York (in 678; *Vita Sancti Wilfrithi* chap. 25) – and thus soon attracted the attention of the Merovingian major-domo Pepin II of Herstal and came under his control (Malbos 2017: 210). Displays of power in Quentovic's surroundings suggest that the emporium had a strong political involvement – such as a the royal villa at Attin or in the churches of Saint-Josse of the Abby of Fontenelle/Saint-Wandrille, next to Rouen, and the monk's cell of Saint-Josse of the Abby of Ferrières-en-Gâtinais, close to Orléans; even the customs privilege of the Abby of Saint-Germain-des-Prés in Paris should be mentioned in this context (Malbos 2017: 69, 105, 113, 115–17, 128, 218–19, 235, 285–8 maps 8–9). The effects of a Viking raid on the *emporium Quantovicus* in 842 (*Annales Bertiniani*, entry 842 CE) seem to have been limited.[3] Yet, by the early tenth century, the emporium was succeeded by the *castrum* at Montreuil-sur-Mer. Another emporium, Domburg-Walichrum, was located at the border between Austrasia and Frisia. Originally situated immediately inland from the sand dunes on the island of Walcheren in the Scheldt estuary, the site, which is nowadays submerged, has never appeared in historical records. Yet, despite its immediate vicinity to a Roman temple of the (Germanic?) goddess Nehalennia – the patron of merchants and mariners – there does not seem to be any direct links between the two. The assumption that Domburg was indeed an active emporium between the second half of the eighth and the first half of the ninth century, however, is clearly corroborated through a great number of coin finds from its mint (van Heeringen et al. 1995: 42–9 figs. 31, 33, 35–6; cf. Capelle 1976; Lebecq 1995). Its demise may be connected to the Viking raid on Walcheren in 837 (*Annales Xantenses*, entry 837 CE), while its successor, the ring fortress of Domburg (Dut. *Duinenburg*; 'dune-fortress') dates to 835–8 (Ufkes 2011: 185, 190; cf. van Heeringen 1995: 28–32 fig. 17).

One of the most important border harbours of the Frankish Empire was Dorestad, which was situated at the confluence of the rivers Kromme Rijn and Lek, at present-day Wijk bij Duurstede in the Dutch province of Utrecht. This emporium was active between c.675 and 875. It is assumed that the as yet unidentified Roman *castellum Levefanum* at the river confluence played a decisive role in the emergence of Dorestad (van Es & Verwers 2010: 19–20). Earlier evidence, at least since the second half of the sixth century, for an elite agrarian domain/ *curtis* in the area has been derived from the earthwork at Dorestad-De

---

[3] A presumed 'economic renaissance' of Quentovic, which was suggested to have occurred after its last historical mention in the *Edict of Pîtres* of Charles the Bald from 864 (Coupland 2002: 218–20, 227), is linked to the fact that mints struck with the name Quentovic continued even after the shift towards Montreuil. It is likely that the recorded Viking raid in 898 on the *Castrum Mostorio vel Inguer* (*Annales Vedastini*, entry 898 CE) – a castle 'Montreuil-in-Quentovic'? (cf. Barbier 2010: 22) – was actually already directed on Montreuil-sur-Mer, instead of Quentovic (Malbos 2017: 364 n. 26).

Geer (van Es & Verwers 2010: 14–19; van Doesburg 2010: 55).[4] Even more astonishing are the oak finds from reused barrels – deriving from Steinbach in the Rhine-Main area – which suggest a very early seventh-century involvement in the bulk goods trade that went via a long-distance trade corridor on the Rhine (Jansma & van Lanen 2016: 4–5 fig. 5, tabs. 5–7; Jansma et al. 2017: 38; cf. Tys 2020: 773–4). After Pepin II's victory at the Battle of Dorestad in 689, the Franks took control of the Frisian site. Dorestad is known not only as the tragic victim of a total of *seven* Viking attacks in the course of the ninth century[5] but also for its extensive harbour facilities at Dorestad-Hoogstraat. There, installations made from earthen embankments extended into the Kromme Rijn and followed its continuously shifting riverbed, reaching up to 200 metres in length during the latest phase of settlement (van Es & Verwers 1980, 2009; Kalmring 2010b, 2012a). Research, published in one of the more recent Dorestad Hoogstraat publications (van Es & Verwers 2009) has even managed to reveal information about the early phases of the emporium: at the beginning of occupancy in the late Merovingian period, when the left bank of the Rhine still lay immediately east of Hoogstraat (zone 1), the oldest features in the river-bank area were bank revetments made of wickerwork, as demonstrated by the Hoogstraat II trench. As at many other sites, these revetments were probably meant to stabilise the shoreline in an effort to raise the ground level of the soggy but crucial waterside plots. Such efforts seem to have started immediately after the mid-seventh century, meaning that these bank revetments predate the construction of the first dams, which began in the last quarter of the century (van Es & Verwers 2009: 84–5, 290). It seems no coincidence that it was there – as well as on slightly later 'land abutments' (continuations of the earliest plot system on the riverbank), almost coinciding temporally with the old bank revetments – that the oldest coins from

[4] Topographically, the location of De Geer in relation to the emporium at Hoogstraat displays certain similarities with the detached relationship between the manor at Skiringssal and Kaupang (Skre 2007: 223–47), as well as the one between the manor at Korshamn and Birka (Kalmring et al. 2017).

[5] Viking raids took place in 834, 835, 836 and 837, followed by the ones in 846 and 847 as well as a final one in 863.

Dorestad, six sceattas, were found (van Gelder 1980, 2009; van Es & Verwers 2009: 311–12). These early riverine construction activities, which predate the embankments, and the distribution of sceattas limited to the old riverbank, seem to indicate a landing site connected to commercial activities. Even though there is no proof of seasonality, these features support theories about an antecedent beach market even at Dorestad.

The classic example of a seasonal beach market, however, is undoubtedly Ribe, which developed by the banks of the river Ribe Å, approximately 6 kilometres inland from the North Sea coast in south-western Jutland. There, navigable waters met the overland route Ravvejen/Drivvejen (Søvsø 2020: 84–7, 133 fig. 96). The topography is defined by a series of small sandy islands in an otherwise flat moorland, where a salt marsh cuts extraordinarily deep into the Jutland peninsula. Ribe's emergence is connected to the 'Dankirke dynasty', the manorial site of Dankirke and its likely replacement, Okholm (Søvsø 2020: 115, 127, 152, 172). The earliest traces of activities were found north of the Ribe Å. Here, a series of initial and irregular ditches were met, which predate the renowned *emporium* by one to five years (Feveile 2006a: 74 fig. 9). The so-called marketplace itself is dated to around 705. The site would have been systematically subdivided into regular plots forming rows on either side of a central pathway or road. The documented stretch is 110 metres long and contained at least twenty-five to thirty plots. These oblong plots, approximately 6–8 metres wide and up to 30 metres long, were separated by dug ditches and wattle fences (Feveile 2006a: 74–5 fig. 10). From these plots, only a few pit houses have been identified, which possibly could have served as permanent dwellings for year-round habitation. Consequently, the activities at the site were appraised as remnants of annually recurring seasonal market activities: 'As far as the cultural layers are concerned, they are either examples of refuse layers or of layers which present some open-air activity, or perhaps in the shade of light structures such as windbreaks or tents. In other words, activities of a short-lived character, possibly seasonal and recurrent: a marketplace' (Bencard & Bender Jørgensen 1990: 144).[6] It seems as though a transition from seasonal activities to year-round occupation with permanent buildings happened around the turn of the Viking Age, in about 780–800 (phase E/F; Feveile 2006a: 78–9). Judging by Croix's (2014) reassessment of the excavations of ASR 7 Sanct Nikolajgade 8 (cf. Frandsen & Jensen 1987: 187 fig. 17), however, larger permanent buildings may have existed even earlier, as she was able to identify one single wall of a 6-metre-long house of urban fabric dated to between 710 and 730, around the time when the plot system was established (phase 1a; Croix 2014: 10–12 fig 4). Hence, with certain reservations, she does suggest a permanent settlement on the early eighth-century marketplace (Croix 2014: 21). Even in the most recent excavation in 2017/18 at SJM 3 Posthustorvet, an early building (K2) with a roof-bearing post was identified and dated to the decade around 700, while the scale of activities in this phase (F3) was characterised as still being extensive (Croix et al. 2022: 64–71; cf. Sindbæk 2018; 164 fig. 2; cf. Søvsø 2020: 169). Remarkably, a 'small fragile house or hut' had previously been identified at ASR 9 Posthuset (feature A110 from phase B; Feveile 2006a: 77). Søvsø recently stated – possibly somewhat conflictingly – that the earliest phases with their irregular ditches were indications of initial seasonal activities but also that the existence of the oldest well in Dommerhaven, dated to 704, demonstrated long-term or even permanent activities (Søvsø 2020: 150, 156). Other factors also seem to support the latter, for example that a large proportion of the early inhabitants of Ribe were women and children, which suggests that 'Ribe was already permanently occupied from early in the 8th century' (Søvsø 2020: 169).[7] Interestingly, with its emerging

---

[6] Åhus in Scania should also be considered in this discussion, initially as Åhus I, a non-permanent trading place from the period 700–50 'with only flimsy constructions' (Callmer 2002: 127; cf. Callmer 1991a: 34–8). For a comparison with Ribe, see Søvsø (2018: 83; 2020: 228, 230).

[7] While these new data increasingly challenge the traditional notion of seasonal origins of market activities in Ribe, it should be pointed out that historically attested Viking camps as seasonal, multifocal entities also actually fulfilled some market functions (*The Annals of St-Bertin*, entry 873 CE; cf. Cooijmans 2021: 202) and, for the contemporary observer, could even resemble 'something like a permanent settlement' (*The*

permanent structures, Ribe has been described as an 'outpost of Dorestad' or even as a 'mini-Dorestad in Scandinavia' (Søvsø 2020: 22, 171). Surprisingly, the landing site associated with Ribe's marketplace has not yet been identified.[8] In fact, so far, the only evidence pointing to maritime activities is an iron-stocked anchor found subsequent to the excavations at Dommerhaven 5M74 (Rieck 2004).

The time span of Birka's existence is set to 750–975 and has been subdivided into an early Birka period (*'ältere Birka-Stufe'* (ÄBS), c.750–860) and a late Birka period (*'jüngere Birka-Stufe'* (JBS), c.860–975). However, it was not until Birgit Arrhenius' study of Birka's oldest artefacts published in 1976 that the earliest settlement activities before 800 were acknowledged. Not only was she able to identify reworked Migration- and Vendel-period artefacts within Viking-age burial contexts (group B) but she was also able to pinpoint three true Vendel-period burials (group A: burials Bj. 349, 1009, 1055), as well as scattered Vendel-period single finds from the Black Earth settlement area that had not been reworked (group C). She suggested that, in particular, the latter two indicated the existence of three to four early farmsteads on the island at least one generation prior to the Viking-age settlement occupation (Arrhenius 1976: 193). Later excavation of a monumental mound at Ormknös A revealed a primary burial from the early Roman Iron Age (Arrhenius 1990: 71), providing further evidence from Björkö's 'colonisation epoch' (Arrhenius 1990: 74). The so-called moose-man burial, found underneath remnants of a longhouse on a building platform next to the town wall, dates from the transition between the late Vendel period and early Viking Age (Holmquist Olausson 1990; Fennö Muyingo & Holmquist Olausson 1995), while the shaft grave of a male with his horse buried in a mound – later integrated in the ramparts of

---

Annals of St-Bertin, entry 843 CE). This insight not only means that the boundaries between seasonal marketplaces and Viking-age winter camps are blurring but also urges us to reconsider the physical nature of seasonal type-A emporia themselves.

[8] Søvsø (2020: 135–7, 157–9 figs. 98, 123) argued for a former elongated lake (south-) east of Ribelund, which may or may not have constituted a natural harbour at the southern tip of the *'uferparallele Einstrassenanlage'* (cf. Søvsø 2018: 80). So far, however, no hard evidence has been found to support this theory (cf. Bani-Sadr 2016).

the hillfort *Borg* – is dated to the first half of the eighth century (Fennö Muyingo 2000). As for the origins of Birka, Lena Holmquist (Holmquist Olausson 2002a: 157–9) suggests that a couple of longhouses were located on the prominent ridge near the later town rampart, which displayed 'considerable similarity with the more everyday settlement buildings of the surrounding countryside' (Holmquist Olausson 2002a: 158). This means that there is growing evidence for pre-Viking-age settlements on Björkö, with an obvious affinity for the elevated landmarks on the island. It seems reasonable to assume that it was these initial settlements that provided incentives for occasional beach markets at the island's landing sites.

Thanks to the careful work of the Kaupang excavation project, for Kaupang an initial seasonality has been demonstrated, too. Through a study of the entire artefactual spectrum from the most recent excavations in 2000–2, Pedersen and Pilø (2007) divided the settlement development into three main phases: the latest phase, site period III, from c.840/50 until the settlement demise in around 960–80 is a rather artificial one, since – with the exception of a few deeper pits – it basically corresponds with the modern plough horizon. Site period II, with two sub-phases, began in 805–10 and is characterised by the structural remains of a permanent settlement. However, during a short preceding period between 800 and 805–10, referred to as site period I, the authors suggested an initial phase with only seasonal settlement. This earliest phase is also evident in the discussion of the settlement features, revealing a plot system marked by fences and indicated by fire-cracked stone piles but otherwise without any permanent building features. Interestingly, and in retrospect, this pattern of plots without permanent buildings from an initial seasonal settlement occupation is also recognisable in Charlotte Blindheim's excavation trench from 1956 to 1974 (Pilø 2007: 192–5).

In Hedeby, no conclusive evidence for an early beach market has been found so far, although several indicators have emerged that would suggest a similar development there: the late Merovingian evidence – the burial ground on the hillfort Hochburg from the second half of the seventh century as well as early artefacts from metal-detecting surveys found inside the semi-circular rampart and in the Southern Settlement – has already been mentioned in Section 5.1. Moreover, there is the well-known Wodan/Monster sceatta from pit house 1 in the Southern Settlement (Steuer 1974: 28; Schietzel 2014: 86) as well as plough marks from an agricultural phase from the lowermost strata of the settlement excavations (Schietzel 1969: 50 fig. 39; 2014: 86–7; cf. Schultze 2017: 567, 573; Wouters 2020: 92–3, 97). Finally, there is evidence of pre-Viking-age activity from the harbour basin, not least the so-called Nydam plank from the hull of a boat, which has been dendrochronologically dated to around or after 749 (Kalmring 2010a: 111–12, 155–6 fig. 118). The excavator Schietzel (2014: 35 figs. 86–7) suggested that Hedeby was initiated 'by the arrival of individual persons or small groups ... whose business was in trade and craft and for that reason were applying for temporary residency' (my translation). More recently, his assumptions have been reinforced by the identification of a seasonal 'first main phase' of settlement development in the second half of or the late eighth century. It was characterised by a grid of plots without permanent dwellings that was found along a main road parallel to the shoreline (Schultze 2017: 567, 573).

Although in each case the specific seasonal element must be critically scrutinised (cf. Croix 2014; Scull 2002: 308–9), it becomes apparent that Viking-age towns emerged through quite ordinary beach markets and thus as integral parts and everyday institutions of the traditional rural society.[9] This leads to the questions of how and why these particular sites developed into towns when the overwhelming majority of beach markets did not.

6.2 TRANSFORMATION FROM LANDING SITES TO EARLY TOWNS: IMPETUS OF ROYAL POWER

As outlined in Section 6.1, even the few existing Viking-age towns developed from ordinary landing sites where beach markets were held, as was common throughout early medieval north-western Europe

---

[9] For the Slavonic southern Baltic Sea coast, it has been suggested that both Reric/Groß Strömkendorf and Menzlin also evolved from seasonally occupied sites (Kleingärtner 2014: 35).

(Jahnke 2019: 184, 196–7).[10] Considering these ordinary origins, the question is whether and if that were the case at what point did local chieftains, petty kings or kings became involved in the transformation of these sites. In Norway, there is an old and extensive historical debate regarding the origins of the Norwegian towns, which is characterised by the antipodes of the so-called *strandstedsteorien* ('beach-site theory') and *kongestadteorien* ('royal-town theory') (cf. Helle 1982: 95) that also highlight possible basic scenarios debated in the past. The *strandstedsteori* by Munch (1849) is based on the idea that towns 'grew' naturally from maritime trading places (Nrw. *strandsteder*) and only later received town rights and privileges from the king. With reference to Snorri's *Heimskringla*, the *kongestadteori* by Storm (1899), on the other hand, argues that towns were actively founded by the king on royal demesnes. It is certainly no coincidence that Andrén (1983) chooses to begin his influential article 'Städer och kungamakt' ('Towns and Royal Power') with a discussion of these antipodes in order to circumscribe the debate on medieval urbanisation.

During the 1990–5 *Svarta Jorden* ('Black Earth') excavations in Birka, a fragment of a grave or stone orb (Swd. *gravklot*) was found in a stone cairn located by a former shoreline in front of the initial plots by the beach (Ambrosiani & Eriksen 1996: 50–7; Ambrosiani 2013: 45–8). The orb depicts three horses and an eagle, which are known from Vendel-period imagery. The eagle in particular often symbolises the god Óðinn, who, according to Snorri's *Heimskringla*, was the

[10] Recent research suggests that some of these early landing places, such as Ribe, Reric/Groß Strömkendorf and Åhus, might not have been so ordinary after all (Søvsø 2018: 83–5; Feveile 2019; cf. Theuws 2018). Early numismatic evidence seems to support the idea that these sites were in fact royal emporia with an existing coin economy based on series X or vernacular Wodan/Monster sceattas. This particular sceatta issue might thus not be a genuine Ribe coin but actually represent a royal Danish coinage. It has been suggested that such an eighth-century border-zone trade network may have been controlled from Gammel Lejre, which would have been its geographic centre. Note that according to Søvsø's model another site to the north-east, presumably around the Göta älv, remains unidentified (Søvsø 2018: fig. 9). In this context, the discussion on the origins of early Scandinavian 'network kingdoms' might be of further relevance (Blomkvist 2008: 172–4 fig. 6; cf. Hennius 2021: 85–6).

mythological ancestor of the Ynglinga dynasty (cf. *Heimskringla*, chap. 5). Since the orb was found in Birka, it has been interpreted as a heraldic symbol and as an 'allegory for the Uppsala kings' presence in the oldest town setting' (Ambrosiani & Eriksen 1996: 56; cf. Hillerdal 2009: 262). However, whether the stone orb should be regarded as evidence for a royal foundation or rather of a rapid royal engagement after an initial autonomous emergence is not explicitly stated. In the case of Kaupang, the excavator Skre (2007: 463) was more assured, suggesting that it was intentionally founded next to an already existing central place – notwithstanding direct evidence of an initial seasonal phase by the project itself. Skre argued that Kaupang was founded near Skiringssal on the initiative of the Danish king around 800, when the ruling Norwegian Ynglinga dynasty had temporarily withdrawn from the area (Skre 2007: 466–8). He even goes one step further and claims that both Kaupang and Hedeby were founded simultaneously by the Danish king Godfred, who at the same time also turned Ribe from a seasonal trading place into a permanent one (Skre 2007: 461).

For a long time, Ribe was considered the most prominent example of a royal foundation of a trading place. Here, a massive layer of yellow, sterile drift sand was originally considered to be anthropogenic backfill placed on top of an earlier surface during the preparation of the marketplace area (Feveile 2006a: 70–1 fig. 8). It was therefore assumed that the supposed backfill had been placed there on the initiative of an early 'Danish' king, who would have been the only person with the authority to order such a huge undertaking. Moreover, it was suggested that the regular plot system of the marketplace was already laid out before the arrival of the first crafters and merchants in Ribe. Further, the establishment of the regular plot system of the marketplace itself was believed to be laid out before the arrival of the first craftsmen and merchants in Ribe. Based on the earliest archaeological datings from 705, the early eighth-century ruler Ongedus – who is mentioned in Alcuin's hagiography, *Saint Willibrord's Life* – was identified as the founder of the market site. A competing interpretation, suggesting that the site was founded by Frisian merchants, was promptly dismissed (Bencard & Bender Jørgensen 1990: 161–2; cf. Feveile 2006a: 73–5). Interestingly, although both arguments that supported a royal initiative for the market site have been dismissed – that is, the anthropogenic backfill and the preparation of the plot system – the involvement of some kind of authority in Ribe's emergence continues to be discussed (most recently Søvsø 2018: 83–5; 2020: 151–3). Sindbæk (2005: 166–72) argued that, although there is clear documented evidence for an eighth-century west Danish royal power, there is no proof of it interfering in trade matters. Instead, he suggests that it was long-distance merchants from the Rhineland who took the initiative for trade in the area. As a synthesis, Feveile (2006a: 76) argues for a more differentiated development:

> One could imagine a development that began with Frisian merchants settling on the banks of the River Ribe to establish a seasonal market there with both Frisian and Danish tradesmen and craftsmen taking part. When they had been there for a couple of years – perhaps with increasing success? – certain Danish authorities (a local leader or a king) saw the potential and chose to take a controlling hand in the matter.

Regarding the origins, or rather 'rebirth', of English towns in post-Roman England (cf. Crabtee 2018), Fleming (2009) reassessed evidence from Kent and argued against earlier assumptions that suggested that the towns were founded by kings who wanted to monopolise a trade that was largely based on the exchange of prestige goods. She found that sites such as Gipeswic/Ipswich, Hamwic/Southampton and Lundenwic/London had undergone significant changes by the eighth century, three generations after their re-emergence. By that time, they had developed into 'proper' towns with permanent populations. Based on the distribution of imports in eastern Kent, she saw the influx of Frankish material in the sixth and seventh centuries not only as a result of elite communication but also as a consequence of the active participation of the coastal population, who engaged in genuine trade across the English Channel (cf. Loveluck & Tys 2006; Loveluck 2013: 178–212). By using Ipswich as an example (cf. Scull 2002), Fleming suggested that its origins go back to periodical gatherings at a landing site by the river Orwell, set up by local farmers intending to exchange their rural surplus produce for goods brought by foreign traders. This exchange became more and more formalised and eventually, around 600, resulted in a substantial permanent settlement that included Franks and Frisians. As proposed for Ribe, Fleming, for her part, suggested that in early seventh-century England 'different groups of outsiders, and the competition ..., is a more likely driving force behind the rebirth of towns ... than is monopolistic trade' (Fleming 2009: 415). These developing trading sites in turn stimulated the development of multiple other market and craft sites in the hinterland that were controlled by elite households. However, it was not until the last quarter of the seventh century that royal authorities established themselves in these towns in order to monopolise the trade with prestige goods and to collect duties, resulting in further infrastructure development and settlement expansion.

This general assessment, however, must be partially revised in the light of recent research findings, and in the case of Gipeswic/Ipswich this is mirrored in its burial grounds: it is evident that while the Boss Hall burial ground still reflects the rural occupation of the late fifth and sixth centuries, the seventh-century St Stephen's Lane/Buttermarket burial ground already belonged to a precursor with a permanent population that had some limited connections to Merovingian Continental Europe (graves 1306, 2297 and 3871). However, it was not until the eighth century that the Buttermarket burial ground became abandoned, making way for the settlement occupation and craft activities of the 'classic' emporium (Scull 2009, 2013). Scull concluded:

> It [early seventh-century Ipswich] served to channel exchange with the Continent ... and it seems unlikely that it could have been established, functioned and developed without paramount sanction, although whether this amounted to more than the

extraction of tolls and an understanding that the place was under royal protection remains open to question. It can be argued that the immediate property and economic interests were most likely vested in the magnates or magnate lineage able to extract and redeploy landed surplus [of the Orwell estuary] on the scale necessary to make long-distance bulk trade viable, and who constituted the market for elite and luxury imports. (Scull 2013: 222–3)

Despite this assessment, the importance of the emerging coastal societies is still recognised – as is a possible temporary increase in the otherwise permanent population of Ipswich's precursor during the trading season (Scull 2013: 223, 227; cf. Loveluck & Tys 2006). Moreover, it is not until its expansion and reorganisation into the emporium Gipeswic in the early eighth century that there is any true indication of a royal initiative, possibly by Ælfwald of East Anglia (Scull 2013: 227–8; cf. Naylor 2016: 61). The seventh-century so-called Stadium Cemetery in Hamwic/Southampton displayed similarities with Ipswich-Buttermarket as well as contemporary rural cemeteries. Owing to its relatively large amount of weapon burials, even here an affiliation to some – as yet unidentified – royal estate has been suggested. Such an estate may have controlled the trade resulting from the surplus of a well-developed hinterland of the upper Itchen Valley from an early stage (Stoodley 2005; cf. Birbeck et al. 2005). The development of Hamwic into a 'classical' emporium, however, only seems to have started after the area was annexed by the West Saxons in 686 (Bede, book 4, chaps. 15–16). Even London had at least two burial grounds dating to the late sixth and seventh centuries, before the settlement developed into Lundenwic: one dispersed burial ground near Convent Garden, that is, at Long Acre – Royal Opera House – Jubilee Hall, which may have belonged to a small settlement close to the waterfront near the Strand, the other – only documented by antiquarian finds – at St Martin-in-the-Fields (Blackmore 2002: 278–81, 294; cf. Cowie & Harding 2000; Malcom et al. 2003). According to Blackmore (2002: 281, 284), the initial settlement associated with these early burial grounds may well have been a seasonal type-A emporium, possibly consisting of several polyfocal centres. This initial settlement did not display any signs of planning or deliberate foundation. Consequently, the local elites seem to have exploited pre-existing conditions rather than creating them themselves (Naylor 2016: 61–2). There are no indications of royal incentives until the development of a 'classical' emporium along the Strand in the late seventh or early eighth century conceivably by Wulfhere of Mercia.

Already in 1986, Sawyer (1986: 73) suggested that 'there was a natural tendency for rulers to claim authority over the more successful places and to provide protection in return for a share of the profits of trade. Scandinavia can, indeed, offer a very early parallel to the efforts of English rulers to extend their regalia rights.' The source on Scandinavian conditions to which he refers is, of course, the enlightening entry in the *Royal Frankish Annals* describing the events in 808 that led to the destruction of Reric (Figure 11). At the end of a Danish campaign against the Slavic Obotrites – then allies of Charlemagne – King Godfred turned his fleet against Reric at the Bay of Wismar, an act that was to become the initial spark for the emergence of Hedeby as an early town: 'But Godofrid [Godfred] before his return destroyed a trading place on the seashore, in Danish called Reric, which, because of the taxes [*vectigalium*] it paid, was of great advantage to his kingdom. Transferring the merchants from Reric he weighed anchor and came with his whole army to the harbour of Sliesthorp [Hedeby]' (*Royal Frankish Annals*, entry 808 CE). Archaeologically, Schultze (2017: 574) links this historical event to his suggested 'second main phase' of development in Hedeby, which saw a fundamental shift from seasonal site activities on a parcelled-out area ('first main phase')[11] to a permanent trading site with permanent dwellings on plots and further subdivision of the area by minor byways. This last event of Godfred's campaign against the Obotrites clearly displayed traits of a conscious

---

[11]   See also plot-ditch feature N1 from the northern shore area of the 1979/80 harbour excavation in Hedeby and a suggested initial seasonal 'Ribe-phase' belonging to a landing site with beach market (Kalmring 2010a: 258, 452, 269; 2011: 248).

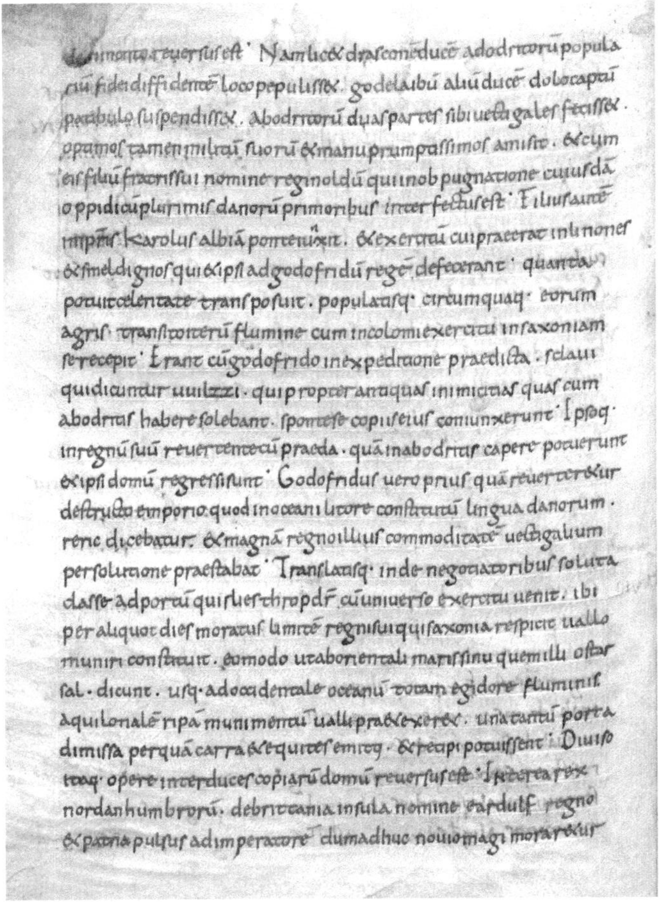

FIGURE 11 *Royal Frankish Annals* (*Annales Laurissenses*). Entry for the year 808 on the destruction of Reric and the transferral of its merchants to 'Sliesthorp' (Hedeby) (Codex 473, folio 139v; Österreichische Nationalbibliothek).

and active economic policy implemented by military means. The destruction of Reric and the transfer of its merchants to Hedeby, a site closer to his own dominion, allowed him stricter control and extended possibilities to collect taxes.[12] The trading site of Reric has been

12 The source also mentions that Godfred expelled the Obotrite duke Thrasco (Drasko) and that another Slavonic duke, Godelaib (ON *Guðleifr*), was hanged at Reric for

identified as today's Groß Strömkendorf, where extensive excavations were conducted between 1995 and 1999 (cf. Müller-Wille 2009; Kleingärtner 2014: 303–15). How important Reric actually was as an economic factor – and thus also what triggered the hostile takeover and the relocation closer to the Danish sphere of influence – has, based on its archaeological evidence, hitherto been difficult to understand. With the most recent finds from metal-detector surveys, however, this picture has changed completely: the amount of known sceatta coins from the site – previously three in number (Jöns 1999: 208) – has literally multiplied fifteenfold with forty-three newly discovered specimens from the area of the trading site, *Handelsplatz Fpl. 3* (Jöns 2015: 247 fig. 2; Wiechmann 2021; Ilisch & Wiechmann In press). Although this is still a minor number compared to the 281 sceattas known from Ribe (Bendixen 1981 (excavations 1970–6); 1994 (excavations 1985–6); Feveile 2006 (excavations 1989–2000); Feveile 2023 (excavation 2017/18); cf. Søvsø 2018: 81; 2020: 163–5 tab. 10; Feveile 2019: tab. 1), it is a significant increase that brings Reric closer to Ribe in its economic importance.

Based on the evidence presented in this chapter, there is expanded evidence that the Viking-age towns, too, developed from beach markets held next to landing sites and initiated under the agency of local maritime communities and long-distance merchants. A few trading places, however, caught the attention of the potentates due to their specific topographical conditions in certain border regions and/or their commercial success, which led to either their destruction – as in the case of Reric/Groß Strömkendorf – or their deliberate promotion, by elevating them out of their surrounding rural traditional societies. This promotion equates to a transition that Callmer (1994: 63–8) calls the 'heyday phase' of early urbanisation, which entailed a hierarchical differentiation between different trading sites; another way of expressing this development is Hodges' (1982: 50–3; cf. 2012: 102–3) 'classical' type-B

treason (cf. Lübke 2001: 30). Why Godfred – even though two-thirds of the Obotrites were already obliged to pay him tribute – did not restore control over the trading site at Reric but instead chose to destroy it remains unclear. Was it due to Drasko's presumed 'policy of expansion' or the Frankish claim to supremacy over their Obotritic allies (Helten 2019: 45–8)?

emporia, which evolved from seasonal type-A emporia. This development corresponded with Continental European trends as well, and Verhulst (2002: 129) suggested that:

> The flowering of markets during the ninth century was certainly not the result of any direct intervention by the king inspired by a policy in matters of trade and commerce. This does not mean that markets where not the king's concern. He 'legalised' markets, controlled their number and existence, and in order to fight the evading of market tolls, ordered that all business should be done on a 'legal' market.

7 Jurisdiction and Taxes

By deliberately promoting certain trading sites, rulers extended their regalia rights in terms of the control and taxation of long-distance trade (Sawyer 1986: 73), a development that was initiated by providing a few selected places with a very distinct legal status that separated them from the context of ordinary society and triggered the transformation into early towns. Yet what this legal status entailed is hard to ascertain due to the dearth of contemporary sources, while in the case of later, high medieval law codes, one can only speculate about possible older origins. However, a closer look – both at written sources and archaeological evidence – reveals a whole range of clues that can help illuminate the existence and nature of this important judicial framework, which was an important part of the distinctiveness of these towns.

7.1 DEFENSIVE FORTIFICATIONS AND CUSTOMS BORDERS

In archaeology, small boundary ditches around market sites are well-known features, not least from a range of eighth-century *wik* sites. They are narrow and shallow ditches that separate these sites from their surroundings, and it is doubtful whether they ever had any defensive function. On the contrary, Verheaghe emphasises that 'In the early phases, the ['classical'] type-B emporia do not seem to have been systematically defended. ... The defensive-works protecting the other active towns date from the second half of the ninth century or slightly later, and have to be interpreted in the light of new threats, notably Viking raids' (Verheaghe 2005: 274). Hence, it seems likely that these very modest ditches were there for other reasons, for example as legal boundaries, which provides archaeologists with another indicator suggesting that such sites possessed their own specific jurisdiction.

In England, Middle Anglo-Saxon Hamwic/Southampton had a boundary ditch that enclosed an area of between 42 and 45 hectares. It has been identified at the Six Dials site but also at Cook Street, as well as by means of geomagnetic surveys. The shallow boundary ditch had a V-shaped cross-section and was 3 metres wide and 1.5 metres deep. Judging by its backfill, it dates to around 700 and had already been backfilled by the mid-eighth century. Remarkably, an earlier 'gulley', about 0.5 metres wide and 0.15 metres deep only, may also have already served as a field or boundary marker. Since there were no traces of a rampart by the ditch, it has not been regarded as a defensive structure but rather a major boundary feature between the settlement and the surrounding cultivated land. However, the idea of the ditch having some symbolic function – emphasising Hamwic's status – has also been considered (Andrews 1997: 22–30 fig. 8; cf. Morton 1992: 30–1 fig. 9b; see also Brisbane 1988: 102–3; Hinton 2000a: 220). Notwithstanding more recent assessments of the genesis of this emporium (cf. Birbeck et al. 2005: 192–6), it has been assumed that the limits of the settlement had been determined by the ditch since some very early development stage, suggesting that a large trading port had been envisaged all along (Andrews 1997: 252). Excavations at Fishergate in Eorforwic/York also revealed a boundary ditch, which ran in a gentle curve – with a north–south alignment – almost entirely around the site. The ditch varied in shape and dimensions, beginning with a width of 0.4 metres and a depth of 0.45 metres in the north and gradually extending to a maximum width of 2.1 metres and a depth of 0.7 metres before it once again narrowed to a width of 1 metre and a depth between 0.15 and 0.3 metres. At the bottom of the ditch, a row of minute postholes was exposed (Kemp 1996: 18–22). This main ditch, which is attributed to site period 3a, has been interpreted as a 'property demarcation'. Interestingly, soil analysis has suggested that the Anglian settlement was not established until a year after the boundary ditch was dug. Although this is a rather weak indicator, it has been proposed that the settlement was laid out 'according to a plan of some kind' (Kemp 1996: 22, 67). But, even for York, more recent research tends to assume origins in a polyfocal settlement group, including the

Northumbrian royal palace, which would have been situated somewhere between the Roman *principia* and the Anglo-Saxon minster, as well as the episcopal centre around the church of Paulinus of York (cf. Loveluck 2013: 150, 171, 173–4, 307–8).

On the other side of the North Sea, excavations in Ribe provided an almost model version of a legal boundary ditch. The so-called *bygrøft A* ('town ditch A') was about 1.5 to 2 metres wide and 1 metre deep (Figure 12). It has been estimated that it enclosed the approximately 12-hectare area of the marketplace area and the adjacent settlement over a length of 475 metres; in Rosenallé ASR 8, it was uncovered over a continuous stretch of 40 metres. Beyond the ditch were situated the town's burial grounds, but no evidence has been

FIGURE 12 Ribe, western Denmark. The shallow boundary ditch *bygrøft A* demarking the marketplace and indicating 'the peace of the town' within (© Sydvestjyske Museer). Note that only half of the ditch has been emptied by excavation.

found for other contemporary settlement activities. The earth from the ditch was used to build a 0.5-metre-high and 2–3-metre-wide embankment (*vold A*/'rampart A') on the inside of it. The embankment has been dated to the early ninth century and was probably only in use for a few years before being replaced at the end of the ninth century by a more substantial *voldgrav B* ('moat B') with an accompanying rampart built of turf (Feveile 2006a: 81–2; 2009).[1] Already in 1991, St Jensen had suggested that the initial town ditch must have had a symbolic significance, marking the town limits, since its dimensions indicate that it would not have been sufficient to stop an enemy attack: 'To use terms that belong to a later date, within the moat ran the Laws, the Rights and the Obligations of the town. Here, the king guaranteed the peace of the market [ON *kaupfrið*], and in return the traders paid their dues' (Jensen 1991: 55). The ditch constituted the judicial boundary between 'the peace of the town' (*byfreden*), that is, within the trading site, and the surrounding countryside (Søvsø 2020: 173, 202). Rösch (2019: 267, 269) recently suggested a possible link between the so-called spatial *Bannbezirke* ('ban or interdiction district') found in Ottonian market legislation and the initial symbolic town ditch in Ribe. A ditch similar to the one in Ribe has also been found in Truso/Janów Pomorski, where it so far has been described as a 'drainage ditch' (Brather & Jagodziński 2012: 102–4; cf. Kalmring 2015: 399, 402).

Besides boundary ditches, other types of barriers that surrounded trading sites may also indicate the existence of a divergent jurisdiction within them. Since Viking-age urbanisation was highly dependent on harbours (see Chapter 6), potential evidence for prevailing legislation and customs can also be surmised here. In the case of Hedeby, the harbour palisade seems to have had such a legal function, although a simultaneous defensive function should not be completely

---

[1] During recent excavations at Rosenallé II in 2014 another short-lived town ditch was documented, K200, predating moat B. Its dating to the second half of the ninth century probably means that moat B itself was not dug until the tenth century, before being backfilled in the first half of the eleventh century (Søvsø 2020: 177–9, 207–8).

ruled out: the physical nature of this barrier is still unclear. When it was discovered in 1933, it was interpreted as a seaward equivalent to Hedeby's semi-circular ramparts. Since then, it has been investigated through several underwater and seismic surveys, but the results remain inconclusive and difficult to piece together (Kalmring 2010a: 63–104; Müller et al. 2013), probably due to its multiphase construction over the approximately 250 years of the town's existence. Nevertheless, Hedeby's inner harbour at Haddebyer Noor, a sheltered bay at the inner end of the Schlei fjord, was restricted by some kind of structure. The fjord itself cuts 40 kilometres inland from the Baltic Sea, and along the sea route towards Hedeby (and its high medieval successor Slesvig) several naval defences and beacon sites have been identified (cf. Kalmring 2010a: 35–40; Lemm 2016a, 2019). Against this background, one can indeed ask whether a last line of defence around the inner harbour of Hedeby made sense if an enemy fleet could not have been repelled on its long way into the innermost fjord. Also, if earlier defences were breached a more reasonable last line of defence would have been where the fjord meets the bay of Haddebyer Noor, an area that is currently covered by a road embankment – it seems to be no coincidence that in the sixteenth and seventeenth centuries there were reports of alleged 'bridge foundations' at this very spot. This suggests that Hedeby's harbour palisade was an actual judicial boundary, within which traders were offered protection in exchange for harbour duties. One of the wooden features, at the port entrance, has been discussed as a *Baumhaus* – a tower that secured floating wooden logs, or boom chains – which would have been used to close the entrance at nights and at the same time a place where duties could be collected (cf. Kalmring 2010a: 102–3; for *Baumhäuser* as customs facilities, see Deggim 2005: 20).

Harbour chains are known to have been in existence since antiquity and are mentioned in Vitruvius' chapter on harbours, breakwaters and shipyards: 'Round them [harbours], of course, ... towers must be set up on both sides, from which chains can be drawn across by machinery' (Vitruvius, book 4, chap. 12.1). Among examples contemporary with Hedeby, the most prominent one would be the chains across the Golden Horn, between the towers of Kentenarion and Galata, in Byzantine Constantinople (cf. *Nuremberg Chronicle*: fol. CCLXXIIII). These were first mentioned in written sources from 717 describing the second Arab siege of Constantinople (Bury 1912: 92–3). They may also be what is referred to in *The Russian Primary Chronicle* when the Varangian Prince Oleg (ON *Helgi*) of Novgorod is said to have raided Miklagård/Constantinople in 907. The chronicle was written shortly after 1060 and is preserved in a manuscript from 1116 (cf. Müller 2002: 96–7). It reports that 'the Greeks fortified the strait and closed up the city' so that Prince Oleg had to disembark his fleet (*The Russian Primary Chronicle*, entry 6412–15 [904–7 CE]; cf. Vasiliev 1951). Constantinople's harbour chains are also mentioned in Snorri Sturluson's *Saga of Harald Hardrada* (chap. 15), describing King Harald's spectacular escape from the Byzantine court in 1042, when one of his two galleys was split in two when trying to escape from the *Sjáviðarsund*/Golden Horn as it attempted to cross the 'iron chain' (ON *járnrekendr*) before entering the Bosporus. A similar navigational barrier is documented for the early twelfth century for Slesvig, which blocked the Schlei fjord for reasons of defence but also to levy taxes on incoming traffic. The reference is handed down in the *Knýtlinga saga*, which was written down in the middle of the thirteenth century (cf. Simek & Páulsson 1987: 211–12), and the passage in question reads:

> After Lord Knut [Lavard; 1096–1131] had been back in his province a short while, he hired some builders and had two castles constructed on either side of Slesvigen at the narrowest part of the sound which stretches out from Hedeby [Slesvig]. Next, he had iron chains and timber structures [*járnrekendr, en sumt með viðum*] placed across the sound that no ships could sail through apart from those they wanted: and so they charged toll on every ship that sailed in. (*Knýtlinga saga*, chap. 86)

Simpler harbour chains than the one recorded for Slesvig seem to have existed even in Viking-age Birka and consisted of floating tethered logs, which would have been connected to the individual pilings, together forming the harbour palisade. With regard to Birka, Ambrosiani (1988) suggested that 'Such pole barriers consist of simple, or pairs of [vertical] poles, which are connected by floating tree trunks, and can be opened or closed when needed' (Ambrosiani 1988: 28; my translation). Interestingly for this context, some large logs with dovetailed endings have been found in more recent marine-archaeological surveys (Olsson 2017: 46 fig. 37). This type of joint would hardly be found in a Viking-age dwelling built with mortise and tenon joints, or in a log house, but – when connected by ropes – might very well have constituted the logs of a harbour chain.[2] Apart from a defensive function of Birka's harbour barrier, some role as a judicial and fiscal boundary must be considered, too.

7.2 SHIPPING DUTIES AND PORT ADMINISTRATION IN THE POST-ROMAN WORLD

This section addresses the core of the epigraph on harbours by Ambrose Bierce's: 'Habour, n. A place where ships taking shelter from storms are exposed to the fury of the customs.' As a historian, Jahnke (2010) suggested a legal definition of a port as a place where the sovereign granted periodical or permanent legal protection to merchants and markets as well as an exemption of the custom of *jus naufragii* (right of shipwreck), in exchange for customs duties (*ripatica*), including in particular market tithes (*decima* in Francia, and *dekateia* in Byzantium; cf. Jahnke 2019: 188, 190). The Roman Empire developed a complex harbour administration (Figure 13) with a multitude of different imperial civil servants such as *quaestores* and *procuratores portus* but also *annonae* and *tabularii* and *dispensatores* (Hirschfeld 1905: 246–51; Rougé 1966: 201–11), as well as specialised dock workers,

---

[2] In Olaus Magnus' sixteenth-century *Description of the Northern Peoples*, such floating log booms are repeatedly referred to (book 9, chap. 28; book 10, chap. 5; book 10, chap. 12 and book 11, chap. 18; cf. Rieck 1991: 83 fig. 1).

FIGURE 13 Portus, Ostia Antica, Italy. Third-century relief with Roman harbour administration (Museo Torlonia: Inv. no. 428 iDAI.objects Arachne, ID 1086724; German Archaeological Institute/DAI [Deutsches Archäologisches Institut] [BY-NC-ND 3.0]). An imperial civil servant (*tabularius*) – supported by two assistants – is recording the freight while one longshoreman receives a token; two longshoremen (*saccarii*) unloading wine from a trading vessel.

such as various specific longshoremen (*phalangarii, saccarii*), officials in charge of measurements (*mensores*), boat builders (*naualia*), skippers (*scapharii* and *lyntrarii*) and even harbour divers (*urinatores*) (Rougé 1966: 179–201). In the following post-Roman period, harbour administration seems to have diminished, although Italian harbours in the kingdom of the Ostrogoths were still controlled by royal agents titled *comitiacus portus* and *vicarius portus* during the first half of the sixth century (Cassiodorus, book 7, chap. 9.23; cf. Claude 1985: 130). This suggests that in the Mediterranean some harbour administration endured in spite of the collapse of the Western Roman Empire. And for the early eighth century, a treaty between the Lombardic King Liutprand and the Byzantine border port Comacchio confirmed the levying of navigation fees (*ripatica*) for salt shipments, which – based on 'ancient custom' (*antiqua consuetudo*) – were collected in the ports by the river Po in Lombardy. On behalf of Comacchio, this treaty was signed by the royal agents, the *magister militum* Bertarene and his *comites* Mauro and Stephano (source in Hartmann 1904: 123–4; cf. Costambeys et al. 2011: 359–61). Other surviving features were the *cellarium fisci* and *cellarium telonei* – storehouses for goods claimed by tax authorities – that are documented from the Merovingian ports of Marseille in 692 and Fos-sur-Mer in 716, which also underlines their continued status as important Mediterranean customs harbours, retaining at least some of the earlier administration (Loseby 2000: 176–8).

This implies that commercial tariffs, rooted in Roman traditions, are documented from the Frankish world since the seventh century (Ganshof 1959: 493; Sawyer 1979: 142). In her study *Das Zollwesen im fränkischen Reich und das spätkarolingische Wirtschaftsleben* (*Customs in the Frankish Empire and Late Carolingian Economic Life*), Adam (1996) compiled an impressive collection on Merovingian and Carolingian traffic duties, market and trading tariffs, including customs legislation and its organisation. Generally, matters concerning transport duties or trading tariffs were referred to as *telonium* (Ganshof 1959: 293–4; Adam 1996: 38–41). The specific nature and function of such customs become evident in various charters dealing with trading privileges granted to ecclesiastical institutions. Charters on privileges regulating the payment of maritime tariffs for riverine traffic were particularly common, especially those dealing with salt shipments. In written sources, shipping duties appear as *navigia, telonea de navi* or *ripatici*, where they may refer to rights of use or certain counter-performances. Shipping duties can be subdivided into either tolls for navigable fairway use and passing fees or mooring and anchoring tariffs (Adam 1996: 117–18). Among the latter, *portaticum* dealt with the tariffs for right of access, mooring and anchoring in a harbour, but it was also meant to contribute to the maintenance and good repair of the harbour facilities (Ganshof 1959: 493; Jahnke 2019: 187–9). Sometimes it could even include the right to trade, since harbours – as an evolution from simple beach markets – could simultaneously fulfil the function of harbour markets (Adam 1996: 125 n. 321; cf. Kalmring 2010a: 443–50; 2011: 254–5). Originally, the term *portaticum* may actually be derived from the Latin word for 'gate', indicating a link between fees at town gates and those at lockable harbour entrances (Falke 1869: 17; Adam 1996: 57–8 n. 326; see Section 7.1). Specific but less common fees were the *palifictura* for making fast at a mooring pole in a harbour and the *plantaticum* for anchoring (Adam 1996: 53–4, 56). For this review, the *salutaticum* is of special interest since it was a specific maritime tariff for harbour markets through which the rulers, in exchange for granting market rights and safe passage, levied taxes on merchants and their trade goods, as well as on ships and their crews (Adam 1996: 62–3, 136). Unless it was a mere stopover on a journey, mooring duties were even collected at landing sites as *ripaticum* or sometimes *laudaticum* if the intention was to hold a beach market (Adam 1996: 49, 60–1, 127–8, 136–7). For matters regarding how harbour administration was organised and which officials were involved, the first volume of *The Miracles of Saint Benedict*, from the last quarter of the ninth century, provides invaluable information: the episode in question tells of a ship belonging to the monastery of Fleury which had been loading salt in Nantes and was confiscated in the customs harbour (*portus fiscalis*) of Orléans, despite having rights to travel on the river Loire issued by Emperor Louis the Pious. In the end, it was only through the actions of Benedict of Nursia that the ship miraculously managed to slip out of the harbour during Sunday Mass. In this context, the text also details how the duties were collected by an *exactor*, who belonged to the *telonarii civitatis*, and that after the ship was confiscated it was placed under the supervision of a *procurator portus*, who was in charge of the harbour (*Miracula Sancti Benedicti*, book 1, chap. 19; cf. Ganshof 1959: 487–8; Adam 1996: 132–3, 227).

For Britain, too, it has been suggested that the royal agents and the levying of shipping duties mentioned in Anglo-Saxon charters were apparently based on a system which 'derive[d] from Roman arrangements that survived the collapse of Imperial authority in the fifth century' (Sawyer 1986: 62). Another possibility, however, is that they were inspired by Frankish models, which in turn had been influenced by Lombardic customs and interactions with the Byzantine world (Middelton 2005: 315, 319; cf. Sawyer, 1979: 143–4). Be that as it may, from the eighth century at the latest there is evidence of a developed customs system, which once again features the transfer of shipping duties on laden ships to various abbeys and diocese, which were otherwise levied by royal *thelonarii*. It is noteworthy that these fees were not regularly called *teloneum* but were referred to by terms such as *vectigal*, *censum* or *tributum* (Sawyer 1979: 144 n. 19); unfortunately, the charters do not mention which of these fees relate to which trade goods. The documents in question were issued by Æthelbald of Mercia (S86–88, S91, S98, S103a, S1788; cf. Sawyer 1968: 93–6; Kelly 1992: 27–8) and Offa of Mercia (S143; cf. Sawyer 1968: 107–8) and dealt with the arrangements at the toll station at *portus* Lundonia/London. Eadberht II of Kent (S29, S1612; cf. Sawyer 1968: 78–9) issued trading privileges at the *loci* Fordwic/Fordwich, the principal port for Canterbury, and Seorre/Sarre-on-Thanet, by the former Wantsum Channel. Although the Anglo-Saxon shipping duties remain unspecified and its toll system seems to have been less ostentatious than its Frankish counterparts, Kelly (1992) suggested that there was royal interest in 'exploiting the great emporia and the long-distance trade-routes', with a special focus on the merchant ships, with charges applying to both transport and cargo, depending on the vessels' cargo capacity (Kelly 1992: 17). Apart from customs tariffs there is evidence of an early Kentish royal right of pre-emption (S29) and charges for granted *incessum* ('entry') to the harbour of London, as described in charter S88 from the year 733 – although this may actually relate to an existing separate port tax (Kelly 1992: 21; Middelton 2005: 331–3). Finally, as to harbour markets in ninth-century London, all evidence suggests that there was a strict separation in customs regulations between harbour and town (Middelton 2005: 335–6; cf. Kalmring 2010a: 443–50).

7.3 AN OWN JURISDICTION IN VIKING-AGE MARITIME TRADING TOWNS?

Based on the ample evidence for a sophisticated contemporary harbour administration and taxation in Continental Europe and Britain and archaeologically corroborated legal land and sea boundaries surrounding major trading sites, it seems evident that the Viking-age towns also must have their own jurisdiction, separating them from the surrounding countryside. Given the largely preliterate culture of the Viking Age, the question is whether there is evidence to help us form an opinion about the prevailing legislation.

The Bjarkey laws (ON *Bjarkeyjarréttr*, Swd. *Bjärköarätt*) as privileges for trading places are preserved in fragments in a law book of Nidaros/Trondheim from the time after 1164, although it was first mentioned in the privileges for Iceland issued by Olaf II of Norway around 1020 and can probably even be linked back to the foundation of Nidaros by Olaf Tryggvason in 997 (Müller-Boysen 1990: 31, 117–21; Jahnke 2017: 576; Sanmark 2017: 10; Semple et al. 2020: 74). For a long time, academics have debated whether the original Bjarkey laws were derived from Birka and the island of Björkö, suggesting that the name *Birca*, which is found in these written sources, might in fact be a latinised version of an Old Norse *Bjarköj* (Wessén 1923; Arbman 1939: 41–3). The confirmed existence of a specific Birka *thing* (mentioned in Section 4.2) provides reliable evidence for a separate jurisdiction on the island (Arbman 1939: 41) and Müller-Boysen (1990: 121) suggested that the Bjarkey laws, as privileges for trading places, would have applied to sites like Birka and Hedeby. However, given the diversity of the Bjarkey laws preserved in various town laws, to him it seems questionable whether there was ever an original Bjarkey law that was then transferred to other trading places. Rather, to Müller-Boysen they seem to be associated with a common, specific legal sphere that generally designated the market rights of the individual trading places.

Specific regulations can only be deduced from later law codes or possibly from Icelandic sagas. Elementary for such laws were the rules pertaining to foreign merchants – that is, those who travelled outside their own legal jurisdictions – who, as guests, were provided with an on-site legal status that simultaneously granted legal security for their transactions (Müller-Boysen 1990: 109–15, 117–52). In the initial version of the town law of Slesvig (*Slesvig stadsret*) from c.1200, paragraph 29 deals with the 'right of purchase' (ON *laghkøp*), which was a general legal protection that merchants acquired from the king. In the context of the oldest town law of Slesvig, it seems more likely to be a relic of a privilege dating back to early medieval trading places, not least Hedeby itself (Müller-Boysen 1990: 113, 126; Gelting 2016: 215–16).

Little information can complement this source: both the *Magnus Håkonssons bylov* ('town law') from 1276 (chap. 9, §§14–15) and the Icelandic *Jónsbók* from 1281 (chap. 9, §§15–16) list 'harbour theft' (ON *hafnarrán*) as an offence, which pertains to stealing the berth of another ship by force. At the same time, another law stipulated that ships that had already unloaded their cargo had to make room for newcomers by leaving their berths and anchoring in the harbour basin (*Magnus Håkonssons bylov*, chap. 6, §§14–15). Although it has not been established whether such harbour laws already existed in the Viking Age, it is very likely that similar conflicts must also have arisen in Viking-age towns and that they would have been settled at the *thing* (Falk 1912: 23; Müller-Boysen 1990: 130–1). In contrast, we are well informed about the royal customs tariffs (*vectigalia*) which were levied at major trading places from the beginning of the ninth century at the latest due to the events connected with the destruction of Reric. Furthermore, Jankuhn (1958: 480) suggested an event from *Njáls saga* (chap. 31), penned c.1280 – when Gunnarr Hámundarson, on this way back from a Viking raid in the Baltic Sea, attains the court of King Harald Bluetooth in Hedeby and gifts one ship of his ten-vessel fleet to the king – could represent the payment of a *tithe* ('tenth') as a tax. This

FIGURE 14 Hedeby, present-day northern Germany. Miniature lead anchor as a 'customs stamp' for paid harbour fees? (inventory no. KSD 381.113 © Museum für Archäologie, Stiftung Schleswig-Holsteinische Landesmuseen, Schleswig).

interpretation, however, must be regarded as highly speculative, for, according to the saga, it is its hero Gunnarr who was invited to Hedeby at the king's request and in turn also received rich gifts himself (cf. Hilberg & Kalmring 2014: 223).

Material evidence for an existing harbour jurisdiction in Viking-age towns may be visible through an inconspicuous artefact group found in Hedeby, namely twelve crudely worked miniature lead anchors, which have puzzled scholars ever since (Figure 14). Drescher (1983: 184) suggested an affiliation with the known toy ship models from the site (cf. Kalmring 2010a: 398–9 fig. 293), although with the caveat that the anchors could also be Christian amulets. Without reaching a clear conclusion, Koktvedgaard Zeitzen (2002: 76; cf. Jensen 2010: 78–80) suggested a number of interpretations, ranging from amulets with either Christian or pagan connotations to profane insignias as marks of group affiliation or even as some kind of 'customs stamp', that is, as a token certifying that some form of customs payment has been made. Finally, Anspach (2010: 55–7) chooses to argue for a profane utilisation in the context of harbour operations, which corresponds to the idea that these miniature anchors were proof of payment of harbour fees.[3] If this is true, these fees may have been paid upon entry into the designated harbour area, but they may also simply have been payment for the use of harbour facilities (Kalmring 2010a: 416–17). It seems no coincidence that other miniature anchors are currently only known from distinctly urban sites, such as Dublin with four (Wallace 2016: 343) and York (Mainman & Rogers 2000: 2562), Slesvig (Koktvedgaard Zeitzen 2002: 71) and Sigtuna (Edberg 2011: 156) with one specimen each – which could suggest that they were part of a significant widespread customary harbour practice.

7.4 THE KING'S REPRESENTATIVE ON-SITE: ROYAL ADMINISTRATION

As demonstrated in the previous section (see also Section 5.2), Viking-age towns were exterritorial sites with their own jurisdiction. Although such towns were deliberately promoted by kings, they had no direct royal presence on-site but resided on estates in the immediate vicinity during their stays. Instead, the actual administration of the towns was subject to officials who represented the royal power on the ground. Some of these royal officials have already been mentioned, such as King Beorhtric's hapless reeve Beaduheard in 789, as well as the royal agent Herigar in Birka in 830 and 845, and Tolir, the bailiff of King Håkan, mentioned in the runic inscription on *Hovgårdstenen* from the last quarter of the eleventh century (Figure 15). For a more profound understanding of Viking-age towns, the significance of these royal officials has to be considered carefully.

In his role as royal prefect in Birka, Herigar is mentioned twice in *Vita Ansgarii* (Rimbert, chap. 11, 19; cf. Kalmring et al. 2017: 134–6).

---

[3] In this case, it may even be possible to link these lead anchors to the crudely made ship-shaped lead seals (Fre. *plombs naviformes*) from the river Charente at Taillebourg in Aquitania (Dumont & Mariotti 2013: 197–223). There, however, they have previously been considered as fishing-net sinkers, although interpretations as lead ingots from the nearby mines of Melle or simply as merchandise seals have also been suggested (Dumont & Mariotti 2013: 215).

FIGURE 15 Hovgården, Uppland, Sweden. Rune stone U 11 from Adelsö, mentioning the royal representative Tolir as King Håkan's bailiff (photo ID: KMB_16000300040790_085W0507; Swedish National Heritage Board/ RAÄ [Riksantikvarieämbetet], Photo: B. A. Lundberg 2004 [CC BY]).

While the designation of his official title changes somewhat from *praefectus vici* to *praefectus loci*, the first mention also contains another valuable addition: not only was Herigar *praefectus* but he was also the *consiliarius regis*, the advisor to the king. One of the first candidates for baptism after Ansgar's first arrival on Björkö was 'the prefect of this town [*praefectus vici*] named Herigar, who was a counsellor of the king [*consiliarius regis*] and much beloved by him [Björn at Haugi]' (Rimbert, chap. 11). A hundred years after Birka's demise, another such royal representative named Tolir is mentioned on *Hovgårdstenen* from the royal estate at Adelsö. In Indigenous Old Norse, his official title is *bryte* (cf. Wessén 1940: 17; Swd. *ombudsman*).[4] Originally, the term *bryte* was used for an unfree foreman of a farmstead, but in the king's service the title later came to signify an administrative position, which, for example, dealt with tax and fines collection (Wührer 1981; cf. Brink 2012: 139–49). Almost

---

[4] Immediately south of *Fornsigtuna*, a predecessor to late Viking-age Sigtuna, the place name *Bryttiaholm* recorded from 1348, indicates the presence of another royal representative in Old Sigtuna (Björklund 2014: 66).

contemporaneously with the *praefectus vici* in Birka, a royal official named Hovi is also mentioned for Hedeby in *Vita Ansgarii*. Designated as *comes vici*, Hovi appears after the death of King Horik the Elder in 854 and the subsequent pagan uprising when Ansgar's church was destroyed: 'Accordingly the headman of the village [*comes vici*] of Sliaswich [Hedeby], whose name was Hovi, who was specially opposed to this religion, urged the king [Horik the Younger] to destroy the Christian faith, and he ordered the church that had been built there to be shut and forbade the observance of the Christian religion' (Rimbert chap. 31).[5]

Unfortunately, neither of these sources mention the main duties of the royal officials in Birka and Hedeby. Arbman (1939: 39; 1943: xvi) suggested that Herigar was a 'commander' (Swd. *hövitsman*) whose main duty – based on an analogy to a much later Scandinavian term for a tax collector, *gælkaren* – was to collect duties for the king but also that he was in charge of Birka's defences and, in the absence of the king, presided over the *thing* (cf. Schück 1926: 57–60). Previously, Bolin (1933: 118–32) had presented the same line of argument, although he was in some doubt whether the presence of such officials was enough to prove the administrative and judicial autonomy of these sites (Bolin 1933: 131). Based on historical evidence, for Hedeby, Scheel (1938: 240–1; cf. Jankuhn 1949: 55; Jahnke 2019: 191) argued for a royal administration led by a 'prefect', who would have collected duties and tolls, a theory that also included the existence of a particular market legislation. As late as the 1970s, however, Jankuhn urged caution, noting: 'On the institution of the *comes vici* [in Hedeby] and the *praefectus* [in Birka] ... much has been said, yet so far clarity on the function and constitutional status of these authorities does not exist [and will remain unclear] until an elaborate analysis of the terms, based on comprehensive source reviews, has been undertaken' (Jankuhn 1972: 142; my translation). While Arbman (1939: 42) sought parallels with

---

[5] While no written sources mention a royal representative for Ribe, Søvsø (2020: 173) argued for a royal control of the site from 725 onwards, which would have included the presence of a *comes vici*.

Eastern Europe and made an analogy to the title *posadnik* (посадник) used for the highest representative of Grand Prince Vladimir (ON *Valdamarr*) the Great in Novgorod (*The Russian Primary Chronicle*, entry 6486–8 [978–80 CE]),[6] Jankuhn (1971: 29–30; 1972: 142) suggested western continental parallels, such as *comes* Bernhar of Hamburg, who held the town's *praefectura* but due to absence could not fulfil his task of defending it when it came under Viking attack in 845 (Rimbert, chap. 16).

Judging by the previously described deep chronological roots of shipping duties and port administration, it is quite likely that even the antetypes of the royal representatives may share the same judicial origins. From the time of the Roman Empire, among other imperial servants, the *procuratores portus* have already been mentioned. For late Roman conditions, the fourth-century handbook *Notitia dignitatum* (*The List of Offices*) lists the *comites commerciorum* as heads of trading towns of the three eastern frontier provinces 'Oriens and Egypt', 'Illyricum' and 'Moesia and Pontus', who were likely entrusted with the supervision over foreign trade (Jones 1964: 826–7). The role of the Byzantine fiscal official *kommerkiarios* (κομμερκιάριος), who was evidently responsible for the collection of the imperial export duties, seems indeed to originate from the Roman office *comes commerciorum* (Kazhdan & Oikonomides 1991); the activities of the Byzantine *kommerkiarioi* are well attested by the finds of their leaden customs seals. It is certainly not a coincidence that parallels to these late antique conditions in Continental Europe and Anglo-Saxon England are restricted to major commercial ports: in the eighth century, the shipping duties imposed by the Lombards were negotiated with two *comites* from Comacchio. In the English Channel, both Dorestad and Quentovic had officials called *procuratores* (cf. Jankuhn 1949: 55; Verhulst 2000: 111; Middelton 2005: 321), who, in at least one case, can be

---

[6] An addition to the *Medieval Russian Laws* (art. 19–21), the *Pravda of Yaroslav's Sons* from c.1072, included fines for manslaughter on princely bailiffs. Here, the *ognishchanin* (огнищанин) was the general manager of princely estates (*Medieval Russian Laws*, art. 19 footnote), which may have been a similar role to that of the king's *bryte* in Scandinavia.

directly linked to the collection of taxes and other dues. For Dorestad, a charter issued by Louis the Pious in 815 mentions the presence of *procurators rei publice* (Diplomata Belgica no. 179). In an entry for the year 787, the *Gesta abbatum Fontanellensium* (book 12, chap. 2) mentions that the abbot Gervold of Fontanelle/Saint Wandrille, in his role as *procurator*, collected tolls and dues (*tributa atque vectigalia*) in different ports and towns (*portus ac civitates*) but mostly in Quentovic. Remarkably, however, the *procurator* of Quentovic does not seem to have lived on-site, for as the abbot of Saint Wandrille, Gervold would still have been based at the monastery some 125 kilometres south-west of there. In 858–68, it was no longer a *procurator* but a *praefectus emporia* named Grippo who performed such duties in Quentovic (Malbos 2017: 278, 280), and his tasks even included negotiations on behalf of Emperor Charles the Bald at the court of King Offa of Mercia (*Miracula Sancti Wandregisili*, chap. 15; cf. Lebecq 1983: 164–5; 1991: 422; 1993: 79; 2006: 247–9). The source does not reveal what Grippo's task entailed, but since the emperor sent his *praefectus* of Quentovic it is likely that it dealt with a mutual agreement on cross-channel trade. On the other side of the English Channel, the term *wicgerefas* was used for royal officials,[7] and according to the ninth-century *Old English Martyrology* (chap. 190) the term for customs official, *thelonarius*, corresponded to the role of tax collector and *wic* reeve (*theloniarius, þæt is gafoles moniend ond wicgerefa*). *The Laws of Hlothhere and Eadric* (chap. 16) from c.673–85 state that men from Kent intending to buy property in Lundenwic/London had to bring either two to three trustworthy men or the *wicgerefa* as witnesses (cf. Campbell 2000: 51). In the late ninth century, *The Anglo-Saxon Chronicle* (AD 897) mentions Boernwulf, the *wicgerefa* of Winanceastre/Winchester, who died of disease. Later, the title changed to *portgerefa*,

---

[7] For both Ipswich-Buttermarket and Hamwic-Stadium Cemetery, it has been suggested that studs with Germanic animal-style II ornamentations on the scabbards of scramasaxes, found in one outstanding seventh-century weapon grave each, may indicate burials belonging to the king's reeves at these *wics* (Hinton 2005: 75 fig. 3.1: 930–4; cf. Hodges 2012: 104–5).

linking the office even closer to the harbour. *Portgerefas* appear in a whole series of eleventh-century charters issued for several English river ports: Ælfsige, Swetman, Leofstan and Ulf are known from London (*Codex diplomaticus* nos. 856–7, 861, 871), Godric, Leofstan and Æðelred from Canterbury (*Codex diplomaticus* nos. 789–99, 929), Leafcild from Bath (*Codex diplomaticus* no. 933) and Ælfsige from Bodmin (*Codex diplomaticus* no. 981).

However, although there is plenty of evidence of high-ranking royal officials linked to a specific administration in major *emporia*, their responsibilities remain somewhat unclear. Malbos (2017: 278) suggested that while the abbot Gervold, as *procurator*, was a mere tax official who functioned as an *exactor* of dues, his successor Grippo, the *praefectus* of Quentovic, was a royal official with many administrative, judicial, tax and military duties. Regarding the roles of officials in Viking-age towns, Norr (1998: 160–3) argued that the *praefectus* of Birka probably had a role equivalent to the one of the *comes* known from, for example, Hedeby. And with the roles of the latter, thanks to Merovingian sources, we are indeed much more acquainted: Weidemann (1982: 66–7) specified that the domain of a Merovingian *comes* – comparable to that of a bishop – was the *civitas*, in which he also had his official residence. The *comites* were appointed by the king and their terms of service was thus tied to the reign of their respective regents. The actual responsibilities of a Merovingian *comes* are well-understood and indeed seem to correspond to those previously suggested for the officials of Viking-age towns:

> In the *civitas* the *comes* was in charge of justice, administration and warfare. In the *civitas* or the *comiat* respectively, the *comes* was judge ... and in this capacity was called '*iudex*' ... In the field of administration, the *comes* was responsible for the collection of dues and other fees and to deliver them to the king's court. ... *Comites* are surprisingly seldom referred to as military leaders of the troops in their *civitas*. ... The military leader of larger armies

was usually the *dux*, to whom additional contingents from other duchies were only rarely assigned. Such additional troops were always led by the *comes*, as were the smaller armies that only consisted of the levy of his *civitas*. (Weidemann 1982: 66; my translation)

8 Free Trade within Narrow Boundaries

As discussed in previous chapters, the spatial exclusion of Viking-age towns from the surrounding rural societies can be complemented by strong arguments for a separate jurisdiction enforced by the king's reeve, with laws distinctly different from the provincial laws, as reflected in the later high medieval *landskapslagar*. This can be demonstrated both archaeologically through evidence of custom boundaries and historically through suggested analogies with contemporary continental and Anglo-Saxon trade legislation as well as from the substratum of later Scandinavian law codes. During this period, not only would the royal officials of merchant towns all over Europe have been responsible for defence issues and judicial matters but their primary responsibility would have been the collection of customs duties for their royal patrons. It was the kings who, acting in the background, purposely granted space for international trade in their realms and provided the compulsory judicial and administrative framework. However, as will be demonstrated in the following, this space provided for free trade in Viking-age towns was at the same time a very strictly restricted one.

8.1 AN ACTIVE SCANDINAVIAN TRADE POLICY

As a major player in early medieval Europe, the Carolingian Empire followed a very conscious trade policy, authorising and controlling markets for both political and fiscal reasons (Verhulst 2002: 129–30). In this context, reference should be made to Charlemagne's trade embargo against Offa of Mercia in c.790 (*Alcuin*, no. 7; cf. Middelton 2005: 324), Charlemagne's Capitulary of Thionville/Diedenhofen with its arms embargo from 805 (*Karoli Magni Capitularia*, no. 44; cf. Kalmring 2010c: 285) and the Raffelstetten customs regulations of Louis the Child from 903 to 906 (*Inquisitio de theloneis Raffelstettensis*; cf.

Adam 1996: 121–4), to mention but a few. Generally, Carolingian trade regulations were based on protectionism in an attempt to confine the circle of Carolingian commodity products to domestic commerce. This policy was enforced by the introduction of high export duties on cross-border trade:

> Rather unfavourable to commerce was their concern with the frontiers of the empire, whether in the emporia on the North Sea and Channel coast, where even royal merchants had to pay the 10 per cent tax, or at the Alpine passes and in the border region with the Avars. We can assume that all these frontier posts, and also on the Elbe, trade ... was severely controlled. Importation however, for example along the Danube, upstream from the Avar frontier, well known from the famous Raffelstetten inquiry, was favoured by lower toll tariffs. (Verhulst 2002: 130, cf. 92).

Verhulst's assessment was mainly based on the *Praeceptum negotiatorum* of Louis the Pious from 828 (*Formulae Imperiales e curia Ludovici Pii*, no. 37; cf. Ganshof 1957), which explicitly, although solely by name, mentions the royal customs facilities Quentovic and Dorestad as the major gateways to England and Scandinavia for the extraction of the *decima* or market tithe. In fact, from the ninth century onwards the use of the *decima* was an important transaction levy that not only was used in the Carolingian Empire but can be traced across large parts of early medieval Europe (Middelton 2005: 324–30 fig. 2).[1]

The previously described destruction of Reric in 808, for the sake of gaining control over customs duties, is an obvious testimonial to a distinctly active trade policy, albeit with warfare as its ultimate political means. Furthermore, the Scandinavians not only came to terms with

---

[1] Even for the Khazar Khaganate, with its capital Atil at the Volga delta, there are accounts of shipping duties and tithes since the second half of the ninth century (see Ibn Fadlān, chap. 'Taxes and Custom Duties'), which were also adapted by the Volga Bulghars (cf. Noonan 2007: 213). In this context, it is noteworthy that at the burial ground of Timerëvo, in chamber-grave kurgan no. 100, a scale bearing the Arabic inscription 'tax' or 'toll' (ضريبة) on its weighting pans was found (Fekhner & Yanina 1979: fig. 1).

the protective Carolingian trade policies and introduced customs duties of their own but also attempted to conclude their own commercial trade agreements. The most illustrative example from written sources is without a doubt the events of 873, as transmitted through *The Annals of Fulda*, which describes how envoys of the co-ruling Danish kings Sigfrid and Halfdan (cf. Lund 1995: 211) appeared at the court of Louis the German, king of East Francia (Ganshof 1958: 29–30; Müller-Boysen 2007: 180). In April 873, the envoys of King Sigfrid attended the imperial assembly at Bürstadt near Worms 'seeking to make peace over the border disputes between themselves and the Saxons and so that merchants of each kingdom might come and go in peace to the other, bringing merchandise to buy and sell' (*The Annals of Fulda*, entry 873 CE). Although Louis had assured the envoys that this would be the case, only four months later, in August, Halfdan had to send further envoys to the imperial assembly at Metz, this time with a diplomatic gift – a sword with a golden hilt – proposing a summit at the border river Eider south of Hedeby in order to reach a peace agreement: 'Halfdan ... also sent his messengers to the king asking the same things which his brother had asked, namely, that the king should send his ambassadors to the River Eider, which separates Danes and Saxons, and that they should meet them there and ratify a perpetual peace on both sides' (*The Annals of Fulda*, entry 873 CE). The source clearly states the reasons for the Danish peace proposals, which were unmistakably linked to commercial interests. Moreover, it is quite likely that there was even a direct fiscal interest from the Danish co-rulers themselves, since they personally advocated the matter twice at the court of King Louis. As early as 829, the *Vita Ansgarii* mentions another delegation visiting the court of Emperor Louis the Pious, this time from Sweden: 'Meanwhile it happened that Swedish ambassadors [*legatos Sueonum*] had come to the Emperor Louis, and, amongst other matters which they had been ordered to bring to the attention of the emperor, they informed him that there were many belonging to their nation who desired to embrace the Christian religion' (Rimbert, chap. 9). Considering the nature of the text, it is not surprising that Rimbert emphasises the burning wish of many *Svear* to become Christian, and indeed this visit must be seen as a prelude to Ansgar's missionary attempts in Birka one year later. It is, however, quite possible that King Björn at Haugi had to accept a Christian mission as an imperial prerequisite for negotiating the 'other matters', which are likely to have had a political and/or commercial background (cf. Arbman 1943: xv; 1965: 19). It is not unlikely that these trade delegations, the Swedish one in 829 and the two Danish ones in 873, were even directly linked to efforts relating to Birka and Hedeby, where foreign merchants were particularly desired. Additionally, many of the Scandinavian kings, such as Horik the Elder, Harald Fairhair, Harald Bluetooth, Erik Segersäll ('the Victorious') and Knut the Saint, are known to have campaigned against domestic Viking pirates, who threatened important shipping routes and long-distance trade in their own realms (Müller-Boysen 1990: 97–9).

Commercial endeavours were not restricted to north-western Europe but also included the Byzantine Empire. According to *The Russian Primary Chronicle*, the Rurik dynasty was eager to come to commercial agreements with none other than the Byzantine emperors themselves. After the alleged raid on Miklagård/Constantinople in 907, Prince Oleg (ON *Helgi*) and Emperor Leo VI the Wise, with his co-ruling brother Alexander, agreed upon these terms:

> Your prince shall personally lay injunction upon such Russes as journey hither that they shall do no violence in the towns and throughout our territory. Such Russes as arrive here shall dwell in the St. Mamas quarter. Our government will send officers to record their names, and they shall then receive their monthly allowance, first the natives of Kiev, then those from Chernigov, Pereyaslavl', and the other cities. They shall not enter the city save through one gate, unarmed and fifty at a time, escorted by an agent of the Emperor. They may conduct business according to their requirements without payment of taxes.
>
> (The Russian Primary Chronicle, entry *6412–15 [904–7* CE*]*)

In 912, a delegation of fifteen Varangians commissioned by Prince Oleg appeared at the Byzantine court to reconfirm this trading peace (*The Russian Primary Chronicle*, entry 6420 [912 CE]). This time, the source makes a detailed account of all aspects of the agreement concerning common, criminal and mercantile law – for example, in cases where 'Greek' trading vessels were wrecked in Rus' territory – as well as matters dealing with the legal framework for commerce and legal protection for merchants abroad. The chronicle also describes that in 945 a Byzantine delegation was sent to Grand Prince Igor (ON *Ingvar*) of Kiev/Könugård to renew the treaty, whereupon Igor sent a delegation to the court of Emperor Romanos I Lekapenos and his co-ruling sons Stephen and Constantine. Here, it is particularly noteworthy that Igor's delegation included not only twenty-five envoys consisting of various princes and nobles (boyars), representing the grand prince himself, but also a group of twenty-five merchants (*The Russian Primary Chronicle*, entry 6453 [945 CE]). With additions, the agreed contract essentially confirms the agreements made in 907 and 912, such as the restriction to stay in the St Mamas quarter and the procedures for wrecked Byzantine ships. New

FIGURE 16 Berezan, Dnieper-Bug Estuary, Ukraine. Ukraine's sole rune stone, raised in the eleventh century by Grani for his deceased trading partner Karl on the island of Berezan (photo ID: KMB_16001000167644_PNN02691; Swedish National Heritage Board/ RAÄ [Riksantikvarieämbetet], photo: P.-N. Nilsson [CC BY]).

items were the promise that the Rus' may send as many ships with agents and merchants as they desired, as long as they were able to produce an official certificate issued by their prince, as well as the ban on wintering in Belobereg and St Eleutherius/Berezan by the mouth of the river Dnieper, paired with the obligation for ships to return to Rus' territory in the autumn. It was certainly no coincidence that the only rune stone ever found in Ukraine (Figure 16) was discovered in 1905 on the island of Berezan (Arne 1914).

8.2 PROTECTION OF FOREIGN MERCHANTS DURING TRADING VOYAGES

The famous travel account of Wulfstan, included in the Old English translation of Paulus Orosius' *Historiarum adversum paganos libri septem* (*Seven Books of History against the Pagans*; cf. Wulfstan's Report: 15), and his journey from Hedeby to Truso/Janów Pomorski illustrate the dangers at sea for independent traders. The fact that it took the Anglo-Saxon merchant Wulfstan an unusually long time to get from Hedeby to Truso – seven whole days, sailing both night and day – has led to assumptions that he may have first joined a merchant convoy (ON *samfloti*; cf. Falk 1912: 22) towards Scania. This way, Wulfstan stayed in Denmark waters as long as possible before heading south towards the Pomeranian coast and successfully reaching his final destination at the Vistula Lagoon. Such precautions may have been necessary because of the late ninth-century activities of Slavonic pirates along the southern Baltic Sea coast, blocking a more direct route from Hedeby (Ulriksen 2009; Englert & Ossowski 2009: 268–9 fig. 18). In fact, Wendish Vikings – along with Courlanders and 'many others from the eastern Baltic' – are mentioned in *The Saga of Harald Hardrada* (chap. 48), while 'Vikings from Estonia' appear in *The Saga of Olaf Tryggvason* (chap. 6); both sagas have been handed down in the *Heimskringla* by Snorri Sturluson (cf. Lind 2012: 156). Unlike Wulfstan, Ansgar and his companion Witmar were not as fortunate when they travelled as passengers in a convoy of merchant vessels – most likely with Hedeby as their port

PLATE 1 Viking-age town of Hedeby, present-day northern Germany (© J. Stuhrmann & T. W Wehrmann for GEO Epoche: Picture Press).

PLATE II Viking-age town of Ribe, western Denmark (illustration: © F. Bau).

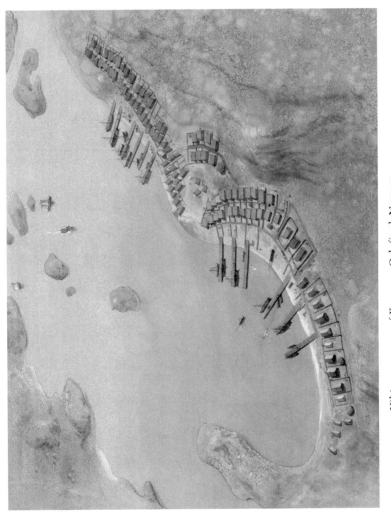

PLATE III Viking-age town of Kaupang, Oslofjord, Norway (illustration: © F. Bau).

PLATE IV Viking-age town of Birka, eastern middle Sweden (The Swedish History Museum/SHM [CC BY 4.0]).

of departure – during their first missionary voyage to Birka in 830. Halfway to Birka their convoy fell prey to a Viking (*pyratis;* 'pirates') attack and lost all its ships; the missionaries were deprived of all the royal gifts and their precious books and had to continue the journey overland (Rimbert, chap. 10). Hence, before returning to Francia – after having spent a year and a half evangelising on Björkö – they requested written (runic?) royal guarantees, conforming to local traditions (*litteris regia more ipsorum deformatis*) (Rimbert, chap. 12). Before his second missionary journey to Birka in 852, Ansgar took even further precautions when he secured the company of an envoy and a royal token (*missum partier et signum*) from King Horik the Elder, which guaranteed safe passage (Rimbert, chap. 26). Around 1070, Adam of Bremen (book 1, chap. 26) refers to the same event reporting that: 'Without delay the intrepid champion [Ansgar] asked king Horik for an escort and safe-conduct [*missum rogavit atque sigillum*] and, putting off from the Danish shore, came to Sweden.'

Already in 1977, Sawyer drew attention to the fact that

> merchants who traded in more than one kingdom were necessarily strangers somewhere, and as such they lacked the normal protection afforded in the Dark Ages by lords and kinsmen. ... Traders therefore needed protection and ... it was best provided by kings who could do so by extending their peace to cover such men. (Sawyer 1979: 150)

Strangers and foreigners would generally have been associated with the unknown and therefore possibly perceived as potential threats to the prevailing local social order. By acting outside their own legal sphere, as subjects of foreign kings, these 'aliens' – regardless of being refugees, slaves, pilgrims or merchants – enjoyed virtually no legal protection, which exposed them to the risks of theft, slavery and manslaughter (Ganshof 1956). Consequently, seeking royal protection constituted a vital assurance, either by becoming *mundeburdis* ('legal guardian') of a royal *patronus* or else – in the case of long-distance traders (Figure 17) – by paying fees in order to enjoy the legal protection of the *salutaticum* or *laghkøp* on-site (Jahnke 2019: 186; cf. Sections 7.2–7.3). Similar royal protection would have been essential for foreign merchants travelling not only through Viking-age Scandinavia but through other parts of early medieval Europe as well. This was certainly the case in the Carolingian and Byzantine Empires, as attested in the *Annales Bertiniani* for the year 839, when the Annals mention a couple of Varangians attending the court of Louis the Pious at Ingelheim as part of an entourage of a Byzantine delegation sent by Emperor Theophilus (Shepard 1995). These Varangians, referred to as *Rhos*, had been sent as envoys to Theophilus but were unable to return home via the Russian river system. Hence:

FIGURE 17 Viking-age long-distance merchant from the Baltic, with folding scales and precious furs as merchandise (drawing: Å. Gustavsson).

Theophilus requested in his letter that the Emperor [Louis the Pious] in his goodness might grant them safe conducts to travel through his empire and any help or practical assistance they needed to return home, for the route by which they had reached Constantinople had taken them through primitive tribes that were very fierce and savage and Theophilus did not wish them to return that way in case some disaster befell them.

However, when Louis discovered that the Varangians in fact 'belonged to the people of the Swedes [*Sueonum*]', he suspected them of being spies and requested assurances from Theophilus, although not without declaring that 'if they were found to be genuine, he would supply them with means to return to their own fatherland without any risk of danger and send them home with every assistance' (*Annales Bertiniani*, entry 839 CE).

Sawyer also pointed to the fact that, as late as in the eleventh century, the penalty for breaking a peace granted directly by the king was far higher than one granted by one of his agents (Sawyer 1979: 150). A breach of peace against merchants or trading places under royal protection was regarded as a felony against the king himself, whose vows included the personal pursuit of violators (Müller-Boysen 1990: 93). An example of the severe consequences of a violation of royal protection is found in *Bjarnar saga Hítdœlakappa* (chaps. 7–8), recorded in c.1220, when an envoy of Olaf II of Norway (995–1030) and the merchants travelling with him were robbed on their way home from Denmark. Since the envoy Þórður Kolbeinsson had been issued a sealed letter (ON *brév*) by King Olaf, the perpetrators – once they realised their mistake – subjected themselves to the judgement of the king, who then decided on a mutual settlement and the return of the looted merchandise. Similar information is found in the *Færeyinga saga* (chap. 19), penned around 1200, which mentions how Sigmundur Brestisson was tasked to avenge twelve slain Norwegian merchants in the name of Earl Håkon Sigurdsson († 995). The Norwegians merchants had previously been executed by the Swedish King Erik Segersäll after one of them had violated the market peace and killed a Swede at a local fair (ON *kaupstefna*) (cf. Müller-Boysen 1990: 93–5).

8.3 COSMOPOLITAN TRADING CENTRES WITH RIGID BOUNDARIES

From *The Saga of the People of Laxardal*, we learn of an event which allegedly took place around 956, when Olaf 'the Peacock' Hǫskuldsson, on his voyage from Norway to the court of this grandfather King Mýrkjartan (OI Muircheartach), was stranded on the Irish shore. Upon this misfortune, his companion Orn cautions that they would not be well received and their cargo would be seized according to Irish law, for 'We're far from any port or merchant town where foreigners are assured of trading in peace' (*The Saga of the People of Laxardal*, chap. 21). As demonstrated in Section 7.2, the legal protection granted by the rulers of Viking-age towns was essential for attracting foreign long-distance merchants, who otherwise had no legal security and risked not only their commodities but also their personal freedom and lives. In return, they would willingly have paid taxes and customs duties that guaranteed this royal privilege, levied by the *praefectus* or *comes* at the few commercial 'nodal points' situated outside the boundaries of traditional society and protected by a specific commercial legislation. The tax revenues these sites generated must have been so substantial that Scandinavian kings were prepared to eliminate competitors and sometimes even to actively campaign for trade peace with the Carolingian and Byzantine Empires. Against this background, the conclusion 'that they [foreign traders] tended to do their business not in the countryside but in special trading places that were easily accessible by boat' (Sawyer 1979: 151) is more than evident. It was these places where foreign merchants were more than welcome and even sought after; and the results of these frameworks to promote long-distance trade can be found in the sources mentioned at the beginning of this volume (see Chapter 2): in Hedeby, foreign merchants from all known parts of the world gathered, and Birka attracted rich merchants from Frisia,

Denmark, Norway, the Slavic countries, Sambia and even 'Scythia',[2] contributing to an 'abundance of goods' and 'a large amount of money' (cf. Rimbert, chaps. 19, 24) which could be siphoned off by the towns' patrons.

However, these parallel communities, with their cosmopolitan open spaces, were rigidly controlled and the movements of visiting merchants were limited by strict boundaries. To prove this argument, we must first turn to the Mediterranean: the most famous examples of contemporary restrictions for foreign merchants derive from the Byzantine Empire and its capital Constantinople. As already quoted from *The Russian Primary Chronicle* (entries 6412–15 [904–7 CE] and 6453 [945 CE]) and its descriptions of the treaties between the Rus' and Byzantine authorities, Varangian merchants were only allowed to dwell in one specified quarter of Constantinople, on its south-western margin around the monastery of St Mamas. Moreover, they were only allowed to enter the capital through one specified gate – possibly the Xylokerkos/Belgrade Gate of the Theodosian Land Walls (Figure 18) – and were not allowed to carry arms and move in groups larger than fifty merchants and even then only when escorted by imperial representatives. Even more noteworthy is that the time they were allowed to stay within the city walls was limited: after the names of the merchants had been recorded, temporary residence permits or 'monthly allowances' were issued by Byzantine imperial officials. The time allowances afforded by such permits depended on the status of the visitors and differed between Rus' ambassadors and common merchants, who were only granted the 'usual amount' (cf. Laiou 2002: 724). In the Byzantine sources themselves, we find additional first-hand information on the temporal restrictions of visits from foreign merchants in Constantinople: *The Book of the Eparch* (Τὸ ἐπαρχικὸν βιβλίον), written during the reign of Emperor Leo VI the Wise in 911/12 (cf. Dagron 2002: 407), states that traders from 'Syria' – that is, Arab merchants from the Muslim world – could generally only acquire three-month permits. The corresponding paragraph reads:

[2] For a discussion of the *scithiae populi* (Adam of Bremen, book 1, chap. 60) and the early medieval concept of Scythia, see Jansson (2011: 46–9).

FIGURE 18 Theodosian Land Walls, Istanbul, Turkey. Xylokerkos/Belgrade Gate within the late antique walls of Constantinople, leading to the Rus' commercial hostels at the St Mamas quarter (Wikimedia Commons).

> He [the Eparch] shall not permit any person so arriving to remain in the city for more than three months. And he must tell them that within that time they are to dispose of their goods and purchase what they want and leave the city. Should he find any who have outstayed their permission they shall be flogged, shaved, their goods shall be confiscated and they shall be expelled from the city.
>
> (The Book of the Eparch, book 5, §2)

During their limited stays, foreign merchants could not just settle in any part of Constantinople but – as in the case of the Syrian silk merchants – were assigned areas where they lodged in specific supervised commercial hostels, so-called *caravanserais* or Greek *mitata* (Μιτάτα) (Dragon 2002: 441; cf. Middelton 2005: 355–6).

Claude (1985) elaborated on these Byzantine *mitata* restrictions for foreign merchants and stated that, since we lack sources for analogous regulations from western Europe, the existence of such administrative constrictions – although not impossible – is less likely (Claude 1985: 125–6). By contrast, Middelton (2005: 348–9; cf. Jahnke 2019: 188) argued that the term *mansio* found in Frankish sources is in fact a synonym for *metatus*, from which the Byzantine *mitaton* is derived. Furthermore, he suggested that the suffix *-wic*, which is generally considered to be derived from the Latin *vicus*, could in fact derive from a direct translation of *mansio* into Old English. In that context, the resulting *wic* would refer 'to a hostel for overseas travellers ... If this is the case, then in the context of ports and markets, *wic* may have acquired the meaning of "a place where hostels for foreign traders (and other visitors) are located"' (Middleton 2005: 349). Later, in the twelfth or thirteenth century at the latest, evidence from London suggests that the wine merchants from Lower Lorraine were not allowed to stay more than forty days in town and that the same applied for merchants from Gascony as well as for woad-dye traders. Additionally, the sources report that foreign merchants from Lorraine had to inform the local sheriff in which hostels – owned by local merchants – they were staying, who then inspected their merchandise and collected customs (Middleton 2005: 336–9 n. 108). This practice is also known from the Swedish urban law of King Magnus Eriksson from c.1360, stating that foreign merchants or 'guests' had to be able to supply the name of their hosts for tax purposes. The town hosts, often trading partners of the foreign visitors, also had a legal responsibility for their guests (cf. Roslund 2007: 143). Against this background, the question is whether we can presuppose such regulations already for the Viking Age. Apart from possible analogies suggested by the Byzantine evidence,[3] there is no contemporary evidence for time-restricted residence permits issued by the *praefectus* or *comes* for visits to Viking-age towns. In north-western

---

[3] The concept of being hosted in order to be able to conduct trade abroad – albeit apparently without temporal limitations – is even reported for the 'Turks' (Khazars) in Ibn Fadlān's contemporary account (chap. 'Hospitality') from 921/2: 'No Muslim can cross their country without having made friends with one of them, with whom he stays.'

Europe, however, similar obligations for local hosts to take responsibility for (legally ambiguous and potentially harmful) strangers can be traced as far back as to the late seventh century. In the Kentish *Laws of Hlothhere and Eadric,* the relevant paragraph reads:

> If a man entertains a stranger [OE feormæþ; a trader or anyone else who has come over the border] for three days in his own home, and then supplies him with food from his own store, and [if] he [the stranger] then does harm to anyone, the man shall bring the other to justice, or make amends on his behalf.
>
> (The Laws of Hlothhere and Eadric, *chap. 15; cf. Sawyer 1986: 60; Middelton 2005: 338*)

To try to explain the limited possibilities for long-distance merchants to operate and continue trade in the hinterlands of urban communities through reasons of cost-effectiveness would be misguided for the western Mediterranean (Claude 1985: 125–6) just as it would be for the North Sea and Baltic Sea. It actually had more to do with their ambiguous legal status as strangers operating outside the boundaries of the emporia and thus no longer under direct royal protection. As desirable as the presence of long-distance traders was at maritime trading places it was equally undesirable outside of these international trade enclaves, that is, to have foreigners within the limits of traditional society. Outside of those designated sites for international commerce, travelling merchants would have been immediately recognised as strangers or perhaps even as suspicious characters due to reasons such as their physical appearance or portable and mobile lifestyle, which, as previously mentioned, may have been perceived as a threat to traditional local societies. As masterless men, they were not integrated within the constraints of traditional social networks and thus potentially endangered the prevailing local social order (Loveluck 2013: 208; Abels 2008: 151). That this attitude actually prevailed is evident from legal texts from Wessex dating from c.694. The corresponding passage states unequivocally: 'If a man from afar, or a stranger, travels through a wood off the highway and neither shouts or blows his horn, he shall be assumed to be a thief, and as such may be either slain or put to ransom' (*The Laws of Ine*, chap. 20; cf. Middelton 2005: 338–9). It is possible that it was such a signal instrument, an iron bell, that was found among the grave goods in an isolated, mid-seventh-century burial of an itinerant smith at Tattershall Thorpe in Lincolnshire (Hinton 2000b; cf. Loveluck 2013: 208–9). However, if foreign merchants decided to leave the jurisdiction of the trading centres in order to pursue their commercial interests further inland, they first had to announce their intentions to the king's reeve during a public assembly, where they would declare which men would accompany them. They would then be legally responsible for these men during the journey. This is described in *The Doom Book of Alfred the Great* from around 893:

> Further, with regard to traders [*ciepemonnum*], it is decreed: they shall bring before the king's reeve [*kyninges gerefan*], at a public meeting [*folcgemote*], the men they are taking with them up into the country [*to ryhte brengan*; rather: 'to bring on the ride'], and declare how many of them they are; and they shall take with them [only] such men as they can bring to justice again, at a public meeting. And when they need to have more men on their journey, a similar declaration shall always be made to the king's reeve, before the assembled company, as often as need arises.
>
> (*The Laws of Alfred*, chap. 34)

There even seems to be archaeological evidence of the actual confinement of foreign long-distance merchants to Viking-age towns that were located in no man's land and deliberately separated from the surrounding traditional society. Even in a microcosm such as the island of Björkö, foreigners and locals seem to have been perceived and treated differently. Almost a century ago, Schück (1926: 57) drew attention to Rimbert's specific wording when describing the conditions in Birka in connection with the attack on Birka by the exiled King Anund and his Danish allies in c.844: with regard to the inhabitants of Birka, Rimbert (chap. 19) differentiated between *populi* and *negociatores*, which Schück understood as a distinction between 'permanent resident inhabitants' and '"guests" from abroad or from other Swedish places'. Yet even in death – and thus archaeologically traceable – foreigners and locals seem to have been separated from each other. In her doctoral thesis on the burial customs of Birka, Gräslund (1980) categorised the approximately 1,100 burials that Hjalmar Stolpe excavated between 1873/4 and 1888 and separated them into inhumation and cremation burials. The inhumations were then subdivided into graves with coffins, graves without coffins and chamber graves, as well as indeterminate inhumation burials and possible inhumation burials, while the cremations were subdivided into cremation deposits – such as urns and cremation pits – and other cremation burials, that is, cremation burials without cremation deposits (Gräslund 1980: 87; cf. Arwidsson 1984: tab. 2). Despite two enclosed maps displaying the burial grounds *Norr om Borg* ('North of [the] Hillfort') 2A–2B and *Hemlanden* ('The Home-fields') 1A–1 C (Gräslund 1980: maps 1–2), the spatial distribution of the different burial customs was not entirely apparent. However, a general review based on Birka town geographic information system (GIS) data (Kalmring 2012b), displaying the proportions of burial types within separate single grave districts, strikingly revealed that the inhumations were more or less restricted to *Stadsvallen* ('The Town Rampart') and to the burial ground *Norr om Borg*, whereas cremations were limited to the eastern *Hemlanden* districts, the hillfort *Borg* itself and particularly south of it in *Borgshage* and *Kvarnbacka*.[4] By accepting cremation burials as an expression of indigenous traditions and inhumations as an alien element (Ambrosiani 1992: 20), it must be concluded that while the burials of the local population are located at a distance from the town, those of the 'strangers' have a closer relationship to the settlement area of *Svarta Jorden* ('The Black

[4] An exception to this pattern is seen in the burial grounds of *Grindsbacka* (5) and *Lilla Kärrbacka* (6A), where inhumations are oriented east–west and only small amounts of grave goods dominate. Generally, these are presumed to be later Christian village cemeteries from the time after Birka's demise and as such rather related to the hamlet of Björkö (cf. Stolpe 1882: 62; Hallström 1913: 10–11; Arbman 1939: 79–80, 87–8; 1943: xxiii).

Earth'), that is, they are more or less exclusively dispersed along the town limits (Kalmring 2016b: 207 fig. 3).

If this pattern, which is evident in Birka, is a general one, it should consequently also be observable in other Viking-age towns. In Hedeby, however, such burial patterns are much less distinguishable due to its vicinity to the Continent and earlier impacts of Christianity, which also affected funeral rites. In addition, the significantly longer time span of Hedeby must be taken into account – while Birka was abandoned around 975 and Kaupang around 960–80, Hedeby persisted until c.1066, that is, long after Denmark's official conversion to Christianity around 965. The main burial grounds of Hedeby are namely the burials on top of the hillfort *Hochburg* north of the town, the chamber burial ground (Ger. *Kammergräberfeld*), the inhumation burial ground (Ger. *Flachgräberfeld*) inside the semi-circular rampart and finally the southern burial ground (Ger. *Südgräberfeld*), which included a chambered boat burial (Ger. *Bootkammergrab*). Additional smaller groups of graves have been found at the foot of the hillfort (Ger. *Gräber am Fuße der Hochburg* or '*Nordgräberfeld*') and inside the settlement near the Haddebyer Noor (Ger. *Gräber am Noor*). Of the 1,348 excavated burials in Hedeby, only 98 were cremation burials (Arents & Eisenschmidt 2010: 181–6). Despite the more complex initial situation described here and the low number of cremation burials, it can be observed that these are restricted to the *Hochburg* (Kalmring 2014/15) and the western part of the southern burial ground (Ger. *Südgräberfeld-West*; Arents & Eisenschmidt 2010: map 10), which were situated on the outskirts of the later fortified main settlement.[5] In the case of Hedeby, however, its cremation burials cannot be linked exclusively to an indigenous population, since cremation pits are rather common in the West Slavonic area and cremations in egg-shaped urns are characteristic for the Frisian North Sea coast; only the unseparated cremation deposits, as found on the hillfort, are considered

---

[5] From within the semi-circular ramparts only two cremations are known: Grave Hb. 309 was a cremation pit found on the chamber burial ground in 1931 (Arents & Eisenschmidt 2010: 39); another single cremation pit was found during a recent pit house excavation 2005–10 (Hilberg, personal communication, 19 March 2015).

to be a typical local early Viking-age phenomenon in Old Denmark (Arents & Eisenschmidt 2010: 212, 282–6).

In Kaupang, there are cautious estimates of c.700 burials, of which 204 have been excavated so far (Stylegar 2007: 75–7 fig. 5.2). They are distributed over two main burial grounds, *Nordre Kaupang* ('Northern Kaupang') and one on the island of Lamøya; in addition, there are also a few smaller burial grounds such as *Hagejordet* and *Bikjholberget*, *Søndre Kaupang* and *Vikingholmen*, as well as *Bjønnes*. The vast majority of the graves from *Nordre Kaupang*[6] and *Hagejordet*, north of the town, are mounds with cremations, as are those at *Søndre Kaupang*, south of the settlement area. Accordingly, Skre (2007: 382) argued that both *Nordre* and *Søndre Kaupang* had a 'connection with the local rural society'. On Lamøya, these links to some local population are less obvious, since the burial ground features cremation graves and inhumations, as well as mounds and flat graves – although the different modes of burial seem concentrated in clusters or groups. For our concern, however, the burial ground of *Bikjholberget*, situated on a former headland extending from the northern settlement area down to the town's harbour (Stylegar 2007: 68), is the most interesting: this isolated and clearly delimited burial ground is a flat-grave cemetery exclusively with inhumations, comprising a vast variety of foreign burial customs, such as boat graves, chamber graves, a wagon-body burial, graves with sledges, as well as coffin graves and graves without coffins. It is no coincidence that Stylegar (2007: 100–1) seeks a parallel with Birka when he commented:

> [T]here seem to be very clear similarities between *Hemlanden* and *Nordre Kaupang* on the one hand and between the cemetery immediately to the south of the settlement area [i.e. *Norr om Borg*] and *Bikjholberget* on the other – the first two dominated by barrows and cremations, the latter two by different kinds of richly furnished inhumations.

[6] To be more precise, in *Nordre Kaupang* there were thirty-nine cremations and thirty-two seemingly empty barrows but no inhumations whatsoever (Stylegar 2007: 69–70).

9 Special Economic Zones of Their Time

The previous chapters have outlined the special topographical locations and distinct characteristics of the Viking-age towns, which were sharply contrasted with the main features of the surrounding rural Viking-age society. The case was made for a deliberate separation of the towns from the surrounding local societies not only geographically by their strategic locations in no man's land but also legally through their own *things* and a separate jurisdiction and finally by the exclusive, restricted and controlled alien presence at these sites. Since these few Viking-age towns, actively developed and promoted by their respective rulers, were thus clearly the exception to the rule defined by the surrounding social structures, it was certainly not the result of, as Randsborg (1989: 191) suggested, 'the economic and social development [that] led e.g. to the growth of market towns on the coasts', reversing cause and effect in his conclusion. On the contrary, as will be demonstrated in what follows, their establishment took place against a background of economic backwardness and tenacious social development as instruments to accelerate local economic development. In other words, the towns became political, administrative and economic tools for a controlled influx of funds and innovations from abroad.

9.1 THE HINTERLAND QUESTION

Geographically separated from the ordinary Viking world as they already were, and actively restraining foreign merchants from roaming the countryside, the rigid boundaries created around Viking-age towns made them almost parallel societies. This certainly raises questions regarding the extent of the influence that these sites had on their immediate hinterlands. Given the evidence presented in previous chapters, Skre's conclusion 'Nor does it appear as if there was any apparatus in the towns that exercised administrative functions over the immediate hinterland of the town, as [it] was the case in Scandinavia from the 11th/12th centuries onwards' (Skre 2007: 45) is hardly surprising. Against the background of the previous discussion, it seems rather obvious that these early towns functioned only in a very limited sense as centres for their regional surroundings. However, opinions about the actual influence these towns had on their hinterlands, even for those in Continental Europe and in the British Isles, diverge widely. While Verhaeghe (2005: 270) stated that 'as we learn more about these sites and their hinterlands, it is becoming increasingly clear that other roles [such as long-distance trade] were just as important; these emporia also seem to have acted as central points for craft production and regional trade, and they may also have functioned as nodal centres of regional power', Wickham (2005: 685–7), on the other hand, suggested that 'their general lack of territorial hinterlands further explains why so many of them failed as economic centres'.

Verhaeghe (2005), however – who mainly relied on van Es' (1990) observations from Dorestad – was certainly not mistaken when he emphasised that 'however important the overseas trade and exchange [was], the international urban networks are not the only ones linking the individual towns of the period. Most of them relied heavily on the countryside for basic supplies and they must also have had regional functions' (Verhaeghe 2005: 281). This is particularly evident in the case of Birka, which was situated on the small island of Björkö, formerly only 150 hectares in size, in the midst of Lake Mälaren (Bäck 1997: 131). Consequently, in the context of the discussion on the vital connection of Birka with its hinterland, Bäck (1997) aptly titled his contribution 'No Island Is a Society'. To accommodate for an urban population specialised in long-distance trade and crafts, a daily supply of agrarian surplus produce relying on regional exchange with its hinterland would have been essential and would have included edibles such as meat, fish, grains and fruits, as well as firewood and peat for fuel. In order to supply a population of c.1,000 inhabitants on a daily basis, three to five wagonloads of fuel and another wagonload of grain would have been needed. This corresponds quite well with the calculated population density of Birka, estimated at 900 individuals, which would have required this very amount of supplies. Hedeby is estimated to have had an average population of 1,500 (Clarke & Ambrosiani 1991: 156–8), and to cater for the needs of such a town required a catchment area with a diameter of at least 16 kilometres (Kalmring 2010a: n. 210 with reference therein). In urban environments, such amounts of consumables would leave traces, such as vast quantities of discarded animal and fish bones (cf. Kalmring 2010a: 425–9 maps 40–2). However, while for the hinterland the material expressions of such exchanges are far more difficult to grasp, in urban contexts it is often difficult to discern between domestic craft products and those originating from regional – or even supra-regional – trade (Verhaeghe 2005: 279).

The development of Hedeby's hinterland in Anglia and the Schwansen peninsula has been thoroughly studied, albeit before the introduction of metal-detector surveys, by Willroth (1992: 444–73 maps 69–71). Through a study of the spatial distribution of Viking-age sites, he demonstrated that the post-Migration-period land seizure of the eighth and ninth centuries – ideas that today are only accepted with constraints (cf. Kalmring 2014/15: 281; Lemm in press) – initially focussed on the area of Hedeby itself, including both sides of the Schlei fjord, as well as the shores of Lake Langsee in Anglia. The tenth century was characterised by a consolidation phase (Ger. *Landesausbau*) with a clear inland expansion, predominantly expressed through rich equestrian graves (cf. Pedersen 2014: 49–51 plates 46–54; Lemm 2016b). Surprisingly, rural sites such as Kosel (Meier 1994; Schade 2010/11), Schuby (Meier 2007) and maybe even the newly discovered Ellingstedt (Siegloff 2014; Siegloff & Wolpert 2018: 182–8), situated in the immediate hinterland of Hedeby, have turned out to be more than mere farming villages engaged in the production of edibles for the supply of Hedeby. To some extent, they even displayed evidence of involvement in long-distance trade:

imported goods such as Norwegian whetstones, soapstone vessels from western Sweden or south-eastern Norway, basalt quern stones from Mayen, as well as a few Tating jugs from the Vorgebirge region near Cologne have been found not only in Hedeby but at various sites along the Schlei fjord and across Anglia (Müller-Wille 2002b: 23–9 figs. 16–19). The distribution of younger Hedeby coins in Schleswig-Holstein even led Wiechmann (2007a, 2007b) to the assumption that the area around Hedeby formed a 'local numismatic region' of its own. The younger Hedeby coins belong to the so-called Early Nordic coins, which were previously categorised by Malmer (1966) into the 'combination groups' (Swd. *kombinationsgrupper*) KG 1–2 (Dorestad deniers), KG 3–6 (ninth-century coins) and KG 7–12 (mainly tenth-century coins). Malmer argued that while KG 5–6 (c.825 and 840–60) may have been minted in Ribe, KG 3–4 (c.825) and KG 7–9 (around 900–80) were struck on-site in Hedeby. After a hiatus in coinage in the late ninth century, coins of the 'younger Carolingian type', also referred to as 'Hedeby half-bracteates' (KG 7–9), were issued. These younger Hedeby coins have occasionally been found in Slavonic eastern Holstein in the form of hack silver but are otherwise exclusively found in Anglia (Figure 19), where they occur as coinage that replaced both hack silver and foreign currencies (Wiechmann 2007a: 191–4 fig. 8; 2007b: 35–7 fig. 3.6; more differentiated Hilberg 2011, 2014: 170–88). Obviously, Hedeby did not only function as a *bureau de change* where foreign merchants were forced to exchange their own coins into local currency against payment of fees (Fre. *Seigniorage*, Ger. *Schlagschatz*) to the royal minting authority (Garipzanov 2008: 139–40; Hilberg 2014: 185).[1] Instead, the entire 'local numismatic region' and its spread throughout Anglia must be understood as a direct reflection of an ongoing market trade between Hedeby and agents from its local hinterland.

As far as the Birka hinterland is concerned, Bäck (1997) also tried to trace the underlying social and economic relationships of the town

---

[1] The same practice (cf. Jahnke 2019: 191) was suggested for Ribe (Søvsø 2018: 81; 2020: 166–8, 172–3), Sigtuna (Runer 2006) and medieval Slesvig (Radtke 2006: 147–8).

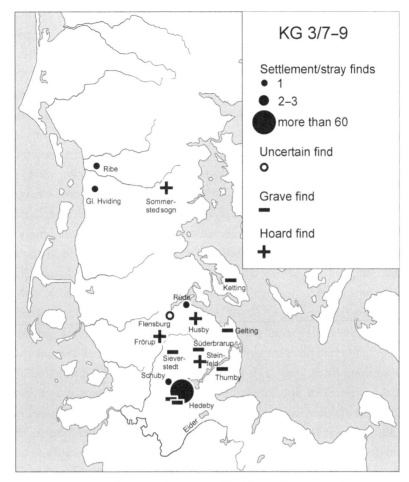

FIGURE 19 'Early Nordic coins' in Hedeby and its hinterland. Distribution of Hedeby coins KG 3 and KG 7–9 in Hedeby and its 'local numismatic region' (after Hilberg 2011: fig. 10.1; with kind permission).

through the diffusion of some key artefact groups in order 'to illustrate the importance of the countryside ..., the first emergence in Sweden of an urban community in an otherwise completely agrarian society' (Bäck 1997: 130). Of course, a basic prerequisite for Birka's ability to exist was the surplus production of commodities in the surrounding 'traditional agrarian society' (Bäck 1997: 135). The study area for his research on Birka's hinterland was the whole of eastern central Sweden, which was reviewed for the particular distribution patterns of Islamic silver as well as oval brooches as two case studies. Regarding the distribution of Islamic dahārim coins (digital data set provided by Kenneth Jonsson, Stockholm), it is apparent that they were predominately found on the island of Björkö itself, as well as in the eastern Lake Mälaren area, and from there they follow the river courses towards Gamla Uppsala and further north. Additional isolated clusters have been observed southwest of Örebro in Närke, west of Nyköping in Södermanland and around Norrtälje in Uppland. Unless they are all the direct outcome of Viking expeditions to the east, these coins may well have been dispersed through trade with Birka, implying that these farmsteads or villages were involved in the local trade that supplied the town with edibles and fuel on a regular basis. The distribution pattern of oval brooches in eastern central Sweden, published by Jansson (1985: 152–62 fig. 118), can be seen as evidence both of wealthy women from 'the upper stratum of society' and of specialised handicraft predominantly executed in Birka, rather than in the hinterland (Bäck 1999: 145–6). The number of finds is dominated by Birka, where 302 specimens of oval brooches have been found, but there are also dense distribution patterns along the northern shores of Lake Mälaren towards Västmanland. Further north, there are small clusters around Lake Siljan in Dalarna, at Gävle in Gästrikland and on the Åland islands. When combined with a map of presumed trade routes and iron production sites in northern Svealand and Närke, the distribution of brooches displays a striking coherence with the homesteads of middlemen involved in the down-the-line trade in iron directed towards Birka. However, since the distribution pattern of these oval brooches only reaches the fringes of the actual iron production areas in Bergslagen, it has been suggested that the miners themselves did not benefit from that trade (Bäck 1997: 146–50 figs. 3–4). The fact that almost no oval brooches have been found south of Lake Mälaren in Södermanland could be an indication that the mere supply of Birka with food and firewood did not generate any larger surplus either.

Finally, quite similar to the Hedeby hinterland, small quantities of imported pottery from Western Europe are even found in Birka's hinterland at sites such as Pollista, Gredelby, Sanda, Säby and Valsta in Uppland and must have passed through the town (Bäck 1997: 144; 1999: 124 fig. 162).

A crucial piece of evidence for understanding the relationships between the hinterlands and Viking-age towns – and even for the understanding of their *raison d'être* for the Viking-age society surrounding them – has only recently been presented (Pedersen 2015): it demonstrated that their purpose was much more complex than that of simple import hubs for desirable goods, which then penetrated to a certain extent into their spatially limited hinterlands, and that their role in the transfer of innovation to the surrounding societies was equally important. In what manner the latter was achieved, considering the topographical seclusion and legal restrictions for foreign merchants and crafters in these towns, is illustrated by the introduction and dissemination of expert knowledge in non-ferrous metalworking technologies. Non-ferrous metalworkers were highly specialised crafters not only in working different metals and alloys but also in the composition and adaption of the required moulds for their own requirements (Pedersen 2015: 59–61). However, their specialist work also required one or two assistants – for example, to operate bellows – who at the same time would have served as apprentices to their metalworking masters (Pedersen 2015: 56–7; 2016: 263–4). Evidence from Ribe and Birka suggests that these masters were for the most part permanently based in their respective towns, although there are also examples of urban metalworkers travelling, at least for a time, as itinerant crafters between major centres around the Baltic Sea. As a synthesis, Pedersen (2016: 264–6) argued that specialist urban metalworkers did indeed have their permanent bases, to which they returned regularly, but also that they occasionally travelled to other urban centres as 'guests'. The Viking-age towns could act as meeting places for crafters and provided opportunities for dialogue and learning, not least for the local apprentices of the visiting metalworkers. In this context, her example from

Barva, about 40 kilometres west of Björkö in Södermanland, is enlightening (Dunér & Vinberg 2006; cf. Pedersen 2016: 265–6). There, a few casting moulds for oval brooches were found at the ninth-century rural settlement: two for P37 brooches and one for a P27 brooch. Chronologically, both date from the early Birka period (c.750–860), with P37 brooches belonging to the latter part of the period (Jansson 1985: 226). While P27 brooches appear almost as frequently in Sweden as in Norway, the brooches of type P37 are among the most common examples of older oval brooches and it is quite likely that this type was created on Björkö or in its immediate vicinity (Jansson 1985: 42, 51). In a bronze-caster workshop found during the Birka-*Svarta Jorden* excavations in 1990–5, situated on a plot north of the former stone jetty, around 1,800 fragments of clay moulds for casting oval brooches were discovered. Interestingly, the lion's share derived from the production of the two types in question: around 44 per cent of the mould fragments could be assigned to type P27, while 17 per cent belonged to the oval brooches of type P37 (Ambrosiani 2013: 223 fig. 10.11). Turning back to Barva, it is striking that the petrological and metallurgical analyses of the moulds from here showed no difference from the signatures of moulds found in Birka, which led Dunér and Vinberg (2006: 20–1) to the conclusion that the casting moulds must have come ready-made from Birka. Consequently, although with caveats for other scenarios, Pedersen (2016: 266) suggested that 'Bearing in mind that team work is necessary for successful metalworking, it is possible that the mould-maker could have stayed in Birka while other members of the team visited Barva'. In the case of an itinerant craftsman attending Birka as a guest – and who, like any stranger, was legally restricted to the boundaries of the town – this would imply that his knowledge must have been transferred into the hinterland through his local apprentices.

9.2 SPECIAL ECONOMIC ZONES

At the end of Chapter 2 on the context and academic debate of Viking-age towns, it was stressed that the aim of this book was not to come up with yet another term for the first sparks of the urban phenomenon in the north but rather to contribute to the understanding of the specific nature of these sites, as well as to their function within Viking-age society. Quite accurately, in the case of Birka, Bäck (1997: 151) argued that

> One of the most fundamental preconditions for people from a 'civilised' Europe venturing into the heart of the barbarous north is that there must have been a place where they could safely transact [conduct] their business, a kind of free zone.... The fact of Birka being situated on an island also helped to create a neutral space, segregated from the mainland.

His appraisal can be understood as an adjusted restatement of Polanyi's (1963) cultural-historical concept of 'ports of trade', which, as neutrality devices, offered secure environments for oversea trade in an era described as the dawn of a fully developed system of market economy. However, to be able to describe the generally presupposed distinct otherness of the Viking-age towns and their assumed exceptional position within their societies, it is indispensable to review the keystones of the Viking world.

In order to support the argument, the most important facts from earlier chapters shall be briefly summarised once again: it has been demonstrated that Viking-age Scandinavia was still largely rooted in the societal structures of the preceding younger Iron Age; it was a rural, agrarian society based on communities living in individual farmsteads or small hamlets, where the population was subdivided into distinct regional groups. The traditional centres of power and cult that were still in use had emerged during the earlier Roman Iron Age and in the Migration period and were used to legitimise royal power but also for gathering the population during religious feasts, which at the same time provided an opportunity for legal and political assemblies (*things*) and for holding regional fairs. Seasonal fairs and occasional religious feasts were also held at periodically occupied royal manors of itinerant kings. Against this background, the emerging Viking-age towns with their vast and multi-ethnic populations, and their permanent long-distance market trade, constituted utterly alien elements, which were only allowed to exist at the fringes of traditional society: royal manors (and early churches; see Section 10.2.2 and Chapter 10, Note 8) were not situated within the boundaries of these towns but only in the immediate vicinity to these new urban communities. And though these towns were favourably positioned in terms of transport topography, their geographic situation in the borderlands was at the same time administratively detached from the traditional power structures of the surrounding countryside; the latter is emphasised by evidence that these towns had their own assemblies. In their initial stages, Viking-age towns also began as ordinary beach markets, and as such they would have been everyday institutions and part of the regular societal structure. However, due to their favourable geographical locations and/or success in trade and commerce they attracted the attention of local magnates, who intervened and deliberately promoted a few selected sites, most likely by providing them with a divergent and specific legal status.

Archaeologically, the divergent jurisdiction is indicated both by symbolic boundary ditches around the trading sites and, most likely and at a later stage, by floating log booms or harbour chains. Furthermore, from both the contemporary Frankish world and Anglo-Saxon England we know of the levying of royal shipping duties and the implementation of trading tariffs, as well as of the existence of an effective port administration administrated by a variety of officials with different tasks. For Scandinavia, such analogous legal regulations can only be deduced from younger law books and Icelandic sagas; however, corresponding royal officials with titles such as *comes* or *praefectus vici* are attested for the Viking-age towns, suggesting that a similar administration existed here as well. As representatives of royal power, these officials were probably responsible for jurisdiction, defence and – most notably – the collection of customs duties. Scandinavian magnates not only adapted the use of customs duties but also tried to arrange commercial agreements with Frankish and Byzantine rulers themselves – which included that they sometimes actively campaigned against Viking pirates threatening important trade routes. To be able to attract merchants from abroad, the kings guaranteed and granted market peace within the Viking-age towns and occasionally even provided royal personal protection on sea routes. This was necessary, since otherwise anyone who travelled outside their own native legal sphere would have lacked legal protection and would have been considered easy prey. But while long-distance merchants were highly desirable at these almost exterritorial free spaces for trade, analogies to other areas as well as the observed separation between various burial grounds suggest that their presence was also rigidly controlled and limited to the Viking-age towns themselves; these foreign merchants and crafters were considered to be lordless men who constituted a potential threat to the surrounding traditional society, and thus in most cases they were prevented from roaming the countryside. And even though these emerging urban communities relied heavily on their hinterlands for consumables, the archaeological footprints of the towns on the material culture of the hinterlands are rather limited. However, there seems to be faint indications of a diffusion of innovation. The latter corresponds with insights from modern cultural geography, which argues that innovations initially spread via supra-regional centres and only then diffuse hierarchically from there (Kulke 2009: 258).

At first glance, the evidence from Northern Europe seems to correspond with Verhaeghe's (2005) assessments of the Carolingian attitude towards their towns:

> [W]e still know too little about royal perceptions of, and attitude towards, towns. Indirect intervention seems clear – notably by influencing the economy with measures related to coinage, tolls and markets – but that is about as far as we can go at present. ... In fact, it is also quite possible that the Carolingians had only a *limited or perhaps even parasitic interest in the urban phenomenon*, given their predilection for the rural world that was the basis of their power and income, and where they chose to build their palaces.
>
> (Verhaeghe 2005: 284; my emphasis)

If this is true, one would have to ask what exactly the 'parasitic interest' might have consisted of. For Viking-age Scandinavia, one obvious and very true answer is that the kings were perpetually obliged to be ostentatious and generous in order to command the allegiance of their retainers and to establish and maintain political alliances (cf. Näsman 2000: 67). From skaldic poetry and sagas, it is evident that gift-giving was one of the major social principles in Old Norse societies. On one hand, gift-giving accumulated social prestige and created bonds between people; on the other, if the principle was violated, it could just as well lead to a negation of social communication, feuds and even wars (Vestergaard 1991). In his influential article on wealth and gift bestowal, Gurevich (1968) emphasised that the acceptance of any gift would have required a reciprocal action from the recipient to the donor – for example, to pledge one's servitude to the king – unless it was compensated by a return gift. These were ways in which retainers became obliged to pledged allegiance and loyalty to wealthy and generous lords. Moreover, a successful and generous king was considered to be a guarantor of peace, good harvest and abundance in his domain. Since objects were believed to magically absorb some of their owner's personal qualities, the perpetual accumulation of wealth was intended not only for enrichment but more importantly as a means of preserving and increasing one's own success and good fortune. Thus even gifts had this magical connotation and retained a part of the donor's success and good fortune, making them even more desirable (Gurevich 1968). Consequently, the Scandinavian kings, in their role as ostentatious gift bestowers, would have been in permanent need of new means and objects of value, either through warfare and looting or else through the control of trade and the resulting income from customs duties and other trade tariffs collected by their reeves in return for maintaining market peace (Figure 20); additional means could – as in the case of Hedeby – also be accumulated through the operation of a mint and the associated collection of seigniorage.

But is there more to the matter? In the light of the evidence, it is becoming increasingly clear that Viking-age towns and their

FIGURE 20 Hedeby, present-day northern Germany. The harbour and its jetties as the marketplace and arena for major economic activities (© J. Stuhrmann & T. Wehrmann for GEO Epoche: Picture Press).

interdependence with the traditional conservative social order of their surroundings shared many characteristics with what in modern economics is termed a 'special economic zone'. Today, most special economic zones are found in developing countries (Moberg 2014: 171); they are universally defined as:

> demarked geographic areas contained within a country's national boundaries where the rules of business are different from those that prevail in the national territory. The differential rules principally deal with investment conditions, international trade and customs, taxation, and the regulatory environment; whereby the zone is given a business environment that is intended to be more liberal from a policy perspective and more effective from an administrative perspective than that of the national territory.
> (Farole 2011: 23)

In their article 'Special Economic Zones: Shortcut or Roundabout Way towards Capitalism?', Ahrens and Meyer-Baudeck (1995) use a definition that in many aspects is akin to Farole's definition, but they also introduce some important additional facets:

> SEZs [special economic zones] are *geographically or functionally limited parts of an economy* in which rules and other institutions concerning the production and the distribution of goods and services *differ from those in the rest of the economy*. These special institutions are realised in order to *promote and favour economic activities in a specific area*. Generally, they offer both financial incentives, such as lower taxes and tariffs, and subsidies as well as the substantial deregulation of the legal and administrative framework or the *provision of legal privileges*.
> (Ahrens & Meyer-Baudeck 1995: 88; my emphasis)

In terms of political economical and institutional setting, privately developed special economic zones – in contrast to government-developed ones – tend to minimise both the knowledge and the so-called incentive problem, that is, on how to promote technological progress (via investments and resource allocation) and the prevention of opportunities for rent-seeking and corruption by government officials (Moberg 2014). While they persist, special economic zones seem characterised by permanent change, adjustment and expansion, and thus seem rather to circumscribe processes. And when they eventually diminish and lose relevance for their respective economies, they have served their purpose in successfully introducing comprehensive reforms to commercial policies in their larger areas (Moberg 2014: 169, 175). In terms of the Viking-age towns, this seems to have been the case in the last quarter of the tenth century (see Chapter 10). On top of these overarching characteristics and

> in addition to the direct economic benefits that can be derived from boosting trade ... SEZs also can carry indirect economic benefits, which in turn can drive local innovation. Indeed, while attracting 'content-rich' FDI [foreign direct investment] and stimulating trade, SEZs tend to favour the acquisition of international knowledge and

know-how, which are crucial to the development of innovation capabilities. (White 2011: 184)

In this context, Justine White defines these new innovations as the 'implementation of new or improved products, processes, marketing, or organizational methods in business practices and workplace organization', which, if they are considered as radical innovations, can be 'the creation of "new-to-the-world" innovations'; but if they are considered to be incremental innovations, they merely deal with 'applying existing global technologies that are new to the local context or bringing small improvements to existing technologies' (White 2011: 183). Through the diffusion of innovation, the development of shielded special economic zones is also likely to initiate a favourable development of local conditions in the respective hinterlands and thus act as a catalyst for promoting innovations, especially in developing countries (White 2010: 305, 329). Interestingly, for the seasonal type-A emporia, Hodges suggested something very similar, namely that 'they were not towns so much as gatherings, the result of the *economic underdevelopment* of the post-classical world' (Hodges 2000: 120; my emphasis). And regarding the Viking-age urban settlements of the Danelaw, he stated elsewhere:

> Indeed, the Vikings, when as conquerors and kings rather than raiders they took command of regions, conspicuously adopted the portus model, creating solar central-places [= class C sites, after 850] such as Ipswich, Norwich, Stamford, Lincoln and York. Their leadership led to an infusion of economic activity *in previously underdeveloped regions* like East Anglia and Northumbria.
> (Hodges 2006: 70; my emphasis)

Admittedly, today these general suggestions would have to be nuanced on the basis of more recent research (cf. Loveluck 2013: 16–18). In fact, Naylor (2016: 60) points to the possibility that that the changes, or innovations, in the organisation of rural settlement and economy may already have taken place prior to the initial activities in the *emporia*. And using the examples of Gippeswic/Ipswich, Lundenwic/London and Hamwic/Southampton, Palmer (2003) was able to demonstrate that even the emerging *emporia* – as much as ecclesiastical and royal sites – actually had some basic rural hinterlands along their navigable waterways. However, it also seems as if these Middle Saxon 'multi-settlement focal areas' only developed fully later on, that is, during the heyday of the *emporia* in the eighth and ninth centuries (Palmer 2003: 56; cf. Naylor 2016: 62–3).[2] Thus, even if signs of underdevelopment may by more palpable for sites in the Baltic Sea region, in some respect it also seemed true for British sub-Roman conditions, which triggered the introduction of *emporia* – even if their biographies today prove to be more individual and complex than previously presumed.

9.3 DESIRABLES IN 'UNDERDEVELOPED' SCANDINAVIA

The royal interest in the Viking-age town thus seems to have been twofold: firstly, to ensure the acquisition of additional means and funds for the rulers' obligations as gift givers and, secondly, to ensure a steady influx of innovation to a lesser developed part of Europe. To substantiate this argument, one has to ask what kind of innovation – be it new or even radical – was so desirable in Scandinavia that its rulers sought to establish and protect these free zones for international long-distance trade. Was the Carolingian Empire really so much more developed than Scandinavia? And if so, what kind of innovations, ideas and technologies can be identified archaeologically?

First, we shall briefly turn to the economic situation of the Carolingian Empire, where the eighth century was a time of consolidation of royal power and expansion of the Frankish sphere of influence. These developments led to an economic surge, which intensified trade between the Rhine and Loire and extended into the North Sea area (Adamczyk 2014: 89). By the ninth century, the classical villa system was replaced by a bipartite manorial system: one was the

---

[2] Here, note Naylor's (2016: 64–6) advocacy for a multifocal thematic approach by differentiating between impact, productive, subsistence and social hinterlands.

mansus indominicatus or demesne, which was overseen by a lord or abbot, while the second relied on small plots of land – the *mansi* – which were given to (mostly) free tenant farmers in exchange for various obligations such as tribute but above all assignments on the demesne itself (Verhulst 2002: 31–60). This reorganisation resulted in a self-supported productive labour force which could also be used as seasonal farm labour on the aristocratic demesnes. As such, developments must be perceived as an attempt to maximise the efficiency of manorial production. These alterations, along with the adoption of a three-course crop rotation system – the cultivation of summer grain, barley and oats – resulted in a remarkable increase in agricultural production, which even generated a surplus. However, the economic success was not limited to agricultural production but also affected craft and industrial manufacture, which was executed predominantly in a rural and manorial context (Verhulst 2002: 72). Salt was one of the most important commodities, and its production reached an industrial scale in the Carolingian period. Wine production also exceeded the needs of its cultivating monasteries, and the surplus was fed into the commodity cycle. In addition, Frisian wool production, glass production and the Mayen lava quern stone manufacture reached industrial levels. Improvements were also made to the fabrication of pottery, in terms of both quality and quantity, and iron production was also increased due to a higher demand for weapons (Verhulst 2002: 61–113; cf. Janssen 1983). The export of all these surpluses stimulated interregional as well as long-distance trade of bulk commodities via the central hubs of Quentovic and Dorestad.

The resulting economic interplay with Northern Europe, triggered by the developments on the Continent, has been aptly outlined by Näsman (2000: 35):

> The peripheral geographical as well as economic position of the regions of Scandinavia makes them ... very sensitive to changes in the European economic exchange systems. Studies of Scandinavian external contacts are thus important contributions to the

> understanding of the distribution of goods and the economic as well as political network that in the Early Middle Ages connected European realms with one another as well as Byzantium. One important aspect of the problem of production, distribution, and demand is the prelude of urbanism outside the former Roman Empire ... The long eighth century saw the establishment of the first proto-urban sites in South Scandinavia and their subsequent growth into early towns.

With this paragraph, Näsman (2000) begins his article in the anthology *The Long Eighth Century*, in which he emphasised both the particular peripheral geographical and economic position of the Scandinavian world and its dependency on developments in Continental Europe in terms of urbanisation and the exchange of goods. Naturally, the above-mentioned crop rotation (Øye 2013: 301–3) would eventually be adopted in Scandinavia as well, although in this case Viking-age towns would probably not have been essential for the diffusion of this particular agrarian innovation. The question is, still, what exactly was it that made the establishments of towns – or special economic zones – worthwhile?

The import of cutting-edge products from continental workshops in itself was nothing new to the Viking Age and, as a trade in prestige goods, had already been transacted through the central places in the centuries before. One luxury item of the early Middle Ages was without doubt the so-called Ulfberht swords, which were characterised by a welded blade signature, probably naming the overseer of an arms workshop in the Lower Rhine region (Stalsberg 2008). This was a sought-after brand which was imitated and subject to forgery on numerous occasions. Modern metallurgical analyses have shown that Ulfberht blades were in fact not made of iron but were the only swords of their era already made of steel (Williams 2009).[3] What is

---

[3] Since the steel used for the Ulfberht swords may or may not have been imported from the Samanid town of Herat, Williams (2009: 143) misleadingly concluded that the manufacture, as the starting point of the so-called 'Route from the Varangians to the Greeks', should instead have been 'located in the Baltic area'.

particular for the Viking Age, however, is not the trade in prestige goods but the emerging large-scale long-distance trade in bulk goods. This included the aforementioned commodities from the Carolingian Empire, such as quern stones and pottery, which were traded and distributed via the early towns. All this has been discussed at length in the academic debate for decades already (cf. Steuer 1987). But would it also be possible to provide evidence of real innovation in the sense of active knowledge transfer? There are, in fact, a few striking examples, and an early one was an unsuccessful attempt to introduce new technology from the early *emporium* of Ribe and its immediate surroundings: instead of local hand-built pottery, coarsely tempered wheel-turned vessels with flat bottoms were produced both in Ribe and in Okholm, situated some 8 kilometres south-west of it (cf. Feveile 2001), since c.720–50. A magnetic susceptibility analysis has revealed that, although the technology obviously seemed to derive from the Rhine Valley, this manufacture was in fact related to domestic Frisian *Muschelgrus* pottery and not to the Rhinish Badorf pottery. However, after only thirty years of local manufacture in the Ribe area, the knowledge of the potter's wheel seems to have disappeared, and it would be another 450 years before it was reintroduced (Feveile et al. 1998). Another, in this case successful, innovation deals with highly skilled glass manufacture in Hedeby and the production of mixed-glass vessels. Instead of exclusively using the novel and locally producible pure (beech) wood-ash glass, which turned out to be quite brittle, about a quarter of all sampled vessels featured a blend of 60 per cent rare but durable soda-lime glass – with sodium (Lat. *natrium*) oxide from the Egyptian Wadi El Natrun – and only 40 per cent of wood-ash glass. This technique ensured a firmness similar to that of pure soda-lime glass but reduced the need for the increasingly rare pure glass of that kind. Apart from at Carolingian abbeys such as Fulda and Lorsch, this technique was used exclusively in Hedeby (Kronz et al. 2015; Hilberg 2018: 150).

Another prominent innovation dealt with building technology and the so-called Hedeby house from 874 (Schultze 2008: 160–201).

This decidedly urban dwelling only measured 12 by 5.5 metres and was built using a frame construction, with the characteristic supporting posts angled against the outside of its wattle-and-daub walls. The outside supports became necessary because in this building, for the first time, the load-bearing roof posts were integrated into the walls themselves in an effort to maximise the inside living space. However, this also meant that the entire roof load of a rafter roof without pediment rested solely on the walls alone, which therefore needed additional support for the lateral pressure of the roof. Dwellings with outer supporting posts of the 'Warendorf' type are well-known from the Frisian-Westphalian area since the seventh century (Speckmann 2005: 94–5). In most parts of Scandinavia, this innovative building technique, which can be observed in the Trelleborg houses, is only known since the second half of the tenth century – which is roughly seventy-five years later than its first appearance in the urban fabric of Hedeby (Schultze 2012: 100–1). Although this dwelling may very well have been erected by a Frisian tradesman and modelled after the houses in his place of origin, this kind of innovation is a vivid example of important by-products of international trade channelled through Viking-age towns due to the agency of foreigners. It seems to be no coincidence that major innovations are particularly associated with Hedeby, as it was located immediately on the border between Continental Europe and Scandinavia and thus served as a prime gateway for novelties from the Carolingian world. However, even Birka may serve as an example of how urban dwellings developed and of how these techniques diffused from there into its hinterland. Innovative examples of single-aisled two-room houses in Birka – such as house B263 from c.790–810/15, house B523a from c.835/40–60 and even one dwelling from outside the ramparts at Grindsbacka from c.850 (cf. Bäck 2009) – eventually also begin to appear in Pollista in Uppland, where they seem to have replaced the traditional three-aisled longhouses with their internal roof-bearing posts (c.760–1100; Hållans & Svensson 1999: 29–31, 67 fig. 34A). In the meantime, other examples of small, single-aisled dwellings also emerged elsewhere in Uppland, such as in Gamla Uppsala (c.850–1000; Ljungkvist 2000: 21–3 fig. 8) and Skäggesta (Göthberg 1995: 81–2 cat. 212 [house XXI]). Thus, just like Hedeby, Birka may also have functioned as 'a centre of innovation for building techniques in its hinterland' (Ambrosiani 2013: 218).

An oak-pulley block was found during settlement excavations in Hedeby in 1967 (excavation area 2, grid square 22; cf. Westphal 2006: 67; Crumlin-Pedersen 1997: 134).[4] Its stocky forked frame measured 23.2 centimetres, was tapered above the fork arms and featured a suspension hole (eye) on its widening crown. A grooved block sheave with a diameter of 3.7 centimetres, which was spinning on a metal axle, was inserted between the cheeks of the fork (Figure 21(a)). First, the pulley block was considered to be part of the rigging of a boat, yet this initial interpretation was quickly dismissed and instead it was identified as a pulley for a treadle loom (Grenander Nyberg 1984: 145; Schietzel 2014: 364). The pulley was originally attached to the mounting of the heddle shafts with a string; aided by a treadle, one heddle shaft was lowered while the other was simultaneously lifted. Since the suspension hole of the Hedeby pulley showed no sign of wear from a string, it has been assumed that it was instead suspended from a bar running at a right angle to the sheave itself. In contrast to the (vertical) warp-weighted loom, a treadle loom had a horizontal warp which doubled its efficiency and accelerated the working process tremendously; this was achieved not only by the simultaneous shifting of the shafts but also by the benefits of the treadle that enabled the weaver to have both hands free when operating the shuttle with the weft yarn (Grenander Nyberg 1984, 1994). Chronologically, Grenander Nyberg (1984: 148; 1994: 204) dates the Hedeby pulley to the first half of the eleventh century or possibly to the tenth century. In the Mediterranean

---

[4] In subsequent publications, the pulley was pictured together with a block sheave, which was found in 1969 (Grenander Nyberg 1984: 147 fig. 1.1; 1994: 203–5). However, since block sheaves appear in six specimens from the settlement excavations and another eleven specimens from the harbour excavation, Crumlin-Pedersen (1997: 136 tab. C2.7; cf. Kalmring 2010a: 346, 394 map 3) rather assumed a use in various contexts, including seafaring.

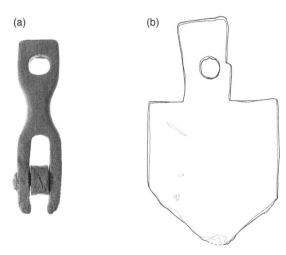

FIGURE 21 Hedeby, present-day northern Germany. Technical innovations pointing to an active knowledge transfer via Viking-age towns: (a) pulley of a treadle loom (inventory no. HbS 429.001; after Grenander Nyberg 1984: fig. 1); (b) blade of a water wheel (inventory no. HbS 116.002; after Westphal 2013: fig. 1) (© Museum für Archäologie, Stiftung Schleswig-Holsteinische Landesmuseen, Schleswig).

region, treadle looms are attested from the seventh century at the latest, while north of the Alps they possibly appeared as early as the seventh or eighth century but certainly by the ninth or tenth century. They become more common in the eleventh and twelfth centuries but coexisted for quite some time with the conventional warp-weighted looms (Cardon 1999: 393; Windler 2008: 215 fig. 4). For Northern Europe, the tenth-century pulley from Hedeby is by far the earliest remnant of a treadle loom in the area (Windler 2008: 207–8). The chronologically closest remnant of a treadle loom from other parts of Northern Europe is dated between the late eleventh and early thirteenth centuries and comes from Coppergate in York, where a heddle cradle was found (Walton Rogers 1997: 1763–6 fig. 822.6654; Morris 2000: 2335–6 fig. 1148.6654). Otherwise, in Scandinavia treadle looms do not seem to appear until the twelfth century, as indicated by pulley finds from Sigtuna, Lund and Bergen (Grenander Nyberg 1994: 205 with reference therein).

Another major innovation may be indicated by a rather inconspicuous undated wooden artefact of formerly unknown function (Westphal 2006: plate 87.1) which was found during settlement excavations in Hedeby in 1963 ('Old Excavation Area' Jankuhn/Schietzel, grid square 90). The 31.2-centimetre object, which had a spade-blade shape, was 2.8 centimetres thick and had a 3-centimetre drilled aperture in its shaft-like end (Figure 21(b)). It was found immediately north of the stream *Haddebyer Bach* that flows through the settlement, right next to a bridge from 819 (cf. Schietzel 1969: 21–6; 2014: 113–15; Schultze 2005: 369–71; 2008: 240). Today, although with reservations, the blade has been interpreted as part of a water wheel – or more specifically as a blade from a vertical undershot mill wheel; previously suggested weirs (Ger. *Stauanlagen*) in the course of the stream could indicate that it may have been channelled specifically for milling purposes (Westphal 2013; cf. Hübener 1959: 56, 61). Typologically, the closest parallels to this object are found among the blades of the water mill at Großhöbing in the Schwarzach Valley in Franconia, where a dendrochronological analysis revealed a remarkably long period of use, stretching from the late Merovingian to the early Carolingian period (site 74; Herzig et al. 1997 fig. 94.4). In scholarly discourse, there is general agreement that water mills survived the end of antiquity and that they were continuously in operation through the Middle Ages and beyond (Kind 2007: 379–83; Westphal 2013: 139). Early north-western European finds of medieval water mills, from the period 600–1000, were mapped by Kind (2007: fig. 8) in connection with investigations of the mill from the monastery of Fulda. From all of Scandinavia – apart from the Hedeby example – only two early medieval sites with vertical undershot wheels are known,[5] and both were situated in rural western Jutland: one in Ljørring, where a mill race including a wooden trough for a vertical water wheel was encountered, whose parts were dated to 935±70 (sample K-2817) and 965±85 (sample K-2716), the other at the homestead of Omgård, where a mill

---

[5] On the original map by Kind (2007: fig. 8), the water mill at Ljørring was erroneously indicated as having a 'horizontal wheel' (cf. Eriksen et al. 2009: cat. no. 58, 298).

race and two wheel blades were found, one dendrochronologically dated to c.950 (and the other as late as the fifteenth century) (Eriksen et al. 2009: 79–85, 297–300). These examples demonstrate that vertical water mills were operated as early as the late Viking Age. However, for a more profound understanding of the diffusion of this radical innovation via Viking-age towns – which is nothing less than the introduction of the earliest engines in the Viking world – a dating of the wheel blade from Hedeby would be essential.

10 Development after the Inception Phase

As shown in the previous chapters, only a juxtaposition of the local, traditional Viking-age societies with the innovative, largely detached cosmopolitan Viking-age towns may help to resolve the seemingly incompatible scholarly views of the Scandinavians as 'brutal Vikings and gentle traders' (Staecker 1997). This ambivalence is not so much a question of two sides of the same coin but instead represents two very different phenomena that need to be treated separately in future Viking-age research (see also Hillerdal 2009: 253). Apart from this appeal to the research community, another frequent inaccuracy also needs to be addressed when discussing early Scandinavian urbanisation: for far too long, Viking-age towns have been perceived as monolithic entities, a perception that neglected their considerable chronological depth of up to 250 years, suggesting dynamically changing conditions rather than static idleness. In fact, a few scholars reached and shared this insight several decades ago, as they tried to tackle this very problem: Hodges (1982: 50–2) introduced development phases, which discerned between type-A (seasonal beach markets), type-B (classical *emporia*) and type-C *emporia* (regional administrative centres). In the case of Birka, an admittedly rough distinction between an early Birka period (c.750–860) and a late Birka one (c.860–975) was employed (Arwidsson 1984; cf. Janson 1985: 176–86), approximately separated by predominately early western and later eastern trade contacts. For Hedeby, Radtke (2009) attempted to characterise change using systems theory by outlining the prevalent conditions in the decades around 800, 900 and 1000. Finally, in an attempt to illustrate change in the entire Baltic Sea area, Callmer (1994) proposed a series of phases based on fifty-year time slices, covering the period from 700 to 1100. Obviously, a diligent review with such short time intervals cannot be accomplished within the scope of this volume. Nevertheless, a brief outlook on the development of the towns following their inception phase, that is, the royally initiated transformation from everyday beach markets to early towns at the beginning of the ninth century, will be given. The ensuing question, however, is how to identify critical turning points and breaks in this urban development. In what follows, two examples are given that had wide-reaching consequences.

10.1 IMPACT OF THE 850S CRISIS AND A SHATTERED BALANCE OF POWER

One such critical turning point in the development of these towns seems to have occurred in the third quarter of the ninth century. After half a century of prosperity under royal patronage, the crisis of the North Sea *emporia*, accompanied by a stagnating influx of Islamic silver in parts of the Baltic, must have had a negative effect on trade networks and the economic state of the Viking-age towns. The decline and, in some cases, abandonment of the North Sea *emporia* on both sides of the English Channel around 850 (Figure 22) is a generally accepted fact among scholars, which is testified through the archaeological records of formerly flourishing sites such as Dorestad, Hamwic/Southampton, Eoforwic/York and Lundenwic/London (cf. Hodges 1982: 151–61; Verhulst 2000: 114–15; 2002: 135; Loveluck 2013: 302–5). The commonly used antipodes for discussing the actual reasons behind this development have been summarised by Griffiths (2013: 3):

> A significant problem with evolutionary notions of proto-urbanism is that few of the trading sites that showed significant signs of urbanism in the 8th or 9th centuries went on to become fully fledged towns in the 10th or 11th centuries. The North Sea emporia, with one or two exceptions, failed in the mid-9th century, becoming derelict and abandoned, and later urban activity took place on different (in some cases nearby) sites.... The decline was, ironically, blamed by historical commentators such as Peter Sawyer (1982) on the effects of North Sea Viking raids, although Hodges [1982] and

FIGURE 22 *The Normans at Dorestad* (Dut. *De Noormannen voor Dorestad*). History wall chart by J. H. Isings Jr (1927) (inventory no. Z 2009/9.1; National Museum of Antiquities/RMO [Rijksmuseum van Oudheden]).

others preferred to point to system collapse due to changing emphases in early state formation, and the decline of the Carolingian Empire.

In any case, after c.850, with a few exceptions from Hedeby and the Schleswig Isthmus, late Carolingian coins became rare in Scandinavia (Hilberg 2014: 162, 187 with references therein). Also, for the Baltic Sea – and similar to the one in the North Sea region – Callmer (1994: 66–8) suggested a contemporary collapse of the so-called second-level trading places such as Åhus, Trelleborg, Menzlin, Rostock-Dierkow, Ralswiek, Truso and Grobin due to 'political instability', ultimately triggered by the Treaty of Verdun in 843, which was followed by internal struggles and the final fall of the Carolingian Empire after the death of Charles the Fat in 887 (cf. MacLean 2003).

Although the North Sea *emporia* crisis and that of the second-level trading places along the southern Baltic coast occurred roughly at the same time, the reasons were not necessarily the same. The latter is more likely to correlate with an ebbing away of Islamic silver in the Baltic Sea region, which is becoming increasingly evident. Noonan (1981: 69–71; 1985) and others considered that there was a general and major silver crisis in Russia and the Baltic region during the second half of the ninth century. Although the production of dahārim had resumed after a reduced mintage during the reign of the sons of Hārūn al-Rashīd in the 'Abbāsid Caliphate, these new coins did not seem to have reached Eastern Europe, which seems evident by the fact that they are only sparsely represented in contemporary silver hoards. This interruption is also observable in the import of oriental beads, such as carnelian and millefiori beads with layered eyes, which came to an 'abrupt and complete or almost complete end' around the 860s or 870 at the latest (Callmer 1991b; 1997: 199; 2004: 44; cf. Delveaux 2017: 23). Kilger (2007: 228–35), however, argued that

> The theory of a silver crisis is [only] partially correct insofar as it works to explain the reduction in the *supply* of dirhams struck post-875: that is, there was a break in contacts between the Caliphate and some networks through which dirhams were distributed in the East. But the theory is utterly misleading as an account of the access to silver and the *actual quantity* of dirham silver that remained in circulation in Scandinavia after 875. (p. 232)

On the other hand, Gustin (2011) suggested that the low quantity of dahārim, which is observed from the second half of the ninth century in Birka, as well as in, for example, Uppåkra, Truso and Arkona, was actually a result of a 'general disruption in the dirham network between the Russian region and the southern Scandinavia centres' (Gustin 2011: 238). This disruption to the eastern trade network may well have been triggered by the failed attack on Constantinople in 860 and the subsequent destruction of the trade centres of Staraja Ladoga/ Aldeigjuborg, Pskov and Rjurikovo Gorodišče/Holmgård, prior to the rise of the Rurik dynasty (Gustin 2011: 238-9; cf. Callmer 2000: 38, 50). A more nuanced perspective on the 'silver crisis' was presented by Adamczyk (2014), who demonstrated that the dirham influx into the Baltic Sea region shifted considerably between 840/1 and 896/7. And while the number of available dahārim in the North Sea area, along the southern Baltic coast and in the eastern parts of the central Polish inland, in fact decreased by 16 per cent, there was a remarkable increase of 34 per cent in Scandinavia, especially in the period around 850/60; for Adamczyk, it was this increased yet spatially limited influx that was the actual trigger for the resulting 'intensity of the Viking-expansion towards the East' (Adamczyk 2014: 102–4 tab. 43).

The numismatic evidence from Birka, however, shows a considerable decrease in the coin influx between 844 and 890, which is visible both in the Garrison area (Swd. *övre-* and *nedre terassen*; 'upper' and 'lower terrace') and in the settlement area, as well as in the absence of such coins in grave contexts of the island's many burial grounds (Gustin 2011; Jonsson 2001: 33 fig. 1; cf. Arwidsson 1989; Wiséhn 1989: 22–39). Considering the general development in the North Sea and the Baltic Sea, it does not seem surprising that Birka, with its strategic position in eastern central Sweden, swiftly realigned its trade networks from Western Europe and the Southern Baltic towards the territories of the Rus', Byzantium and the Caliphate, exactly in the period 'since the mid- and towards the end of the ninth century' (cf. Ambrosiani 2002: 342). Hedeby, on the other hand, situated in the south-western Baltic Sea, having built its success as a gateway between Scandinavia, the Carolingian Empire and the North Sea, did not have quite the same options. In southern Scandinavia, domestic early Nordic coins of Brita Malmer's 'pictorial and older Carolingian types' were minted from c.825 onwards; in Ribe they were modelled after Frisian Wodan-Monster sceattas (combination groups KG 5–6), in Hedeby as imitations of Dorestad denarii (combination group KG 3 [as well as the rare KG 4?]) (Malmer 1966, 2007; Hilberg 2014: 176–82). Even more remarkable for our concern, however, is the following development, which has so far only been mentioned *en passant* in the specialist literature: while Malmer (1966: 341) saw evidence that 'During the years *c*. 850–900 there is a gap in the finds with Scandinavian coins. There is a corresponding scarcity of hoards with Frankish and Anglo-Saxon coins. The import of Arab coins appears to come partly to a standstill *c*. 870–890', Wiechmann (2007b: 32) noted that 'After a hiatus at the end of the ninth century, it has been proved that intensive minting took place, especially in the tenth century'. We may thus conclude that there was an actual gap in early Nordic coinage in the later part of the ninth century, which may have lasted only a few decades. With the appearance of the so-called Hedeby half-bracteates of Malmer's 'younger Carolingian types' (combination groups KG 7–9a–d), and from c.900–20 at the latest, there is renewed evidence that the minting resumed in Hedeby, whereas this was not the case in Ribe (Malmer 1966; Wiechmann 2007b: 42; for a more restricted time frame, cf. Hilberg 2011: 211–14; 2014: 181–2, 184–6). In light of this evidence from Hedeby, it seems to be no coincidence that the Danish petition for trade peace, recorded in *The Annals of Fulda* for the year 873, falls precisely in the decades of the observed hiatus in early Nordic coinage.

The question is how the Viking-age towns recovered from this crisis and what the consequences were. The massive harbour development in Hedeby from 886 onwards (Kalmring 2010a: 241–2 fig. 324) suggests that the crisis was over by then (cf. Hilberg 2018: 150–1). Also, since the development of certain harbour facilities has to correspond to a need from contemporary shipping, Hedeby's late ninth-century harbour development points to the presence of the first pure cargo vessels at the site – and allows us to predate this crucial specialisation in shipbuilding in general (cf. Kalmring 2010a: 352 n. 154 fig. 269). The economic revival of Hedeby coincides with the establishment of an alleged 'Swedish' Olof dynasty, whose kings Gnupa and Sigtrygg are manifested by two rune stones, DR 2 and DR 4, in the immediate vicinity of the town (lastly Myhre 2015: 167–8 with references therein). Remarkably, it is this very period that is otherwise regarded as one of diminishing royal power by historians, prior to a resurgence with the establishment of the Jelling dynasty (Lund 1995: 211), or alternatively as a phase when 'Danish history is plunged in darkness' (Skovgaard-Pedersen 2003: 174). The reorientation of the Birka trade, on the other hand, coincided with the time when, according to *The Russian Primary Chronicle*, entry (6388–90 [880–2 CE]), the Varangian Prince Oleg (ON *Helgi*) initiated the unification of the Kievan Rus' by conquering Kiev/Könugård in 882 and shifting his power base there from Novgorod.

There also seems to be evidence of increasing self-organisation among independently acting merchants: Scandinavian guilds, such as the well-known *Frisa gilda*R, the Frisian guild – mentioned on two rune stones in Sigtuna (U 379 and U 391) – appear in the second half of the eleventh century at the latest (Roslund 2010: 239–40), although guild-like brotherhoods may have much older origins. Although they were limited to specific time frames or enterprises, communities of property, ON *félagi*, were already formed before the year 1000 not only for Viking expeditions or associated mutual husbandry but also as trading companies (Müller-Boysen 1990: 80–1, 127–30; 2007: 182–3); none of them, however, can be dated with certainty to the end of the ninth century. The formation of tradeship fleets or convoys, ON *samfloti*, described in the Icelandic Sagas (Falk 1912: 22; Müller-Boysen 1990: 64), seems to have been vital and is likewise indicated in the travel account of Wulfstan from the 890s. As described in Section 8.2, the duration of his trip from Hedeby to Truso/Janów Pomorski – seven days and nights – suggests a detour from a more direct route along the southern Baltic coast. Because of threatened sea routes, it is likely that the Anglo-Saxon merchant joined a trade convoy in Hedeby. Pirate fleets then forced the convoy north along the coast of Scania before it was able to set a direct course on the Vistula Lagoon (Ulriksen 2009; Englert & Ossowski 2009: 268–9). Such assumptions are supported by a passage in *The Saga of the Sworn Brothers* (chap. 8), which suggested that the Wendish coast was still haunted by Slavonic Vikings in the early eleventh century: 'He [Þorgeirr] went on a trading journey south to Vindlands [the land of the Wends], where at that time there was little personal security for merchants.' Wulfstan's late ninth-century travel account, as well as Ansgar's first missionary voyage in 830 to Birka mentioned in Section 8.2, suggests that organised merchant efforts (with consequent convoys) already emerged in the decades around the 850s crisis and its subsequent demise of the second-level trading places along the southern Baltic coast.

10.2 BIRKA'S FALL AND HEDEBY'S TRANSFORMATION

Another clear break rather than a mere turning point in Scandinavian urban development was, beyond doubt, the eventual demise of the Viking-age towns. This final development and the perception of these towns as a discontinuous phenomenon was the point of departure for Hillerdal's (2009; cf. Hillerdal 2010) doctoral thesis. Hillerdal argued that purely functionalistic explanations (e.g. changing trade routes or new developments in shipbuilding) were hardly purposeful for describing this process and, since towns as new living environments would trigger the formation of new communities that are different from the surrounding rural society, suggested a more identity-based perspective (Hillerdal 2009: 205–8, 221, 250–2, 274–6). She concluded that the abandonment of the first Viking-age towns was primarily an ideological necessity and should be perceived as a result of political conflicts between a strengthened royal power and urban dwellers who had become largely autonomous from the king and the hinterland:

> This autonomy was the determining factor when they [the Viking-age towns] were dismissed and relocated by the new 'national' royal power. The history of the townspeople had to be rewritten to fit into medieval society; they could no longer be allowed to work within a system of their own, but needed to be reorganised to submit to the hierarchical order of the king and his realm.
>
> (Hillerdal 2009: 208, see also 272–3, 276–8)

In Denmark, it is obvious that the emerging Jelling dynasty accomplished a consolidation of royal power (cf. Lund 1995: 215–20; Roesdahl 2008).[1] The inscription on Harald Bluetooth's rune stone (DR 42) from c.965 – often referred to as the 'birth certificate' of Denmark – states that 'Haraldr ... won for himself all of Denmark [including Scania and Halland] and Norway [i.e. the province of Viken] and made the Danes Christian' (cf. Jacobsen & Moltke 1941–2). During the reign of Harald Bluetooth, Denmark experienced a virtual building boom for monumental structures, including not only the Jelling monument itself but also the bridge of Ravning Enge, the royal strongholds of the Trelleborg fortresses and probably even the construction of the linear *Kovirke* within the Danevirke fortification system (Roesdahl 2002; Andersen 2003). By contrast, however, it should also be pointed out that it was to take until the thirteenth century for feudal traits to take hold in Sweden, and attempts to strengthen the royal power would still have been a very precarious undertaking (cf. Sundqvist 2002: 183, 306, 314, 329). But even though some of Hillerdal's arguments are certainly contestable, her conclusion is highly convincing:

> [The early towns] created new opportunities for people to organize a social structure *separate from traditional power structures based on family, kin and land*. In that capacity, as *autonomous communities*, they posed a potential threat to an emerging consolidating royal power trying to take control of the land. In this light, the discontinuation of the towns can be ascribed to an ideological change. (Hillerdal 2009: 278; my emphasis)

Consequently, in the course of the state formation process, Viking-age towns had to be either assimilated or destroyed (Hillerdal 2009: 279).

---

[1] For a critical discussion of the alleged temporary setback for king Harald Bluetooth's centralistic tendencies by the rebellion of Sven Forkbeard, which was supported by disempowered pagan magnates and ultimately led to Harald's death in Jumne/Wolin in c.985 (Adam of Bremen book 2, chap. 27), see Lund (2002).

10.2.1 The Fall of Birka

The ideological conflict between consolidating royal powers, and increasingly autonomous urban communities, as suggested by Hillerdal (2009), seems to become apparent in the decades before Birka's abandonment around 975. Under the heading *Olika tider – olika Birka* ('Different Times – Different Birka'), in her article 'Birkafolket' ('The People of Birka'), Hedenstierna-Jonson (2012) suggested that wholesale merchants became increasingly wealthy and powerful towards the end of the ninth century:

> The structural power still lay with the king and chieftains in the region, but they were unable to exercise direct power on the extensive network Birka belonged to. Instead the real power shifted towards trading families. They owned the resources and contacts abroad, they were flexible and they could provide themselves with the required military power to guard the commercial traffic. In the tenth century, Birka appears to have become increasingly self-governed. (Hedenstierna-Jonson 2012: 215; my translation)

That this was a volatile situation with an immediate potential for conflict also finds archaeological support, as manifested in two examples from late Birka.

From Birka's final phase, there are strong indications of distinctly pagan expressions. One of the primary objectives of scholarly efforts in Birka has been the quest to identify Christian artefacts and 'true' Christian burials (cf. Gräslund 1980: 83–5; 2001: 58–63, 69–78; Trotzig 2004). Ansgar's second visit to Birka in 852 was followed by the presence of the priests Erimbert (c.856), Ansfrid (856–9) and Rimbert (shortly after 860)[2] (cf. Rimbert chap. 33). After this concentrated missionary attempt 'no teacher had dared to go in the [following] seventy years' before another missionary, the archbishop Unni of Hamburg-Bremen, attempted to revive the 'long neglected' Christian

---

[2] Probably not the same person as the archbishop of Hamburg-Bremen, who wrote *Vita Ansgarii*.

mission on Björkö (Adam of Bremen, book 1, chaps. 60–1; cf. Tegnér 1995). Unni died in Birka on 17 September 936 and was buried on the island; only his head was transferred to St Peters' Cathedral in Bremen, attested by a lead epitaph found in the high choir of St Peter's (Brandt 1976: 332; 1979: 71–4 cat. no. 2). He is the last missionary we learn about from the written sources, and after the mid-930s missionary efforts on Björkö seem to have ceased. As a result, pagan elements seem to have become more explicit. This is indicated by archaeological finds from the last phases of Birka, including an iron-amulet ring with sickle and fire-steel pendants (F23362), as well as a miniature iron axe (F24070). These were found in a roadbed (stratigraphic unit S5)[3] that led towards the Black Earth and aligned with an abandoned jetty by the waterfront. Price (1995) suggested that these pagan amulets were part of a unique 'foundation offering, during the construction of a major work of civic engineering', and thus 'evidence for the active practice and patronage of paganism during the final phases of Birka's occupation' (Price 1995: 76). Further evidence for a significant pagan resurgence has been found in the Garrison area, where four spearheads had been deposited as building sacrifices: while two spearheads were found next to and below the Garrison ramparts, respectively, on the lower-house terraces 0 (Swd. *nedre terrassen*), two more were part of a hoard with a *terminus post quem* 922–32 that was found in one of the postholes (feature A 9) of the central roof-bearing double posts of the 'warriors house'. Besides the two spearheads, the

[3] This stratigraphic unit was mentioned in the interim report from the first year of excavations, where it was attributed to feature A2, a 'ditch or passage across the trench', together with the stratigraphic unit S15 (Ambrosiani 1995: 44). In the recently published second volume of the Black Earth excavations, the mentioned stratigraphic units S5 (sublevel L4) and S15 were attributed to feature B919a–b (A [= excavation area 1990]), which was described as 'filling, and the large coin hoard in JP [jetty passage]'. More specifically, the amulet ring from the stratigraphic unit S5 belonged to feature B919 of sublevel B91, described as 'Waste and ash layers and a ["ceremonial"] building [= B91S1–2a] with a post-supported roof' and as a part of phase B9 (Ambrosiani 2021: 101, 176 fig. 20.9, tab. 26.1). While the large coin hoard from 1991 itself has a *terminus post quem* of 945–50 (Rispling 2004: 30–1; cf. Ambrosiani 2021: 98), phase B9 is chronologically placed in the period c.940–50/70 (Ambrosiani 2021: 130), making it part of Birka's final occupation phase.

hoard comprised a sword chape, a Þórr's hammer from antler, three hones, four knives, a padlock, two dirhams and a comb case (Kitzler 2000). From the other posthole of these roof-bearing double posts, which had already been excavated by Stolpe in 1877 as a part of a putative *liksbränningsplats* ('cremation site'), there even seems to be evidence of an additional building sacrifice ('burial' Bj. 596 f; Stolpe 1888: 14; cf. Hedenstierna-Jonson 2006: 64). If it was not just a weapon that once leaned against the wall of the hall, even a fifth spearhead found in the debris on the north-western side of the house could have been among these building sacrifices. Through their contexts, these spearheads have been interpreted as attributes of Óðinn and thus as parts of sacrifices performed by an Odin cult within a warrior ideology (Kitzler 2000). Hedenstierna-Jonson (2006: 64–6) suggested that: 'Perhaps the manifestation of pagan fervour should be seen as an *expression of resistance against the rise of Christianity*, an expression that did not require complete polarization away from all aspects of the new religion ... The Birka warriors distanced themselves from some group of Christians *for political rather than religious reasons*' (Hedenstierna-Jonson 2006: 65; my emphasis; see also Hedenstierna-Jonson 2012: 215). Her quote emphasised the conflict between the town's people and the royal power, which increasingly legitimised itself through Christianity. Ultimately, this conflict is likely to have been a major contributing reason for Birka's violent destruction (see later in this section) and for the politically motivated restart in Sigtuna, which was founded as an expressly Christian town under direct royal control. This conclusion is underlined by the fact that the first Swedish coins were struck in Sigtuna in c.995 during the reign of King Olof Skötkonung ('the Treasurer') (Malmer 1989, 1991), son of the aforementioned Erik Segersäll, and that Svealand's first diocese was established there around 1070 before being transferred to Gamla Uppsala c.1130 (Ros 2008: 143; cf. Holmquist Olausson 2001; Runer 2014). The novel religious aspect is also evident by the fact that Adam of Bremen called Sigtuna a *civitas magna* ('large episcopal town'; Adam of Bremen, book 4, chap. 25), and that the legends on some of

Olaf Skötkonung's coins – of the English Long Cross–type B:II in the early Sigtuna style – even promoted it as *Situne Dei* ('God's Sigtuna'; cf. Malmer 1989: 19 plate 3.21).

In Birka, the second manifestation of this ongoing conflict also emanates in part from the so-called Garrison, pointing to a violent destruction of the Viking-age town: the bailey-like Garrison, located next to the hillfort *Borgen* and its gate *kungsporten* ('the King's Gate'), consisted of several artificially erected house terraces on a slope facing Lake Mälaren which were protected behind further ramparts (for a summary, see Bergström 2015). The prominent *krigarnas hus* ('House of the Warriors'), also referred to as *ceremonihuset* ('the Ceremonial House'), was situated centrally on the most pronounced terrace, terrace I (Holmquist Olausson 2002a: 161–3; 2002b: 163–5; Holmquist 2010). The house – a double-walled three-aisled hall – was only built in the second half of the tenth century and thus belongs to the final construction phase on that terrace. With a size of approximately 19 by 9 metres, its dimensions were rather squat, while the type itself ties in with the floor plans of houses from the Migration and Vendel periods and thus appears quite archaic, which has been interpreted as a politically and ideologically motivated design for such a high-status building (Holmquist Olausson & Kitzler Åhfeldt 2002: 22–3). The artefact assemblage from the hall had a distinctly martial and professional character and consisted of spear and arrowheads, axes and swords, as well as shields, chain mail and lamellar armour (Hedenstierna-Jonson 2006: 54–60). But after less than half a century, the hall burnt down in a large fire, as evidenced both by a soot and charcoal rich cultural layer and by the find of a head of a flaming arrow. Even the parapet of the hillfort may have been affected by the same fire (Holmquist 2010). The analysis of the strikingly large number of arrowheads from the Garrison area as a whole (Lindbom 2009) revealed the presence of predominantly Eastern European or Russian arrowhead types. Lindbom (2009: 92–8) suggested that these artefacts were remnants of a major naval attack on both Helgö and Birka during the mid-970s, during which Birka's Garrison was destroyed. Although simple pirates were also discussed as possible attacking enemies, it was considered more likely to be none other than 'the founding father of Sigtuna, Erik Segersäll', reinforced by the exiled Prince Vladimir (ON *Valdamarr*) of Novgorod. Consequently, Lindbom suggested that the merchants in Birka had become a threat to Erik's plans to reclaim control over trade and that this was the reason for his efforts to relocate trade to the newly founded Sigtuna (Lindbom 2009: 98–9). In such a scenario, the professional mercenaries of the Garrison, the 'Birka warriors' (cf. Hedenstierna-Jonson 2006) would have fought in opposition to the king and thus may have been employed by the Birka merchants in their pursuit of autonomy. The large silver hoard found in 1872 in the Black Earth settlement area (Stolpe 1873: 18–31; 1874: plates. I–II; cf. Zachrisson 1992: 53–4) has also been discussed in a very similar scenario: the hoard, consisting of 2.16 kilograms of silver, was found on an iron dish and comprised approximately 450 dirhams, as well as 15 arm rings, a bracelet, ringed pins, silver rods and half an ingot. It even contained the youngest coin ever found on Björkö, which was either a Hamanid issue of Emir Sayf al-Dawla minted in al-Masisah in 963–7 or a Samanid issue of Emir Abu Salih Mansur from the period 961–77 (Wiséhn 1989: 32). The hoard and its terminal coin played a decisive role in setting the date of Birka's fall to around 975. On the circumstances of the deposition of the hoard, Arbman (1939: 132) stated that 'Obviously somebody had hidden his wealth there, which he could never claim back. Perhaps it was buried when the town was threatened and destroyed by enemies for the last time, or maybe it was hidden amongst the ruins of the recently abandoned town' (my translation).

Another strong indicator for a violent end to the activities on Björkö comes from a more unexpected context: when Callmer published his doctoral thesis on trade beads and bead trade in 1977, he dedicated a few pages to the Birka beads, discussed as 'zone 19' (Callmer 1977: 155–6). Callmer's catalogue included finds from eighty-four graves that contained sets of beads consisting of more than nine specimens, to which he added another thirty-eight burials with smaller sets of beads (Callmer 1977: 27–32; cat. no. 219–302).

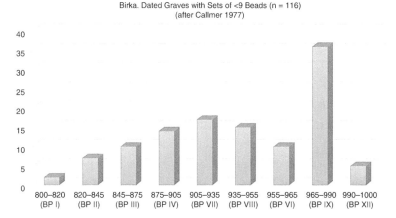

FIGURE 23 Birka, Uppland, Sweden. Graves with sets of beads assigned to J. Callmer's (1977) bead periods (BP) (bar chart: S. Kalmring). Note the standard normal distribution and the deviating peak of interments in BP IX, coinciding with Birka's fall in c.975.

These bead sets were then assigned to his general bead periods (BP), which provided precise chronological time frames for dating the discussed burials themselves.[4] When this information on the 116 discussed graves[5] is converted to a simple graph the results are staggering (Figure 23): at first glance, the diagram describes an ordinary standard normal distribution, with a maximum of seventeen bead-bearing burials in the period 905–35 (BP VII). However, there is another significant peak on this otherwise predictable curve – with a total of thirty-six graves, more than 31 per cent of the burials with beads belong to the period 965–90 (BP IX). It hardly seems a coincidence that this phase includes the suggested date for Birka's fall around 975. In the following

[4] Note that the Roman pagination of Callmer's bead periods does not correspond to their actual chronological sequence (cf. Kalmring et al. 2021: 89–101). In his thesis, Callmer differentiates between a 'Hypothetical Dating' (Callmer 1977: 77), a 'Revised Chronology' based on coin-dated find assemblages (Callmer 1977: 168–70) and finally an 'Absolut Chronology' (Callmer 1977: 170). The latter one is used here.

[5] Of the analysed burials, 6 of the 122 had to be excluded due to uncertain dating. These are Bj. 131 (BP IV or IX; 875–905 or 965–90), Bj. 161 (possibly BP IX; 965–90), Bj. 306B (possibly BP IX; 965–90), Bj. 332 (BP IV or IX; 875–905 or 965–90), Bj. 457 (BP II or III; 820–45 or 845–75) and Bj. 606 (unclassified).

period, BP XII, represented by five bead-bearing burials, the graph returns to the normal curve in the short interval of 990–1000, which may indicate that Birka once again became an ordinary rural settlement (cf. Bäck 2012). This basic compilation is thus able to demonstrate a significant increase in deaths during Birka's final phase, which coincides with the other indications of violence listed in this section. Harder to corroborate, but still tempting, would be to even link the mass grave in the St Lawrence churchyard in Sigtuna to the violent end of Birka and an execution of captives from Björkö. It contained nineteen individuals – thirteen men, five women and one child – of which at least eleven displayed fatal traumata from bladed weapons, predominantly directed towards the throat and neck (Kjellström 2005: 58–61 fig. 4.12; 2014: 246–7). Chronologically, the mass grave was only roughly dated to the period 880–1000 by radiocarbon dating.

The shift, however, that the relocation from Birka to Sigtuna represented was not unique to eastern central Sweden but was part of a general trend in Scandinavia, which has been referred to as the 'second wave of urbanisation' that took place in the decades around the turn of the first millennium (Skre 2007: 45; Hillerdal 2009: 253). As Näsman (2000: 66) accurately put it, 'the rapid urbanisation ... from the tenth century went hand in hand with the conversion and the spread of direct royal rule'. Almost at the same time as Sigtuna, medieval towns such as Lund, Roskilde, Odense, Slesvig, Aarhus and Viborg, as well as Oslo and Nidaros/Trondheim, were all founded as new royal, ecclesiastical and administrative centres, which, more closely embedded in the regional settings, integrated all three sovereign functions in one and the same place (cf. Andrén 1985). This development was not just limited to Northern Europe alone; a second wave of urbanisation can also be identified in north-western Continental Europe. There, following the heyday of the *emporia*, a change in socio-economic contexts in the sense of a growing importance of regional functions and an increased orientation towards regional trade can already be observed from the second half of the ninth century onwards. These changes prepared the ground for the new dynamic and multifunctional urban centres of the tenth and eleventh centuries (Verhaeghe 2005: 271–2). In the late ninth century, the trading places that had survived the crisis of the North Sea *emporia* slowly developed an increasingly urban character, while at the same time ecclesiastical centres and royal residences with attached manors formed further nuclei for emerging urban settlements. During the tenth century, other types of urban settlements also emerged, which evolved from the duality of the feudal castles of territorial lords and adjacent crafter settlements; in their economies, long-distance trade no longer played a significant role. It was not until the eleventh century, in the course of an advancing feudalisation and a dwindling manorial system, that increased production on an almost industrial scale – brought about by division of labour and serial production – managed to get a foothold in the towns, and international trade once again became the main economic pillar of urban communities (Verhulst 1999: 68–70, 113–18).

10.2.2 *The Transformation of Hedeby*

Despite Hillerdal's stimulating and plausible approach on the demise of Viking-age towns discussed at the beginning of Section 10.2, she accepts a certain chronological vagueness regarding the demise of the first Scandinavian towns by dating it generally to 'the turn of the first millennium' or 'by the early 11th century' (Hillerdal 2009: 205, 253, 276). The demise of Birka and Kaupang, however, was already a fact by the end of the tenth century – c.975 and c.960–80 (Pedersen & Pilø 2007: 186), respectively. Developments in Ribe are less obvious: after the sack of Reric in 808, Hedeby's subsequent rise was clearly at the expense of Ribe's trade volume, which is particularly evident in the period from 850 to 900 (Søvsø 2020: 17, 23, 175–6, 200–1, 204, 254). And in spite of the historically corroborated foundation of a diocese in Ribe in 948 (Adam of Bremen, book 2, chap. 4), hardly any archaeological support has been found to suggest that it was still a major site in the period between the late ninth or early tenth century (on the eastern bank of the river Ribe Å) and the end of the eleventh century (on the western bank of the river) (Feveile 2006a: 52–3). Even recent excavations at SJM 3 Posthustorvet could merely verify continuous activities up to the time of c.860–80 (phase F13), whereas in the following period, c.880–900/20 (phase F14), only fragments of the former town life were traceable (Croix et al. 2022: 192–205). However, this general picture must be adjusted due to excavations at *Lindegården* west of the Ribe Å, where a Christian cemetery from the ninth to the eleventh century was revealed, right next to the cathedral (Søvsø 2010, 2014, 2020: 184–200). This early Christian cemetery, enclosed by a circular ditch, suggests that even Angar's first church from c.855 (Adam of Bremen, book 1, chap. 29) was located in its immediate vicinity, most likely underneath the present cathedral (Søvsø 2014: 254 fig. 11; 2020: 182, 203).[6] Judging by the still weak archaeological evidence in Ribe for the period in question, this church may have functioned as a minster church for all of northern Jutland (Søvsø 2020: 203). The town itself does not seem to have shifted across the river and towards the cathedral until the 1050s (Søvsø 2020: 215–24). As for Hedeby, however, historical records of events in 1050 and 1066 strongly suggest that it persisted continuously into the mid-eleventh century (Hilberg 2016) – and thus close to a whole century longer than Birka and Kaupang. This putative anachronism demands further attention.

For the late tenth century in question, it has been suggested that Hedeby experienced an economic decline (cf. Hilberg 2016: 65–7 with references therein). The account of the Jewish diplomat Ibrâhîm ibn Ya`qûb al-Ṭurṭûshî on his visit to *Šilšwīq* ('Slesvig', i.e. Hedeby) in 965 has been interpreted as a sign of this recession (cf. Adamczyk 2014: 152): Although al-Ṭurṭûshî described it as 'a very large town at the extreme end of the world ocean', at the same time he characterised it as only being 'poor in goods and riches'. However, ongoing field research and recent scientific analyses have shown that this account

---

[6] This insight cannot be overstated, for it is the first time not only that archaeology has been able to pinpoint the location of one of the first churches in Scandinavia but also that it was spatially separated from the early town on the eastern side of the river.

must rather be understood as an expression of the cultural gap experienced by a visiting envoy from the highly developed Caliphate of Córdoba; both the late coins finds and standardised weights demonstrate that, even in the early eleventh century (Hilberg 2022), Hedeby was by no means only a 'centre of power with perhaps garrison-character', as argued by Radtke (2009: 152). It seems as though it was still a flourishing centre for long-distance trade, whose relocation to high medieval Slesvig during the reign of king Svend Estridsen (1047–76) (Gelting 2016: 200) does not seem to have been based on an economic crisis (Hilberg 2016: 74–5). On the other hand, Birka was not abandoned because of an *economic* recession either but rather from the necessity to establish a true Christian town under direct royal control. For Hedeby, therefore, the question still remains by what means – in contrast to the other Scandinavian Viking-age towns – was it able to persist that much longer. A sensible way to proceed would be to seek possible reasons in the events around 975 which were linked to the demise of Birka and Kaupang. Around the same time Birka and Kaupang were abandoned, in 974 to be precise, Thietmar of Merseburg notes that Hedeby was conquered by Emperor Otto II (see later in this section). However, a general problem in considering the later settlement development of Hedeby is the fact that the younger archaeological remains have often decayed due to insufficient soil moisture and because of the effects of modern deep ploughing, which was employed until the 1970s; the few remaining exceptions are dug-in, deeper features such as pit houses and wells or features from the submerged harbour area (Hilberg 2018: 130 fig. 6; 2016: 68–9 figs. 4–5; Schietzel 2014: 72–5, 95; Schultze 2008: 64–71 fig. 29). Yet important clues can also be found by shifting the focus from Hedeby itself to its immediate surroundings.

The extensive fortifications of the Danevirke have already been discussed in relation to Hedeby's location south of it, as an exterritorial site in the political no man's land between Scandinavia and Continental Europe (Kalmring 2016a: 15–16; Dobat 2008; cf. Section 5.2). Even with its incorporation into the Danevirke in the mid-tenth century – accomplished through the erection of the semi-circular rampart around the town and via the Connecting Wall, linking it to the Main Wall/Northern Wall section of the Danevirke at Lake Dannewerk – the town merely 'moved' onto the very border itself instead of, as a true part of the Danish realm, being withdrawn behind the fortifications themselves. At this point, it should be noted that the monument of the Danevirke itself can and has been discussed between the antipodes of a 'border fortification or boundary mark of a territory' (Schietzel 2014: 587). This question actually mirrors a more general debate in early medieval studies, which deals with two competing concepts of territorial frontiers, either as distinct linear boundaries – in this case, political rather than cultural or economic borders – or alternatively as wider frontier zones. The frontiers of the Carolingian Empire seem to have been quite permeable and flexible and would probably have been easier to recognise from afar than for the people actually living in the border area. Pohl (2001: 254–5) argued that:

> Even without taking symbolic, religious, moral, cultural or linguistic frontiers into account, the political geography of early medieval Europe can hardly be reduced to a clear pattern of proto-national boundary lines. This does not mean that no theoretical, or symbolical notion of a frontier existed ... Neither does it mean that on the level of states, the concept of realm and frontier was lacking.

Interestingly, however, he also acknowledged that: 'When frontiers changed, that was usually perceived in terms of gain or loss of *civitates* or provinces, not shifting frontiers. It may be no coincidence that it was beyond the post-Roman world of, however rudimentary, *civitates* that we find ... indications that linear frontiers were negotiated' (Pohl 2001: 255). Although due to recent excavations at the historically attested main gate of Danevirke, the so-called *Wieglesdor* (Thietmar of Merseburg, book 3, chap. 6; cf. *The Royal Frankish Annals*, entry 808 CE), discussions regarding the earliest origins of the Danevirke have resumed (Tummuscheit & Witte 2014: 156–7; 2018: 70–3), the observations made by Harck (1998) on the monument's impact on local settlement patterns are still valid: while the settlement indicators for the inner Schlei Fjord in the pre-Roman Iron Age were still evenly distributed across the landscape, this picture changed markedly in the course of the Roman Iron Age, and there is less and less evidence of settlements immediately south of Danevirke and along its Eastern Wall (Harck 1998: 131–4 fig. 3). However, during the Viking Age the situation along the Danevirke frontier is much less obvious. While Dobat (2008: 46) suggested a 'rather clear-cut demarcation line', Lemm (2013a: 362) argued 'that the Saxon–Danish frontier, despite two prominent linear structures – the river Eider and the Danevirke – was recognised as a *Flächengrenze* ['frontier zone']' (my translation). A more dynamic way of looking at this dilemma would be to link these linear earthworks with chronologically changing defence strategies ('From Frontier to Border'; see Baker & Brooks 2011). A reconsideration of the narrower sphere of activity of the Danish 'commander of the Norse border' (*custos Nordmannici limitis*) named Gluomi (*The Royal Frankish Annals*, entry 817 CE; cf. Dobat 2022: 15), who is mentioned in connection with the Obotrites abandoning their alliance with the Franks and a subsequent joint Slavonic-Danish attack on the Saxon castle of Esesfelth in 817 (Lemm 2013a: 266, 357–8; cf. 2013b: 221–6), could also provide further clues to this debate.

Already the first mention of Hedeby in the written sources in 804 was connected with a boundary dispute when the Carolingian Empire, with the incorporation of Nordalbingia in the aftermath of the Saxon Wars (which also entailed an expulsion of the local Saxons as well as a relocation of Slavic Obotrites there), extended its dominion to the southern border of the Danish territory. The Danish King Godfred reacted to this threat by concentrating his troops in Hedeby, which is said to have been situated on the border between his realm and Saxony: 'At the same time king Godofrid [Godfred], king of the Danes, came with his fleet and the entire cavalry of his kingdom to Sliesthorp [Hedeby] on the border of his kingdom and Saxony' (*The Royal Frankish Annals*, entry 804 CE). However, only four years later the river Eider, which runs some 21–33 kilometres south of Hedeby, was mentioned as the frontier:

'[Godfred] decided to fortify the border of his kingdom against Saxony with a rampart, so that a protective bulwark would stretch from the eastern bay, called Ostarsalt [Baltic Sea], as far as the western sea, along the entire north bank of the River Eider' (*The Royal Frankish Annals*, entry 808 CE). However, the notion 'north bank of the river Eider' is problematic, as no such archaeological traces of ramparts have so far been identified along the river course. It may in fact be a rather vague description referring to the entire frontier zone north of the river and consequently to the fortifications of the Danevirke themselves.[7] The river Eider, in turn, is also mentioned as a border river in Adam of Bremen's *Descriptions of the Islands of the North*: 'The principal part of Denmark, called Jutland, extends lengthwise from the Eider river toward the north' (Adam of Bremen, book 4, chap. 1). Then again, when Otto II was fighting a Danish uprising in 974, the battle took place by the Danevirke itself:

> At a second [campaign] he [the Emperor] hastened to Sleswic [Hedeby] in order to attack the rebellious Danes. There he discovered that his enemies anticipated him armed in the occupation of the ditch erected for the defence of their country and its access, the so-called Wieglesdor; following the advice of duke Bernhard [II of Saxony] and my grandsire, the count Henry [the Fowler], he subdued all these defences ... The Emperor built a town [urbs] at this border and secured it with a garrison. (Thietmar of Merseburg, book 3, chap. 6)

A larger frontier zone remained contested for another half a century until the later Salian Emperor Conrad II officially dropped his claim on 'Slesvig and the [associated] march across the Eider' in c.1025 (Adam of Bremen, book 2, chap. 55; for a more elaborate discussion on the Danish–Saxon frontier, see Lemm 2013a: 356–62).

---

[7] Indications for a 'Southern Danevirke' along the Eider can only be deduced from fifteenth-century sources and later maps naming a *Landscheide* ('tariff walls') (Kühl & Hardt 1999: 85–7).

Regardless of how the borderland between Danevirke and Eider was actually perceived, the erection of the Kovirke defence line constituted a clear novelty in the development of the Danevirke. As it is dated to c.980 and the latter part of Harald Bluetooth's reign, it may be perceived as a direct Danish measure to secure the reconquered territory after they successfully thwarted Ottonian efforts for hegemony in 983 with the destruction of the above-mentioned *urbs* (commonly identified with the so-called margrave's castle of Duke Bernhard; cf. Kalmring 2014/15: 247–9) – an effort which was deliberately synchronised with the *Lutizenaufstand* ('the Great Slavic Revolt') (Thietmar of Merseburg, book 3, chap. 24; cf. Lemm 2013a: 360; Andersen 1998: 168; Erlenkeuser 1998: 193–4). As a shortening of the front, the Kovirke constituted an alternative line of defence 1.5 kilometres south of Hedeby. It ran dead straight over a distance of 6.5 kilometres from the innermost end of the *Selker Noor* ('Selk inlet') towards the boggy flats of the river Rheider Au next to the hamlet of Kurburg. In terms of construction, it consisted of a remarkably uniform rampart 7 metres wide and about 2 metres high with three rows of posts and a 3-metre-deep, V-shaped ditch. Since only one single construction phase has been detected – exactly as for the contemporary Trelleborg-ring fortresses – the structure must have been rather short-lived (Andersen 1998: 153–68 plates 22–3), implying that it was only significant for Hedeby but no longer for high medieval Slesvig. Why, then, is exactly this observation so important for the assumed changes in late Viking-age Hedeby? As demonstrated, Viking-age towns were only able to develop in political no man's lands, where they formed almost parallel societies, separated from the surrounding traditional agrarian world (see Section 5.2). With the construction of Kovirke, however, all of sudden the town found itself behind by the very physical Danevirke border (figure 24), depriving it of its former status as a special economic zone. The implications were dramatic indeed: Henceforth, Hedeby was incorporated into a territorial realm (Dobat 2008: 59) and was reduced to an admittedly very large, and certainly royal, but otherwise regular Danish town.

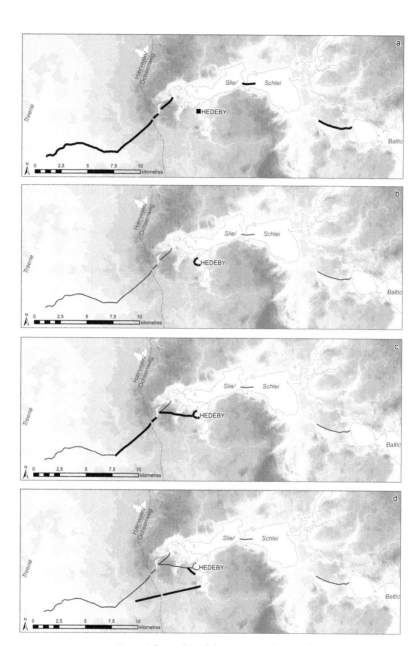

FIGURE 24 Danevirke and Hedeby, present-day northern Germany. Phases of development with new or reinforced sections highlighted in bold (adapted from Dobat 2008: fig. 8) (Map: S. Kalmring).
Note the position of Hedeby in the no man's land south of the border fortifications (phases a–b) and as part of the borderline (phase c). Only with the establishment of the Kovirke does Hedeby fall behind the actual border (phase d).

Against the background of the largely lacking archaeological features from late Viking-age Hedeby and in order to get an idea of what these late tenth- and early eleventh-century towns looked like – and what demands were made on their infrastructure – it seems, at least at first glance, useful to consider the evidence from the nearby Jutish towns of Ribe and Aros/Aarhus. For Ribe, we must therefore briefly recapitulate some of the most important facts mentioned in this section: evidence for the late tenth and early eleventh century has only recently come to light thanks to the efforts of the *Lindegården* excavations near the cathedral (Søvsø 2010, 2014, 2020: 184–200); prior to this, there was little archaeological evidence for the period between the late ninth or early tenth century and the late eleventh century (Feveile 2006a: 52–3; for a more nuanced timeline, see Croix et al. 2022: 200–5). With regard to the historically attested diocese in 948 (Adam of Bremen, book 2, chap. 4) during this archaeologically elusive transitional period, it had therefore been suggested that it not only served Ribe but may have been an equivalent to an English minster for the whole of northern Jutland (Søvsø 2020: 203). The shift of the main settlement activities east of the Ribe Å, across to the western shore of the river, however, did not take place prior to the 1050s (Søvsø 2020: 215–24), that is, not until Hedeby's demise was initiated by Harald Hardrada of Norway's attack on the town in 1050 (Adam of Bremen, book 3, chap. 12). Aarhus, despite its roots as a trading place from c.770 onwards, is generally not counted as part of the canon of Viking-age towns. In spite of attested close contacts with Norway, traces of its imports are not considered to reflect the same scale of long-distance trade as that seen in, for example, Ribe or Hedeby. Aarhus is not mentioned in written sources before 948, when a diocese was established there at the same time as in Hedeby and Ribe. The first town ramparts in Aarhus are assumed to have been built shortly after 934 in response to the seizure of Hedeby by the East Francian ruler Henry the Fowler (cf. Widukind of Corvey, book 1, chap. 40; Adam of Bremen, book 1, chap. 59); a second phase is dendrochronologically dated to after

957 – and often specified to around 970, that is, the time of the Trelleborg-ring fortresses (cf. Roesdahl & Sindbæk 2014: 206–7). Aarhus' initial cathedral, St Nicholas, dated to around 1070, is partially preserved in the Dominican Abbey of Our Lady (Dan. *Vor Frue Kirke*) but may even date back to a stave church built during the reign of Harald Bluetooth. When it was built, the cathedral was situated outside the town ramparts, across the former ford (ON *vað*) Immervad.[8] When Harald Hardrada attacked Hedeby in 1050, he also attacked Aarhus, events that were linked to his succession conflict with Svend Estridsen (Adam of Bremen, book 3, chap. 12). Despite the attack, however, it is assumed that the town – apart from an extramural growth around the churches of St Nicholas and St Olaf – maintained its basic Viking-age structure until the end of the twelfth century. No major restructuring of the urban space is evident before the 1190s, when the cathedral was relocated from the area of the later Dominican priory to the area inside the town ramparts, where it was consecrated to St Clement (Skov 2005, 2008: fig. 3c; cf. Andersen et al. 1971).

While the evidence from Ribe and Aarhus is of limited significance for illuminating conditions in late Viking-age Hedeby, Sigtuna may serve as a better comparison. Sigtuna's urban topography was characterised by distinctive 20–30 by 8 metre town plots (Swd. *stadsgårdar*) protruding from either sides of the main road *Stora gatan*, which still runs east to west parallel to the shoreline, but also by its many cemeteries and rapidly emerging ecclesiastical architecture, which meant that seven churches were built along the rear side of the elongated settlement (Tesch 2007). Excavations at the town quarter *Trädgårdsmästaren* (cf. Wikström 2011) revealed that *Stora gatan* was lined with rows of buildings built gable to gable (Tesch

[8]   With its spatial position, it shares characteristics with the early churches of Ribe and maybe even Hedeby, which are only found at some distance from the trading places (see Note 6, this chapter). For Aarhus, such a spatial separation may also apply to the town and its royal administration (see Section 5.1), as the example of the manorial complex of Lisbjerg, some 7.5 kilometres north-west of the town, suggests (Jeppesen & Madsen 1995/6; cf. Kalmring et al. 2017: 130).

2007: 82-90). During the first main phase I, which covered the brief period 985-1000, there was probably only one single row of plots, each with two buildings facing the shore, and a possible initial road along the lakeshore. However, from the eleventh century onwards, in main phase II, the new main road *Stora gatan* was built on the rear side of the initial plots, where new plots became available, creating a two-sided urban development (Tesch 2007: 89 fig.; 2016: 118-22). Henceforth, these plots would house four to five buildings that each had specific functions: next to the main road, each plot possessed a small simple workshop (zone I), followed by modest granaries or multifunctional buildings (zone II); only then came the actual residential homes with sitting rooms (Swd. *dagligstuga*) featuring corner fireplaces and seat/bed platforms (zone III), which were finally followed by proprietors' halls (zone IV) as the largest dwellings on the plots (Tesch 2007: 88 fig.; 2016: 120-1).[9]

Against this background, closer scrutiny even reveals glimpses of a similar internal settlement layout of late Viking-age Hedeby as well: geomagnetic surveys conducted in 2002 (cf. Neubauer et al. 2003) revealed, among other things, a main road running roughly north to south, which crossed the Haddeby stream at the above mentioned bridge excavated in 1963 (cf. Section 9.3; Schietzel 1969: 21-6; 2014: 113-15). The survey demonstrated that particularly the northern stretch of this road was lined with matching minor anomalies on both sides (Schultze 2008: 235-43 figs. 161, 163). Some of these had been excavated earlier as part of Schietzel's excavation area 4 and were attributed to 'a relatively late phase ... of settlement development', possibly dating from around 900, although certain artefacts were even dated to the early tenth century or as late as the first half of the tenth century (Schultze 2008: 240-1). Excavations proved them to be small rectangular buildings, about whose exact purpose the author at first

[9] Similar town plots with a specific multipart development may even have existed in Nidaros/Trondheim as well, where they are attributed to its third development phase from the end of the eleventh century onwards (Mokkelbost forthcoming; Christophersen & Nordeide 1994: 212; Christophersen: 1989: 117-27 fig. 16; cf. Tesch 2016: 129; 2001b: 733).

remained reserved: 'since fire places are missing the question arises, whether they are dwellings or outbuildings' (Schultze 2008: 241; my translation). Among other characteristics, these (out-) buildings displayed comparably high levels of magnetisation, but they also featured evidence of many types of handicrafts on the inside and immediately outside (Schultze 2008: 242–3); the latter was also confirmed through micromorphology (Wouters 2020: 91–4 [core 502, stratigraphic unit SU9]). More recently, Schultze (2017) attributed these features to a 'third main phase' of settlement development in Hedeby, chronologically placed in the mid-to-late ninth century, with town plots comprising workshops closest to the road and (presumably) larger main dwellings at their far side (Schultze 2017: 571, 574). Volker Hilberg was able to demonstrate that a few of the actual workshops, which coincided with the geomagnetic anomalies, had in fact been excavated on the western side of the main road as early as 1911/13 (Hilberg 2009: 89–90 fig. 8; Hilberg & Kalmring 2014: 231–2 fig. 16.4). Apart from the features of the workshops themselves, other finds included a glass oven and crucibles for metal casting of a whole range of artefacts dating from the second half of the ninth and first half of the tenth century. Hilberg concluded that: 'We get a picture that the settlement area in the decades around AD 900 was divided into long rectangular plots measuring 6–9 m. in width, where workshops and ovens were situated immediately on both sides of a main street [which was] no wider than *c.* 2 metres running N–S across the site' (Hilberg & Kalmring 2014: 232).

These small workshop buildings facing the main street at the front of elongated town plots are strongly reminiscent of the eleventh-century urban fabric of Sigtuna.[10] They seem to suggest that Hedeby had already undergone a major structural and spatial reorganisation in the first half of the tenth century – a process which may have been completed prior to or with the construction of Kovirke around 980 and

[10] This suggestion and the following comparison with parallels from northern France have previously been presented by the author at lectures in Visby (2013) and Vilnius (2016); later, it was adopted by Schultze (2017).

the incorporation of the formerly free trade zone into the Danish realm proper.[11] Conclusions regarding the general settlement pattern of Hedeby are admittedly difficult, as it has so far only been exemplified by a building sequence from Schietzel's excavation area 5, which measured 10 by 15 metres, and only represented a rear development oriented towards an easterly running road (Schultze 2008: 217–34). However, this section provides an impression of a rather rapid building succession: in the process, the floor plans of the subsequent buildings were repeatedly shifted and even an east to west running lane was built over several times, a development that clearly contradicts the existence of fixed plot boundaries. In another area, although 'House 2' from 833 was rebuilt on-site in no less than three rapid successive phases, the subsequent building development changed its general orientation from east–west to north–south. As a matter of fact, only a few structures such as a picket fence displayed continuity of place during the entire ninth century. However, a settlement transformation as indicated by the establishment of workshops along the main road may provide the key to the putative anachronism of Hedeby's continued existence beyond the last quarter of the tenth century and well into the eleventh century.

An argument that contradicts a 'Sigtuna phase' in Hedeby is the fact that the presumed major reorganisation of Hedeby predates the town development in Sigtuna by several decades, which can therefore hardly have served as a model (cf. Schultze 2017: 575). A more plausible interpretation, however, is that this is rather a matter of cultural transfer: it seems unlikely that Sigtuna was built according to an indigenous pioneer ideal, nor was this the case with Hedeby, which – considering the chronological framework – is more likely to have served as a model for Sigtuna than vice versa. Once again, the antetypes are much more likely to come from Continental Europe: at the site of *La Fonderie*

---

[11] Note that even Rösch (2018) considered an urban reorganisation of late Viking-age Hedeby when he suggested that 'one possible scenario would be that Hedeby, like Ribe and Aarhus, was in the process of being restructured and was forced to abandon the plans during the attacks in 1050 and 1066' (Rösch 2018: 314).

('the Foundary') in Douai in northern France, four Carolingian town plots were excavated between 1976 and 1981 (Demolon & Louis 1991; cf. Schofield & Steuer 2007: 125–6 fig. 4.5). They were located inside semicircular ramparts next to the river Scarpe and orientated at right angles to a 2.5-metre-wide central corduroy road. The elongated plots measured 5 by 25 metres, and all had a narrow sequence of three buildings aligned gable to gable. Right next to the road, there was in each case a 2.5 by 4 metre small shallow pit house (Fre. *fond-de-cabane*) which may have been used as a granary. The second, central building measured 3 by 4–5 metres and covered almost the whole breadth of the plot. At the far end, by the foot of the ramparts, another somewhat deeper pit house, which accommodated a weaving loom, was located (Demolon & Louis 1991: 55 fig. 7). This plot development, referred to here as *parcellaires urbain* ('urban plots'), strongly resembles the building pattern from eleventh-century Sigtuna. At *La Fonderie*, the plot system dates from the ninth century and prevailed, separated into two distinct build phases, until around 945, when the ducal residence of Arnulf I of Flanders was erected on the site.

It seems as if this novel building pattern only gradually found its way towards Northern Europe, spreading from ninth-century Flanders to Hedeby, as Scandinavia's most southernmost outpost, by the second half of the ninth or first half of the tenth century. From there, this innovation 'diffused' further north until it was finally implemented on the town layout in Sigtuna around 1000. It might not be by chance that the decades when Hedeby adapted this continental novelty as part of a major structural and spatial reorganisation of the urban space (cf. even Arents & Eisenschmidt 2010: 316, 324) roughly coincide with the phase of Ottonian rule in Hedeby after 934/47. Consequently, the final Danish recapture of Hedeby in 983 – and after half a century under Ottonian rule and development – would have been the reclamation of quite a different town. By then, it had fully transformed into a Christian European town, which as such became incorporated into the Danish realm, as the erection of the Kovirke unmistakably demonstrated.

10.2.3 Implications of a Successful Transformation: Hedeby's Late Viking-Age 'Sigtuna Phase'

If Hedeby actually became an Ottonian-Christian *civitas* in the tenth century, this development would have included churches inside the boundaries of the town. As the example of Ribe illustrates, it must be assumed that the earliest missionary churches were placed at a distance from the Viking-age towns (see Section 10.2.2 and Note 8), as they do not seem to have gone along well with the basic ideas of cosmopolitan trading centres and free trade (cf. Staecker 2009: 313–14). For Hedeby, the existence of a possible early stave church underneath the Romanesque St Andrew's Church, some 735 metres north of the town rampart, has been discussed and may have been Ansgar's missionary church from 849/60 (lastly Staecker 2009: 309–12). For a long time, this hypothesis had also been supported by the suggestion that, before the Reformation, St Andrew's must have been consecrated to the Virgin Mary as its original patron saint (Frahm 1934: 194–5).[12] For late Viking-age Sigtuna, in his subchapter 'Från hallkult till sockenkyrkor' ('From Hall-Cult to Parish Churches'), Tesch (2007: 101–8) suggested that the earliest Christian cult was initially practised in the long houses (zone IV) – as some continuation of earlier pagan practices on rural manors – since no evidence of early wooden stave churches had yet been found; Sigtuna's characteristic ecclesiastical architecture is not evident before the early twelfth century (Tesch 2007: 105–8). However, the excavation of a cemetery at the *Magistern* quarter offered some 'secondary evidence' (Tesch 2016: 125) relating to a presumed initial stave church built on Sigtuna's royal estate (on the museum plot in the *S:ta Gertrud 3* quarter) around 1060. Such a presumed stave church, however, would have been replaced by a stone cathedral by the end of the eleventh century (cf. Tesch 2001a: 16, 19–20).[13] For Hedeby, despite its

---

[12] For the Virgin Mary's central role in Ansgar's faith, next to John the Baptist and the Apostle Saint Peter, see Staats and Weitling (2016: 34–6).

[13] Already towards the end of the thirteenth century, this cathedral was abandoned and replaced by a marketplace (Swd. *Lilla Torget*, cf. Tesch 2001a: 16–17). This development is not totally unlike the insights from Schleswig *Rathausmarkt*, where the Saint

continued existence until 1050/66, no clear traces of a church within the semi-circular rampart have been found to date; in 1978, however, a ringing bell was found in the Haddebyer Noor near the town's harbour (Kalmring 2010a: 80 figs. 50–1).[14] This remarkable object was specifically a bronze bell with clapper, 51.5 centimetres high and weighing 24.3 kilograms, as well as its wooden frame (Figure 25). Due to a failed dendrochronological analysis of the frame, the typo-chronology was rather unsatisfactorily placed between the eighth or ninth and mid-eleventh century, that is, into the general period of the Viking Age as such (Drescher 1984; cf. Kalmring 2010a: 440–1; Schietzel 2014: 424–5). Later, thanks to an elemental analysis, the bronze of the bell was linked to the Rammelsberg mine in the Harz mountains, which opened around 960. Thus the bell's dating was narrowed down to the mid- or second half of the tenth century (Radtke 2009a). Previously, it has been suggested that the bell derived from a raid on Slesvig (Olsen 1981: 250) or that it was even just a profane signal bell at the entrance to Hedeby harbour (Articus 1982). However, as one of the earliest ringing bells found north of the Alps, it must be assumed to have derived from an ecclesiastical context, which strongly supports the argument that it is a genuine church bell originating from an actual church in Hedeby itself, most likely connected to the diocese at Hedeby founded in 948.

And there is further circumstantial evidence that can be added to the argument: Hedeby's extensive inhumation burial ground (Ger. *Flachgräberfeld*), where 322 graves have been excavated so far, was – analogous to the cemeteries of Sigtuna – situated towards the rear of the settlement and indeed displayed a couple of characteristics of a Christian cemetery. The editors U. Arents and S. Eisenschmidt (2010) argued that 'None of Hedeby's burial grounds corresponds to our contemporary picture of a Christian cemetery. ... The *Flachgräberfeld* and especially the burials at the Noor, with their

[14] Trinitatis church (II) was replaced by a marketplace in the early thirteenth century (Lüdtke 1997; cf. Kalmring 2010a: 446–7).
As early as 1710, another broken church bell was found in the valley next to the village of Loopstedt on the northern shore of the Haddebyer Noor, probably almost opposite St Andrew's Church (Schietzel 2014: 425).

FIGURE 25 Hedeby, present-day northern Germany. Bronze bell and wooden frame found in Hedeby harbour. A bell from a church inside an Ottonian-Christian *civitas*? (inventory no. KSD 591.092; © Museum für Archäologie, Stiftung Schleswig-Holsteinische Landesmuseen, Schleswig).

high occupancy and lack of burial mounds, however, do display more Christian features than the chamber-burial ground and the southern burial ground' (Arents & Eisenschmidt 2010: 296; my translation; cf. Müller-Wille 2017). In a previous chapter, they had dared to be more explicit: 'The even, dense occupation [of the inhumation burial ground] and its linear disposition, as well as the absence of grave goods, is typical for Christian cemeteries' (Arents & Eisenschmidt 2010: 292; my translation). The inhumation burial ground was probably established in the second half of the ninth century and was initially only one of many burial grounds in Hedeby. In the tenth century, the adjacent chamber burial ground was abandoned, which meant that the area of the inhumation burial ground was enlarged towards the east, north and west (while the more pagan *Südgräberfeld*, which was located outside of the younger town wall, expanded eastwards towards the Haddebyer Noor, where it replaced the previous Southern Settlement). From the inhumation burial ground, the latest datable interment (coffin grave 33; cf. Arents & Eisenschmidt 2010: 228 plate 6.33) has been dated to the time around 1000 by an Otto-Adelheid-penny as a burial gift, although the presence of even younger eleventh-century burials, which remained unidentified due to the absence of grave goods, cannot be ruled out either (Arents & Eisenschmidt 2010: 323). In this context, a hitherto little-noticed feature should be mentioned, which is only partially known from some trial trenches excavated by Jankuhn in 1931 and was located immediately west of Hedeby's inhumation burial ground near the highest point within the semi-circular rampart. In trial trench I, a 0.8-metre-wide solid boulder-stone packing with a north–south orientation was encountered. Trial trench II revealed another stone assemblage, although the stones were no longer structurally connected. As an extension of this feature, some 'deliberately apposed' bolder stones were also found in a small survey pit excavated around the turn of the last century (F. Knorr, pit II/1903; cf. Jankuhn 1986: 105; Arents & Eisenschmidt 2010: 37 fig. 84). These stone assemblages probably belonged to one single structure, which in that case would have stretched at least 23.5 metres; apart from the individual clay-covered hearths of the dwellings, it is so far the only known boulder-stone construction in all of Hedeby. The immediate vicinity of this linear stone structure, more than 20 metres long, to the inhumation burial ground suggests that it may have been a part of a cemetery wall. Interestingly, in their attempt to distinguish the pagan burial grounds of Hedeby from later medieval churchyards in general, Arents and Eisenschmidt (2010), with reference to the work of Kieffer-Olsen (1993: 156), stated: 'An additional important characteristic of a cemetery is the demarcation of the area, e.g. by a small wall with a ditch or simply by a stone wall.' They elaborated: 'Round about the middle of the enclosure the church is situated' (Arents & Eisenschmidt 2010: 292; my translation). Based on the evidence from *Lindegården* in Ribe, Søvsø (2020: 182, 235–336 fig. 188) recently also emphasised the obvious Christian influences on the *Flachgräberfeld* in Hedeby and suggested that it must have been part of an actual Christian cemetery to an existing church in that area.[15]

In the context of a 'Sigtuna phase' suggested for Hedeby – with a corresponding, imperative ecclesiastical architecture within the limits of the town (see Section 10.2.2) – the bronze bell from Hedeby harbour may thus, in the light of the evidence presented, be regarded as indeed originating from a tenth- or eleventh-century (stave?) church situated inside the town ramparts. While the physical identification of such a church is a task for future archaeological surveys, a suggested location for such a church could be the area of the inhumation burial ground, with its Christian traits and possible stone cemetery wall (Kalmring 2017: 42; 2018: 76). Based on the proposed chronology for such as church, it could be nothing less than the episcopal church of the first bishops of Hedeby/Slesvig founded in 948: on the consequences following the murder of Otto the Great's margrave and legate and Harald Bluetooth's subsequent destruction of the Saxon *colonia* at Hedeby, which the Emperor Otto responded to with a punitive expedition through Jutland at the end of which King Harald was defeated in a battle at '*Silaswig*', Adam of Bremen (book 2, chap. 3) reports: 'At the same time Denmark on this side of the sea, which is called Jutland by the inhabitants, was divided in to three dioceses and subjected to the bishopric of Hamburg.' He continues in the following chapter:

> Our most blessed father [archbishop Adaldag], then, was the first to consecrate bishops for Denmark: Hored for Sliaswig [Hcdcby/Slesvig], Liafdag for Ribe, Reginbrund for Aarhus. ... This was done in the archbishop's twelfth year [948]. And indeed, such increase followed these beginnings of heavenly mercy, God working with them, that the churches of the Danes are seen to abound in the manifold fruits of the northern peoples from that time even to this day. (Adam of Bremen, book 2, chap. 4)

---

[15] According to Søvsø, however, the proposed church should be no less than Ansgar's church from around c.850.

Hedeby's first bishop Hored was followed by Folkbert, Marco and Poppo. The latter went on to baptise Harald Bluetooth in c.960 (Widukind of Corvey, book 3, chap. 65). A few years after his own baptism, Harald in turn proclaimed that he had 'made the Danes Christian', as witnessed by the large Jelling stone (DR 42) from around 965 (see Section 10.2).

According to the *Vita Bernwardi* (chap. 20), however, bishop Ekkehard (†1026), the successor of Poppo, was banished from Hedeby after the destruction of the *civitas* and the abandonment of the church – presumably immediately after the Danish recapture of the town in 983. At the synod of Gandersheim in the year 1000, the bishop complained: 'The borders of my diocese had been laid waste by barbarians, the town [civitas] is deserted, my church is desolate; I have no seat' (*Vita Bernwardi*, chap. 20; my translation). Ekkehard remained titular bishop in exile in Hildesheim, as did his successor Rodulf in the diocese of Cologne. During the time of these two 'shadow bishops' (cf. Gelting 2004: 175, 179–81, 183), the episcopal see in Hedeby remained abandoned, although Canute the Great of England-Denmark – in an attempt to ward off the influence of Hamburg-Bremen and the Holy Roman Empire – tried to establish a church dependent on the archbishopric of Canterbury instead (Gelting 2004: 175–7). According to Gelting (2004, 187–91), it was not until the gathering between Archbishop Adalbert and Svend Estridsen in 1052/3 (cf. Janson 2016: 84–8) that the supremacy of Hamburg-Bremen was recognised and the episcopal see was reinstated through the instalment of bishop Ratolf (†1072) in 1059. Radtke, on the other hand, suggested that the bishops from Hamburg-Bremen were already reinstated with the peace treaty between Conrad II and Canute from c.1025 (Radtke 1992a, 2009b: 152 n. 170 with references therein; cf. Adam of Bremen, book 2, chap. 55). Bishop Ratolf's predecessor Rodulf (†1047), however, was evidentially buried in the church of St Cunibert in Cologne (Schütte 1997: 13–15; Gechter 1997; cf. Weise 2000; Scherping 2003). Gelting (2004, 181) therefore argued that, although bishop Rodulf was undoubtedly present at the negotiations between Adalbrand Becelin and Magnus the Good in 'Sliaswig' in 1042 (cf. Adam of Bremen, book 2, chap. 79), he was only able to attend as a member of the archbishop's retinue.

Be that as it may, with the first Hedeby/Slesvig bishops Hored, Folkbert, Marco and Poppo we have a whole line of at least four ecclesiastical dignitaries who may actually have been active in Hedeby itself. Regarding any Anglo-Danish replacement bishops from Canterbury during the following rule of Canute, there is at least evidence of such bishops for the dioceses in Scania (bishop Bernhard), Zealand (bishop Gerbrand) and Funen (bishop Reginbert) (Adam of Bremen, book 2, chap. 53; cf. Gelting 2004: 175–6), but on Hedeby the sources remain silent. The assumption of an episcopal church in Hedeby itself, however, may even find support in the Icelandic sagas (*Gísli Súrsson's saga*, chap. 38), where the two Islandic women Auður and Gunnhildur visited 'Heiðabæ' as a major ecclesiastical centre of the North in order to be baptised before continuing their pilgrimage to Rome (cf. Radtke 2009b: 154–5; Hilberg & Kalmring 2014: 223). In light of the discussion in this chapter, it seems necessary to re-evaluate the locations of the much-debated negotiations between Archbishop Adalbrand Becelin and Magnus the Good of Norway-Denmark in 1042 (Adam of Bremen, book 2, chap. 79) and those between Archbishop Adalbert and Svend Estridsen in 1052/3 (Adam of Bremen book 3, chap. 18) (cf. Radtke 2007: 320–1 with references therein); it seems perfectly possible that they took place neither in the vicinity of Hedeby nor at an early Slesvig but actually in Hedeby itself. At least for the first event in 1042, Radtke, at some point in time, clearly assumed an actual bishop's see at the location of Hedeby (Radtke 2009b: 156; differently Radtke 1999: 368). Still presuming an earlier reinstitution of the bishops from Hamburg-Bremen, he elaborated:

> This archaeologically insecure period [the eleventh century] coincides with a range of historical events, which for the spheres of power and religion – without being archaeologically verifiable – required a more advanced settlement development: Since the

official peace agreement between Canute the Great of England and Denmark and Conrad II ... from 1026 onwards, the bishop's see is occupied in an unbroken succession, which would be unthinkable without [the presence of] a cathedral. [The existence of an] *Episcopal church* and *royal court*, as well as a relevant infrastructure, *must inevitably be concluded* from the political negotiations and the wedding ceremony in autumn 1042 between the Norwegian-Danish king and the Saxon ducal house, and even more so from the negotiations between King Svend Estridsen and Archbishop Adalbert of Hamburg-Bremen that took place in winter 1052/1053. (Radtke 1999: 367–8; my translation, my emphasis)

It may be assumed that the above-mentioned political wedding in 1042 was the actual occasion for the much-debated negotiations between Archbishop Adalbrand Becelin and Magnus the Good of Norway-Denmark. On this wedding, Adam of Bremen (book 2, chap. 79) reports: 'In that conference King Magnus' sister [Wulfhild of Norway; Nrw. Ulvhild] was betrothed to the duke's [Bernhard II of Saxony] son, Ordulf.' If this event took place in Hedeby itself, as argued in the context of the episcopal church, this high-ranking political event certainly also required a royal manor. If we thus should even assume the existence of a royal palace (Ger. *Königspfalz*) in Hedeby, which – according to Radtke (1999: 367–8; cf. Radtke 2009b: 156) – indispensably corresponded to the inferred cathedral church on-site, the spatial separation between early towns and royal estates (see Section 5.1), characteristic of the earlier special economic zones, must have ceased in the late tenth or early eleventh century before the palace was finally moved to the *Graukloster* site in high medieval Slesvig (Radtke 1977, 2003). While for Sigtuna it is indeed assumed that such a royal manor existed from c.980 onwards – located prominently inside the town on the so-called *äldsta kungsgårdstomten* ('the oldest royal manor plot') (Tesch 2001a: 19–20) – in Hedeby there is even sparser evidence for such a potential royal manor than there is for its implied ecclesiastical architecture. Despite indications of the reorganisation and Christian transformation of Hedeby, which includes the church bell, the inhumation burial ground and the stone cemetery wall, alongside the Sigtuna plot layout, there is as yet no comparable evidence of a royal manor.[16] However, by including archaeological evidence from the harbour there is indeed proof of a late direct royal presence on-site: the elegant, 30-metre-long warship Hedeby wreck 1, which sunk off the town's harbour facilities after it was subject to a major fire (Crumlin-Pedersen 1997: 81–95; Kalmring 2010a: 114–19, 329–36), was considered to be nothing less than a royal vessel. Based on the elaborate execution and the extraordinarily large and high-quality planks used for the ship, Crumlin-Pedersen (1997: 93) argued that: 'The ship excavated in the harbour at Hedeby must therefore be described as "a longship of royal standard", designed for high-speed sailing and rowing in relatively protected waters.' The royal longship was built around 982 and, judging by the wear and some repairs, must have been in service for five to fifteen years before it finally sunk sometime between 990 and 1010 (Crumlin-Pedersen 1997: 94; Kalmring 2010a: 118). Based on its date of construction, it must originally have been commissioned by King Harald Bluetooth. While the date of construction would theoretically even allow for involvement in the reconquest of Hedeby in 983, its estimated loss between 990 and 1010 is more likely to coincide historically with the deployment of the royal fleet, the *Þingmannalið*, for the conquest of England during the reign of Sven Forkbeard, which was based both in London and in Hedeby (*The Saga of the Jómsvíkings*, chap. 50; cf. Radtke 2009b: 153; Kalmring 2010a: 54). Previously, the presence of a royal warship in Hedeby as a cosmopolitan trading centre only governed by a *comes* had to be considered rather an alien element. Such a direct royal presence would

---

[16] Here, a specific settlement area, about which we still know next to nothing, could hold the key for clarifying the question of a late Viking-age manor in Hedeby. It is the area along the shoreline, which must have been one of the most important settlement areas due to its proximity to the communication routes and maritime trade. Since this area is heavily water-saturated as a result of maritime transgression, neither geophysical nor metal-detector surveys were carried out (cf. Hilberg 2018: fig. 4).

be not so strange, however, if we accept a successful transformation from a special economic zone into an Ottonian-Christian *civitas*, which included not only an existent episcopal church within the limits of the town but even an 'indispensable' royal palace in late Viking-age Hedeby.[17]

---

[17] Indeed, the place of discovery of the royal longship could possibly indicate the presence of such a royal palace in in the immediate vicinity (cf. Note 16, this chapter).

11 Discussion: Hedeby's Abandonment and the Foundation of Slesvig

Finally, one might ask why Hedeby, after such a successful transformation as described in the previous chapter, which enabled the town to persist well into the eleventh century, was abandoned after all and finally relocated to present-day Slesvig. Despite comparable topographical conditions – just as Hedeby was located by the Haddeby Noor, Slesvig emerged by the (today silted) Holmer Noor – it is striking that the old town of Slesvig, which was delimited by its 12-hectare pocket-shaped peninsula on the northern shore of the inner Schlei fjord, was in fact only half the size of the urban area of Hedeby. Previously, three partly interdependent main hypotheses for the shift from Viking-age Hedeby to high medieval Slesvig had been put forward: (1) two subsequent devastating attacks in 1050 and 1066 recorded in the written sources; (2) the spatial integration of economical, administrative, and ecclesiastical functions, together with the assumption that the latter two already pre-existed at Slesvig and constituted a pull factor within a 'second wave of urbanisation'; and (3) the assumed preceding economic decline of Hedeby as an *emporium*, which had already commenced in the late tenth century (cf. Hilberg 2007: 189–90; 2016). In the following, these three main points shall be re-evaluated in the light of the implications carved out in Section 10.2.3.

Historically, the transition from Hedeby to Slesvig constitutes a major problem in source criticism: during the Viking Age, Old Norse sources refer to Hedeby as *Heiðabýr*, while contemporary continental sources speak of *Sliesthorp* or *Sliaswich* instead (cf. Kalmring 2010a: 41–2). This duality is best reflected in *The Chronicle of Æthelweard* (book 1, chap. 4) from c.974, which states: 'The old land of the Angles lies between the Saxons and Jutes, and has as its capital the town known in the Saxon language as Slesuuic [Slesvig], but by the Danes as Haithaby

[Hedeby].' To make matters worse, the same duality persisted even after the transition to medieval Slesvig (cf., e.g. Adam of Bremen, book 4, chap. 1). This circumstance makes it hard to discern whether the respective contemporary sources still refer to the Viking-age site south of or to the medieval site north of the Schlei fjord (cf. Radtke 2017). In addition, it is worth noting that Hedeby is referred to as 'Haithabu' in current German literature, which is due to an originally overly literal reading of its spelling 'hiþa:bu' on the Skarthi rune stone (DR 3; Jacobsen & Moltke 1941-2: 9–10). On the whole, this means that the historical records are precarious to use in the quest to discern the shift from Viking-age Hedeby to high medieval Slesvig. However, for the relocation itself, it may not be so far-fetched to seek an explanation in historical events after all: during the battle at the Lürschau/Lyrskov Heath (ON *Hlýrskógsheiði*) in 1043, when an Obotrite army under the command of the sons of the murdered prince Ratibor, was routed by King Magnus the Good upon its return from a vengeance campaign in southern Jutland (Adam of Bremen, book 2, chap. 79; *Heimskringla: The Saga of Magnús the Good*, chaps. 26-8; cf. Radtke 1992b: 71-7), the town of Hedeby apparently remained unharmed. This was, however, not the case when Harald Hardrada of Norway pillaged Hedeby (ON *Heiðabœr*) – 'the lord's town' (ON *bœjar þengils*) – during the succession dispute with King Svend Estridsen in c.1050, as described in Skaldic poetry (Anonymous [HSig], verse 2; Þórleikr fagri, verse 6; cf. Adam of Bremen, book 3, chap. 12), nor when during an Obotrite rebellion in 1066 the commander Blusso – Prince Gottschalk's brother-in-law – raided Hedeby (Lat. '*Sliaswig, civitas Saxonum Transalbianorum*'; 'Slesvig [Hedeby], town of the Nordalbingian Saxons') a final time (Adam of Bremen, book 3, chap. 51, scholium 81) – a raid that may have dealt Hedeby its death blow (cf. Rösch 2018: 280).[1] To date, this

---

[1] Differently, Radtke (2017), who recently suggested that the Norwegian attack from 1050 was directed at *both* the trading centre in Hedeby and a – presumed earlier, although archaeologically not verified (cf. Rösch 2018: 277-81) – royal and ecclesiastical Slesvig (Radtke 2017: 91; differently Radtke 1999: 367-8), which would have developed from after the turn of the millennium. Since in his view this attack had already triggered the transfer to Slesvig, this also implies that the Slavonic attack in

assumption seems to be consistent with the earliest archaeological evidence from Slesvig: in fact, the so far oldest timber dated from high medieval Slesvig – which belonged to a dwelling found in the *Schild* excavation – was still not older than 1071 (Vogel 1991: 269; cf. Rösch 2018: 240, 277–9 fig. 83). Similar dates apply to the minting of local Slesvig coins under royal Danish control, which, as the small finds from the recent *Hafengang 11* excavation demonstrated, only began in the mid-to-late 1070s (Moesgaard et al. 2016: 190).

There is no doubt that the relocation from Hedeby to Slesvig must have taken place during the reign of Svend Estridsen in the period 1047–76 – and judging by the evidence from early Slesvig, it is more likely to have happened only after the devastating attacks by Harald Hardrada and the Obotrites on Hedeby. However, this does not mean that the town of Slesvig was actually founded within the framework of a 'second wave of urbanisation' either (cf. Skre 2007: 45; Hillerdal 2009: 253), since this development had effectively already been completed with the Ottonian-Christian transformation of Hedeby (see Section 10.2.2). But if late Viking-age Hedeby had already housed both administerial and ecclesiastical functions, next to its original role as a superregional centre of commerce, what was the deciding pull factor that actually led to its relocation after all? Using Ribe as his point of origin, Søvsø (2020: 18, 237) argued that either a royal manor or a church (although not Ansgar's church from 850), or perhaps both, must already have existed on the Slesvig peninsula and have 'pulled' Hedeby towards Slesvig around 1050. In fact, this argument might well find support in the Slesvig rune stone (DR 6) found within the foundations of the Cathedral of St Peter at Slesvig where it

1066 would not have been directed at the already abandoned Hedeby but exclusively at Slesvig (Radtke 2017: 88–9). Radtke also claimed that, during the events leading up to the battle at the Lyrskov Heath, Magnus the Good still landed in Hedeby in 1043 but that the events of the previous year – the gathering between Archbishop Adalbrand-Bezelin and Magnus the Good in 1042 – could not have taken place anywhere other than Slesvig itself (Radtke 2017: 85). Central to Radtke's argument is his core hypothesis that 'a sharp breach in the ecclesiastical organisation, such as the relocation of the cathedral including its episcopal annexes from the southern to the northern shore of the Schlei fjord, would presumably have been recorded' (Radtke 2017: 88; my translation).

FIGURE 26 Slesvig, present-day northern Germany. Urnes-style rune stone DR 6 from c.1050 found within the foundations of the Cathedral of St Peter at Slesvig. (Photo ID: DMR-181075; National Museum of Denmark/NMS [Nationalmuseet], photo: R. Fortuna 2014 [CC-BY-SA]).

had been relocated to (Figure 26). It is ornamented in the Urnes style, which places it chronologically from the time around 1050 (Laur 2006: 37–8; cf. Jacobsen & Moltke 1941–2: 17–18; von Liliencron & Wimmer 1898). Although it is only possible to speculate on its original context, the vicinity to the cathedral as well as its date may suggest an affiliation with an early Christian cemetery at Slesvig. On the other hand – as the small Sigtrygg rune stone (DR 4) demonstrates, which was likewise found relocated in the redoubts of Gottorf castle and still belongs to the first third of the tenth century – an original provenance of the Slesvig rune stone (DR 6) from Hedeby itself cannot be completely ruled out either (Imer 2016: 154–8; cf. von Liliencron 1888; Wimmer 1892: 18–35; Jacobsen & Moltke 1941–2: 14–15). In fact, neither can the chronological dating for the shift of Ribe to the western side of the river and towards the cathedral be used as an argument for an earlier relocation of Hedeby, that is, already during the period subsequent to the Norwegian attack in 1050. On closer inspection, with regard to the relocation of Ribe, Søvsø (2020: 219) actually stated that 'The town [of Ribe] had thus moved to the church, and this event or process can be dated to AD 1050±10 years when the radiocarbon datings are considered along with the buried finds from the sealed settlement horizon', which theoretically even leaves a chronological margin for the generally accepted relocation of Hedeby after the Slavonic attack in 1066. Nonetheless, apart from chronological considerations, the hypothesis that administrative and ecclesiastical structures already pre-existed in Slesvig remains central to this argument, which seems to contradict the assumption that these functions already existed in late Viking-age Hedeby. But if, as stated in Section 10.2.2, Hedeby had indeed successfully undergone a 'second wave of urbanisation' – and was thus able to endure for another whole century – are there further 'waves' of urban development that could offer an explanation for the shift to high medieval Slesvig?

For the period around 1050, Søvsø (2020: 255) proposed a fusion between the old *emporia* model and the new *civitates* model as two distinct roots to urban life in southern Scandinavia – that is, a fusion of trade and crafts (*emporia*) with religious and administrative functions (*civitates*). In fact, parallel to the presumed fusion of functions that prompted the shift from Hedeby to Slesvig, a radical reorganisation of urban development is also tangible in other parts of the Danish realm (cf. Gelting 2016: 215) – not only in Ribe (Søvsø 2020: 18) but even in Lund (Carelli 2012: 108–10). It is thus hardly surprising that readjustments to urban networks during the late tenth and early eleventh century can also be observed in England (Astill 2000: 41, 262):

> The intention, stated in Æthelstan's laws, to concentrate the marketing, minting and defensive fortifications in one place was, no doubt, close to being fulfilled. *But* there were still parts in the country ... where these three activities took place in separate locations, reflecting perhaps the low level of economic differentiation which had taken place between towns, burhs and

centres of authority in these regions. That the relocation of some seats into the larger towns occurred only in the eleventh century perhaps indicates how extended was this centralising, urban movement *which was still incomplete at the Norman Conquest* [in the autumn of 1066]. (Astill 2000: 42; my emphasis)

Even during the following period 1050–1100/50, Christopher Loveluck argued for 'different urban worlds' and differentiated between major commercial ports such as London and fiscal and governmental administrative towns such as Winchester, which existed alongside a wide variety of smaller towns that acted as central places for regional land-based territories. It was not until the end of the twelfth century that London had accrued the administrative and fiscal functions from Winchester (Loveluck 2018; 2013: 325–30, esp. 329). In light of the English conditions, one might ask if further impulses might not have come from Continental Europe but also included traits from late Saxon towns in pre-Conquest England, that is, in the wake of the Anglo-Scandinavian 'North Sea Empire' and due to the close contacts that developed across the North Sea during this period.[2] In high medieval Slesvig, prior to the establishment of the late medieval marketplace in the first half of the thirteenth century, such an 'incomplete' development stage – or rather transitional phase – could include the harbour market that consisted, next to the jetties, of a double-sized and 20-metre-wide embankment which housed a custom house and also served as a platform for public trade (Rösch 2018: 255–60 fig. 92;

---

[2] While the North Sea Empire itself collapsed with Canute's death in 1035, the Danish–English link prevailed with the regencies of Canute's sons Harold Harefoot (†1040) and Harthacnut (†1042) (Lund 1995: 221–6; Skovgaard-Petersen 2003: 176–8; Sawyer 2004: 295–7). But even with their deaths and the end of direct English rule, the claim to the English throne did not end: after Harald Hardrada's death at the Battle of Stamford Bridge in 1066, Svend Estridsen turned his attention towards England, having a legitimate claim to the throne himself (cf. Sonne 2016: 31–2, 34–7). In 1069, he supported an invasion fleet belonging to his brother Asbjørn, which also included his own sons and later Danish kings Harald Hen and Canute the Holy (Lund 1983, 2005). However, this invasion only briefly managed to capture the town of York before it had to withdraw the following year. A second, likewise unsuccessful invasion led by Canute the Holy and Jarl Håkon was launched as late as 1075 (Christensen 1981).

2019: 272–3 fig. 8). However, are these mere adjustments of *urbanity* (see Chapter 2, Note 2) – instead of true 'waves of urbanisation' – really enough to account for the shift of the presumed late Viking-age *civitas* Hedeby to high medieval Slesvig?

Are reasons instead to be found in a previous economic decline of the late tenth- or early eleventh-century *civitas* of Hedeby (cf. Radtke 2009b: 151–4), or did such a supposed loss of commercial significance only occur with the shift to high medieval Slesvig in 1066/70, as indicated by the reduction of the urban area by half? On this matter, Hilberg's recently published comprehensive monograph – which compiles and presents the numerous metal-detector finds from Hedeby's plough zone – provides important new clues for the discussion on the final developments in Hedeby and its ultimate abandonment (Hilberg 2022; cf. Hilberg 2018). So far, the archaeological evidence from the harbour of Hedeby, as the economic heart of an active trading town, merely indicates continued building activity after the sinking of the royal longship Hedeby wreck 1 in the years 990–1010. This continued development is further emphasised by the dating of the keel-laying of the heavy high-sea trading vessel Hedeby wreck 3 in 1023 (−0/+12) and, as the traces of repair confirm, its subsequent use over an unknown period of time prior to its loss. The most recent coin from Hedeby harbour, indicating continued commercial activity, was issued by Harthacnut and minted in 1035–42 (Kalmring 2010a: 124, 402). As far as the settlement area is concerned, and as mentioned previously (see Section 10.2.2), evidence of the earliest developments has been severely affected by the plough. The youngest dendrochronological date derived from a dug-in well dated to only 1020 (Eckstein & Schietzel 1977: fig. 11a). While the most recent coin from the settlement is a denarius of Count Herrmann of Jever, minted in 1060–86, at the same time there is also an observable decrease in coins that were issued after 1050 (Hilberg 2007: 202; 2016: 75 fig. 9). It was only recently, in 2017, however, that the excavations of the inhumation burial ground (Ger. *Flachgräberfeld*) revealed a hitherto unpublished Hauberg Svend Estridsen type 66/67 coin (further specification pending),[3] while another Hauberg Svend Estridsen type 67 coin had previously been found during settlement excavations in 1967 (Wiechmann 2007a: 220 cat. no. 133 plate 7:133). Remarkably, these issues have lately been reattributed from a mint in Viborg to one in Ribe and, more importantly, redated to 1065–70 instead of, as previously, to around 1040 (Bengtsson 2021; cf. Horsnæs 2020). This considerably increased the coin stock of very late issues at Hedeby, suggesting some degree of continuous trading activities up to the time around 1066.

To find the answer to the intricate problem of the reasons for the eventual relocation of Hedeby, it may be worthwhile to return to the written records: according to Gelting (2004), the ecclesiastical breach between Hamburg-Bremen and Sven Forkbeard in 987 was followed by a Danish orientation towards the archdiocese of Canterbury, which continued through the reigns of Canute the Great and Harthacnut. During the reign of Svend Estridsen, however, a rapprochement to the archbishopric of Hamburg-Bremen took place, and the ecclesiastical alignment once again changed from England to the Holy Roman Empire and Rome. An associated ease of the political tensions becomes apparent with the peace treaty between Conrad II and Canute around 1025, when the future emperor dropped his claim on the contested borderland north of the river Eider (see Section 10.2.2). However, the Holy Roman Empire's attempts to force the Danes to officially recognise the titular bishops Ekkehard and Rodulf failed, and the (English-) Danish church remained independent until well into the 1050s (Gelting 2004: 181, 187). It was not until the gathering between Archbishop Adalbert – which included Bishop Rodulf in his entourage – and Svend Estridsen in 1052/3 (Adam of Bremen, book 3, chap. 18) that the ecclesiastical supremacy of Hamburg-Bremen was officially recognised by an apparently canonical obedient Danish church. It has been suggested that the purpose for this sudden acknowledgement was part

---

[3] Kind advice from J.-C. Moesgaard, Stockholm, 21 September 2021.

of an initial attempt to create an independent Danish ecclesiastical province, detached from Hamburg-Bremen, through direct negotiations with the pontifex; this, however, did not happen until the elevation of Lund to the Scandinavian archdiocese in 1103/4 (Gelting 2004: 192–3). As part of the reorganisation of the Danish church, subsequent to the treaty between Adalbert and Svend, a subdivision of the Jutish diocese took place in 1059, when new dioceses were created in Aarhus, Viborg and *'Wendila'* (i.e. the district of Vendsyssel), alongside the initial one in Ribe (Gelting 2004: 188–91). This also included a reinstated diocese in *'Sliaswig'* with the instalment of Bishop Ratolf (Adam of Bremen, book 4, chap. 3). Is it possible that Hedeby's relocation to Slesvig was part of Svend Estridsen's church-political arbitration and his decision to realign with Hamburg-Bremen and Rome in 1059 – a realignment which consequently led to the construction of a cathedral on the northern shore of the inner Schlei fjord,[4] after a devastating Norwegian attack on Hedeby in 1050 and as witnessed by the Urnes-style rune stone DR 6 in Slesvig, which is stylistically likewise dated around 1050? In other words, is it conceivable that the existence of a relocated Roman Catholic episcopal church not only formed the origins of Slesvig but also was the decisive pull factor for the relocation of an already faltering Hedeby after the Norwegian raid in 1050 – a relocated church which resulted in a gradual shift to the new (administrative-) ecclesiastical centre from 1059 at Slesvig, which was without alternative after the final pillage of Hedeby in 1066? While such a scenario may offer a tentative, conclusive synthesis to our problem, it seems that definitive answers to these questions can only be found through future studies on the genesis and development of high medieval Slesvig (e.g. Jahnke 2006).

---

[4] By way of explanation, was it about a relocation from Hedeby to Slesvig within a true 'sharp breach in the ecclesiastical organisation' (Radtke 2017: 88; cf. Note 1, this chapter), which indeed remained unrecorded in the historiography of Hamburg-Bremen due to this unwelcome interim period during the Danish liaison with the archdiocese of Canterbury? Or was this relocation even considered to be about a breach, since Slesvig was perhaps not considered to be a new town but rather a continuation of an urban centre that had been, and continued to be, identified by its double name Hedeby/Slesvig in the eyes of its contemporaries?

12 Summary and Conclusions

After a brief introduction to the topic and its objectives (see Chapter 1), *Towns and Commerce in Viking-Age Scandinavia* opened with a general orientation on the debate about terminology and its associated concepts that have been proposed – distinct from the definitions formulated by historians – in order to try to capture the specific nature of Viking-age urbanisation on the eve of the rise of the classical medieval town (see Chapter 2). With this aim, to date two main research avenues have been pursued: on the one hand, through the initial attempt to find an appropriate definition for the phenomenon, along with a corresponding conceptual designation (the *what* – a focus on the result), and, on the other, through the later application of central place and network theory, focussing on the interconnectivity of Viking-age towns as ports for maritime trade and urban production (the *how* – a focus on the process). Since each concept or theory is associated with a number of different aspects of Viking-age urbanisation, urbanism and urbanity, this review simultaneously introduces the reader to the most distinctive features of Viking-age towns. This aim of this volume, however, is not merely an attempt to recapitulate the current debate but above all to address the hitherto unanswered core problem of *why* Viking-age towns emerged. In this way, the *focus* is shifted towards their distinct economic and societal *purpose* for Viking-age society at that particular point of development in European history.

In order to identify and therefore assess the distinct novelty and otherness of the emerging urban communities in the Scandinavian heartlands, the subsequent two chapters provided some background on both everyday living and the omnipresent entanglement of power, religion and economy. The Viking world itself (see Chapter 3) was still deeply rooted in the traditions of the Iron Age and, as a traditional rural and agricultural society, consisted mainly of single farmsteads or small villages. Even the notion of one uniform Viking world can be questioned given the many local variations in dialects as well as funerary, building and household utensil traditions. These indicators of social seclusion and relative isolation suggest that, quite contrary to what is portrayed in the media and popular culture, the vast majority of individuals probably spent most of their lives in the rural local contexts that they were born into, rather than on Viking expeditions or raids. Chapter 4 then introduced some of the most important central places in Scandinavia as focal points for both power and cult, which also displayed profound links to Iron Age predecessors: the example of Gamla Uppsala demonstrates that it not only was the religious centre of the Viking world but also quite deliberately served as part of the political power strategy of a ruling dynasty. Moreover, religious festivals at these traditional centres of power and cult went hand in hand with *things* (assemblies) as the main legal and administrative institutions in Viking-age and medieval Scandinavia. In societies with few or no urban centres, regular assemblies were of particular importance for the inhabitants of the various, often sparsely populated administrative districts – as gatherings, these events simultaneously offered a rare opportunity for local market exchange, not entirely dissimilar to the contemporary Carolingian annual fairs of Continental Europe. Parallel to these dynastical seats of Scandinavian royal dynasties themselves, many manorial estates may also have served as periodical residences for itinerant kings, even in Northern Europe. Elsewhere, such itinerant kingdoms are considered a characteristic feature of societies with rudimentary state structures only. Manorial estates such as Tissø seem to have imitated Carolingian imperial palace architecture and, under pagan auspices, also comprised a clear ritual component. It had been suggested that such manors, as possible assembly sites, even had judicial dimensions. Similar to the traditional centres of power and cult, the periodical attendance at such manorial estates, with a corresponding retinue, thus provided an opportunity not only for ritual acts and assemblies but even for holding seasonal fairs. However, this type of exchange of goods, offered at individual and seasonal fairs, had little in common with the daily and long-distance market trade evidenced by the archaeology of the emerging Viking-age towns. The evolving urban communities, with their comparatively vast and multi-ethnic populations and an enduring engagement in long-distance trade, were by no means an integral part of the rural, agrarian Viking-age world and its existing power structures.

The following chapter (Chapter 5) therefore sought to analyse whether and – if that were the case – how these emerging towns were embedded in the existing societal frameworks. One mutual aspect of the Scandinavian Viking-age towns seems to be that royal manors (and pagan or ecclesial presence) were not found within the boundaries of the towns themselves. Rather, they seem to have constituted religious and political neutral zones. This, however, does not mean that royal administration was totally absent or far away: apart from the historically documented presence of bailiffs as royal representatives in Viking-age towns, the royal estates themselves – although always in a controlling position close by – maintained a certain distance from these religious and political neutral zones. By broadening the topographical perspective, it becomes evident that these communities were not even spatially a part of the surrounding societal framework but merely coexisted on the fringes of traditional society; they literally emerged in no man's land, at the border zones between different natural landscapes, transport zones or ethnic and political entities. In the Scandinavian *seascape*, waterways were essential for any long-distance trade in bulk commodities between Viking-age towns. Hence, it is no coincidence that the introduction of the sail in the North falls exactly in the time of transition between the late Vendel/Merovingian period and the earliest Viking Age. The role of a corresponding maritime infrastructure must therefore be understood as an essential prerequisite for Viking-age urbanisation (see Chapter 6). As early as the sixth or seventh century, landing sites at protected natural harbours – often merely separated by a day's row – formed a dense network across the Baltic Sea. They developed under the influence of local maritime communities and long-distance merchants and, alongside other functions, often served as beach markets and thus as an integral part of everyday society. It seems that even the few emerging Viking-age towns originated from such ordinary, seasonal beach markets and not from some royal greenfield foundations. But what was the spark that transformed only a handful of those many landing sites into proper Viking-age towns? The historical account of the raid on Reric/Groß Strömkendorf in 808 (and the subsequent relocation of its merchants to Hedeby for the sake of the taxes, that is, for a share of the trading profits) strikingly illustrates the causes: it demonstrates that this spark was not just an act of commercial policies but a matter of royal power claiming authority over the most successful trading places. And while competitor sites could even be obliterated in the process, others were deliberately promoted and in this way developed into fully fledged Viking-age towns.

With this extension of the royal regalia rights in terms of taxation and control of long-distance trade, it must be assumed that Viking-age towns even received a very specific legal status, which elevated them beyond the framework of ordinary society (see Chapter 7). Even though there are obviously no indigenous contemporary written sources on this matter, the archaeological record combined with external and/or later indigenous historical sources makes it possible to make assumptions about the jurisdiction and taxation in these emerging towns. The symbolic boundary ditches that are found at all the major *vici* around the North Sea not only separated them legally from the jurisdiction of the surrounding countryside but also seem to have marked the existence of a 'peace of the town' within. Against this background, even sea barriers that surrounded the harbour basins of Viking-age towns – including chains or boom barriers fashioned after antique and East Roman prototypes – should be reassessed in their function as legal and customs boundaries rather than as purely defensive measures. Contemporary written records suggest that, on the Continent, parts of the Roman harbour administration had survived the 'Dark Ages' and that in the Frankish and

Anglo-Saxon world shipping duties were still extracted on a regular basis according to antique models. For Viking-age Scandinavia itself, indications of extracted shipping duties and existing port jurisdictions can be deduced from Icelandic sagas as well as later law codes. The actual administration of the Viking-age towns was the responsibility of historically well-documented regal officials who, as *comites* or *praefecti vici*, represented the royal power on-site. Once again, their counterparts can be traced to major *emporia* on both sides of the English Channel. Unfortunately, apart from being mentioned, the range of their official duties is not visible in the source material. However, older Merovingian sources suggest a rather large set of duties such as administration, legislation and defence. In their capacity as royal administrators, these representatives probably acted as tax officials, extracting tariffs for the king's treasury.

Chapter 8 sought to explore whether there were any other particularities, beyond the mere extraction of custom duties by appointed royal bailiffs in return for the provision of the 'peace of the town', that constituted the distinct novelty and otherness of the emerging Viking-age towns. At frontier trading places, such as Quentovic and Dorestad, the Carolingian Empire attempted to confine the commodity circle to domestic commerce through levies, such as the market tithe, and thus to limit exports. At the same time, Scandinavian rulers and their delegations actively tried to come to commercial agreements and personally campaigned for trade peace with the Carolingian and Byzantine imperial courts in order to attract foreign merchants and gain access to desirable markets. In addition, Scandinavian sovereigns even sought to protect long-distance merchants on their voyages through their realms by issuing writs of protection and, against the payment of a fee, by granting direct royal protection for foreigners on-site. Violations of this type of protection, through piracy or a breach of the market peace, were regarded as felonies against the king himself, who personally ensured the pursuit of the culprits. In this way, the Scandinavian sovereigns prepared the necessary framework to attract foreign merchants, who, since they operated far beyond their own legal spheres, would have widely lacked legal protection during their mercantile expeditions. At the same time, however, the active commercial policy and openness towards foreign merchants in these cosmopolitan Viking-age towns seem to have had quite rigid boundaries, since aliens otherwise appear to have been generally considered as potential threats to the prevailing public order. In Constantinople, where the number of foreign merchants at any given time was regulated, this meant that they had to apply for temporary residency and were only allowed to dwell in specified quarters during their stays. Analogously, the existence of such hostels for foreign merchants in the Frankish and Anglo-Saxon world has been discussed. Middle Anglo-Saxon–period legal texts suggest that foreign merchants were generally not expected to leave the *emporia* and travel the countryside on their own. To avoid being slain on the spot, they had to announce such exploits to the king's reeve in advance, and during their journeys they had to warn locals of their approach, either by shouting or by blowing a horn. While similar historical records do not exist for Scandinavia, the archaeological evidence from burial grounds in Viking-age towns, such as Birka and Kaupang, suggests similar settings: there, the inhumation burial customs, identified as a distinctly foreign element, are segregated from the cremation burials of the locals. In the case of Birka, the archaeological evidence demonstrates that, even in death, strangers were bound exclusively to the boundaries of the town. It would seem that in Viking-age towns – outside the jurisdiction of everyday society – foreign merchants were very welcome and even sought-after, but at the same time, as elsewhere, comparable limiting regulations must have been in place.

While the detachment of Viking towns from the surrounding society was obviously deliberate, the degree of interdependency between the towns and their hinterlands – as well as their limited footprints on their surroundings – remains controversial (see Chapter 9). However, the town dwellers would certainly not have been able to prevail without daily wagonloads of food and fuel from the surrounding countryside. The evidence from Birka's hinterland also provides a glimpse of another essential function of these towns: it seems as though the urban workshops introduced expert know-how to their surroundings by employing local apprentices who would have been indispensable to any foreign master crafter. While the latter were bound to the limits of the towns, the local apprentices could eventually introduce learned skills and technologies to the hinterland, contributing to the diffusion of innovation within rural Viking-age society. By examining the lordly 'parasitic interest in the urban phenomenon' as attested for the Carolingian realm, with regard to the Viking world, this interest hence appears to have been twofold: on the one hand, interest certainly lay in the royal extraction of added value from trade as a steady source of income, but on the other hand, it also lay in the controlled introduction of innovation to the surrounding society in the respective dominions. On a more general level, the characteristics of Viking-age towns and their settings have much in common with the modern concept of 'special economic zones' in economics. Today, the concept of special economic zones is often linked to developing countries. Such zones are located within restricted geographical areas, created to stimulate trade through legal privileges and more liberal rules for business but also with the intention of promoting technological progress and serving as catalysts for the diffusion of innovation to the respective host countries. However, in order to truly be able to make such a comparison, is it really possible to state that Viking-age Scandinavia – with Viking-age towns as some kind of special economic zones of their time – only held a peripheral geographical and economic position? A closer look at the contemporary conditions on the Continent shows that the ninth-century Carolingian Empire had just undergone a major reorganisation of its manorial production. This resulted in increased agricultural production as well as increased craft and industrial manufacture, which generated surpluses that stimulated both intra-regional and long-distance trade. While the import of cutting-edge luxury items from Continental European workshops into Scandinavia certainly had already been practised prior to the Viking Age – via networks of landing sites and their corresponding beach markets – the developments of the Carolingian Empire in the ninth century subsequently made it possible for bulk commodities to reach the Viking-age towns of Scandinavia. And indeed, with wheel-turned pottery, the manufacture of mixed-glass vessels, 'Warendorf'-type houses, treadle looms or water mills, there is even evidence of real innovations, in the sense of an active knowledge transfer, which were first introduced to the Viking-age towns and only eventually diffused into the surrounding everyday society.

With the Viking-age towns firmly established as the special economic zones of their time, Chapter 10 sought to pursue the inherently dynamic nature of these institutions. In order to finally recognise the considerable chronological depth of some 250 years in the development of Viking-age towns – instead of trying to uncover some 'fixed' town plans as in the past – the importance of studying these urban entities through high-resolving time slices has been emphasised recently. By way of example, following the initial inception phase described in detail, this volume discusses two further important caesuras in the urban development which occurred towards the end of the ninth and at the end of the tenth century. The second half of the ninth century saw the decline or abandonment of the North Sea *emporia* due to a changing emphasis on state formation and the fall of the Carolingian Empire. The latter even led to the end of the so-called second-level trading places in the Baltic Sea area, which in turn coincided with a major silver crisis in the Rus' – possibly caused by the destruction of the trading sites in the southern hinterlands of the Gulf of Finland prior to the arrival of the Rurikids. This disruption to the eastern trade networks even caused the influx of Islamic silver to stagnate in certain parts of the Baltic Sea. In Hedeby, this crisis caused a hiatus in the minting of early Nordic coins, and for Birka it meant that the trade networks had to be realigned. The massive development of Hedeby's harbour after 886, however, illustrates a swift and strong determination to overcome this crisis. The late ninth-century account of Wulfstan's voyage also provides evidence for early consortia of self-organising merchants from around that time, which could have been a way to meet the perils of piracy caused by the economic crisis. The second caesura, a century later, dealt with a more severe crisis and represented, rather than a mere turning point, a clear break. This time, however, it was not caused by external factors but rather by a dawning ideological conflict between a consolidating new 'national' royal power and the increasingly autonomous urban population in the Viking-age towns. In Birka, this conflict seems to have been manifested both through a deliberate pagan expression directed against a royal power, which increasingly legitimised itself through Christianity, and through a naval attack on the so-called Garrison in the mid-970s, possibly instigated and commanded by the king himself. Further evidence for this final crisis is suggested by the massive, disproportionate increase in burials dated to 965–90, which coincided with Birka's assumed fall around 975. While Ribe in the long run experienced an economic downfall in the late ninth-century– due to its affinity with the failing North Sea emporia and/or its competitive relationship with Hedeby (from which Ribe did not fully recover before the twelfth century) – Kaupang ceased to exist at the same time as Birka, around 970. According to economic theory, at the time of their demise Viking-age towns – special economic zones as they were – had paved the way for more comprehensive reforms to commercial policies, which ultimately triggered the so-called second wave of urbanisation in Scandinavia. In spite of this, however, the town of Hedeby managed to persist for almost an entire century longer, until c.1066 – a fact which, against this background, is of particular importance and has not been adequately taken into account so far.

Previously, it had been suggested that Hedeby also experienced an economic decline in the late tenth century. Yet, apart from the fact that Birka was not abandoned due to some *economic* decline either, Hedeby actually seems to have continued to flourish. However, archaeological attempts to detail the development that allowed Hedeby's unparalleled continuance are impeded by modern agricultural use and ploughing, which continued until the 1970s and largely destroyed its most recent structural remains. Through a widened perspective, though, we can observe that around 980 – that is, with the addition of the Kovirke line of defence to the Danevirke – Hedeby, for the first time in its existence, fell behind the border fortifications. This development not only dramatically concluded its long-standing status as a special economic zone in a political no man's land but even emphasises the fact that it was incorporated into a territorial realm and thus turned into a true Danish town. Further clues regarding late Viking-age Hedeby's transformation may be found through a comparison with the town plots of its contemporary Sigtuna. There, elongated plots included the proprietors' hall at the rear, a residential building and a granary/multifunctional building in the middle, as well as a small workshop closest to the main street. Geophysical surveys suggest that this pattern – particularly the small workshops along a main street but also the elongated town plots – may have been present in Hedeby as well, thus providing another key to Hedeby's continued existence. Interestingly, the spatial reorganisation of the urban space in Hedeby, which can be dated to the second half of the ninth or first half of the tenth century, seems to predate the development of eleventh-century Sigtuna. This means that rather than being inspired by Sigtuna, the reverse seems to be the case. The original influences for the novel town plots in Hedeby, in turn, probably came from Continental Europe, in this case ninth-century Flanders. The suggested major structural and spatial reorganisation of Hedeby roughly coincided with the Ottonian dominance over the town after 934/47, which would imply that the Danes encountered quite a different Hedeby after their final recapture of the town in 983, perhaps in the shape of an Ottonian-Christian *civitas*. In fact, despite the generally poor preservation conditions for tenth- or eleventh-century Hedeby, it is possible to identify some historical and archaeological clues for an existing novel ecclesiastical (diocese of 948; bronze bell from the harbour; Christian cemetery requiring chapel/church) and royal (political wedding of 1042; 'longship of royal standard') presence within the limits of the late Viking-age town itself.

The penultimate chapter (Chapter 11) discussed why Hedeby, despite its suggested successful transformation into a *civitas*, was finally relocated across the inner Schlei fjord to present-day Slesvig after all. Was it due to the obvious, historically recorded raids on Hedeby in 1050 and 1066, or perhaps because of a putative economic downfall in the late tenth or early eleventh century – as indicated by the fact that the urban area of later Slesvig comprised only half the area of the former Hedeby? The proposed presence of an episcopal church and royal court within an already transformed Christian Ottonian Hedeby could explain how it endured beyond 970/5 but conflicts with earlier ideas, which suggested that early ecclesiastical and administrative structures existed in the location of the later Slesvig and that they acted as decisive pull factors for Hedeby's relocation within some 'second wave of urbanisation'. This leads to questions about whether the final demise actually depended on other factors influencing the late urban development, perhaps triggered by Anglo-Saxon impulses in the aftermath of the Danish 'North Sea Empire'? Or was it dependent on the later ecclesiastical and political rapprochement to Hamburg-Bremen and Rome, resulting in a re-erected diocese in 1059? A hypothesis that could offer a tentative conclusive synthesis would be that an earlier, Ottonian-period episcopal church was relocated from Hedeby to Slesvig in the context of the latter events – a scenario which may find chronological support in the Norwegian raid on Hedeby in 1050 and the presence of a rune stone in Slesvig from around 1050. It would imply that, from 1059, this new cathedral in Slesvig could have attracted the population of an – in consequence of the events in 1050 – already faltering Hedeby to this new location, who, after the final attack in 1066, remained without an alternative. For the time being, however, the ultimate reasons and the closer time frame of the final relocation of Hedeby to Slesvig during the reign of Svend Estridsen, during the period between 1050/66 and 1070, remain elusive due to a lack of hard reliable archaeological facts.

In conclusion, when the Viking Age is envisaged, it might be through fierce Viking raids, which spread terror throughout Europe, or through the courageous voyages of trade and discovery, which led to all the corners of the then known world and even beyond. Also, it might be through prominent archaeological sites such as Hedeby, Ribe, Kaupang and Birka with their remarkable archaeology and material culture. With regard to the latter, however, we must start to recognise that these Viking-age towns were not at all representative of Viking-age society. These novel urban environments without indigenous predecessors and with – for that time – vast and multi-ethnic populations were only allowed to blossom on the very fringes of everyday Viking-age society because they served a specific *purpose*. Through the promotion of royal sovereigns and the provision of appropriate frameworks, Viking-age towns were able to evolve from seasonal landing sites, integrate into long-distance trade networks and attract foreign merchants and crafters. In the Viking-age towns, for the first time in Scandinavian history, market trading was not just an occasional event; it formed the daily basis of operations. This way, they obviously safeguarded an influx of sought-after imported goods, which to a certain extent even penetrated into the surrounding countryside. Also, against the background that pre-Christian royal power was dependent on a perpetual influx of wealth to maintain the expected lavishness towards their retinues, royal patronage of Viking-age towns – in contrast to occasional raids, protection rackets or ransoms – generated a reliable income. This source of income was sustained by guaranteeing trading peace in exchange for the payment of custom duties and, in the case of Ribe and Hedeby, seigniorage from coinage issued on-site. Most importantly, however, as international trade hubs, they formed gateways for new technologies and innovations, which then diffused and contributed to the development of the hinterland. After almost a century of debating appropriate designations for the *results* of Viking-age urbanisation (the *what*), followed by decades of meticulous mapping of the outcome of the Viking-age town's wide-ranging economic networks, that is, putting the focus on the *process* of interconnectivity (the *how*), we are finally able to reach the core of the reversed golden circle model and embark on providing initial answers to the central question of the *why* and thus to the actual *purpose* of Viking-age towns. Through the evidence presented in this volume, it is possible to conclude that Viking-age towns served very much the purpose of special economic zones of their time. Even the growing understanding that Viking-age towns were by no means static during their existence, but on the contrary were very dynamic entities, corresponds to the characteristics ascribed to modern special economic zones, namely that they are subject to permanent change, adjustment and expansion. And just like modern special economic zones, the Viking-age towns of Birka and Kaupang were disbanded and disappeared by the late tenth century, after having fulfilled their purpose for their respective political economies towards more comprehensive forms of commercial policy. While around the same time, Ribe apparently suffered a severe economic blow through the loss of this very function, only Hedeby managed to persist for another century – a fact that demands further explanation. It appears as though Hedeby must have pursued a successful transformation that resulted in it becoming the first fully fledged Danish medieval town, which, for the moment, is still very elusive archaeologically. The incentive for its ultimate relocation to the nearby town of Slesvig, during the reign of Svend Estridsen (1047–76) after attacks in 1050 and 1066, remains a pivotal research avenue to pursue and is particularly dependent on further efforts in the urban archaeology of the earliest Slesvig.

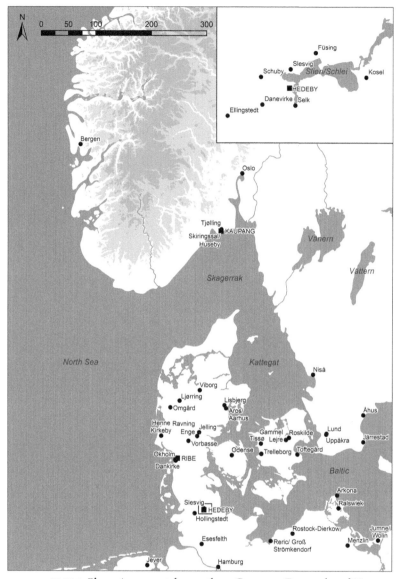

MAP 2 Places in present-day northern Germany, Denmark and Norway mentioned in the text (S. Kalmring).

SUMMARY AND CONCLUSIONS 211

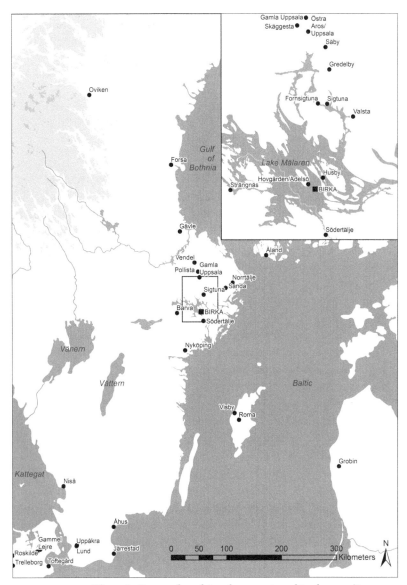

MAP 3 Places in Denmark and Sweden mentioned in the text (S. Kalmring).

References

PRIMARY SOURCES

Adam of Bremen: *History of the Archbishops of Hamburg-Bremen*, trans. F. J. Tschan. New York: Columbia University Press, 2002.

Alcuin: *Alcvini sive Albini epistolae*, ed. E. Dümmler. Monumenta Germaniae Historica. Epistolae (in quart) 4: 2. Epistolae Karolini aevi (II): 1–481. Berlin: Weidmann, 1895.

The Anglo-Saxon Chronicle: ed. and trans. M. Swanton. New York: Routledge, 1998.

Annales Bertiniani: *The Annals of St-Bertin*, trans. J. L. Nelson. Ninth-Century Histories 1. Manchester Medieval Sources. Manchester: Manchester University Press, 1991.

Annales Vedastini: *Annales Vedastini*. In *Annales Xantenses et Annales Vedastini*, ed. B. von Simson. Monumenta Germaniae Historica. Scriptores rerum Germanicarum in usum scholarum separatim editi 12: 40–82. Hannover: Hahn, 1909.

Annales Xantenses: *Annales Xantenses qui dicuntur*. In *Annales Xantenses et Annales Vedastini*, ed. B. von Simson. Monumenta Germaniae Historica. Scriptores rerum Germanicarum in usum scholarum separatim editi 12: 1–39. Hannover: Hahn, 1909.

The Annals of Fulda: trans. T. Reuter. Ninth-Century Histories 2. Manchester Medieval Source Series. Manchester: Manchester University Press, 1992.

Anonymous (HSig): *Lausavísur* from *Haralds saga Sigurðarsonar*. In K. E. Gade (ed.), *Skaldic Poetry of the Scandinavian Middle Ages, Vol. 2: Poetry from the Kings' Sagas: From c. 1035 to c. 1300*: 815–23. Turnhout: Brepols, 2009.

Bede: *Ecclesiastical History of the English People*, trans. L. Sherley-Price, rev. R. E. Latham. Penguin Classics. London: Penguin, 1990.

Bjarnar saga Hítdœlakappa: *Saga of Bjorn, Champion of the Hitardale People*, trans. A. Finlay. Hisarlik Press: Enfield Lock, 2000.

The Book of the Eparch: *To Eparchikon vivlion = The book of the Eparch = Le livre du préfet*, ed. and trans. I. Dujčev, J. Nicole & E. Hanson Freshfield. Collected Studies B1. London: Variorum Reprints, 1970.

Cassiodorus: *Variae*, trans. S. J. B. Barnish. Liverpool: Liverpool University Press, 1992.
The Chronicle of Æthelweard: *Chronicon Æthelweardi*, ed. and trans. A. Campbell. Nelson's Medieval Texts. London: Thomas Nelson, 1962.
Codex Diplomaticus: *Codex Diplomaticus Aevi Saxonic*. Tomus IV, ed. J. M. Kemble. London: Sumptibus Societatis, 1846.
Diplomata Belgica: *Diplomata Belgica ante annum millesimum centesimum scripta*, ed. M. Gysseling & A. C. F. Koch. Bouwstoffen en studien voor de geschiedenis en de lexicografie van het Niederlande 1. Brussels: Belgisch Inter-Universitair Centrum voor Neerlandistiek, 1950.
Egil's Saga: trans. B. Scudder. In *The Sagas of the Icelanders*: 3–184. New York: Penguin Books, 2001.
Færeyinga Saga: *The Tale of Thrond of Gate, Commonly Called Færeyinga Saga*, trans. F. York Powell. Northern Library 2. London: David Nutt, 1896.
Formulae Imperiales e curia Ludovici Pii: ed. K. Zeumer. Monumenta Germaniae Historica. Leges, Formulae Merovingici et Karolini aevi 1: 285–327. Hannover: Hahn, 1886.
Gesta abbatum Fontanellensium: Gesta sanctorum patrum Fontanellensis coenobii, ed. F. Lohier & J. Laporte. Paris: Société de l'histoire de Normandie, 1936.
Gisli Sursson's Saga: trans. M. S. Regal. In *The Sagas of the Icelanders. A Selection*: 496–557. New York: Penguin Books, 2000.
Heimskringla: Snorri Sturluson, *Heimskringla: History of the Kings of Norway*, trans. L. M. Hollander. Austin: University of Texas Press, 2009.
Helmold of Bosau: *The Chronicle of the Slavs*, trans. F. J. Tschan. New York: Octagon Books, 1966.
Ibn Fadlān: *The Book of Ahmad ibn Fadlān. Ibn Fadlān and the Land of Darkness: Arab Travellers in the Far North*, trans. P. Lunde & C. Stone: 1–58. London: Penguin Classics, 2012.
Inquisitio de theloneis Raffelstettensis: ed. A. Boretius & V. Krause. Monumenta Germaniae Historica. Leges (in Folio) 2, Capitularia regum Francorum 2, XIX. Additamenta ad Capitularia regum Franciae orientalis, no. 253: 249–252. Hannover: Hahn, 1897.
Karoli Magni Capitularia: trans. A. Boretius. Monumenta Germaniae Historica. Capitularia regum Francorum 1: 44–186. Hannover: Hahn, 1883.
Knýtlinga saga: *The History of the Kings of Denmark*, trans. H. Páulsson & P. Edwards. Odense: Odense University Press, 1986.
The Laws of Alfred: ed. and trans. F. L. Attenborough. *The Laws of the Earliest English Kings*: 62–93. Cambridge: Cambridge University Press, 1922.

The Laws of Hlothhere and Eadric: ed. and trans. F. L. Attenborough. In *The Laws of the Earliest English Kings*: 19–23. Cambridge: Cambridge University Press, 1922.

The Laws of Ine: ed. and trans. F. L. Attenborough. In *The Laws of the Earliest English Kings*: 36–61. Cambridge: Cambridge University Press, 1922.

Medieval Russian Laws: trans. G. Vernadsky. Records of Civilization: Sources and Studies XLI. New York: Columbia University Press, 1947.

Miracula Sancti Benedicti: *Miracula Sancti Benedicti auctore Adrevaldo Floriacensi*, ed. G. H. Pertz. Monumenta Germaniae Historica. Scriptores (in Folio) 15: 1. Supplementa tomorum I–XII, pars III: 474–97. Hannover: Hahn, 1887.

Miracula Sancti Wandregisili: ed. O. Holder-Egger. Monumenta Germaniae Historica. Scriptores (in Folio) 15: 1. Supplementa tomorum I–XII, pars III: 406–9. Hannover: Hahn, 1887.

Njáls saga: ed. and trans. R. Cook. London: Penguin Books, 2001.

Nuremberg Chronicle: Hartmann Schedel, *Liber Chronicarum cum figuris et imaginibus ab Inicio Mundi*. Nürnberg, 1493.

Olaus Magnus: *Description of the Northern Peoples: 1555*, Vol. 1, trans. P. Fisher & H. Higgens; ed. P. Foote. London: The Hakluyt Society, 1996.

The Old English Martyrology: ed. and trans. C. Rauer. Cambridge: Boydell & Brewer, 2013.

Rimbert: *Vita Ansgarii. Anskar: The Apostle of the North, 801–865*, trans. C. H. Robinson. London: Society for the Propagation of the Gospel in Foreign Parts, 1921.

Royal Frankish Annals: trans. B. W. Scholz & B. Rogers. *Carolingian Chronicles: Royal Frankish Annals & Nithard's Histories*. Ann Arbor, MI: Ann Arbor Paperback, 1972.

The Russian Primary Chronicle: Laurentian Text, ed. and trans. S. H. Cross & O. P. Sherbowitz-Wetzor. Cambridge, MA: The Medieval Academy of America, 1953.

The Saga of the Jómsvíkings: trans. L. M. Hollander. Austin: University of Texas Press, 1995.

The Saga of the People of Laxardal: trans. K. Kunz. In Ö. Thorsson (ed.), *The Sagas of the Icelanders: A Selection*: 270–421. New York: Penguin Books, 2000.

The Saga of the Sworn Brothers: trans. L. M. Hollander. *The Sagas of Kormák and The Sworn Brothers*: 83–176. Princeton, NJ: Princeton University Press, 1949.

The Saga of Yngvar the Traveller: trans. P. Tunstall. In G. Larsson (ed.), *Between East and West: Early Contacts between Scandinavia and the Caucasus*. Revita Archaeology and History: 21–6. Uppsala: Uppsala University, 2013.

Thietmar of Merseburg: *Ottonian Germany: The Chronicon of Thietmar of Merseburg*, ed. and trans. D. A. Warner. Manchester: Manchester University Press, 2001.

Vita Bernwardi: *Vita Bernwardi episcopi Hildesheimensis auctore Thangmaro*, trans. D. G. Waitz. Monumenta Germaniae Historica. Scriptores (in Folio) IV: Annales, chronica et historiae aevi Carolini et Saxonici: 754–82. Hannover: Hahn, 1841.

Vita Sancti Wilfrithi: *The Life of Bishop Wilfrid by Eddius Stephanus*, trans. B. Colgrave. Cambridge: Cambridge University Press, 1927.

Vitruvius: *The Ten Books on Architecture*, trans. M. H. Morgan. Cambridge, MA: Harvard University Press, 1914.

Widukind of Corvey: *Deeds of the Saxons*, ed. B. S. Bachrach & D. S. Bachrach. Washington, DC: The Catholic University of America Press, 2014.

Wisby Town-Law on Shipping: *Codex iuris Visbyensis urbici et maritime*. In *The Black Book of the Admiralty*, Vol. 4, ed. T. Twiss. Cambridge Library Collection: 385–414. Cambridge: Cambridge University Press, 2012.

Wulfstan's Report: ed. and trans. J. Bately Wulfstan's Voyage and His Description of Estland: The Text and the Language of the Text. In A. Englert & A. Trakadas (eds.), *Wulfstan's Voyages: The Baltic Sea Region in the Early Viking Age As Seen from Shipboard*. Maritime Culture of the North 2: 15–17 [14–18]. Roskilde: The Viking Ship Museum, 2009.

SECONDARY SOURCES

Abels, R. 2008. Household Men, Mercenaries and Vikings in Anglo-Saxon England. In J. France (ed.), *Mercenaries and Paid Men: The Mercenary Identity in the Middle Ages*. History of Warfare, Vol. 47: 143–65. Leiden: Brill.

Adam, H. 1996. *Das Zollwesen im fränkischen Reich und das spätkarolingische Wirtschaftsleben: Ein Überblick über Zoll, Handel und Verkehr im 9. Jahrhundert*. Vierteljahresschrift für Sozial- und Wirtschaftsgeschichte. Beihefte 126. Stuttgart: Franz Steiner Verlag.

Adamczyk, D. 2014. *Silber und Macht: Fernhandel, Tribute und die piastische Herrschaftsbildung in nordosteuropäischer Perspektive (800–1100)*. Deutsches Historisches Institut Warschau. Quellen und Studien 28. Wiesbaden: Harrassowitz Verlag.

Ahrens, J. & Meyer-Baudeck, A. 1995. Special Economic Zones: Shortcut or Roundabout Way towards Capitalism? *Intereconomics: Review of European Economic Policy* 30(2): 87–95.

Alkarp, M. & Price, N. 2005. Tempel av guld eller kyrka av trä? *Fornvännen* 100: 261–72.

Ambrosiani, B. 1957. Birka – Sigtuna – Stockholm. Ett diskussionsinlägg. *TOR* 3: 148–58.

Ambrosiani, B. 1988. *Birka*. Svenska kulturminnen 2. Stockholm: Riksantikvarieämbetet.

Ambrosiani, B. 1989. Vattenlederna och omlandet: Birka. *Marinarkeologisk Tidskrift* 3: 4–7.

Ambrosiani, B. 1992. What Is Birka? In B. Ambrosiani & H. Clarke (eds.), *Early Investigations and Future Plans*. Birka Studies 1: 11–22. Stockholm: Riksantikvarieämbetet & Statens Historiska Museer.

Ambrosiani, B. 1995. Excavations at Birka 1990. Interim Report. In B. Ambrosiani & H. Clarke (eds.), *Excavations in the Black Earth 1990*. Birka Studies 2: 19–48. Stockholm: The Birka Project.

Ambrosiani, B. 2001. The Birka Falcon. In B. Ambrosiani (ed.), *Excavations in the Black Earth 1990–1995. Eastern Connections Part One: The Falcon Motive*. Birka Studies 5: 11–27. Stockholm: The Birka Project.

Ambrosiani, B. 2002. Osten und Westen im Osteseehandel zur Wikingerzeit. In K. Brandt, M. Müller-Wille & C. Radtke (eds.), *Haithabu und die frühe Stadtentwicklung im nördlichen Europa*. Schriften des Archäologischen Landesmuseums 8: 339–48. Neumünster: Wachholtz.

Ambrosiani, B. 2013. *Stratigraphy, Vol. 1: Part One: The Site and the Shore. Part Two: The Bronze Caster's Workshop. Excavations in the Black Earth 1990–1995*. Birka Studies 9. Stockholm: The Birka Project.

Ambrosiani, B. 2021. *Stratigraphy, Vol. 2: Part Three: The Later Part of the Birka Period. Part Four: The Finds. Excavations in the Black Earth 1990–1995*. Birka Studies 10. Stockholm: The Birka Project.

Ambrosiani, B. & Erikson, B. G. 1996. *Vikingastaden lever upp igen i TV: smodell av 800-talets Birka!* Birka Vikingastaden 5. Stockholm: Sveriges Radios förlag.

Andersen, H. 2003. Den byggeglade konge. *Skalk* 2003(1): 20–7.

Andersen, H. H. 1998. *Danevirke og Kovirke: Arkæologiske undersøgelser 1861–1993*. Moesgård Museums Skrifter. Aarhus: Jysk Arkæologisk Selskab.

Andersen, H. H., Crabb, P. J & Madsen, H. J. 1971. *Århus Søndervold: En byarkæologisk undersøgelse*. Jysk Arkæologisk selskabs skrifter 9. Copenhagen: Gyldendal.

Andersson, H. 1979. *Urbaniseringsprocessen i det medeltida Sverige: En forskningsöversikt*. Medeltidsstaden 7. Gothenburg: Riksantikvarieämbetet & Statens historiska museer.

Andersson, T. 2000. s.v. 'Hundare'. In H. Beck, D. Geuenich & H. Steuer (eds.), *Reallexikon der Germanischen Altertumskunde* 15: 233–8. Berlin: De Gruyter.

Andersson, T. 2004. Svethiudh, det svenska rikets kärna. *Namn och bygd* 92: 5–18.

Andrén, A. 1983. Städer och kungamakt: en studie i Danmarks politiska geografi före 1230. *Scandia: Tidskrift för historisk forskning* 49(1): 31–76.

Andrén, A. 1985. *Den Urbana Scenen: Städer och Samhälle i det Medeltida Danmark*. Acta Archaeologica Lundensia. Series in 8°, No. 13. Bonn and Malmö: Rudolf Habelt and C. W. K. Glerup.

Andrews, P. 1997. *Excavations at Hamwic, Vol. 2: Excavations at Six Dials*. CBA Research Report No. 109. Southampton Archaeology Monographs 7. York: Council for British Archaeology.

Androshchuk, F. 2009. Vikings and Farmers: Some Remarks on the Social Interpretation of Swords and Long-Distance Contacts during the Viking Age. In L. Holmquist Olausson & M. Olausson (eds.), *The Martial Society: Aspects of Warriors, Fortifications and Social Change in Scandinavia*. Theses and Papers in Archaeology B11: 93–104. Stockholm: Stockholm University Archaeological Research Laboratory.

Androshchuk, F. 2014. *Viking Swords: Swords and Social Aspects of Weaponry in Viking Age Societies*. The Swedish History Museum Studies 23. Stockholm: Historiska museet.

Anspach, B. 2010. Die Bleifunde von Haithabu. In C. von Carnap-Bornheim (ed.), *Studien zu Haithabu und Füsing*. Ausgrabungen in Haithabu 16: 11–126. Neumünster: Wachholtz.

Arbman, H. 1937. *Schweden und das Karolingische Reich: Studien zu den Handelsverbindungen des 9. Jahrhunderts*. Stockholm: Bokförlags Aktiebolaget Thule.

Arbman, H. 1939. *Birka: Sveriges äldsta handelsstad*. Från forntid och medeltid 1. Stockholm: Bokförlags Aktiebolaget Thule.

Arbman, H. 1943. *Birka I: Die Gräber. Text*. Stockholm: Kungl. Vitterhets historie och antikvitets akademien.

Arbman, H. 1955. *Svear I Österviking*. Stockholm: Natur och Kultur.

Arbman, H. 1965. Birka, handelsstaden. In B. Arrhenius (ed.), *Ansgars Birka: En vikingatida handelsplats*: 19–26. Stockholm: Riksantikvarieämbetet och Statens historiska museum.

Arbman, H. 1973. s.v. 'Adelsö'. In H. Beck, H. Jankuhn, K. Ranke & R. Wenskus (eds.), *Reallexikon der Germanischen Altertumskunde* 1: 77–8. Berlin: De Gruyter.

Arents, U. & Eisenschmidt, S. 2010. *Die Gräber von Haithabu*. Ausgrabungen in Haithabu 15. Neumünster: Wachholtz.

Arne, T. J. 1914. Den Svenska runstenen från ön Berezanj utanför Dnjeprmynningen. Referat efter prof. Brauns redogörelse i Ryska arkeol. Kommissionens meddelanden 1907. *Fornvännen* 9: 44–8.

Arrhenius, B. 1976. Die ältesten Funde von Birka. *Prähistorische Zeitschrift* 51: 178–95.

Arrhenius, B. 1990. Utgrävningen av den östligaste storhögen på gravfältet Ormknös. RAÄ 111, Björkö, Adelsö sn, Uppland. *Laborativ Arkeologi* 4: 65–80.

Articus, R. 1982. Die Glocke von Haithabu. *Hamburgs Museen* 6: 10.

Arwidsson, G. (ed.) 1984. *Systematische Analysen der Gräberfunde. Birka. Untersuchungen und Studien II*: 1. Stockholm: Almqvist & Wiksell International.

Arwidsson, G. 1989. Die Münzen der Gräber von Birka: Ein Kommentar. In G. Arwidsson (ed.), *Systematische Analysen der Gräberfunde. Birka. Untersuchungen und Studien II* 3: 137–42. Stockholm: Almqvist & Wiksell International.

Ashby, S., Coutu, A. N. & Sindbæk, S. M. 2015. Urban Networks and Arctic Outlands: Craft Specialists and Reindeer Antler in Viking Towns. *European Journal of Archaeology* 18(4): 679–704.

Astill, G. 2000. General Survey 600–1300. In D. M. Palliser (ed.), *The Cambridge Urban History of Britain, Vol. 1: 600–1540*: 27–50. Cambridge: Cambridge University Press.

Astill, G. 2009. Medieval Towns and Urbanization. In R. Gilchrist & A. Reynolds (eds.), *Reflections: 50 Years of Medieval Archaeology, 1957–2007*. Society for Medieval Archaeology Monograph 30: 255–70. Leeds: Maney Publishing.

Augé, M. 1995. *Non-places: Introduction to an Anthropology of Supermodernity*, trans. J. Howe. London: Verso.

Bäck, M. 1997. No Island Is a Society: Regional and Interregional Interaction in Central Sweden during the Viking Age. In H. Andersson, P. Carelli & L. Ersgård (eds.), *Visions of the Past: Trends and Traditions in Swedish Medieval Archaeology*. Lund Studies in Medieval Archaeology 19. Riksantikvarieämbetet Arkeologiska undersökningar, Skrifter nr 24: 129–61. Stockholm: Almqvist & Wiksell International.

Bäck, M. 1999. Vikingatida och tidigmedeltida keramik i Pollista. In A.-M. Hållans & K. Svensson, *Pollista – bo och bruka under 1200 år*. Arkeologi på väg – E18. Riksantikvarieämbetet. Arkeologiska undersökningar. UV Mitt Rapport 1998: 110. Stockholm: Riksantikvarieämbetet.

Bäck, M. 2009. Vikingatida bebyggelse funnen utanför Birkas stadsvall. *Fornvännen* 104: 262–73.

Bäck, M. 2012. På andra sidan Birka. Södra Björkös arkeologiska potential. In C. Hedenstierna-Jonson (ed.), *Birka nu. Pågående forskning om världsarvet Birka och Hovgården*. The National Historical Museum Studies 22: 45–68. Stockholm: Historiska museet.

Baker, J. & Brookes, S. 2011. From Frontier to Border: The Evolution of Northern West Saxon Territorial Delineation in the Ninth and Tenth Centuries. *Anglo-Saxon Studies in Archaeology and History* 17: 108–23.

Bani-Sadr, N. 2016. A Study of the Evidence for the Viking Age Harbour at Ribe, Denmark. Master's thesis, University of Southern Denmark.

Barbier, J. 2010. Du vicus de la Canche au castrum de Montreuil, un chaînon manquant: Le fiscus d'Attin? In S. Lebecq, B. Béthouart & L. Versype (eds.), *Quentovic: Environnement, Archéologie, Histoire*. Collection traveaux et recherches. Éditions du Conseil Scientifique de l'Université Lille 3: 459–74. Lille: Charles de Gaulle University – Lille 3.

Baug, I., Skre, D., Heldal, T. & Jansen, Ø. J. 2019. The Beginning of the Viking Age in the West. *Journal of Maritime Archaeology* 14: 43–80.

Bencard, M. & Bender Jørgensen, L. 1990. Excavations and Stratigraphy. In M. Bencard, L. Bender Jørgensen & H. Brinch Madsen (eds.), *Ribe Excavations 1970–76: Text*, Vol. 4: 15–167. Esbjerg: Sydjysk Universitetsforlag.

Bender Jørgensen, L. 2002. Rural Economy: Ecology, Hunting, Pastoralism, Agriculture and Nutritional Aspects. In J. Jesch (ed.), *The Scandinavians from the Vendel Period to the Tenth Century: An Ethnographic Perspective*. Studies in Historical Archaeoethnology 5: 129–44. San Marino: The Boydell Press.

Bendixen, K. 1981. Sceattas and Other Coin Finds. In M. Bencard (ed.), *Ribe Excavations 1970–76*. Vol. 1: 63–101. Esbjerg: Sydjysk Universitetsforlag.

Bendixen, K. 1994. The Coins from the Oldest Ribe (Excavations 1985 and 1986, 'Ribe II'). *Nordisk Numismatisk Årsskrift* (1989–90): 27–44.

Bengtsson, K. 2021. Sven Estridsen Hbg. 66 och 67, ett tillägg. *Nordisk Numismatisk Unions Medlemsblad*: 101–7.

Bergström, L. 2015. Husen i Birkas garnison, mellan atavism och förnyelse. *Situne Dei*: 44–59.

Beronius Jörpeland, L., Göthberg, H., Seiler, A. & Wikborg, J. (eds.) 2017. *At Upsalum – mäniskor och landskapande. Utbyggnad av Ostkustbanan genom Gamla Uppsala*. Arkeologisk undersökning. Report No. 2017: 1.1. Stockholm: Arkeologerna.

Biddle, M. 1976. Towns. In D. M. Wilson (ed.), *The Archaeology of Anglo-Saxon England*: 99–150. London: Methuen & Co.

Bill, J. & Clausen, B. L. (eds.) 1999. *Maritime Topography and the Medieval Town: Papers from the Fifth International Conference on Waterfront Archaeology in Copenhagen, 14–16 May 1998*. Publications from the National Museum. Studies in Archaeology and History 4. Copenhagen: Nationalmuseet.

Birbeck, V., Smith, R. J. C., Andrews, P. & Stoodley, N. 2005. *The Origins of Mid-Saxon Southampton: Excavations at the Friends Provident St. Mary's Stadium 1998–2000*. Salisbury: Wessex Archaeology.

Björklund, A. 2014. *Håbo härad och Sigtuna stad*. Uppland I. Det medeltida Sverige 10. Stockholm: Riksarkivet.

Blackmore, L. 2002. The Origins and Growth of Lundenwic, a Mart of many Nations. In B. Hårdh & L. Larsson (eds.), *Central Places in the Migration and Merovingian Periods: Papers from the 52nd Sachensymposium Lund, August 2001*. Uppåkrastudier 6. Acta Archaeologica Lundensia. Series in 8°, Vol. 39: 273–301. Lund: Almqvist & Wiksell International.

Blomkvist, N. 2008. Spåren av en svunnen världskonjunktur. In A.-M. Pettersson (ed.), *Spillingsskatten: Gotland i vikingatidens världshandel*: 155–85. Visby: Länsmuseet på Gotland.

Bolin, G. 1933. *Stockholms uppkomst: Studier och unersökningar rörande Stockholms förhistoria*. Uppsala: Apelbergs boktryckeri.

Brandt, K. H. 1976. Zur karolingischen und ottonischen Baugeschichte des Bremer St Petri-Domes. *Archäologisches Korrespondenzblatt* 6: 327–34.

Brandt, K. H. 1979. Ausgrabungen im Bremer Dom 1973–1976. In A. Löhr (ed.), *Der Bremer Dom: Baugeschichte, Ausgrabungen, Kunstschätze*. Hefte des Focke-Museums 52: 56–85. Bremen: Focke-Museum.

Brather, S. 2003. Lindisfarne 793 als Beginn der Wikingerzeit? Kulturentwicklung und Ereignisgeschichte im Vergleich. *Zeitschrift für Archäologie des Mittelalters* 31: 39–60.

Brather, S. & Jagodziński, M. F. 2012. *Der wikingerzeitliche Seehandelsplatz von Janów (Truso). Geophysikalische, archäopedologische und archäologische Untersuchungen 2004–2008 = Nadmorska osada handlowa z okresu Wikingów z Janowa (Truso). Badania geofizyczne, archeo-pedologiczne i archeologiczne w latach 2004–2008*. Zeitschrift für Archäologie des Mittelalters. Beiheft 24. Bonn: Habelt Verlag.

Brink, S. 2002. Law and Legal Customs in Viking Age Scandinavia. In J. Jesch (ed.), *The Scandinavians from the Vendel Period to the Tenth Century: An Ethnographic Perspective*. Studies in Historical Archaeoethnology 5: 87–117. San Marino: The Boydell Press.

Brink, S. 2007. Skiringssal, Kaupang, Tjølling: The Toponymic Evidence. In D. Skre (ed.), *Kaupang in Skiringssal*. Kaupang Excavation Project Publication Series, Vol. 1. Norske Oldfunn XXII: 53–64. Aarhus: Aarhus Universitetsforlag.

Brink, S. 2008. Law and Society. In S. Brink & N. Price (eds.), *The Viking World*: 23–31. London: Routledge.

Brink, S. 2012. *Vikingarnas slaver: Den nordiska träldomen under yngre järnålder och äldsta medeltid*. Stockholm: Atlantis.

Brisbane, M. 1988. Hamwic (Saxon Southampton): An 8th Century Port and Production Centre. In R. Hodges & B. Hobley (eds.), *The Rebirth of Towns in the West: AD 700–1050*. CBA Research Report No. 68: 101–8. London: Council for British Archaeology.

Brookes, St. 2001. Reflections on 'The Archaeology of Inland Markets, Fairs and "Productive Sites" c.650–850', Worcester College, Oxford, 15th–17th December 2000. *Papers from the Institute of Archaeology* 12: 124–7.

Brundstedt, S. 1996. *Alsnu Kungsgård. Forskningsprojekt Hovgården. Uppland, Adelsö socken, RAÄ 46 m fl. Arkeologisk undersökning*. UV Stockholm, Report No. 1996: 71/1. Stockholm: Riksantikvarieämbetet.

Bur, M. 1995. s.v. 'Saint-Denis'. In N. Angermann, R.-H. Bautier & R. Auty (eds.), *Lexikon des Mittelalters*, Vol. 8: 1145–8. Munich: Lexma Verlag.

Burström, M. 1988. Regional identitet och territoriell organisation: Exemplet inre Sydsverige under järnålder. In Å. Hyenstrand (ed.), *Samhällsteori och källmaterial – aktuell arkeologi II*. Stockholm Archaeological Report No. 21: 113–26. Stockholm: University of Stockholm.

Bury, J. B. 1912. *A History of the Eastern Roman Empire: From the Fall of Irene to the Accession of Basil I. (A.D. 802–867)*. London: Macmillan & Co.

Byock, J. L. 2013. *Viking Language 1: Learn Old Norse, Runes and Icelandic Sagas*. Pacific Palisades, CA: Jules William Press.

Callmer, J. 1977. *Trade Beads and Bead Trade in Scandinavia ca. 800–1000 A.D*. Acta Archaeologica Lundensia. Series in 4°. No. 11. Bonn: Habelt & Gleerup.

Callmer, J. 1991a. Platser med anknytning till handel och hantverk i yngre järnålder: Exempel från södra Sverige. In P. Mortensen & B. M. Rasmussen (eds.), *Fram Stamme til Stat i Danmark, Vol. 2: Høvdingesamfund og Kongemagt*. Jysk Arkæologisk Selskabs Skrifter XXII: 2: 29–47. Højbjerg: Jysk Arkæologisk Selskab.

Callmer, J. 1991b. Beads as a Criterion of Shifting Trade and Exchange Connections. *Studien zur Sachsenforschung* 7: 25–38.

Callmer, J. 1992. Interaction between Ethnical Groups in the Baltic Region in the Late Iron Age. In B. Hårdh & B. Wyszomirska-Werbart (eds.), *Contacts across the Baltic Sea during the Late Iron Age (5th–12th centuries)*. Baltic Sea Conference, Lund October 25–27, 1991. Institute of Archaeology Report Series No. 43: 99–107. Lund: University of Lund.

Callmer, J. 1994. Urbanisation in Scandinavia and the Baltic Region c. CE 700–1100: Trading Places, Centres and Early Urban Sites. In B. Ambrosiani & H. Clarke (eds.), *Developments around the Baltic and North Sea in the Viking*

Age. Birka Studies 3 (= The Twelfth Viking Congress): 50–90. Stockholm: The Birka Project.

Callmer, J. 1997. Bead and Bead Production in Scandinavia and the Baltic Region *c*. CE 600–1000: A General Outline. In U. von Freeden & A. Wieczorek (eds.), *Perlen: Archäologie, Techniken, Analysen.* Akten des Internationalen Perlensymposiums in Mannheim vom 11. bis 14. November 1994. Kolloquien zur Vor- und Frühgeschichte 1: 167–202. Bonn: Habelt.

Callmer, J. 2000. The Archaeology of the Early Rus' *c*. CE 500–900. *Medieval Scandinavia* 13: 7–63.

Callmer, J. 2002. North-European Trading Centres and the Early Medieval Craftsmen: Craftsmen at Åhus, North-Eastern Scania, Sweden ca. CE 750–850. In B. Hårdh & L. Larsson (eds.), *Central Places in the Migration and Merovingian Periods: Papers from the 52nd Sachensymposium Lund, August 2001.* Uppåkrastudier 6. Acta Archaeologica Lundensia. Series in 8°, Vol. 39: 125–57. Lund: Almqvist & Wiksell International.

Callmer, J. 2004. Beads in Scandinavia in the Early and High Medieval Periods, ca. CE 400–1200. In I. Glover, H. Hughes-Brock & J. Henderson (eds.), *Ornaments from the Past: Bead Studies after Beck: A Book on Glass and Semiprecious Stone Beads in History and Archaeology for Archaeologists, Jewellery Historians and Collectors*: 38–46. London: Bead Study Trust.

Campbell, J. 2000. Power and Authority 600–1300. In D. M. Palliser (ed.), *The Cambridge Urban History of Britain, Vol. 1: 600–1540*: 51–78. Cambridge: Cambridge University Press.

Capelle, T. 1976. *Die frühgeschichtlichen Metallfunde von Domburg auf Walcheren*, Vol. 1. Nederlandse oudheden 5. Amersfoort: Rijksdienst voor het Oudheidkundig Bodemonderzoek.

Cardon, D. 1999. *La draperie au Moyen Âge: Essor d'une grande industrie européenne.* Paris: CNRS Éditions.

Carelli, P. 2012. *Lunds historia – staden och omlandet, Vol. 1: Medeltiden. En metropol växer fram.* Lund: Elanders Sverige.

Carlsson, D. 1998. *Vikingehamnar: Ett hotat kulturarv.* ArkeoDok Skrifter 1. Visby: ArkeoDok.

Carver, M. 2015. Commerce and Cult: Confronted Ideologies in 6th–9th Century Europe. *Medieval Archaeology* 59: 1–23.

Cense-Bacquet, D. 2016. L'occupation du haut Moyen Âge sur le site de La Calotterie, 'Chemin de Visemarais' (France, Pas-de-Calais): Premiers résultats de la fouille réalisée sur les parcelles AC 40 et AC 3p. In I. Leroy & L. Verslype (eds.), *Les cultures des littoraux au haut Moyen Âge: Cadres et modes de via dans l'espace maritime Manche-mer du Nord du IIIe au Xe s.* Revue du Nord.

Collection Art et Archéologie 24: 187–216. Villeneuve-d'Ascq: Université de Lille – Sciences humaines et sociales.

Christaller, W. 1933. *Die zentralen Orte in Süddeutschland eine ökonomisch-geographische Untersuchung über die Gesetzmäßigkeit der Verbreitung und Entwicklung der Siedlungen mit städtischen Funktionen.* Jena: Fischer.

Christensen, A. E. 1981. s.v. 'Knud (II) den Hellige'. In S. Cedergreen Beck (ed.), *Dansk Biografisk Leksikon* 8: 58–60. Copenhagen: Gyldendal.

Christensen, T. 2015. *Lejre bag myten: De arkæologiske udgravninger.* Jysk Arkæologisk Selskab Skrifter 87. Højbjerg: Roskilde Museum & Jysk Arkæologisk Selskab.

Christiansson, H. & Nordahl, E. 1989. Tingshögen and Kundsgårdsplatåerna in Gamla Uppsala. *TOR. Tidskrift för nordisk fornkunskap* 22: 245–58.

Christophersen, A. 1989. Dwelling Houses, Workshops and Storehouses: Functional Aspects of the Development of Wooden Urban Buildings in Trondheim from *c.* A.D. 1000 to A.D. 1400. *Acta Archaeological* 60: 101–29.

Christophersen, A. & Nordeide, S. W. 1994. *Kaupangen ved Nidelva. 1000 års byhistorie belyst gjennom de arkeologiske undersøkelsene på Folkebibliotekstomta i Trondheim 1973–1985.* Riksantikvarens skrifter 7. Trondheim: Strindheim.

Clarke, H. & Ambrosiani, B. 1991. *Towns in the Viking Age.* Leicester: Leicester University Press.

Claude, D. 1985. *Der Handel im westlichen Mittelmeer während des Frühmittelalters: Untersuchungen zu Handel und Verkehr der vor- und frühgeschichtlichen Zeit in Mittel- und Nordeuropa II. Abhandlungen der Akademie der Wissenschaften in Göttingen.* Philologisch-historische Klasse. Dritte Folge No. 144. Göttingen: Vandenhoeck & Ruprecht.

Coojmans, C. 2021. Down by the River: Exploring the Logistics of Viking Encampment across Atlantic Europe. In 'Viking Wars', ed. F. Iversen & K. Kjesrud, special volume, *Viking Wars* 84(1): 187–206. Oslo: Norwegian Archaeological Society.

Costambeys, M., Innes, M. & Maclean, S. 2011. *The Carolingian World.* Cambridge Medieval Textbooks. Cambridge: Cambridge University Press.

Coupland, S. 2002. Trading Places: Quentovic and Dorestad Reassessed. *Early Medieval Europe* 11(3): 115–232.

Cowie, R. & Harding, C. 2000. Saxon Settlement and Economy from the Dark Ages to Domesday. In M. Kendall (ed.), *The Archaeology of Greater London: An Assessment of Archaeological Evidence for Human Presence in the Area Now Covered by Greater London*: 171–206. London: Museum of London.

Crabtee, P. J. 2018. *Early Medieval Britain: The Rebirth of Towns in the Post-Roman West*. Cambridge: Cambridge University Press.

Croix, S. 2014. Permanency in Early Medieval Emporia: Reassessing Ribe. *European Journal of Archaeology* 18: 1–27.

Croix, S., Deckers, P., Feveile, C. et al. 2022. Excavation Atlas. In S. M. Sindbæk (ed.), *Northern Emporium, Vol. 1: The Making of Viking-Age Ribe*. Jysk Arkæologisk Selskabs Skrifter 122: 49–218. Aarhus: Aarhus University Press.

Crumlin-Pedersen, O. 1991. Søfart og samfund i Danmarks vikingetid: Ships and Shipping in Viking Age Denmark. In P. Mortensen & B. M. Rasmussen (eds.), *Fram Stamme til Stat i Danmark, Vol. 2: Høvdingesamfund og Kongemagt*. Jysk Arkæologisk Selskabs Skrifter XXII:2: 181–208. Højbjerg: Jysk Arkæologisk Selskab.

Crumlin-Pedersen, O. 1997. *Viking-Age Ships and Shipbuilding in Hedeby/Haithabu and Schleswig*. Ships and Boats of the North 2. Schleswig and Roskilde: Wikinger Museum Haithabu and The Viking Ship Museum.

Crumlin-Pedersen, O., Porsmose, E. & Thrane, H. 1996. *Atlas over Fyns kyst i jernalder, vikingetid og middelalder*. Odense: Odense universitersforlag.

Dagron, G. 2002. The Urban Economy, Seventh–Twelfth Centuries. In A. E. Laiou (ed.), *The Economic History of Byzantium: From the Seventh through the Fifteenth Century*. Dumbarton Oaks Studies 39: 393–461. Washington, DC: Dumbarton Oaks.

Damell, D. 1991. Fornsigtuna: A Royal Seat and Precursor of an Urban Settlement. In K. Jennbert, L. Larsson, R. Petré & B. Wyszomirska-Werbart (eds.), *Regions and Reflections in Honour of Märta Strömberg*. Acta Archaeologica Lundensia. Series in 8°, Vol. 20: 291–6. Lund: Almqvist & Wiksell International.

Deggim, C. 2005. *Hafenleben in Mittelalter und Früher Neuzeit. Seehandel und Arbeitsregelungen in Hamburg und Kopenhagen vom 13. bis zum 17. Jahrhundert*. Schriften des Deutsches Schiffahrtsmuseums 62. Hamburg: Convent Verlag.

Delvaux, M. 2017. Patterns of Scandinavian Bead Use between the Iron Age and Viking Age, ca. 600–1000 C.E. *Beads: Journal of the Society of Bead Researchers* 29: 3–30.

Demolon, P. & Louis, E. 1991. Naissance d'une cite médiévale flammande: L'exemple de Douai. In P. Demolon, H. Galinié & F. Verhaeghe (eds.), *Archéologie des villes dans le Nord-Ouest de l'europé (VIIe–IIIe siècle)*. Actes du IVe Congrès International d'Archéologie Médiévale: 47–58. Douai: Société Archéologique de Douai.

Denecke, D. 1973. Der geographische Stadtbegriff und die räumlich-funktionale Betrachtungsweise bei Siedlungstypen mit zentraler Bedeutung in Anwendung auf historische Quellen. In H. Jankuhn, W. Schlesinger & H. Steuer (eds.) *Vor- und Frühformen der europäischen Stadt im Mittelalter I*. Abhandlungen der Akademie der Wissenschaften in Göttingen. Philologisch-historische Klasse. Dritte Folge. No. 83: 33–55. Göttingen: Vandenhoeck & Ruprecht.

Dengsø Jessen, M., Kähler Holst, M., Lindblom, C., Bonde, N. & Pedersen, A. 2014. A Palisade Fit for a King: Ideal Architecture in King Harald Bluetooth's Jelling. *Norwegian Archaeological Review* 47(1): 42–64.

Dilcher, G. 1973. Rechtshistorische Aspekte des Stadtbegriffs. In H. Jankuhn, W. Schlesinger & H. Steuer (eds.) *Vor- und Frühformen der europäischen Stadt im Mittelalter I*. Abhandlungen der Akademie der Wissenschaften in Göttingen. Philologisch-historische Klasse. Dritte Folge. No. 83: 12–32. Göttingen: Vandenhoeck & Ruprecht.

Dobat, A. S. 2003. angulus non desertus! Kontinuität und Zentralität in der jüngeren Eisenzeit Südschleswigs. *Archäologie in Schleswig/Arkæologi i Slesvig* 10: 113–36.

Dobat, A. S. 2004. Hedeby and Its Maritime Hinterland: The Schlei Fjord As an Early Medieval Communication Route. *Jahrbuch der Bodendenkmalpflege in Mecklenburg-Vorpommern* 51: 419–35.

Dobat, A. S. 2006. Angulus non desertus! II. Erste Ergebnisse der Suche nach Siedlungen des 6. bis 7. Jahrhunderts in Südschleswig. *Archäologie in Schleswig/Arkæologi i Slesvig* 11: 87–94.

Dobat, A. S. 2008. Danevirke Revisited: An Investigation into Military and Socio-political Organisation in South Scandinavia (c. CE 700 to 1100). *Medieval Archaeology* 52: 27–67.

Dobat, A. S. 2010. Füsing. Ein frühmittelalterlicher Zentralplatz im Umfeld von Haithabu/Schleswig. Bericht über die Ergebnisse der Prospektionen 2003–2005. In C. von Carnap-Bornheim (ed.), *Studien zu Haithabu und Füsing*. Ausgrabungen in Haithabu 16: 129–256. Neumünster: Wachholtz.

Dobat, A. S. 2022. Finding Sliesthorp? The Viking Age Settlement at Füsing. *Danish Journal of Archaeology* 11: 1–22.

Drescher, H. 1983. Metallhandwerk des 8.–11. Jahrhunderts in Haithabu aufgrund der Werkstattabfälle. In H. Jankuhn, W. Janssen, R. Schmidt-Wiegand & H. Tiefenbach (eds.), *Das Handwerk in vor- und frühgeschichtlicher Zeit II. Archäologische und philologische Beiträge*. Abhandlungen der Akademie der Wissenschaften in Göttingen. Philologisch-historische Klasse. Dritte Folge. No. 123: 174–92. Göttingen: Vandenhoeck & Ruprecht.

Drescher, H. 1984. Glockenfunde aus Haithabu. Das archäologische Fundmaterial 4. *Berichte über die Ausgrabungen in Haithabu* 19: 9–62. Neumünster: Wachholtz.

Duczko, W. 1996a. Uppsalahögarna som symboler och arkeologiska källor. In W. Duczko (ed.), *Arkeologi och miljögeologi i Gamla Uppsala. Studier och rapporter. Volym II.* Occasional Papers in Archaeology 11: 59–93. Uppsala: Societas Archaeologica Upsalensis.

Duczko, W. 1996b. Kungsgården. In W. Duczko (ed.), *Arkeologi och miljögeologi i Gamla Uppsala. Studier och rapporter. Volym II.* Occasional Papers in Archaeology 11: 37–51. Uppsala: Societas Archaeologica Upsalensis.

Dumont, A. & Mariotti, J.-F. 2013. Le mobilier découvert dans le fleuve à Taillebourg – Port d'Envaux. In A. Dumont & J.-F. Mariotti (eds.), *Archéologie et histoire du fleuve Charente. Taillebourg – Port d'Envaux: Une yone portuaire du haut Moyen Âge sur le fleuve Charente*: 127–230. Dijon: Éditions Universitaires de Dijon.

Dunér, J. & Vinberg, A. 2006. *Barva – 2000 år vid Mälarens södra strand. E20, sträckan Eskilstuna Arphus. Södermanland, Barva socken, Säby 4:1, RAÄ 17, RAÄ 36, RAÄ 53, RAÄ 55–57, RAÄ 66, RAÄ 150 och RAÄ 153.* UV Mitt Rapport No. 20. Riksantikvarieämbetet: Hägersten.

Eckstein, D. & Schietzel, K. 1977. Zur dendrochronologischen Gliederung und Datierung der Baubefunde von Haithabu. Untersuchungen zur Anthropologie, Botanik und Dendrochronologie. *Berichte über die Ausgrabungen in Haithabu* 11: 141–64. Neumünster: Wachholtz.

Edberg, R. 2011. Fynd. In A. Wikström (ed.), *Fem stadsgårder – arkeologisk undersökning i kv. Trädgårdsmästaren 9 & 10 i Sigtuna 1988–90.* Rapport Arkeologisk Undersökning. Meddelanden och Rapporter från Sigtuna Museum No. 52: 141–66. Sigtuna: Sigtuna Museum.

Ellmers, D. 1990. Die Verlagerung des Fernhandels vom öffentlichen Ufermarkt in die privaten Häuser der Kaufleute. *Lübecker Schriften zur Archäologie und Kulturgeschichte* 20: 101–18.

Endemann, T. 1964. *Markturkunde und Markt in Frankreich und Burgund vom 9. bis 11. Jahrhundert.* Vorträge und Forschungen 4. Konstanzer Arbeitskreis für Mittelalterliche Geschichte. Konstanz: Thorbecke.

Englert, A. & Ossowski, W. 2009. Sailing in Wulfstan's Wake: The 2004 Trial Voyage Hedeby-Gdańsk with the Skuldelev 1 Reconstruction, Ottar. In A. Englert & A. Trakadas (eds.), *Wulfstan's Voyages: The Baltic Sea Region in the Early Viking Age As Seen from Shipboard.* Maritime Culture of the North 2: 257–70. Roskilde: The Viking Ship Museum.

Ennen, E. 1972. *Die europäische Stadt des Mittelalters.* Göttingen: Vandenhoeck & Ruprecht.

Eriksen, P., Egeberg, T., Helles Olesen, L. & Rostholm, H. 2009. *Vikinger i vest: Vikingetiden i Vestjylland.* Højbjerg: Jysk Arkæologisk Selskab.

Erlenkäuser, H. 1998. Neue C14-Datierungen zum Danewerk, Schlswig-Holstein. In H. H. Andersen (ed.), *Danevirke og Kovirke: Arkæologiske undersøgelser 1861–1993*. Moesgård Museums Skrifter: 189–201. Aarhus: Jysk Arkæologisk Selskab.

Ethelberg, P. 2003. Gården og landsbyen i jernalder og vikingetid (500 f.Kr. – 1000 e.Kr.). In P. Ethelberg, N. Hardt, B. Poulsen & A. B. Sørensen (eds.), *Det Sønderjyske Landbrugs Historie. Jernalder, Vikingetid och Middelalder*. Historisk samfund for Sønderjylland 82: 123–373. Haderslev: Haderslev Museum & Historisk samfund for Sønderjylland.

Fabech, C. 1999. Centrality in Sites and Landscapes. In C. Fabech (ed.), *Settlement and Landscape: Proceedings of a Conference in Aarhus, Denmark, May 4–7, 1998*. Jutland Archaeological Society: 455–73. Aarhus: Aarhus University Press.

Falk, H. 1912. *Altnordisches Seewesen*. Wörter und Sachen 4. Heidelberg: Carl Winter's Universitätsbuchhandlung.

Falke, J. 1869. *Die Geschichte des deutschen Zollwesens: Von seiner Entstehung bis zum Abschluß des deutschen Zollvereins*. Leipzig: Veit.

Fallgren, J.-H. 2008. Farm and Village in the Viking Age. In S. Brink & N. Price (eds.), *The Viking World*: 67–76. London: Routledge.

Farole, T. 2011. *Special Economic Zones in Africa: Comparing Performance and Learning from Global Experiences*. Washington, DC: World Bank.

Fekhner, M. V. & Yanina, S. A. 1979. Vesy s arabskoy nadpis'yu iz Timerevo [Scales with Arabic Letters from Timerevo]. In Akademiya nauk SSSR [Academy of Sciences of the USSR] (ed.), *Voprosy drevney i srednevekovoy arkheologii Vostochnoy Yevropy [Questions of Ancient and Medieval Archaeology of Eastern Europe]*: 184–92. Moscow: Izdatel'stvo nauka.

Fennö Muyingo, H. 2000. *Borgvallen II. Utvidgad undersökning av Borgvallen och underliggande grav 1997. Arkeologisk undersökning 1997, Uppland, Adelsö socken, RAÄ 34*. Birkas Befästning 3. Stockholm: Stockholm University.

Fennö Muyingo, H. & Holmquist Olausson, L. 1995. *Rapport från en arkeologisk undersökning vid Birkas stadsvall 1995. Björkö, Adelsö sn, Raä 188, Uppland*. Birkas befästning 1. Stockholm: Stockholm University.

Feveile, C. 2001. Okholm – en plads med håndværksspor og grubehuse fra 8.–9. århundrede. *By, marsk og geest* 13: 5–32.

Feveile, C. 2006a. Ribe på nordsiden af åen, 8.–12. Århundrede. In C. Feveile (ed.), *Ribe Studier. Det ældeste Ribe. Udgravninger på nordsiden af Ribe Å 1984– 2000 1.1*. Jysk Ark. Selskabs Skr. 51: 13–63. Højbjerg: Jysk Arkæologisk Selskab.

Feveile, C. 2006b. Mønterne fra det ældste Ribe. In C. Feveile (ed.), *Ribe Studier. Det ældeste Ribe. Udgravninger på nordsiden af Ribe Å 1984–2000 1.1*. Jysk Ark. Selskabs Skr. 51: 279–312. Højbjerg: Jysk Arkæologisk Selskab.

Feveile, C. 2009. The Fortifications of Viking Age Ribe. In M. Segschneider (ed.), *Ringwälle und verwandte Strukturen des ersten Jahrtausends n.Chr. an Nord- und Ostsee*. Schriften des Archäologischen Landesmuseums. Ergänzungsreihe 5: 71–85. Neumünster: Wachholtz.

Feveile, C. 2019. Sceattas i Sydskandinavien – fra ekspanderende frisere til kontrollerende kongemagt. *By, marsk og geest* 31, 21–43.

Feveile, C. 2023. The Numismatic Evidence from Posthustorvet. In S. M. Sindbæk (ed.), *Northern Emporium, Vol. 2: The Networks of Viking-Age Ribe*. Jysk Arkæologisk Selskabs Skrifter 123: 115–46. Aarhus: Aarhus University Press.

Feveile, C., Jensen, S. & Lund Rasmussen, K. 1998. Produktion af drejet keramik i Ribeområdet i sen yngre germansk jernalder. Proveniensbestemmelse ved hjælp af magnetisk susceptibilitet og termoluminiscens. *KUML: Årbok for Jysk Arkæologisk Selskab*: 143–59.

Fleming, R. 2009. Elites, Boats and Foreigners: Rethinking the Birth of English Towns. In A. Castagnetti (ed.), *Città e Campagna nei Secoli Altomedievali*. Settimane di Studio della Fondazione Centro Italiano di Studi Sull'alto Medioevo LVI: 393–425. Spoleto: Centro Italiano di Studi Sull'alto Medievo.

Frahm, F. 1934. Schleswig-Haithabu und die Anskarkirche in Haddeby. *Zeitschrift der Gesellschaft für Schleswig-Holsteinische Geschichte* 62: 156–212.

Franck Bican, J. 2010. Bulbrogård, the first aristocratic complex at Tissø – and a new approach to the aristocratic sites. In E. Strahl (ed.), *Herrenhöfe und die Hierarchie der Macht im Raum südlich und östlich der Nordsee von der Vorrömischen Eisenzeit bis zum frühen Mittelalter und zur Wikingerzeit = Herrenhöfe and the Hierarchy of Power in the Region to the South and East of the North Sea from the Pre-Roman Iron Age until the Early Middle Ages and the Viking Age*. Siedlungs- und Küstenforschung im südlichen Nordseegebiet= Settlement and Coastal Research in the Southern North Sea Region 33: 147–54. Rahden: Marie Leidorf.

Frandsen, L. B. 2018. Henne Kirkeby Vest: A Fortified Settlement on the West Coast of Denmark. In J. Hansen & M. Bruus (eds.), *The Fortified Viking Age: 36th Interdisciplinary Viking Symposium*. Kulturhistoriske studier I centralitet. Archaeological & Historical Studies in Centrality 3: 8–15. Odense: Odense City Museums and University Press of Southern Denmark.

Frandsen, L. B. 2020. Henne Kirkeby: A Special Viking-Age Settlement on the West Coast of Denmark. In A. Pedersen & S. M. Sindbæk (eds.), *Viking Encounters: Proceedings of the Eighteenth Viking Congress*: 495–504. Aarhus: Aarhus University Press.

Frandsen, L. B. & Jensen, S. 1987. Pre-Viking and Early Viking Age Ribe: Excavations at Nikolajgade 8, 1985–86. *Journal of Danish Archaeology* 6: 175–89.

Friðriksson, A. & Vésteinsson, O. 1992. Dómhringa saga: Grein un fornleifaskýringar. *Saga* 30: 7–79.

Gammeltoft, P., Jakobsen, J. G. G. & Sindbæk, S. M. 2012. Vikingetidens bebyggelse omkring Kattegat og Skagerrak: Et forsøg på kortlægning. In A. Pedersen & S. M. Sindbæk (eds.), *Et fælles hav – Skagerrak og Kattegat I vikingetiden*. Nordlige Verdener: 6–36. Copenhagen: Nationalmuseet.

Ganshof, F. L. 1956. *Het Statuut van de vreemdeling in het Frankische Rijk*. Mededelingen van de Koninklijke Vlaamse Academie voor Wetenschappen, Letteren en schone Kunsten van België. Klasse der Letteren. Jaargang XVIII: 3: Brussels: Koninklijke Vlaamse Academie.

Ganshof, F. L. 1957. Note sur le 'Praeceptum Negotiatorum' de Louis le Pieux. In A. Noto (ed.), *Studi in onore di Armando Sapori* 1: 101–12. Milan: Istututo Editoriale Cisalpino.

Ganshof, F. L. 1958. L'étranger dans la monarchie franque. In La Société Jean Bodin (ed.), *L'Étranger 2*. Recueils de la Société Jean Bodin 10: 5–36. Brussels: Librairie encyclopédique.

Ganshof, F. L. 1959. À propos du tonlieu à l'époque Carolingienne. In Centro Italiano di Studi sull'Alto Medioevo (ed.), *La Città nell'Alto Medioevo*. Settimane di studio del Centro Italiano di Studi sull'Alto Medioevo 6: 485–508. Spoleto: Presso La Sede del Centro.

Garipzanov, I. H. 2008. Frontier Identities: Carolingian Frontier and *Gens Danorum*. In I. H. Garipzanov, P. J. Geary & P. Urbańczyk (eds.), *Franks, Northmen, and Slavs: Identities and State Formation in Early Medieval Europe*. Cursor mundi 5: 113–43. Turnhout: Brepols.

Gechter, M. 1997. Die Grablege des Bischofs Rudolf von Schleswig in St. Kunibert. *Colonia Romanica* 12: 17–20.

Gechter, M. 2009. Coins. In W. A. van Es & W. J. H. Verwers (eds.), *Excavations at Dorestad, Vol. 3: Hoogstraat 0, II–IV*. Nederlandse Oudheden 16: 257–9. Amersfoort: Rijksdienst voor Archeologie.

Gelting, M. H. 2004. Elusive Bishops: Remembering, Forgetting, and Remaking the History of the Early Danish Church. In S. Gilsdorf (ed.), *The Bishop: Power and Piety at the First Millennium*. Neue Aspekte der europäischen Mittelalterforschung 4: 169–200. Münster: LIT Verlag.

Gelting, M. H. 2010. Poppo's Ordeal: Courtier Bishops and the Success of Christianization at the Turn of the First Millennium. *Viking and Medieval Scandinavia* 6: 101–33.

Gelting, M. H. 2016. Kong Svend, Slesvig Stadsret og arvekøbet i de jyske købstæder: af Danmarks ældste købstadprivilegier. In L. C. A. Sonne & S. Croix (eds.), *Svend Estridsen. Studies in History and Social Sciences 528*: 195–216. Odense: Syddansk Universitetsforlag.

Göthberg, H. 1995. Huskronologi i Mälarområdet, på Gotland och Öland under sten-, brons- och järnålder. In H. Göthberg, O. Kyhlberg & A. Vinberg (eds.), *Hus & gård i det förurbana samhället: Rapport från ett sektorsforskningsprojekt vid Riksantikvarieämbetet. Arkeologiska undersökningar.* Skrifter No. 13/14: 65–109. Stockholm: Riksantikvarieämbetet.

Göthberg, H., Kyhlberg, O. & Vinberg, A. (eds.) 1995. *Hus & gård i det förurbana samhället: Rapport från ett sektorsforskningsprojekt vid Riksantikvarieämbetet. Arkeologiska undersökningar.* Skrifter nr 13/14. Stockholm: Riksantikvarieämbetet.

Gräslund, A.-S. 1980. *The Burial Customs: A Study of the Graves on Björkö.* Birka IV. Stockholm: Almqvist & Wiksell International.

Gräslund, A.-S. 2001. *Ideologi och Mentalitet. Om religionsskiftet I Scandinavien från en arkeologisk horisont.* Occasional Papers in Archaeology 29. Uppsala: Uppsala University.

Grenander Nyberg, G. 1984. Eine Schaftrolle aus Haithabu als Teil eines Trittwebstuhls mit waagerecht gespanner Kette. Das archäologische Fundmaterial 4. *Berichte über die Ausgrabungen in Haithabu* 19: 145–50. Neumünster: Wachholtz.

Grenander Nyberg, G. 1994. Prehistoric and Early Medieval Features in the Construction of the Oldest North European Treadle Looms. In G. Jaacks & K. Tidow (eds.), *Archäologische Textilfunde – Archaeological Textiles. Textilsymposium Neumünster = North European Symposium V*: 203–12. Neumünster: Textilmuseum Neumünster.

Griffiths, D. 2013. Living in Viking-Age Towns. In D. M. Hadley & L. ten Harkel (eds.), *Everyday Life in Viking-Age Towns: Social Approaches to Towns in England and Ireland, c. 800–1100*: 1–13. Oxford: Oxbow Books.

Gurevich, A. J. 1968. Wealth and Gift-Bestowal among the Ancient Scandinavians. *Scandinavica* 7(2): 126–38.

Gurevich, A. J. 1985. *Categories of Medieval Culture*, trans. G. L. Campbell. London: Routledge.

Gurevich, A. J. 1993. s.v. 'Land Tenure and Inheritance'. In P. Pulsiano (ed.), *Medieval Scandinavia: An Encyclopedia*: 372–3. New York: Garland.

Gustafsson, N. B. 2013. *Casting Identities in Central Seclusion: Aspects of Non-ferrous Metalworking and Society on Gotland in the Early Medieval Period.* Theses and Papers in Scientific Archaeology 15. Stockholm: Stockholm University.

Gustafsson, N. B. 2020. On the Significance of Coastal Free Zones and Foreign Tongues: Tracing Cultural Interchange in Early Medieval Gotland. In L. Kitzler Åhfeldt, C. Hedenstierna-Jonson, P. Widerström & B. Raffield (eds.), *Relations and Runes: The Baltic Islands and Their Interactions during the Late Iron Age and Early Middle Ages*: 79–90. Visby: Swedish National Heritage Board.

Gustafsson, N. B. & Östergren, M. 2017. Weights and Values in the Gotlandic Heartland. *Lund Archaeological Review* 23: 95–105.

Gustin, I. 2011. Coin Stock and Coin Circulation in Birka. In J. Graham-Campbell, S. M. Sindbæk & G. Williams (eds.), *Silver Economies, Monetisation and Society in Scandinavia CE 800–1100*: 227–44. Aarhus: Aarhus Universitetsforlag.

Hållans, A.-M. & Svensson, K. 1999. *Pollista – bo och bruka under 1200 år*. Arkeologi på väg – E18. Riksantikvarieämbetet. Arkeologiska undersökningar. UV Mitt Rapport No. 1998: 110. Stockholm: Riksantikvarieämbetet.

Hallström, G. 1913. *Birka I: Hjalmar Stolpes Grafundersökningar*. Första Häftet. Stockholm: Ivar Haeggströms.

Harck, O. 1998. Anmerkungen zum Primärwall des Danewerks. In A. Wesse (ed.), *Studien zur Archäologie des Ostseeraumes: Von der Eisenzeit zum Mittelalter*: 127–35. Neumünster: Wachholtz.

Hartmann, L. M. 1904. *Zur Wirtschaftsgeschichte Italiens im frühen Mittelalter*. Gotha: Friedrich Andreas Perthes Aktiengesellschaft.

Hedenstierna-Jonson, C. 2006. *The Birka Warrior: The Material Culture of a Martial Society*. Theses and papers in Scientific Archaeology 8. Stockholm: Stockholm University.

Hedenstierna-Jonson, C. 2009. Rus', Varangians and Birka Warriors. In L. Holmquist Olausson & M. Olausson (eds.), *The Martial Society: Aspects of Warriors, Fortifications and Social Change in Scandinavia*. Theses and papers in Archaeology B11: 159–78. Stockholm: Stockholm University.

Hedenstierna-Jonson, C. 2012. Birkafolket. In C. Hedenstierna-Jonson (ed.), *Birka nu. Pågående forskning om världsarvet Birka och Hovgården*. The National Historical Museum Studies 22: 213–26. Stockholm: Historiska museet.

Hedenstierna-Jonson, C. & Holmquist Olausson, L. 2006. *The Oriental Mounts from Birka's Garrison: An Expression of Warrior Rank and Status*. Antikvariskt arkiv 81. Kungl. Vitterhets Historie och Antikvitets Akademien. Stockholm: Almqvist & Wiksell International.

Hedlund, G. 1993. Södra Kungsgårdsplatån. Utgrävningen 1992. In W. Duczko (ed.), *Arkeologi och miljögeologi i Gamla Uppsala. Studier och rapporter*. Vol. 1. Occasional Papers in Archaeology 7: 64–9. Uppsala: Societas Archaeologica Upsalensis.

Helle, K. 1982. *Kongssete og kjøpstad: Fra opphavet til 1536.* Bergen Bys historie 1. Bergen: Universitetsforlaget.

Helten, V. 2019. *Zwischen Kooperation und Konfrontation: Dänemark und das Frankenreich im 9. Jahrhundert.* Berlin: Springer Gabler.

Hennius, A. 2021. Outlanders? Resource Colonisantion, Raw Material Exploitation and Networks in Middle Iron Age Sweden. Occasional Papers in Archaeology 73. Uppsala: Department of Archaeology and Ancient History.

Herzig, F., Liebert, T. & Nadler, M. 1997. Die Müller Karls der Großen – Frühmittelalterliche Wassermühlen im Schwarzachtal bei Großhöbing. Stadt Greding, Landkreis Roth, Mittelfranken. *Das Archäologische Jahr in Bayern*: 143–146.

Hilberg, V. 2007. Haithabu im 11. Jahrhundert. Auf der Suche nach dem Niedergang eines dänischen *emporiums* der Wikingerzeit. In M. Posselt, B. Zickgraf & C. Dobiat (eds.), *Geophysik und Ausgrabung. Einsatz und Auswertung zerstörungsfreier Prospektion in der Archäologie*: 187–203. Rahden: Leidorf.

Hilberg, V. 2009. Hedeby in Wulfstan's Days: A Danish *emporium* of the Viking Age between East and West. In A. Englert & A. Trakadas (eds.), *Wulfstan's Voyage: The Baltic Sea Region in the Early Viking Age As Seen from Shipboard.* Maritime Culture of the North 2: 79–113. Roskilde: The Viking Ship Museum.

Hilberg, V. 2011. Silver Economies of the Ninth and Tenth Centuries CE in Hedeby. In J. Graham-Campbell, S. M. Sindbæk & G. Williams (eds.), *Silver Economies, Monetisation and Society in Scandinavia, CE 800–1000*: 203–25. Aarhus: Aarhus University Press.

Hilberg, V. 2014. Zwischen Innovation und Tradition: Der karolingische Einfluss auf das Münzwesen in Skandinavien. In K. P. Hofmann, H. Kamp & M. Wemhoff (eds.), *Die Wikinger und das Fränkische Reich. Identitäten zwischen Konfrontation und Annäherung.* Mittelalterstudien 29: 133–215. Munich: Wilhelm Fink Verlag.

Hilberg, V. 2016. Hedeby's Demise in the Late Viking Age and the Shift to Schleswig. In L. Holmquist, S. Kalmring & C. Hedenstierna-Jonson (eds.), *New Aspects of Viking Age Urbanism, c. CE 750–1100: Proceedings of the International Symposium at the Swedish History Museum, April 17–20th 2013.* Theses and Papers in Archaeology B12: 63–80. Stockholm: Stockholm University Archaeological Research Laboratory.

Hilberg, V. 2018. Detektoruntersuchungen in Haithabu 2003–2015: Aussagemöglichkeiten und Erkenntnisgewinn für die Entstehung eines wikingerzeitlichen Handelszentrums. In V. Hilberg & T. Lemm (eds.), *Viele Funde – große Bedeutung? Potenzial und Aussagewert von Metalldetektorfunden für die siedlungsarchäologische Forschung der Wikingerzeit.* Bericht des 33. Tværfaglige Vikingesymposiums 9. Mai 2014, Wikinger Museum Haithabu: 125–54. Kiel: Ludwig.

Hilberg, V. 2022. *Haithabu 983–1066. Der Untergang eines dänischen Handelszentrums in der späten Wikingerzeit.* Ausgrabungen in Haithabu 19.

Hilberg, V. & Kalmring, S. 2014. Viking Age Hedeby and Its Relations with Iceland and the North Atlantic. Communication, Long-distance Trade and Production. In D. Zori & J. Byock (eds.), *Viking Archaeology in Iceland: Mosfell Archaeological Project.* Cursor mundi 20: 221–45. Turnhout: Brepols.

Hildebrand, H. 1879. *Sveriges medeltid.* Kulturhistorisk skildring I. Stockholm: P. A. Norstedt & Söner.

Hill, D., Barrett, D., Maude, K., Warburton, J. & Worthington, M. 1990. Quentovic Defined. *Antiquity* 64: 51–8.

Hillerdal, C. 2009. *People In Between: Ethnicity and Material Identity, a New Approach to Deconstructed Concepts.* Occasional Papers in Archaeology 50. Uppsala: Institutionen för arkeologi och antik historia.

Hillerdal, C. 2010. Early Urbanism in Scandinavia. In P. J. J. Sinclair, G. Nordquist, F. Herschend & C. Isendahl (eds.), *The Urban Mind: Cultural and Environmental Dynamics.* Studies in Global Archaeology 15: 499–525. Uppsala: Uppsala University.

Hinton, D. A. 2000a. The Large Towns 600–1300. In D. M. Palliser (ed.), *The Cambridge Urban History of Britain, Vol. 1: 600–1540*: 217–43. Cambridge: Cambridge University Press.

Hinton, D. A. 2000b. *A Smith in Lindsey: The Anglo-Saxon Grave at Tattershall Thorpe, Lincolnshire.* Society for Medieval Archaeology Monograph 16. Leeds: Maney Publishing.

Hinton, D. A. 2005. *Gold and Gilt, Pots and Pins: Possessions and People in Medieval Britain.* Medieval History and Archaeology. Oxford: Oxford University Press.

Hirschfeld, O. 1905. *Die kaiserlichen Verwaltungsbeamten bis auf Diocletian.* Berlin: Weidmannsche Buchhandlung.

Hodges, R. 1982. *Dark Age Economics: The Origins of Towns and Trade A.D. 600–1000.* London: Duckworth.

Hodges, R. 2000. *Towns and Trade in the Age of Charlemagne.* London: Duckworth.

Hodges, R. 2006. *Goodbye to the Vikings? Re-reading Early Medieval Archaeology.* London: Duckworth.

Hodges, R. 2012. *Dark Age Economics: A New Audit.* Duckworth Debates in Archaeology. London: Duckworth.

Hodges, R. 2015. The Idea of the Polyfocal 'Town'?: Archaeology and the Origins of Medieval Urbanism in Italy. In S. Gelichi & R. Hodges (eds.), *New Directions in Early Medieval European Archaeology: Spain and Italy Compared*. Collection Haut Moyen Âge 24: 267–83. Turnhout: Brepols.

Hodges, R. & Whitehouse, D. 1983. *Mohammed, Charlemagne and the Origins of Europe: Archaeology and the Pirenne Thesis*. Ithaca, NY: Cornell University Press.

Hohenberg, P. M. & Lees, L. H. 1996. *The Making of Urban Europe 1000–1994*. Cambridge, MA: Harvard University Press.

Holmquist, L. 2010. Pilen som satte Birkas Garnison i brand. *Situne Dei*: 197–204.

Holmquist Olausson, L. 1990. 'Älgmannen' från Birka. Presentationav en nyligen undersökt krigargrav med människooffer. *Fornvännen* 85: 175–82.

Holmquist Olausson, L. 2001. Den förste kände Sigtunabiskopens begravning. In S. Tesch & R. Edberg (eds.), *Biskopen i museets trädgård*. Sigtuna museers skriftserie 9: 45–58. Sigtuna: Sigtuna Museum.

Holmquist Olausson, L. 2002a. Patterns of Settlement and Defense at the Proto-Town of Birka, Lake Mälar, Eastern Sweden. In J. Jesch (ed.), *The Scandinavians from the Vendel Period to the Tenth Century: An Ethnographic Perspective*. Studies in Historical Archaeology 5: 153–67. San Marino: The Boydell Press.

Holmquist Olausson, L. 2002b. The Fortification of Birka: Interaction between Land and Sea. In A. Nørgård Jørgensen, J. Pind, L. Jørgensen & B. Clausen (eds.), *Maritime Warfare in Northern Europe: Technology, Organisation, Logistics and Administration 500 BC–1500 CE*. Publications from The National Museum. Studies in Archaeology & History 6: 159–67. Copenhagen: The National Museum of Denmark.

Holmquist Olausson, L. & Petrovski, S. 2007. Curious Birds: Two Helmet (?) Mounts with a Christian Motif from Birka's Garrison. In U. Fransson, M. Svedin, S. Bergerbrant & F. Androshchuk (eds.), *Cultural Interaction between East and West: Archaeology, Artefacts and Human Contacts in Northern Europe*: 231–7. Stockholm: Stockholm University.

Horsnæs, H. W. 2020. Ny datering af Haubergs Svend Estridsen type 66–67 og en beslægtet gudslam type. *Nordisk Numismatisk Unions Medlemsblad* 3: 77–86.

Hübener, W. 1959. *Die Keramik von Haithabu*. Ausgrabungen in Haithabu 2. Neumünster: Wachholtz.

Hvass, S. 1979. Vorbasse: The Viking-Age Settlement at Vorbasse, Central Jutland. *Acta Archaeologica* 50: 137–72.

Hvass, S. 2006. s.v. 'Vorbasse'. In H. Beck, D. Geuenich & H. Steuer (eds.), *Reallexikon der Germanischen Altertumskunde*, Vol. 32: 595–9. Berlin: De Gruyter.

Ilisch, L. & Wiechmann, R. In press. Münzfunde von Groß Strömkendorf. In H. Jöns (ed.), *Forschungen zu Groß Strömkendorf*. Frühmittelalterliche Archäologie zwischen Ostsee und Mittelmeer. Frankfurt: Römisch-Germanische Kommission.

Ilves, K. 2012. *Seaward Landward: Investigations on the Archaeological Source Value of the Landing Site Category in the Baltic Sea Region*. AUN 44. Uppsala: Uppsala University.

Imer, L. M. 2016. *Danmarks runesten: En fortælling*. Copenhagen: Gyldendal & Nationalmuseet.

Irsigler, F. 1989. Fernhandel, Märkte und Messen in Vor- und Frühhansischer Zeit. In C. Hirte (ed.), *Die Hanse: Lebenswirklichkeit und Mythos* 1: 22–7. Hamburg: LN-Druck.

Irsigler, F. 1996. Jahrmärkte und Messesysteme im westlichen Reichsgebiet bis ca. 1250. In P. Johanek & H. Stoob (eds.), *Europäische Messen und Märktesysteme in Miteelalter und Neuzeit*. Städteforschung A/39: 1–33. Cologne: Böhlau.

Jacobsen, L. & Moltke, E. 1941–2. *Danmarks Runeindskrifter*, Vol. 1: Atlas; Vol. 2: Text. Copenhagen: Ejnar Munksgaard.

Jahnke, C. 2006. 'Und er verwandelte die blähende Handelstadt in ein unbedeutendes Dorf'. Die Rolle Schleswigs im internationalen Handel des 13. Jahrhunderts. In G. Fouquet, M. Hansen, C. Jahnke & J. Schlürmann (eds.), *Von Menschen, Ländern, Meeren*. Festschrift für Thomas Riis zum 65. Geburtstag: 251–68. Tönning: Der andere Verlag.

Jahnke, C. 2010. s.v. 'Hafen'. In A. Cordes, H. Lück, D. Werkmüller & C. Bertelsmeier-Kierst (eds.), Handwörterbuch zur deutschen Rechtsgeschichte 11: 649–52. Berlin: Erich Schmidt Verlag.

Jahnke, C. 2017. The Maritime Law of the Baltic Sea. In C. Buchet & G. le Bouëdec (eds.), *The Sea in History, Vol. 2: The Medieval World = La Mer dans l'Histoire 2. Le Moyen Âge*: 572–84. Woodbridge: The Boydell Press.

Jahnke, C. 2019. Customs and Toll in the Nordic Area c. 800–1300. In B. Poulsen, H. Vogt & J. V. Sigurðsson (eds.), *Nordic Elites in Transformation, c. 1050–1250: Material Resources 1*. Routledge Research in Medieval Studies: 183–211. New York: Routledge.

Jankuhn, H. 1949. Ergebnisse und Probleme der Haithabugrabungen 1930–1939: Ein Beitrag zur Frage der Stadtentstehung im Norden. *Zeitschrift für Schleswig-Holsteinische Geschichte* 73: 1–86.

Jankuhn, H. 1958: Die frühmittelalterlichen Seehandelsplätze im Nord- und Ostseeraum. In T. Mayer (ed.), *Studien zu den Anfängen des Europäischen Städtewesens: Reichenau-Vorträge 1955–1956*. Vorträge und Forschungen 4: 451–98. Lindau: Thorbecke.

Jankuhn, H. 1971. *Typen und Funktionen Vor- und Frühwikingerzeitlicher Handelsplätze im Ostseegebiet*. Österreichische Akademie der Wissenschaften. Philosophisch-historische Klasse. Sitzungsberichte 273, 5. Abhandlung. Vienna: Hermann Böhlaus Nachf.

Jankuhn, H. 1972. Die Bezeichnungen für die Handelspätze der karolingischen Zeit im Ostseegebiet. In Mitarbeiter des Max-Planck-Instituts für Geschichte (ed.), *Festschrift für Hermann Heimpel 3*. Veröffentlichungen des Max-Planck-Instituts für Geschichte 36/III: 135–46. Göttingen: Vandenhoeck & Ruprecht.

Jankuhn, H. 1986. *Haithabu: Ein Handelsplatz der Wikingerzeit*. Neumünster: Wachholtz.

Jankuhn, H., Schlesinger, W. & Steuer, H. (eds.) 1973. *Vor- und Frühformen der europäischen Stadt im Mittelalter I*. Abhandlungen der Akademie der Wissenschaften in Göttingen. Philologisch-historische Klasse. Dritte Folge. No. 83. Göttingen: Vandenhoeck & Ruprecht.

Jansma, E. & van Lanen, R. J. 2016. The Dendrochronology of Dorestad: Placing Early-Medieval Structural Timbers in a Wider Geographical Context. In A. Willemsen & H. Kik (eds.), *Golden Middle Ages in Europe: New Research into Early-Medieval Communities and Identities*: 105–44. Turnhout: Brepols.

Jansma, E., van Lanen, R. J. & Pierik, H. J. 2017. Travelling through a River Delta: A Landscape-Archaeological Reconstruction of River Development and Long-Distance Connections in the Netherlands during the First Millennium CE. *Medieval Settlement Research* 32: 35–9.

Janson, H. 2011. Scythian Christianity. In I. Garipzanov & O. Tolochko (eds.), *Early Christianity on the Way from the Varangians to the Greeks*. Ruthenica. Suppl. 4: 33–57. Kiev: Instytut istoriï Ukraïny.

Janson, H. 2016. Sven Estridsson, Hamburg-Bremen och påven. In L. C. A. Sonne & S. Croix (eds.), *Svend Estridsen. Studies in History and Social Sciences* 528: 81–107. Odense: Syddansk Universitetsforlag.

Janssen, W. 1983. Gewerbliche Produktion des Mittelalters als Wirtschaftsfaktor im ländlichen Raum. In H. Jankuhn, W. Janssen, R. Schmidt-Wiegand & H. Tiefenbach (eds.), *Das Handwerk in vor-und frühgeschichtlicher Zeit 2*. Archäologische und philologische Beiträge. Abhandlungen der Akademie der Wissenschaften. Philologisch-Historische Klasse. Dritte Folge No. 123: Göttingen: 317–94. Vandenhoeck & Ruprecht.

Jansson, I. 1985. *Ovala spännbucklor: En studie av vikingatida standardsmycken med utgångspunkt från Björköfynden = Oval Brooches: A Study of Viking Period Standard Jewellery Based on the Finds from Björkö (Birka), Sweden*. AUN 7. Uppsala: Institutionen för arkeologi.

Jensen, B. 2010. *Viking Age Amulets in Scandinavia and Western Europe*. BAR International Series 2169. Oxford: Archaeopress.

Jensen, S. 1991. *The Vikings of Ribe*. Ribe: Den antikvariske Samling.

Jeppesem, J. 2004. Stormandsgården ved Lisbjerg kirke. Nye undersøgelser. *KUML. Årbok for Jysk Arkæologisk Selskab*: 161–80.

Jeppsesen, J. & Madsen, H. J. 1991. Storgård og kirke i Lisbjerg. In P. Mortensen & B. M. Rasmussen (eds.), *Fram Stamme til Stat i Danmark, Vol. 2: Høvdingesamfund og Kongemagt*. Jysk Arkæologisk Selskabs Skrifter XXII/2: 269–75. Aarhus: Universitetsforlag.

Jeppsesen, J. & Madsen, H. J. 1995/6. Trækirke og stormandshal i Lisbjerg. *KUML. Årbok for Jysk Arkæologisk Selskab*: 149–71.

Jesch, J. 2001. *Ships and Men in the Late Viking Age: The Vocabulary of Runic Inscriptions and Skaldic Verse*. Woodbridge: The Boydell Press.

Jones, A. H. M. 1964. *The Later Roman Empire 284–602: A Social Economic and Administrative Survey*, Vol. 2. Oxford: Blackwell.

Jöns, H. 1999. War das *emporium* Reric der Vorläufer Haithabus? *Bodendenkmalpflege in Mecklenburg-Vorpommern* 47: 201–13.

Jöns, H. 2015. Early Medieval Trading Centres and Transport Systems between Dorestad, Ribe and Wolin: The Latest Results of the Priority Research Programme 'Harbours from the Roman Iron Age to the Middle Ages'. In L. Larsson, F. Ekengren, B. Helgesson & B. Söderberg (eds.), *Small Things, Wide Horizons: Studies in Honour of Birgitta Hårdh*: 245–52. Oxford: Archaeopress.

Jonsson, K. 2001. Mynten: En fyndkatergori som speglar Birkakrigarnas internationella kontakter. In M. Olausson (ed.), *Birkas krigare: 11 artiklar kring Birkas befästningsverk och dess krigare*. Borgar och befästningsverk i Mellansverige 400–1000 e.Kr. (BMS) 5: 29–33. Stockholm: Stockholms universitet.

Jørgensen, L. 2003. Manor and Market at Lake Tissø in the Sixth to Eleventh Centuries: The Danish 'Productive' Sites. In T. Pestell & K. Ulmschneider (eds.), *Markets in Early Medieval Europe: Trading and 'Productive' Sites, 650–850*: 175–207. London: Windgather Press.

Jørgensen, L. 2008. Manor, Cult and Market at Lake Tissø. In S. Brink & N. Price (eds.), *The Viking World*: 77–82. London: Routledge.

Jørgensen, L. 2009. Pre-Christian Cult at Aristocratic Residences and Settlement Complexes in Southern Scandinavia in the 3rd–10th Centuries CE. In U. von Freeden, H. Friesinger & E. Wamers (eds.), *Glaube, Kult und Herrschaft. Phänomene des Religiösen im 1. Jahrtausend n.Chr. in Mittel- und Nordeuropa*. Akten des 59. Internationalen Sachsensymposiums und der

Grundprobleme der frühgeschichtlichen Entwicklung im Mitteldonauraum = Kolloquien zur Vor- und Frühgeschichte 12: 329–54. Bonn: Rudolf Habelt.

Jørgensen, L., Gebauer Thomsen, L. & Nørgard Jørgensen, A. 2019. Accommodating Assemblies, as Evidenced at the 6th–11th-Century AD Royal Residence at Lake Tissø, Denmark. In J. Carroll, A. Reynolds & B. Yorke (eds.), *Power and Place in Europe in the Early Middle Ages*. Proceedings of the British Academy 224: 148–73. Oxford: Oxford University Press.

Kähler Holst, M. 2014. Warrior Aristocracy and Village Community: Two Fundamental Forms of Social Organization in the Late Iron Age and Viking Age. In E. Stidsing, K. Høilund Nielsen & R. Fiedel (eds.), *Wealth and Complexity: Economically Specialized Sites in Late Iron Age Denmark*: 179–97. Aarhus: Museum Østjylland & Aarhus University Press.

Kähler Holst, M., Drengsø Jessen, M., Wulff Andersen, S. & Pedersen, A. 2012. The Late Viking-Age Royal Constructions at Jelling, Central Jutland, Denmark: Recent Investigations and a Suggestion for an Interpretative Revision. *Prähistorische Zeitschrift* 87(2): 474–505.

Källström, M. 2010. Forsaringen tillhör 900-talet. *Fornvännen* 105: 228–32.

Källström, M. 2015. Kungen, bryten och märket. Till tolkningen av runblocket U11 vid Hovgården på Adelsö och något om runstenarnas placering. *Saga och Sed*: 67–86.

Kalmring, S. 2007. Schiff – Hafen – Stadt: Mittelalterliche Hafenanlagen in Nordeuropa. In C. von Carnap-Bornheim & C. Radtke (eds.), *Es war einmal ein Schiff. Archäologische Expeditionen zum Meer*: 171–204. Hamburg: mare.

Kalmring, S. 2010a. *Der Hafen von Haithabu*. Ausgrabungen in Haithabu 14. Neumünster: Wachholtz.

Kalmring, S. 2010b. Dorestad Hoogstraat from a Hedeby/Schleswig Point of View. In A. Willemsen & H. Kik (eds.), *Dorestad in an International Framework: New Research on Centres of Trade and Coinage in Carolingian Times*: 68–81. Turnhout: Brepols.

Kalmring, S. 2010c. Of Thieves, Counterfeiters and Homicides: Crime in Hedeby and Birka. *Fornvännen* 105: 281–90.

Kalmring, S. 2011. The Harbour of Hedeby. In S. Sigmundsson (ed.), *Viking Settlements and Viking Society: Papers from the Proceedings of the Sixteenth Viking Congress*: 245–59. Reykjavík: University of Iceland Press.

Kalmring, S. 2012a. Dorestad Hoogstraat: Ein Diskurs gegen das Verschwinden des Hafens des 'vicus famosus'. In P. Gammeltoft & V. Hilberg (eds.), *29. Tværfaglige Vikingesymposium Schleswig*: 22–49. Højbjerg: Wormianum.

Kalmring, S. 2012b. The Birka Proto-Town GIS: A Source for Comprehensive Studies of Björkö. *Fornvännen* 107: 253–65.

Kalmring, S. 2014/15. Hedeby Hochburg: Theories, State of Research and Dating. With a Contribution by L. Holmquist. *Offa* 71(72): 241–91.

Kalmring, S. 2015. Review on S. Brather & M. F. Jagodziński, Der wikingerzeitliche Seehandelsplatz von Janów (Truso). Geophysikalische, archäopedologische und archäologische Untersuchungen 2004–2008 = Nadmorska osada handlowa z okresu Wikingów z Janowa (Truso). Badania geofizyczne, archeo-pedologiczne i archeologiczne w latach 2004–2008. Zeitschrift für Archäologie des Mittelalters. Beiheft 24 (Bonn 2012). *Germania* 93: 397–402.

Kalmring, S. 2016a. Early Northern Towns As Special Economic Zones. In L. Holmquist, S. Kalmring & C. Hedenstiern-Jonson (eds.), *New Aspects on Viking-Age Urbanism, c. A.D. 750–1000*. Archaeological Research Laboratory. Theses and Papers in Archaeology B: 12: 11–21. Stockholm: Stockholm University Archaeological Research Laboratory.

Kalmring, S. 2016b. Where Do We Go from Here? A Comprehensive Approach into Birka Research. In V. E. Turner, O. A. Owen & D. J. Waugh (eds.), *Shetland and the Viking World: Proceedings of the 17th Viking Congress Lerwick*: 203–10. Lerwick: Shetland Heritage Publications.

Kalmring, S. 2017. Excavations in Hedeby's Flat-Grave Burial Ground: A Preliminary Report. *Jahresbericht Zentrum für Baltische und Skandinavische Archäologie* 2017: 38–42.

Kalmring, S. 2018. Ausgrabungen im Flachgräberfeld von Haithabu: Ein Vorbericht. *Archäologische Nachrichten Schleswig-Holstein* 2018: 68–78.

Kalmring, S. 2020a. 'Without History or Memory, Rituals or Monuments': Viking Harbour Towns As Non-representative Sites. In M. Koçak, T. Schmidts & M. Vučetić (eds.), *Häfen als Orte der Repräsentation in Antike und Mittelalter. Interdisziplinäre Forschungen zu den Häfen von der Römischen Kaiserzeit bis zum Mittelalter in Europa 8*. RGZM-Tagungen 43: 163–73. Mainz: Römisch-Germanisches Zentralmuseum.

Kalmring, S. 2020b. A Different Birka: Emergence of the First Urban Fabric in the Early Birka Period (AD 750–860). *Zeitschrift für Archäologie des Mittelalters* 48 (2020): 1–23.

Kalmring, S., Holmquist, L. & Wendt, A. 2021. *Birka's Black Earth Harbour. Archaeological Investigations 2015–2016: Uppland, Adelsö Parish, Björkö, L2017:1568, RAÄ 119:1*. Theses and Papers in Archaeology B:16. Stockholm: Stockholm University Archaeological Research Laboratory.

Kalmring, S., Runer, J. & Viberg, A. 2017. At Home with Herigar: A Magnate's Residence from the Vendel- to Viking Period at Korshamn, Birka (Uppland/S). *Archäologisches Korrespondezblatt* 47: 117–40.

Kastholm, O. 2014. Under sejlet: Vikingetidens skibe i langtidsperspektiv. In H. Lyngstrøm & L. C. A. Sonne (eds.), *Vikingetidens aristokratiske miljøer*. *Arkæologi på Saxo-Institutet*: 103–12. Copenhagen: Publi@Kom.

Kazhdan, A. P. & Oikonomides, N. 1991. s.v. 'Kommerkiarios'. In A. P. Kazhdan (ed.), *The Oxford Dictionary of Byzantium*, Vol. 2: 1141. Oxford: Oxford University Press.

Kelly, S. 1992. Trading Privileges from Eighth-Century England. *Early Medieval Europe* 1(1): 3–28.

Kemp, R. L. 1996. *Anglian Settlement at 46–54 Fishergate*. Anglian York. The Archaeology of York 7. Dorchester: Council for British Archaeology.

Kieffer-Olsen, J. 1993. *Kirkegårdsudgravninger*. Grav og gravskik i det middelalderlige Danmark 8. Højbjerg: Afdeling for Middelalder-arkæologi og Middelalder-Arkaeologisk Nyhedsbrev.

Kilger, C. 2008. Kaupang from Afar: Aspects of the Interpretation of Dirham Finds in Northern and Eastern Europe between the Late 8th and Early 10th Centuries. In D. Skre (ed.), *Means of Exchange: Dealing with Silver in the Viking Age*. Kaupang Excavation Project Publication Series, Vol. 2. Norske Oldfunn XXIII: 199–252. Aarhus: Aarhus Universitetsforlag.

Kind, T. 2007. Das karolingerzeitliche Kloster Fulda – ein '*monasterium in solitudine*'. Seine Strukturen und Handwerksproduktion nach den seit 1898 gewonnenen archäologischen Daten. In J. Henning (ed.), *The Heirs of the Roman West, Vol. 1: Post-Roman Towns, Trade and Settlement in Europe and Byzantium*: 367–409. Berlin: De Gruyter.

Kitzler, L. 2000. Odensymbolik i Birkas garnison. *Fornvännen* 95: 13–21.

Kjellberg, J. 2021. *Den medeltida stadens dynamic: urbanitet, sociala praktiker och materiell Kultur i Uppsala 1100–1550*. AUN 51. Uppsala: Uppsala University.

Kjellström, A. 2005. *The Urban Farmer: Osteoarchaeological Analysis of Skeletons from Medieval Sigtuna Interpreted in a Socioeconomic Perspective*. Theses and Papers in Osteoarchaeology 2. Stockholm: Stockholm University.

Kjellström, A. 2014. Interpreting Violence: A Bioarchaeological Perspective of Violence from Medieval Central Sweden. In C. Knüsel & M. J. Smith (eds.), *The Routledge Handbook of the Bioarchaeology of Human Conflict*: 237–50. New York: Routledge.

Kleingärtner, S. 2014. *Die frühe Phase der Urbanisierung an der südlichen Ostseeküste im ersten nachchristlichen Jahrtausend*. Studien zur Siedlungsgeschichte und Archäologie der Ostseegebiete 13. Neumünster: Wachholtz.

Kocabaş, U. 2012. The Latest Link in the Long Tradition of the Maritime Archaeology in Turkey: The Yenikapı Shipwrecks. *European Journal of Archaeology* 15(2): 309–23.

Koktvedgaard Zeitzen, M. 2002. Miniaturanker aus Haithabu und Schleswig. Das archäologische Fundmaterial 7. *Berichte über die Ausgrabungen in Haithabu* 34: 69–84. Neumünster: Wachholtz.

Kronz, A., Hilberg, V., Simon, K & Wedepohl, K. H. 2015. Glas aus Haithabu. *Zeitschrift für Archäologie des Mittelalters* 43: 39–58.

Kühl, J. & Hardt, N. 1999. *Danevirke: Nordens største fortidsminde*. Danevikegården: Poul Kristensens Forlag.

Kuhlmann, H. J. 1958. *Besiedlung und Kirchspielorganisation der Landschaft Angeln im Mittelalter*. Quellen und Forschungen zur Geschichte Schleswig-Holsteins 36. Neumünster: Wachholtz Verlag.

Kulke, E. 2009. *Wirtschaftsgeographie*. Grundriss Allgemeine Geographie 2434. Paderborn: UTB Schöningh.

Laiou, A. E. 2002. Exchange and Trade, Seventh–Twelfth Centuries. In A. E. Laiou (ed.), *The Economic History of Byzantium: From the Seventh through the Fifteenth Century*. Dumbarton Oaks Studies 39: 698–770. Washington, DC: Dumbarton Oaks.

Larsson, G. 2013. Ingvar the Fartravellers Journey: Historical and Archaeological Sources. In G. Larsson (ed.), *Between East and West: Early Contacts between Scandinavia and the Caucasus*. Revita Archaeology and History: 36–48. Uppsala: Uppsala University.

Larsson, L. & Hårdh, B. (eds.) 2002. *Central Places in the Migration and Merovingian Periods: Papers from the 52nd Sachsensymposium*. Uppåkrastudier 6. Acta archaeologica Lundensia, Series in 8°, Vol. 39. Stockholm: Almqvist & Wiksell International.

Larsson, L. & Lenntorp, K.-M. 2004. The Enigmatic House. In L. Larsson (ed.), *Continuity for Centuries: A Ceremonial Building and Its Context at Uppåkra, Southern Sweden*. Uppåkrastudier 10. Acta archaeologica Lundensia, Series in 8°, No. 48: 3–48. Stockholm: Almquist & Wiksell International.

Larsson, M. G. 1983. Vart for Ingvar den vittfarne? *Fornvännen* 78: 95–104.

Larsson, M. G. 1986. Ingvartågets arkeologiska bakgrund. *Fornvännen* 81: 98–113.

Laur, W. 1992. *Historisches Ortsnamenlexikon von Schleswig-Holstein*. Veröffentlichungen des Schleswig-Holsteinischen Landesarchivs 28. Neumünster: Wachholtz.

Laur, W. 2006. *Runendenkmäler in Schleswig-Holstein und in Nordschleswig*. Schleswig: Wikinger Museum Haithabu.

Lebecq, S. 1983. *Marchands et Navigateurs Frisons du Haut Moyen âge, Vol. 2: Corpus des Source Ecrites*. Lille: Presses Universitaires de Lille.

Lebecq, S. 1991. Pour une histoire parallèle de Quentovic et Dorestad. In J.-M. Duvosquel & A. Dierkens (eds.), *Villes et Campagnes au Moyen âge: Mélanges Georges Despy*: 415–28. Liège: Éditions du Perron.

Lebecq, S. 1993. Quentovic: Un état de la question. In H.-J. Häßler & C. Lorren (eds.), *Studien zur Sachsenforschung* 8. Beiträge vom 39. Sachsensymposium in Caen, Normandie: 73–82. Hildesheim: Verlag August Lax.

Lebecq, S. 1995. L'emporium proto-médiéval de Walcheren-Domburg: une mise en perspective. In J. M. Duvosquel & E. Thoen (eds.), *Peasants and Townsmen in Medieval Europe: Studia in honorem Adriaan Verhulst*: 73–89. Ghent: Snoeck-Ducaju & Zoon.

Lebecq, S. 2006. L'administration portuaire de Quentovic et de Dorestad (VIIIe–IXe siècles). In S. Lebecq, B. Béthouart & L. Verslype (eds.), Quentovic: Environnement, Archéologie, Histoire. Collection UL3 traveau & recherches: 241–51. Lille: Charles de Gaulle University.

Lemm, T. 2013a. *Die frühmittelalterlichen Ringwälle in westlichen und mittleren Holstein*. Schriften des Archäologischen Landesmuseums 11. Neumünster: Wachholtz.

Lemm, T. 2013b: Graf Egbert und Burg Esesfelth: Überlegungen zu Vorgehensweise und Auswirkungen der fränkischen Annexion Nordelbiens. In B. Ludowici (ed.), *Individual and Individuality? Approaches towards an Archaeology of Personhood in the First Millennium CE*. Neue Studien zur Sachsenforschung 4: 217–32. Hannover: Theiss.

Lemm, T. 2016a. Zum Schutze Haithabus: Die Rekonstruktion eines auf visueller Kommunikation basierenden Verteidigungssystems an der Schlei. *Arkæologi i Slesvig/Archäologie in Schleswig* 16: 27–48.

Lemm, T. 2016b. Husby and the Equestrian Graves in Angeln and Schwansen: Different Chronological Stages in the Development of a Royal Administration? In L. Holmquist, S. Kalmring & C. Hedenstierna-Jonson (eds.), *New Aspects on Viking-age Urbansim, c. A.D. 750–1000*. Archaeological Research Laboratory. Theses and Papers in Archaeology B: 12: 97–113. Stockholm: Stockholm University Archaeological Research Laboratory.

Lemm, T. 2019. Protecting Hedeby: Reconstructing a Viking Age Maritime Defense System Based on Visual Communication. In R. Annaert (ed.), *Early Medieval Waterscapes: Risks and Opportunities for (Im)material Cultural Exchange*. Neue Studien zur Sachsenforschung 8: 101–14. Braunschweig: Braunschweigisches Landesmuseeum.

Lemm, T. in press. 'Tips of Icebergs': Continuity and Change between the 5th and the 8th Centuries in the Hinterland of the Danevirke. In T. Zachrisson &

S. Fischer (eds.), *Changes: The Shift from the Early to Late Iron Age*. Neue Studien zur Sachsenforschung.

Leroy, I. & Verslype, L. 2015. Quentovic: Un portus du haut Moyen Âge aux confins du Ponthieu et du Boulonnais. In P. Demolon (ed.), *Le haut Moyen Âge dans le nord de la France: Des Francs aux premiers comtes de Flandre, de la fin du IVe au milieu du Xe siècle*: 159–60. Douai: Arkeos, Communauté d'agglomération du Douaisis.

Lind, J. 2012. 'Vikinger', vikingetid og vikingeromantik. *Kuml: Årbok for Jysk Arkæologisk Selskab* 61: 151–70.

Lindbom, P. 2009. The Assault on Helgö and Birka and the End of the Iron Age. *Situne Dei*: 83–101.

Lindqvist, S. 1926. *Björkö*. Svenska Fornminnesplatser 2. Stockholm: Wahlström & Widstrand.

Lindqvist, S. 1936. *Uppsala högar och Ottarhögen*. Kungl. Vitterhets Historie och Antikvitets Akademien. Monografier 23. Stockholm: Wahlström & Widstrand.

Lindqvist, S. 1951. Gamla Uppsala kyrka. Bidrag till dess byggnadshistoria. *Fornvännen* 46: 219–50.

Lindqvist, S. 1967. Uppsala hednatempel och första katedral. Gammal stridsfråga i nytt ljus. *Nordisk tidskrift för vetenskap, konst och industri* 43: 236–42.

Line, Ph. 2007. *Kingship and State Formation in Sweden 1130–1290*. The Northern World 27. Leiden: Brill.

Ljungkvist, J. 2000. *I maktens närhet: Två boplatsundersökningar i Gamla Uppsala*. Societas Archaeologica Upsaliensis. SAU skrifter 1. Uppsala: Societas Archaeologica Upsaliensis.

Ljungkvist, J. 2008. Dating of the Two Royal Mounds of Old Uppsala: Evaluating the Elite of the 6th and 7th Century in Middle Sweden. *Archäologisches Korrespondezblatt* 38: 263–82.

Ljungkvist, J. 2013. Monumentaliseringen av Gamla Uppsala. In O. Sundqvist & P. Vikstrand (eds.), Gamla Uppsala i ny belysning. Religionsvetenskapliga studier från Gävle 9: 33–67. Uppsala: Swedish Science Press

Ljungkvist, J. & Frölund, P. 2015. Gamla Uppsala: The Emergence of a Centre and a Magnate Complex. *Journal of Archaeology and Ancient History* 16: 3–29.

Loseby, S. T. 2000. Marseille and the Pirenne Thesis, II: 'Ville Morte'. In I. L. Hansen & C. Wickham (eds.), *The Long Eighth Century*. The Transformations of the Roman World 11: 167–93. Leiden: Brill.

Loveluck, C. 2013. *Northwest Europe in the Early Middle Ages, c. CE 600–1150: A Comparative Archaeology*. Cambridge: Cambridge University Press.

Loveluck, C. 2018. Coopetition and Urban Worlds, c. CE 1050–1150: Archaeological and Textual Case Studies from Northwestern Europe. In R. Le

Jan, G. Bührer-Thierry & S. Gasparri (eds.), *Coopétition: Rivaliser, coopérer dans les sociétés du haut Moyen Âge (500–1100)*. Collection Haut Moyen Âge 31: 295–320. Turnhout: Brepols.

Loveluck, C. & Tys, D. 2006. Costal Societies, Exchange and Identity along the Channel and Southern North Sea Shore of Europe, CE 600–1000. *Journal of Maritime Archaeology* 1: 140–69.

Lübke, C. 2001. Die Beziehungen zwischen Elb- und Ostseeslawen und Dänen vom 9. Bis zum 12. Jahrhundert: Eine andere Option elbslawischer Geschichte? In O. Harck & C. Lübke (eds.), *Zwischen Reric und Bornhöved: Die Beziehungen zwischen den Dänen und ihren slawischen Nachbarn vom 9. bis ins 13. Jahrhundert*: 23–36. Stuttgart: Franz Steiner Verlag.

Ludowici, B., Jöns, H., Kleingärtner, S., Scheschkewitz, J. & Hardt, M. (eds.). 2010 *Trade and Communication Networks of the First Millennium CE in the Northern Part of Central Europe: Central Places, Beach Markets, Landing Places and Trading Centers*. Neue Studien zur Sachsenforschung 1. Hannover: Niedersächsisches Landesmuseum Hannover.

Lüdtke, H. 1997. Die archäologischen Untersuchungen unter dem Schleswiger Rathausmarkt. Kirche und Gräberfeld des 11.–13. Jahrhunderts unter dem Rathausmarkt von Schleswig. *Ausgrabungen in Schleswig. Berichte und Studien* 12: 9–84. Neumünster: Wachholtz.

Lund, N. 1983. s.v. 'Sven (II) Estridsen'. In S. Cedergreen Beck (ed.), *Dansk Biografisk Leksikon*, Vol. 14: 242–3. Copenhagen: Gyldendal.

Lund, N. 1995. Scandinavia, c. 700–1066. In R. McKitterick (ed.), *The New Cambridge Medieval History*, Vol. 2: c. 700–c. 900: 202–27. Cambridge: Cambridge University Press.

Lund, N. 1996. *Lið, Leding og Landværn. Hær og samfund i Danmark i ældre middelalder*. Roskilde: Vikingeskibshallen.

Lund, N. 2002. Harald Bluetooth: A Saint Very Nearly Made by Adam of Bremen. In J. Jesch (ed.), *The Scandinavians from the Vendel Period to the Tenth Century: An Ethnographic Perspective*. Studies in Historical Archaeology 5: 303–15. San Marino: The Boydell Press.

Lund, N. 2005. s.v. 'Sven Estridsen'. In H. Beck, D. Geuenich & H. Steuer (eds.), *Reallexikon der Germanischen Altertumskunde*, Vol. 30: 178–81. Berlin: De Gruyter.

Lundström, F., Hedenstierna-Jonson, C. & Holmquist Olausson, L. 2009. Eastern Archery in Birka's Garrison. In L. Holmquist Olausson & M. Olausson (eds.), *The Martial Society: Aspects of Warriors, Fortifications and Social Change in Scandinavia*. Theses and papers in Archaeology B11: 105–16. Stockholm: Stockholm University Archaeological Research Laboratory.

MacLean, S. 2003. *Kingship and Politics in the Late Ninth Century: Charles the Fat and the End of the Carolingian Empire*. Cambridge: Cambridge University Press.

Magnus, B. 2002. Dwellings and Settlements: Structure and Characteristics. In J. Jesch (ed.), *The Scandinavians from the Vendel Period to the Tenth Century: An Ethnographic Perspective*. Studies in Historical Archaeoethnology 5: 4–33. San Marino: The Boydell Press.

Mainman A. J. & Rogers, N. S. H. 2000. *Craft, Industry and Everyday Life: Finds from Anglo-Scandinavian York*. The Archaeology of York The Small Finds 17/14. London: Council for British Archaeology.

Malbos, L. 2017. *Les Ports des Mers Nordiques à l'Époque Viking (VIIe – Xe Siècle)*. Collection Haut Moyen Âge 27. Turnhout: Brepols.

Malcom, G., Bowsher, D. & Cowie, R. 2003. *Middle Saxon London: Excavations at the Royal Opera House 1989–99*. MoLAS Monograph 15. London: Museum of London Archaeology Service.

Malmer, B. 1966. *Nordiska Mynt före År 1000*. Acta Archaeologica Lundensia Ser. 8°, No. 4. Bonn: Habelt.

Malmer, B. 1989. *The Sigtuna Coinage c. 995–1005*. Commentationes de nummis seaculorum IX–XI. In Suecia repertis. Nova series 4. London: Kungl. Vitterhets Historie och Antikvitets Akademien.

Malmer, B. 1991. *Kung Olofs mynthus i kvarteret Urmakaren, Sigtuna*. Sigtuna museers skriftserie 3. Sigtuna: Sigtuna Museum.

Malmer, B. 2007. South Scandinavian Coinage in the Ninth Century. In J. Graham-Campbell & G. Williams (eds.), *Silver Economy in the Viking Age*: 13–27. Walnut Creek, CA: Left Coast Press.

Matz, E. 1990. Mälaren – vintersjön. In U. Johansson (ed.), *De stora sjöarna = Svenska Turistföreningens Årsbok 1991*: 166–79. Uppsala: Svenska Turistföreningen.

McCormick, M. 2001. *Origins of the European Economy: Communications and Commerce A.D. 300–900*. Cambridge: Cambridge University Press.

Meier, D. 1994. *Die wikingerzeitliche Siedlung von Kosel (Kosel-West), Kreis Rendsburg-Eckernförde*. Siedlungsarchäologische Untersuchungen in Angeln und Schwansen 3. Offa-Bücher 76. Neumünster: Wachholtz.

Meier, U. M. 2007. *Die früh- und hochmittelalterliche Siedlung bei Schuby, Kreis Schlswig-Flensburg, LA 226*. Siedlungsarchäologische Untersuchungen in Angeln und Schwansen 4. Offa-Bücher 83. Neumünster: Wachholtz.

Middelton, N. 2005. Early Medieval Port Customs, Toll and Controls on Foreign Trade. *Early Medieval Europe* 13: 313–58.

Miksic, J. N. 2000. Heterogenetic Cities in Premodern Southeast Asia. *World Archaeology* 32(1) Special Issue, Archaeology of Southeast Asia: 106–20.

Moberg, L. 2014. The Political Economy of Special Economic Zones. *Journal of Institutional Economics* 11(1): 167–90.

Moesgaard, J. C., Hilberg, V. & Schimmer, M. 2016. Mønter fra Slesvigs blomstringstid 1070–1150. *Nationalmuseets Arbejdsmark*: 182–195.

Mogren, M. 2013. The First Sparks and the Far Horizons: Stirring up the Thinking on the Earliest Scandinavian Urbanisation Process – Again. *Lund Archaeological Review* 18(2012): 73–88.

Mohr, A. 2005. *Das Wissen über die Anderen. Zur Darstellung fremder Völker in den fränkischen Quellen der Karolingerzeit*. Studien und Texte zum Mittelalter und zur frühen Neuzeit 7. Münster: Waxmann.

Mokkelbost, M. forthcoming. *The Social Archaeology of Houses: Rural and Urban Households in 800–1350 Central Norway*. Bergen: University of Bergen.

Morris, C. A. 2000. *Craft, Industry and Everyday Life: Wood and Woodworking in Anglo-Scandinavian and Medieval York*. The Archaeology of York The Small Finds 17/13. York: York Archaeological Trust.

Mortensen, P. & Rasmussen, B. M. (eds.) 1991. *Fram Stamme til Stat i Danmark, Vol. 2: Høvdingesamfund og Kongemagt*. Jysk Arkæologisk Selskabs Skrifter XXII: 2. Højbjerg: Jysk Arkæologisk Selskab.

Morton, A. D. 1992. *Excavations at Hamwic, Vol. 1: Excavations 1946–83, Excluding Six Dials and Melbourne Street*. CBA Research Report No. 84, Southampton Archaeological Monographs 5. London: Council of British Archaeology.

Müller, L. 2002. s.v. 'Nestorchronik'. In H. Beck, D. Geuenich & H. Steuer (eds.), *Reallexikon Der Germanischen Altertumskunde*, Vol. 21: 94–100. Berlin: De Gruyter.

Müller, C., Wölz, S. & Kalmring, S. 2013. High-Resolution 3D Marine Seismic Investigation of Hedeby Harbour, Germany. *The International Journal of Nautical Archaeology* 42(2): 326–36.

Müller-Boysen, C. 1990. *Kaufmannsschutz und Handelsrecht im frühmittelalterlichen Nordeuropa*. Neumünster: Wachholtz.

Müller-Boysen, C. 2007. Economic Policy, Prosperity and Professional Traders. In J. Bately & A. Englert (eds.), *Oh there's Voyages: A Late 9th-Century Account of Voyages along the Coasts of Norway and Denmark and Its Cultural Context*. Maritime Culture of the North 1: 180–3. Roskilde: Viking Ship Museum.

Müller-Wille, M. 1973. Zwei wikingerzeitliche Prachtschwerter aus der Umgebung von Haithabu. Das archäologische Fundmaterial 2. *Berichte über die Ausgrabungen in Haithabu* 6: 47–89. Neumünster: Wachholtz.

Müller-Wille, M. 2002a. Schleswig-Holstein: Drehscheibe zwischen Völkern. In U. von Freeden & S. von Schnurbein (eds.), *Spuren der Jahrtausende: Archäologie und Geschichte in Deutschland*: 368–87. Stuttgart: Theiss Verlag.

Müller-Wille, M. 2002b. *Frühstädtische Zentren der Wikingerzeit und ihr Hinterland: Die Beispiele Ribe, Hedeby und Reric*. Akademie der Wissenschaften und der Literatur. Abhandlungen der Geistes- und sozialwissenschaftlichen Klasse. Jahrgang 2002, No. 3. Stuttgart: Franz Steiner Verlag.

Müller-Wille, M. 2009. Emporium Reric. In S. Brather, D. Geuenich & C. Huth (eds.), *Historia archaeologica: Festschrift für Heiko Steuer zum 70. Geburtstag*. RGA Ergänzungsbände 70: 453–73. Berlin: De Gruyter.

Müller-Wille, M. 2017. Unsichtbare Grabhügel. In J. Krüger, V. Busch, K. Seidel, C. Zimmermann & U. Zimmermann (eds.), *Die Faszination des Verborgenen und seine Entschlüsselung: Rāði sār kunni*. Beiträge zur Runologie, skandinavistischen Mediävistik und germanischen Sprachwisschenschaft. Ergänzungsbände zum Reallexikon der germanischen Altertumskunde 101: 261–76. Berlin: De Gruyter.

Munch, P. A. 1849. *Historisk-geographisk Beskrivelse over Kongeriget Norge (Noregsveldi) i Middelalderen*. Moss: Wilhelm Grams Forlag.

Myhre, B. 2015. *Før Viken ble Norge: Borregravfeltet som religiøs og politisk arena*. Norske Oldfunn 31. Tønsberg: Vestfold Fylkeskommune.

Näsman, U. 2000. Exchange and Politics: The Eighth–Early Ninth Century in Denmark. In I. Lyse Hansen & C. Wickham (eds.), *The Long Eighth Century*. The Transformation of the Roman World 11: 35–68. Leiden: Brill.

Naylor, J. 2004. Access to International Trade in Middle Saxon England: A Case of Urban Over-Emphasis? In M. Pasquinucci & T. Weski (eds.), *Sea- and Riverborne Trade, Ports and Hinterlands, Ship Construction and Navigation in Antiquity, the Middle Ages and in Modern Time*. BAR International Series 1283: 139–48. Oxford: Archaeopress.

Naylor, J. 2016. Emporia and Their Hinterlands in the 7th to 9th-Century CE: Some Comments and Observations from England. In I. Leroy & L. Verslype (eds.), *Les cultures des littoraux au haut Moyen Âge: Cadres et modes de via dans l'espace maritime Manche-mer du Nord du IIIe au Xe s*. Revue du Nord. Collection Art et Archéologie 24: 59–67. Villeneuve-d'Ascq: Université de Lille. Siences humaines et sociales.

Neubauer, W., Eder-Hinterleitner, A., Seren, S., Becker, H. & Fassbinder, J. 2003. Magnetic Survey of the Viking Age Settlement of Haithabu, Germany. *Archaeologia Polona* 41: 239–41.

Noonan, T. S. 1981. Ninth Century Dirham Hoards from European Russia: A Preliminary Analysis. In M. A. S. Blackburn & D. M. Metcalf (eds.), *Viking-Age Coinage in Northern Lands: The Sixth Oxford Symposium on Coinage and Monetary History, Part 1*. BAR International Series 122: 47–117. Oxford: Archaeopress.

Noonan, T. S. 1985. The First Major Silver Crisis in Russia and the Baltic c. 875–c. 900. *Hikuin* 11: 41–50.

Noonan, T. S. 2007. Some Observations on the Economy of the Khazar Khaganate. In P. B. Golden, H. Ben-Shammai & A. Róna-Tas (eds.), *The World of the Khazars: New Perspectives*. Handbook of Oriental Studies. Section 8. Central Asia Studies 17: 207–44. Leiden: Brill.

Nordahl, E. 1993. Södra Kungsgårdsplatån: Utgrävningarna 1988–1991. In W. Duczko (ed.), *Arkeologi och miljögeologi i Gamla Uppsala: Studier och rapporter*, Vol. 1. Occasional Papers in Archaeology 7: 59–63. Uppsala: Societas Archaeologica Upsalensis.

Nordahl, E. 1996. *... templum quod Ubsola dicitur ... i arkeologisk belysning*. AUN 22. Uppsala: Uppsala University.

Nordahl, E. 2001. *Båtgravar i Gamla Uppsala. Spår av en vikingatida högreståndsmiljö*. AUN 29. Uppsala: Department of Archaeology and Ancient History.

Nordberg, A. 2006. *Jul, disting och förkyrklig tideräkning. Kalendrar och kalendariska riter i det förkristna Norden*. Acta Academiea Gustavi Adolphi XCI. Uppsala: Kungl. Gustav Adolfs Akademien för svensk folkkultur.

Nørgård Jørgensen, A., Jørgensen, L. & Gebauer Thomsen, L. 2010. Assembly Sites for Cult, Markets Jurisdiction and Social Relations: Historic-Ethnological Analogy between North Scandinavian Church Towns, Old Norse Assembly Sites and Pit House Sites of the Late Iron Age and Viking Period. In *Arkæologi i Slesvig/Archäologie in Schleswig = Det 61. Internationale Sachsensymposion 2010*, Haderslev, Danmark: 95–112.

Norr, S. 1998. *To Rede and to Ropn (w): Expressions of Early Scandinavian Kingship in Written Sources*. Occasional Papers in Archaeology 17. Uppsala: Uppsala University.

Ødegaard, M. 2019. Cooking-Pit Sites As Assembly Sites. Lund in Vestfold, South-East Norway: A Regional Assembly Site in the Early Iron Age? In A. Reynolds, J. Carroll & B. Yorke (eds.), *Power and Place in Europe in the Early Middle Ages*. Proceedings of the British Academy 224: 107–26. Oxford: Oxford University Press.

OED 2010. *Oxford English Dictionary*, ed. A. Stevenson. Oxford: Oxford University Press.

Olsen, O. 1981. Der lange Weg des Nordens zum Christentum. In C. Ahrens (ed.), *Frühe Holzkirchen im nördlichen Europa*. Veröffentlichungen des Helms-Museums 39: 247–61. Hamburg: Helms-Museum.

Olsen, O. 1989. Royal Power in Viking Age Denmark. In H. Bekker-Nielsen & H. F. Nielsen (eds.), *Syvende tværfaglige Vikingesymposium Odense*: 7–20. Højbjerg: Wormianum.

Olsson, A. 2017. *Maritima Birka. Arkeologisk rapport över marinarkeologiska undersökningar av kulturlager och pålanläggning i vattenområdet utanför Svarta jorden på Björkö 2004–2014.* Arkeologisk rapport 2017: 13. Stockholm: Sjöhistoriska museet.

Øye, I. 2009. Settlement Patterns and Field Systems in Medieval Norway. *Landscape History* 30: 37–54.

Øye, I. 2013. Technology, Land Use and Transformation in Scandinavian Landscapes, c. 800–1300 CE. In T. Kerig & A. Zimmermann (eds.), *Economic Archaeology: From Structure to Performance in European Archaeology*: 295–309. Bonn: Habelt.

Palmer, B. 2003. The Hinterlands of Three Southern English *Emporia*: Some Common Themes. In T. Pestell & K. Ulmschneider (eds.), *Markets in Early Medieval Europe: Trading and 'Productive' Sites, 650–850*: 48–61. Macclesfield: Windgather.

Pálsson, H. 2013. The Saga of Ingvar the Fartraveller – Yngvars saga víðförla: The Question of Age and Origin. In G. Larsson (ed.), *Between East and West: Early Contacts between Scandinavia and the Caucasus*. Revita Archaeology and History: 27–30. Uppsala: Uppsala University.

Pedersen, A. 2014. *Dead Warriors in Living Memory: A Study of Weapon and Equestrian Burials in Viking-Age Denmark, CE 800–1000*. Studies in Archaeology and History 22: 1 Jelling Series. Copenhagen: National Museum.

Pedersen, U. 2015. Urban Craftspeople at Viking-Age Kaupang. In G. Hansen, S. Ashby & I. Baug (eds.), *Everyday Products in the Middle Ages: Crafts, Consumption and the Individual in Northern Europe c. CE 800–1600*: 51–68. Oxford: Oxbow.

Pedersen, U. 2016. Non-ferrous Metalworking in Viking Age Scandinavia: A Question of Mobility. In V. E. Turner, O. A. Owen & D. J. Waugh (eds.), *Shetland and the Viking World: Papers from the Seventeenth Viking Congress, Lerwick*: 263–9. Lerwick: Shetland Heritage Publications.

Pedersen, U. & Pilø, L. 2007. The Settlement: Artefacts and Site Periods. In D. Skre (ed.), *Kaupang in Skiringssal*. Kaupang Excavation Project Publication Series, Vol. 1. Norske Oldfunn XXII: 179–190. Aarhus: Aarhus Universitetsforlag.

Pestell, T. & Ulmschneider, K. (eds.) 2003. *Markets in Early Medieval Europe: Trading and 'Productive' Sites, 650– 850*. Macclesfield: Windgather.

Peyer, H.-C. 1964. Das Reisekönigtum des Mittelalters. *Vierteljahresschrift für Sozial- und Wirtschaftsgeschichte* 51: 1–21.

Pilgaard, M. 2013. Farrisskoven. *Skalk* 6: 8–12.

Pilø, L. 2007. The Settlement: Character, Structures and Features. In D. Skre (ed.), *Kaupang in Skiringssal*. Kaupang Excavation Project Publication Series, Vol. 1. Norske Oldfunn XXII: 191–222. Aarhus: Aarhus Universitetsforlag.

Pohl, W. 2001. Conclusion: The Transformation of Frontiers. In W. Pohl, I. Wood & H. Reimitz (eds.), *The Transformation of Frontiers: From Late Antiquity to the Carolingians*. The Transformation of the Roman World 10: 247–87. Leiden: Brill.

Polanyi, K. 1963. Ports of Trade in Early Societies. *Journal of Economic History* 23: 30–45.

Price, N. S. 1995. Pagan Amulets and Cult Objects from the Black Earth: Interim Report on Finds from the 1990 Excavations. In B. Ambrosiani & H. Clarke (eds.), *Excavations in the Black Earth 1990*. Birka Studies 2: 70–8. Stockholm: The Birka Project.

Radtke, C. 1977. Aula und castellum: Überlegungen zur Topographie und Struktur des Königshofes in Schleswig. *Beiträge zur Schleswiger Stadtgeschichte* 22: 29–47.

Radtke, C. 1992a. Sliaswig (Schleswig/Haithabu). In O. Engels & S. Weinfurter (eds.), *Series episcoporum Ecclesiae Catholicae occidentalis: ab initio usque ad annum MCXCVIII* 6.2: 96–116. Stuttgart: Hiersemann.

Radtke, C. 1992b. König Magnus der Gute und Haithabu/ Schleswig. In W. Paravicini, H. Unverhau & F. Lubowitz (eds.), *Mare Balticum. Beiträge zur Geschichte des Ostseeraums in Mittelalter und Neuzeit. Festschrift zum 65. Geburtstag von Erich Hoffmann*. Kieler Historische Studien 36: 67–91. Sigmaringen: Thorbecke.

Radtke, C. 1999. s.v. 'Haiðaby'. In H. Beck, D. Geuenich, H. Steuer & D. Timpe (eds.), *Reallexikon der Germanischen Altertumskunde* 13: 361–81. Berlin: De Gruyter.

Radtke, C. 2003. Das Graukloster in Schleswig: Königspfalz – Franziskanerkloster – Armenhaus – Rathaus. In C. Kimminus-Schneider & M. Schneider (eds.), *Klöster und monastische Kultur in Hansestädten*. Stralsunder Beiträge zur Archäologie, Geschichte, Kunst und Volkskunde in Vorpommern 4: 3–14. Rahden: Marie Leidorf.

Radtke, C. 2006. Money, Port and Ships. In J. Bill & B. L. Clausen (eds.), *Maritime Topography and the Medieval Town: Papers from the 5th International Conference on Waterfront Archaeology in Copenhagen, 14–16 May 1998*. Publications from the National Museum. Studies in Archaeology and History 4: 147–51. Copenhagen: Nationalmuseet.

Radtke, C. 2007. Schleswig ca. 1000–1250: Systemtheoretische Skizzen eines Urbanisierungsprofils. In S. Burmeister, H. Derks & J. von Richthofen (eds.),

Zweiundvierzig: Festschrift für Michael Gebühr zum 65. Geburtstag. Studia honoaria 25: 317–38. Rahden: Marie Leidorf.

Radtke, C. 2009a. Glocke. Katalog: Museum in der Kaiserpfalz. 1009: Meinwerk wird Bischof. In C. Stiegemann & M. Kroker (eds.), *Für Königtum und Himmelreich: 1000 Jahre Bischof Meinwerk von Paderborn*: 284. Paderborn: Schnell & Steiner.

Radtke, C. 2009b. Haithabu. Perspektiven einer Stadtentwicklung in drei Stationen – 800, 900, 1000. *Zeitschrift für Archäologie des Mittelalters* 37: 135–62.

Radtke, C. 2017. Noch einmal Haithabu – Schleswig: Adam von Bremen und die Skalden, Siedlungstransfer und Systemstransformation. *Archäologische Nachrichten Schleswig-Holstein*: 84–103.

Randsborg, K. 1980. *The Viking Age in Denmark: The Formation of a State*. London: Duckworth.

Randsborg, K. 1989. The Periods of Danish Antiquity. *Acta Archaeologica* 60: 187–92.

Reynolds, S. 1977. *An Introduction to the History of English Medieval Towns*. Oxford: Oxford University Press.

Reynolds, S. 1987. Towns in the Domesday Book. In J. C. Holt (ed.), *Domesday Studies*. Royal Historical Society and Institute of British Geographers: 295–309. Woodbridge: The Boydell Press.

Reynolds, S. 1992. The Writing of Medieval Urban History in England. *Theoretische Geschiedens* 19: 43–57.

Richards, J. D. 1999. What's So Special about 'Productive Sites'? Middle Saxon Settlements in Northumbria. In T. M. Dickinson & D. Griffiths (eds.), *The Making of Kingdoms*. Papers from the 47th Sachsensymposium = Anglo-Saxon Studies in Archaeology and History 10: 71–80. Oxford: Oxford University Committee for Archaeology.

Rieck, F. 1991. Aspects of Coastal Defense in Denmark. In O. Crumlin-Pedersen (ed.), *Aspects of Maritime Scandinavia CE 200–1200*: 83–96. Roskilde: Vikingeskibshallen.

Rieck, F. 2004. The Anchor from Sct. Nicolaigade in Ribe. In M. Bencard, A. Kann Rasmussen & H. Brinch Madsen (eds.), *Ribe Excavations 1970–76*, Vol. 5: 173–82. Moesgård: Jutland Archaeological Society.

Rispling, G. 2004. Catalogue and Comments on the Islamic Coins from the Excavation 1990–1995. In B. Ambrosiani (ed.), *Eastern Connections, Part Two: Numismatics and Metrology*. Excavations in the Black Earth 1990–1995. Birka Studies 6: 11–60. Stockholm: The Birka Project.

Roesdahl, E. 1997. Cultural Change: Religious Monuments in Denmark *c*. CE 950–1100. In M. Müller-Wille (ed.), *Rom und Byzanz im Norden. Mission und*

Glaubenswechsel im Ostseeraum während des 8.–14. Jahrhunderts, Vol. 1. Akademie der Wissenschaften und der Literatur Mainz. Abhandlungen der Geistes- und sozialwissenschaftlichen Klasse No. 3/1: 229–48. Stuttgart: Steiner.

Roesdahl, E. 2002. Harald Blauzahn – ein dänischer Wikingerkönig aus archäologischer Sicht. In J. Henning (ed.), *Europa im 10. Jahrhundert. Archäologie einer Aufbruchszeit*. Internationale Tagung in Vorbereitung der Ausstellung 'Otto der Große, Magdeburg und Europa': 95–108. Mainz: Philipp von Zabern.

Roesdahl, E. 2008. The Emergence of Denmark and the Reign of Harald Bluetooth. In S. Brink & N. Price (eds.), *The Viking World*: 652–64. London: Routledge.

Roesdahl, E. & Sindbæk, S. M. 2014. The Dating of Aggersborg. In E. Roesdahl, S. M. Sindbæk, A. Pedersen & D. M. Wilson (eds.), *Aggersborg: The Viking-Age Settlement and Fortress*. Jutland Archaeological Society Publications 82: 203–8. Højbjerg: Jutland Archaeological Society.

Ros, J. 2008. Sigtuna. In S. Brink & N. Price (eds.), *The Viking World*: 140–4. London: Routledge.

Rösch, F. 2018. *Das Schleswiger Hafenviertel im Hochmttelalter. Entstehung – Entwicklung – Topographie*. Zeitschrift für Archäologie des Mittelalters. Beiheft 26. Bonn: Habelt.

Rösch, F. 2019. Medieval Marketplaces in Northern Europe: An Overview with an Emphasis on Merchant Seafaring. In L. Rahmstorf & E. Stratford (eds.), *Weights and Marketplaces from the Bronze Age to the Early Modern Period: Proceedings of two workshops funded by the European Research Foundation (ERC)*. Weight and Value 1: 265–86. Kiel: Wachholtz.

Roslund, M. 2007. *Guest in the House: Cultural Transmission between Slavs and Scandinavians 900 to 1300 CE*. The Northern World 33. Leiden: Brill.

Roslund, M. 2010. Bridging Two Worlds: Tracing Merchants from the Holy Roman Empire in High Medieval Sigtuna. In C. Theune, F. Biermann, R. Struwe & G. H. Jeute (eds.), *Zwischen Fjorden und Steppe*. Internationale Archäologie. Studia honoraria 31: 239–50. Rahden: Marie Leidorf.

Rougé, J. 1966. *Recherches sur l'organisation du commerce maritime en Méditerranée sous l'Empire romain*. École Pratique des Hautes Études. 6e Section. Centre de Recheres Historique: Ports, Routes, Trafics 21. Paris: S.E.V.P.E.N.

Routier, J.-C., Barbet, P. & Foucray, B. 2016. Bilan des opérations archéologique de l'Inrap à La Calotterie (2005–2007). In I. Leroy & L. Verslype (eds.), *Les cultures des littoraux au haut Moyen Âge: Cadres et modes de via dans l'espace maritime Manche-mer du Nord du IIIe au Xe s*. Revue du Nord. Collection

Art et Archéologie 24: 217–54. Villeneuve-d'Ascq: Université de Lille. Siences humaines et sociales.

Runer, J. 2006. Den äldsta svenska myntningen – dess funktion och utveckling. *Situne Dei*: 81–94.

Runer, J. 2014. Om den äldsta kristna miljönpå Sigtuna museums tomt. *Situne Dei*: 70–81.

Rydh, H. 1936. *Förhistoriska undersökningar på Adelsö*. Kungl. Vitterhets Historie och Antikvitets Akademien. Stockholm: Wahlström & Widstrand.

Sanmark, A. 2015. At the Assembly: A Study of Ritual Space. In W. Jezierski, L. Hermanson, H. J. Orning & T. Småberg (eds.), *Rituals, Performatives, and Political Order in Northern Europe, c. 650–1350*. Ritus et Artes 7: 79–112. Turnhout: Brepols.

Sanmark, A. 2017. *Viking Law and Order: Places and Rituals of Assembly in the Medieval North*. Edinburgh: Edinburgh University Press.

Sawyer, P. H. 1968. *Anglo-Saxon Charters: An Annotated List and Bibliography*. Royal Historical Society. Guides and Handbooks 8. London: Royal Historical Society.

Sawyer, P. H. 1973. Västerut över Atlanten – Vikingarna utforskar, driver handel, plundrar och erövrar land från Skottland till Amerika. In B. Almgren (ed.), *Vikingen*: 65–119. Höganäs: Bokförlaget Bra Böcker.

Sawyer, P. H. 1979. Kings and Merchants. In P. H. Sawyer & I. N. Wood (eds.), *Early Medieval Kingship*: 139–58. Leeds: University of Leeds.

Sawyer, P. H. 1982. *Kings and Vikings: Scandinavia and Europe CE 700–1100*. London: Routledge.

Sawyer, P. H. 1986. Early Fairs and Markets in England and Scandinavia. In B. L. Anderson & A. J. H. Latham (eds.), *The Market in History: Papers Presented at a Symposium held 9–13 September 1984 at St. George's House, Windsor Castle*: 59–78. Kent: Mackays of Chatham.

Sawyer, P. H. 2004. Scandinavia in the Eleventh and Twelfth Centuries. In D. Luscombe & J. Riley-Smith (eds.), *The New Cambridge Medieval History, Vol. 4: c. 1024 – c. 1198, Part 2*: 290–303. Cambridge: Cambridge University Press.

Schade, T. 2010–11. Das wikingerzeitliche Gräberfeld von Kosel-Ost (Kosel LA 198), Kreis Rendsburg-Eckernförde. *Offa* 67/68: 203–321.

Scheel, O. 1938. *Die Wikinger: Aufbruch des Nordens*. Stuttgart: Hohenstaufen-Verlag.

Schenk, W. 2010: 'Central Places' as a Point of Discussion from German Geography in (Pre-) Historical Research. In B. Ludowici, H. Jöns, S. Kleingärtner, J. Scheschkewitz & M. Hardt (eds.). 2010. *Trade and Communication Networks of the First Millennium CE in the Northern Part of Central Europe: Central Places, Beach Markets, Landing Places and Trading Centers*. Neue

Studien zur Sachsenforschung 1: 11–13. Hannover: Niedersächsisches Landesmuseum Hannover.

Scherping, R. 2003. Bischof Rudolf von Schleswig: Die Grabtextilien in technischer und kulturhistorischer Perspektive. *Kölner Jahrbuch* 36: 7–149.

Schietzel, K. 1969. Die archäologischen Befunde der Ausgrabung Haithabu 1963–1964. *Berichte über die Ausgrabungen in Haithabu* 1: 9–59. Neumünster: Wachholtz.

Schietzel, K. 2014. *Spurensuche Haithabu. Archäologische Spurensuche in der frühmittelalterlichen Ansiedlung Haithabu. Dokumentation und Chronik 1963–2013*. Hamburg: Wachholtz.

Schjødt, J. P. 1990. Horizontale und verikale Achsen in der vorchristlichen skandinavien Kosmologie. In T. Ahlbäck (ed.), *Old Norse and Finnish Religions and Cultic Place-Names*: 35–57. Åbo: The Donner Institute for Research in Religious and Cultural History.

Schlesinger, W. 1973. Der Markt als Frühform der deutschen Stadt. In H. Jankuhn, W. Schlesinger & H. Steuer (eds.) *Vor- und Frühformen der europäischen Stadt im Mittelalter I*. Abhandlungen der Akademie der Wissenschaften in Göttingen. Philologisch-historische Klasse. Dritte Folge. No. 83: 262–93. Göttingen: Vandenhoeck & Ruprecht.

Schofield, J. & Steuer, H. 2007. Urban Settlement. In J. Graham-Campbell & M. Valor (eds.), *The Archaeology of Medieval Europe: Eighth to Twelfth Centuries CE*. Acta Jutlandica LXXXIII:1. Humanities Series 79: 111–53. Aarhus: Aarhus University Press.

Schück, A. 1926. *Studier rörande det svenska stadsväsendets uppkomst och äldsta utveckling*. Uppsala: Appelbergs boktryckeri.

Schulte, M. 2008. Om å skrive språkhistorie 'nedenfra': Tanker om en ny norsk språkhistorie for tiden 700–1050. *Maal og Minne* 2: 167–88.

Schultze, J. 2005. Zur Frage der Entwicklung des zentralen Siedlungskerns von Haithabu. In C. Dobiat (ed.), *Reliquiae Gentium. Festschrift für Horst Wolfgang Böhme zum 65. Geburtstag* 1: 359–73. Rahden: Marie Leidorf.

Schultze, J. 2008. *Haithabu – Die Siedlungsgrabungen 1. Methoden und Möglichkeiten der Auswertung*. Die Ausgrabungen in Haithabu 13. Neumünster: Wachholtz.

Schultze, J. 2012. Zur konstruktiven Entwicklung des frühstädtischen Hausbaus in Haithabu und Schlewig. *Mitteilungen der Deutschen Gesellschaft für Archäologie des Mittelalters und der Neuzeit* 24: 99–110.

Schultze, J. 2017. Überlegungen zu den frühen Phasen der Entwicklung von Haithabu. In B. V. Eriksen, A. Abegg-Wigg, R. Bleile & U. Ickerodt (eds.), *Interaktion ohne Grenzen. Beispiele archäologischer Forschungen am Beginn des 21. Jahrhunderts*: 565–78. Schleswig: Wachholtz.

Schütte, S. 1997. Zur frühen Baugeschichte von St. Kunibert in Köln und zur Grablege des Bischofs Rudolf von Schleswig. *Colonia Romanica* 12: 9–16.

Scull, C. 2002. Ipswich: Development and Contexts of an Urban Precursor in the Seventh Century. In B. Hårdh & L. Larsson (eds.), *Central Places in the Migration and Merovingian Periods: Papers from the 52nd Sachensymposium Lund, August 2001*. Uppåkrastudier 6. Acta Archaeologica Lundensia. Series in 8°, Vol. 39: 303–16. Stockholm: Almqvist & Wiksell International.

Scull, C. 2009. *Early Medieval (Late 5th–Early 8th Centuries CE) Cemeteries at Boss Hall and Buttermarket, Ipswich, Suffolk*. The Society of Medieval Archaeology Monograph 27. Leeds: Society for Medieval Archaeology.

Scull, C. 2013. Ipswich: Contexts of Funerary Evidence from an Urban Precursor of the Seventh Century CE. In D. Bates & R. Liddiard (eds.), *East Anglia and Its North Sea World in the Middle Ages*: 218–29. Woodbridge: The Boydell Press.

Seiler, A. 2019. Unika båtgravar I Gamla Uppsala. *Populär arkeologi* 6: 8.

Seillier, C. 2010. Rupture et continuité dans le Boulonnais et le Ponthieu entre le Bas-Empire et le haut Moyen Âge. In S. Lebecq, B. Béthouart & L. Versype (eds.), *Quentovic: Environnement, Archéologie, Histoire*. Collection traveaux et recherches. Éditions du Conseil Scientifique de l'Université Lille 3: 125–46. Lille: Charles de Gaulle University – Lille 3.

Semple, S., Sanmark, A., Iversen, F. et al. 2020. *Negotiating the North: Meeting-Places in the Middle Ages in the North Sea Zone*. The Society for Medieval Archaeology Monograph 41. London: Routledge.

Shepard, J. 1995. The Rhos Guests of Louis the Pious: Whence and Wherefore? *Early Medieval Europe* 4(1): 41–60.

Siegloff, E. 2014. Das liegt doch auf dem Weg! Eine neue wikingerzeitliche Siedlung auf der Schleswiger Landenge. *Arkæologi i Slesvig/Archäologie in Schleswig* 15: 163–77.

Siegloff, E. & Wolpert, N. 2018. Zwei neu entdeckte Fundplätze bei Großenwiehe und Ellingstedt auf der Schleswiger Geest – archäologisch-denkmalpflegerische Betrachtungen. In V. Hilberg & T. Lemm (eds.), Viele Funde – große Bedeutung? Potenzial und Aussagewert von Metalldetektorfunden für die siedlungsarchäologische Forschung der Wikingerzeit. Bericht des 33. Tværfaglige Vikingesymposiums 9. Mai 2014, Wikinger Museum Haithabu: 175–91. Kiel: Ludwig.

Simek, R. & Pálsson, H. 1987. *Lexikon der altnordischen Literatur*. Stuttgart: Kröner.

Sindbæk, S. M. 2005. *Ruter og rutinisering: Vikingetidens fjernhandel i Nordeuropa*. Copenhagen: Multivers.

Sindbæk, S. M. 2007a. The Small World of the Vikings: Networks in Early Medieval Communication and Exchange. *Norwegian Archaeological Review* 40(1): 59–74.

Sindbæk, S. M. 2007b. Networks and Nodal Points: The Emergence of Towns in Early Viking Age Scandinavia. *Antiquity* 81: 119–32.

Sindbæk, S. M. 2009. The Lands of Denemearce: Cultural Differences and Social Networks of the Viking Age in Southern Scandinavia. *Viking and Medieval Scandinavia* 4: 169–208.

Sindbæk, S. M. 2010. Re-assembling Regions. The Social Occasions of Technological Exchange in Viking Age Scandinavia. In R. Barndon, A. Engevik & I. Øye (eds.), *The Archaeology of Regional Technologies: Case Studies from the Palaeolithic to the Age of Vikings*: 263–87. Lewiston: The Edwin Mellen Press.

Sindbæk, S. M. 2018. Northern Emporium: The Archaeology of Urban Networks in Viking-Age Ribe. In R. Raja & S. M. Sindbæk (eds.), *Urban Network Evolutions: Towards a High-Definition Archaeology*: 161–6. Aarhus: Aarhus University Press.

Sindbæk, S. M. & Trakadas, A. (eds.) 2014. *The World in the Viking Age*. Roskilde: The Viking Ship Museum.

Skov, H. 2005. Aros in 700–1100 CE. In A. Damm (ed.), *Viking Aros*: 15–38. Højbjerg: Moesgård Museum.

Skov, H. 2008. Det ældste Århus – ca. 770–1200. In H. Andersson, G. Hansen & I. Øje (eds.), *De første 200 årene – nytt blikk på 27 skandinaviske middelalderbyer*. Universitetet i Bergen arkeologiske skrifter. UBAS Nordisk 5: 215–26. Bergen: Universitetet i Bergen.

Skovgaard-Pedersen, I. 2003. The Making of the Danish Kingdom. In K. Helle (ed.), *The Cambridge History of Scandinavia, Vol. 1: Prehistory to 1520*: 168–83. Cambridge: Cambridge University Press.

Skre, D. (ed.) 2007. *Kaupang in Skiringssal*. Kaupang Excavation Project Publication Series, Vol. 1. Norske Oldfunn XXII. Aarhus: Aarhus Universitetsforlag.

Skre, D. 2008. The Development of Urbanism in Scandinavia. In S. Brink & N. Price (eds.), *The Viking World*: 83–93. London: Routledge.

Skre, D. 2020. Rulership and Ruler's Sites in 1st–10th-Century Scandinavia. In D. Skre (ed.), *Rulership in 1st to 14th Century Scandinavia: Royal Graves and Sites in Avaldsnes and Beyond*. Ergänzungsbände zum Reallexikon der Germanischen Altertumskunde: 193–244. Berlin: De Gruyter.

Sonne, L. C. A. 2016. Svend Estridsens politiske liv. In L. C. A. Sonne & S. Croix (eds.), *Svend Estridsen*. Studies in History and Social Sciences 528: 15–38. Odense: Syddansk Universitetsforlag.

Søvsø, M. 2010. Tidligkristne begravelser ved Ribe Domkirke – Ansgars kirkegård? *Arkæologi i Slesvig/Archäologie in Schleswig* 13: 147–64.

Søvsø, M. 2014. Ansgars Kirche in Ribe. In R.-M. Weiss & A. Klammt (eds.), *Mythos Hammaburg. Archäologische Entdeckungen zu den Anfängen Hamburgs*. Veröffentlichungen des Helms-Museum, Archäologisches Museum Hamburg, Stadtmuseum Harburg 107: 245–54. Hamburg: Archäologisches Museum.

Søvsø, M. 2018. Emporia, Sceattas and Kingship in 8th c. 'Denmark'. In J. Hansen & M. Bruus (eds.), *The Fortified Viking Age: 36th Interdisciplinary Viking Symposium*. Kulturhistoriske studier I centralitet. Archaeological & Historical Studies in Centrality 3: 75–86. Odense: Odense City Museums and University Press of Southern Denmark.

Søvsø, M. 2020. *Ribe 700–1050: From Emporium to Civitas in Southern Scandinavia*. Ribe Studier 2. Jutland Archaeological Society Publications 113. Højbjerg: Aarhus University Press.

Speckmann, A. 2005. Ländlicher Hausbau in Westfalen im frühen Mittelalter. *Archäologie in Ostwestfalen* 9: 92–7.

Staats, R. & Weitling, G. 2016. *Ansgar in Haithabu. Anfänge des Christentums in Nordeuropa*. Kiel: Ludwig.

Staecker, J. 1997. Brutal Vikings and Gentle Traders. *Lund Archaeological Review* 3: 89–103.

Staecker, J. 2005. The Concepts of Imitation and Translation: Perceptions of a Viking-Age Past. *Norwegian Archaeological Review* 38: 3–28.

Staecker, J. 2009. The 9th-Century Christian Mission to the North. In A. Englert & A. Trakadas (eds.), *Wulfstan's Voyage: The Baltic Sea Region in the Early Viking Age As Seen from Shipboard*. Maritime Culture of the North 2: 309–29. Roskilde: The Viking Ship Museum.

Stalsberg, A. 2008. Herstellung und Verbreitung der Vlfberht-Schwertklingen. Eine Neubewertung. *Zeitschrift für Archäologie des Mittelalters* 36: 89–118.

Steinsland, G. 2005. The Late Iron Age Worldview and the Concept of 'Utmark'. In I. Holm, S. Innselset & I. Øye (eds.), *'Utmark': The Outfield As Industry and Ideology in the Iron Age and the Middle Ages*. University of Bergen Archaeological Series – International 1: 137–46. Bergen: University of Bergen.

Steuer, H. 1974. *Die Südsiedlung von Haithabu. Studien zur frühmittelalterlichen Keramik im Nordseeküstenbereich und in Schleswig-Holstein*. Ausgrabungen in Haithabu 6. Neumünster: Wachholtz.

Steuer, H. 1987. Der Handel der Wikingerzeit zwischen Nord- und Westeuropa aufgrund archäologischer Zeugnisse. In K. Düwel (ed.), *Untersuchungen zu Handel und Verkehr der vor- und frühgeschichtlichen Zeit in Mittel und Nordeuropa* 4: 113–97. Göttingen: Vandenhoeck & Ruprecht.

Steuer, H. 1995. Freiburg und das Bild der Städte um 1100 im Spiegel der Archäologie. In H. Schadek & T. Zotz (eds.), *Freiburg 1091-1120: Neue Forschungen zu den Anfängen der Stadt*. Archäologie und Geschichte 7: 79-123. Sigmaringen: Thorbecke.

Steuer, H. 1999. s.v. 'Handel'. In H. Beck, D. Geuenich & H. Steuer (eds.), *Reallexikon der Germanischen Altertumskunde* 13: 497-593. Berlin: De Gruyter.

Steuer, H. 2003. s.v. 'Ports of Trade'. In H. Beck, D. Geuenich & H. Steuer (eds.), *Reallexikon der Germanischen Altertumskunde* 23: 292-8. Berlin: De Gruyter.

Steuer, H. 2005. s.v. 'Seehandelsplätze'. In H. Beck, D. Geuenich & H. Steuer (eds.), *Reallexikon der Germanischen Altertumskunde* 28: 20-4. Berlin: De Gruyter.

Steuer, H. 2007. s.v. 'Zentralorte'. In H. Beck, D. Geuenich & H. Steuer (eds.), *Reallexikon der Germanischen Altertumskunde* 35: 878-914. Berlin: De Gruyter.

Stolpe, H. 1873. Naturhistoriska och archæologiska undersökningar på Björkö i Mälaren II. Redogörelse för undersökningarna år 1872. *Öfversigt af Kongl. Vetenskaps Akademiens Förhandlingar* 5: 11-87.

Stolpe, H. 1874. *Björkö-Fyndet. Beskrifning öfver fornsaker från Nordens yngre järnålder funna på Björkö i Mälaren I. Redogörelse för undersökningarna under åren 1871-1873*. Stockholm: Norstedt.

Stolpe, H. 1882. Grafundersökningar på Björkö i Mälaren år 1881. *Svenska Fornminnesföreningens Tidskrift* 13: 53-63.

Stolpe, H. 1888. *Björkö i Mälaren. En vägledning för besökande*. Stockholm: P. A. Norstedt & Söner.

Stoodley, N. 2005. The Origins of Hamwic and Its Central Role in the Seventh Century As Revealed by Recent Archaeological Discoveries. In B. Hårdh & L. Larson (eds.), *Central Places in the Migration and the Merovingian Periods: Papers from the 52nd Sachsensymposium Lund, August 2001*. Uppåkrastudier 6. Acta Archaeologica Lundensia, Series in 8°, Vol. 39: 317-31. Stockholm: Almqvist & Wiksell International.

Storm, G. 1899. De kongelige Byanlæg i Norge i Middelalderen. *Norsk Historisk Tidskrift* 5(3): 433-6.

Strömberg, J. B. L. D. 2004. The Swedish Kings in Progress – and the Centre of Power. *Scandia* 70: 167-217.

Stylegar, F.-A. 2007. The Kaupang Cemeteries Revisited. In D. Skre (ed.), *Kaupang in Skiringssal*. Kaupang Excavation Project Publication Series, Vol. 1. Norske Oldfunn XXII: 65-128. Aarhus: Aarhus Universitetsforlag.

Sundqvist, O. 2001. Feature of Pre-Christian Inauguration Rituals in the Medieval Swedish Laws. In M. Stausberg (ed.), *Kontinuitäten und Brüche in der*

Religionsgeschichte. Festschrift für Anders Hultgård. RGA-Ergänzungsbände 31: 620–50. Berlin: De Gruyter.

Sundqvist, O. 2002. *Freyr's Offspring: Rulers and Religion in Ancient Svea Society*. Acta Universitatis Upsaliensis. Historia Religionum 21. Uppsala: Uppsala University.

Sundqvist, O. 2013. Gamla Uppsala som förkristen kultplats: en översikt och en hypotes. In O. Sundqvist & P. Vikstrand (eds.), *Gamla Uppsala i ny belysning*. Religionsvetenskapliga studier från Gävle 9: 69–111. Uppsala: Swedish Science Press.

Sundqvist, O. 2016. *An Arena for Higher Powers: Ceremonial Buildings and Religious Strategies for Rulership in Late Iron Age Scandinavia*. Numen Book Series. Studies in the History of Religions 150. Leiden: Brill.

Sundqvist, O. 2017. Kultpelare, rituellt hägn och religiösa processioner. In L. Beronius Jörpeland, H. Göthberg, A. Seiler & J. Wikborg (eds.), *At Upsalum – mäniskor och landskapande. Utbyggnad av Ostkustbanan genom Gamla Uppsala*. Arkeologisk undersökning. Report No. 2017: 1.1: 337–48. Stockholm: Arkeologerna.

Svanberg, F. 2003a. *Decolonizing the Viking Age, Vol. 1*. Stockholm: Almqvist & Wiksell International.

Svanberg, F. 2003b. *Decolonizing the Viking Age, Vol. 2: Death Rituals in South-East Scandinavia AD 800–1000*. Stockholm: Almqvist & Wiksell International.

Svensson, G. O. S. 1958. Om namnet Skopinntull. *Fornvännen* 53: 288–91.

Tegnér, G. 1995. s.v. 'Unni'. In C. Orrling (ed.), *Vikingatidens ABC: Ny reviderad upplaga*. Historia i fickformat: 280. Borås: Statens Historiska Museum.

Tesch, S. 2001a. Olof Palme, S:ta Gerturd och Sigtunas medeltida kyrkotopografi. In S. Tesch & R. Edberg (eds.), *Biskopen i museets trädgård: En arkeologisk gåta*. Sigtuna Museers Skriftserie 9: 9–44. Stockholm: Sigtuna Museum.

Tesch, S. 2001b. Houses, Town Yards and Town Planning in Late Viking Age and Medieval Sigtuna, Sweden. In M. Gläser (ed.), *Der Hausbau: Lübecker Kolloquium zur Stadtarchäologie im Hanseraum* 3: 723–41. Lübeck: Schmidt-Römhild.

Tesch, S. 2007. Sigtuna – det maktpolitiska och sakrala stadsrummet under senvikingatid och tidig medeltid (c: a980–1200). In A. Perlinge (ed.), *Människors rum och människors möten: Kulturhistoriska skisser*. Berit Wallenbergs Stiftelse 50 år: 71–121. Stockholm: Berit Wallenbergs stiftelse.

Tesch, S. 2016. Sigtuna: Royal Site and Christian Town and the Regional Perspective, c. 980–1100. In L. Holmquist, S. Kalmring & C. Hedenstierna-Jonson (eds.), *New Aspects of Viking Age Urbanism, c. CE 750–1100: Proceedings of the International Symposium at the Swedish History*

Museum, April 17th–20th 2013. Theses and Papers in Archaeology B12: 115–38. Stockholm: Stockholm University Archaeological Research Laboratory.

Theuws, F. 2004. Exchange, Religion, Identity and Central Places in the Early Middle Ages. *Archaeological Dialogues* 10(2): 121–38.

Theuws, F. 2007. Where Is the Eighth Century in the Towns of the Meuse Valley? In W. Brandes, A. Demandt, H. Krasser, H. Leppin & P. von Möllendorff (eds.), *Post-Roman Towns, Trade and Settlement in Europe and Byzantium, Vol. 1: The Heirs of the Roman West*. Millennium Studies in the Culture and History of the First Millennium C.E. 5/1: 153–64. Berlin: De Gruyter.

Theuws, F. 2018. Reversed Directions: Re-thinking Sceattas in the Netherlands and England. *Zeitschrift für Archäologie des Mittelalters* 46: 27–84.

Thordeman, B. 1920. *Alsnö Hus: Ett svenskt medeltidspalats i sitt konsthistoriska sammanhang*. Stockholm: Norstedt.

Þórleikr fagri: *Flokkr about Sveinn Úlfsson (Þfagr Sveinn)*. In K. E. Gade (ed.), *Skaldic Poetry of the Scandinavian Middle Ages, Vol. 2: Poetry from the Kings' Sagas: From c. 1035 to c. 1300*: 313–22. Turnhout: Brepols, 2009.

Trotzig, G. 2004. Trons försvarare i Birka. *Fornvännen* 99: 197–208.

Tummuscheit, A. 2003. Groß Strömkendorf: A Market Site of the Eighth Century on the Baltic Coast. In T. Pestell & K. Ulmschneider (eds.), *Markets in Early Medieval Europe: Trading and 'Productive' Sites, 650–850*: 208–20. Macclesfield: Windgather.

Tummuscheit, A. & Witte, F. 2014. 'Der einzige Weg durchs Danewerk': Zu den Ausgrabungen am Danewerk im Jahr 2013. *Arkæologi i Slesvig/Archäologie in Schleswig* 15: 153–62.

Tummuscheit, A. & Witte, F. 2018. The Danevirke in the Light of Recent Excavations. In J. Hansen & M. Bruus (eds.), *The Fortified Viking Age: 36th Interdisciplinary Viking Symposium*. Kulturhistoriske studier I centralitet. Archaeological & Historical Studies in Centrality 3: 69–74. Odense: Odense City Museums & University Press of Southern Denmark.

Tys, D. 2020. Maritime and River Traders, Landing Places, and Emporia Ports in the Merovingian Period in and Around the Low Countries. In B. Effros & I. Moreira (eds.), *The Oxford Handbook of the Merovingian World*: 765–96. Oxford: Oxford University Press.

Ufkes, A. 2011. *Een archeologische opgraving in de vroegmiddeleeuwse ringwalburg van Domburg, gem. Veere (Z.)*. ARC-publicaties 223. Groningen: Archaeological Research & Consultancy.

Ulmschneider, K. 2000. Settlement, Economy and the 'Productive' Site: Middle Anglo-Saxon Lincolnshire A.D. 650–780. *Medieval Archaeology* 44(1): 53–79.

Ulmschneider, K. 2002. Central Places and Metal-Detector Finds: What Are the English 'Productive Sites'? In B. Hårdh & L. Larson (eds.), *Central Places in the Migration and Merovingian Periods: Papers from the 52nd Sachensymposium Lund, August 2001*. Uppåkrastudier 6. Acta Archaeologica Lundensia. Series in 8°, Vol. 39: 333–9. Lund: Almqvist & Wiksell International.

Ulriksen, J. 1998. *Anløbspladser: Besejling og bebyggelse i Danmark mellem 200 og 1100 e. Kr. En studie af søfartens pladser på baggrund af undersøgelser i Roskilde fjord*. Roskilde: Vikingeskibshallen.

Ulriksen, J. 2004. Danish Coastal Landing Places and Their Relation to Navigation and Trade. In J. Hines, A. Lane & M. Redknap (eds.), *Land, Sea and Home: Settlement in the Viking Period*. Society for Medieval Archaeology Monograph Series 20: 7–26. Leeds: Maney.

Ulriksen, J. 2009. Viking-Age Sailing Routes of the Western Baltic Sea: A Matter of Safety. In A. Englert & A. Trakadas (eds.), *Wulfstan's Voyages: The Baltic Sea Region in the Early Viking Age As Seen from Shipboard*. Maritime Culture of the North 2: 135–44. Roskilde: The Viking Ship Museum.

Ulriksen, J. 2018. *Vester Egesborg: En anløbs- og togtsamlingsplads fra yngre germansk jernalder og vikingetid på Sydsjælland*. Aarhus: Museum Sydøstdanmark & Aarhus Universitetsforlag.

van Doesburg, J. 2010. Non Modica? Some Thoughts on the Interpretation of a Large Early Medieval Earthwork near Dorestad. In A. Willemsen & H. Kik (eds.), *Dorestad in an International Framework: New Research into Trade Centres in Carolingian Times*: 51–8. Turnhout: Brepols.

van Es, W. A. 1990. Dorestad Centred. In J. C. Besteman, J. M. Bos & H. A. Heidinga (eds.), *Medieval Archaeology in the Netherlands: Studies Presented to H. H. van Regteren Altena*: 151–82. Assen: van Gorcum.

van Es, W. A. & Verwers, W. J. H. (eds.) 1980. *Excavations at Dorestad, Vol. 1: The Harbour: Hoogstraat I*. Nederlandse Oudheden 9. Amersfoort: Rijksdienst voor het Oudheidkundig Bodemonderzoek.

van Es, W. A. & Verwers, W. J. H. 2009. *Excavations at Dorestad, Vol. 3: Hoogstraat 0, II–IV*. Nederlandse Oudheden 16. Amersfoort: Rijksdienst voor Archeologie.

van Es, W. A. & Verwers, W. J. H. 2010. Early Medieval Settlements along the Rhine: Precursors and Contemporaries of Dorestad. *Journal of Archaeology in the Low Countries* 2(1): 5–39.

van Gelder, H. E. 1980. Coins from Dorestad, Hoogstraat I. In W. A. van Es & W. J. H. Verwers (eds.), *Excavations at Dorestad, Vol. 1: The Harbour: Hoogstraat I*. Nederlandse Oudheden 9: 212–24. Amersfoort: Rijksdienst voor het Oudheidkundig Bodemonderzoek.

van Gelder, H. E. 2009. Coins. In W. A. van Es & W. J. H. Verwers (eds.), *Excavations at Dorestad, Vol. 3: Hoogstraat 0, II–IV*. Nederlandse Oudheden 16: 257–9. Amersfoort: Rijksdienst voor Archeologie.

van Heeringen, R. M. 1995. De resultaten van het archeologisch onderzoek van de Zeeuwse ringwallburgen. In R. M van Heeringen, P. A. Henderikx & A. Mars (eds.), *Vroeg-Middeleeuwse ringwalburgen in Zeeland*: 17–39. Amersfoort: Rijksdienst voor het Oudheidkundig Bodemonderzoek.

van Heeringen, R. M., Pol, A. & Buurman, J. 1995. Kolonisatie en bewoning in het mondigsgebied van de Schelde in de vroege Middeleeuwen vanuit archeologisch perspectief. In R. M van Heeringen, P. A. Henderikx & A. Mars (eds.), *Vroeg-Middeleeuwse ringwalburgen in Zeeland*: 40–69. Amersfoort: Rijksdienst voor het Oudheidkundig Bodemonderzoek.

van Houtte, J. A. 1993. s.v. 'Messe (Handelsmesse)'. In N. Angermann, R.-H. Bautier & R. Auty (eds.), *Lexikon des Mittelalters VI*: 558–60. Munich: Artemis & Winkler Verlag.

Varenius, B. 2002. Maritime Warfare As an Organizing Principle in Scandinavian Society 1000–1300 CE. In A. Nørgård Jørgensen, J. Pind, L. Jørgensen & B. Clausen (eds.), *Maritime Warfare in Northern Europe: Technology, Organisation, Logistics and Administration 500 BC–1500 CE*. Publications from the National Museum. Studies in Archaeology & History 6: 249–56. Copenhagen: The National Museum.

Vasiliev, A. A. 1951. The Second Russian Attack on Constantinople. *Dumbarton Oaks Papers* 6: 161–225.

Verhaeghe, F. 2005. Urban Developments in the Age of Charlemagne. In J. Story (ed.), *Charlemagne: Empire and Society*: 259–87. Manchester: Manchester University Press.

Verhulst, A. 1999. *The Rise of Cities in North-West Europe*. Themes in International Urban History 4. Cambridge: Cambridge University Press.

Verhulst, A. 2000. Roman Cities, *Emporia* and New Towns (Sixth–Ninth Centuries). In I. L. Hansen & C. Wickham (eds.), *The Long Eighth Century. The Transformations of the Roman World* 11: 105–20. Leiden: Brill.

Verhulst, A. 2002. *The Carolingian Economy*. Cambridge: Cambridge University Press.

Verlinden, O. 1963. Markets and Fairs. In M. M. Postan, E. E. Rich & E. Miller (eds.), *The Cambridge Economic History of Europe, Vol. 3: Economic Organization and Policies in the Middle Ages*: 119–53. Cambridge: Cambridge University Press.

Vestergaard, E. 1991. Gift-Giving, Hoarding, and Outdoings. In R. Samson (ed.), *Social Approaches to Viking Studies*: 97–104. Glasgow: Cruithne Press.

Vikstrand, P. 2001. *Gudarnas Platser. Förkristna sakrala ortnamn i Mälarlandskapen*. Studier till en Svensk ortnamnatlas 17. Uppsala: Kungl. Gustav Adolfs Akademien.

Vogel, V. 1991. Profaner Holzbau des 11. bis frühen 13. Jahrhunderts in Schleswig. In H. W. Böhme (ed.), *In den nördlichen Landschaften des Reiches: Siedlungen und Landesausbau zur Salierzeit 1*. Monographien des Römisch Germanischen Zentralmuseums 27: 263–76. Sigmaringen: Thorbecke.

Vogel, V. 2002. Archäologische Belege für Fernkontakte der Stadt Schleswig im 11.–13. Jahrhundert. In K. Brandt, M. Müller-Wille & C. Radtke (eds.), *Haithabu und die frühe Stadtentwicklung im nördlichen Europa*. Schriften des Archäologischen Landesmuseums 8: 367–78. Neumünster: Wachholtz.

von Carnap-Bornheim, C. & Kalmring, S. 2011. DFG-Schwerpunktprogramm 1630 'Häfen von der Römischen Kaiserzeit bis zum Mittelalter. Zur Archäologie und Geschichte regionaler und überregionaler Verkehrssysteme' bewilligt. *Jahresbericht Zentrum für Baltische und Skandinavische Archäologie*: 28–31.

von Liliencron, R. 1888. *Der Runenstein von Gottorp. König Sigtrygg's Stein im Schleswig-Holsteinischen Museum Vaterländischer Altertümer zu Kiel*. Kiel: Gesellschaft für Schleswig-Holstein-Lauenburgische Geschichte & Anthropologischer Verein in Schleswig-Holstein.

von Liliencron, R. & Wimmer, L. 1898. *Der Runenstein im Schleswiger Dom*. Kiel: Museum Vaterländischer Alterthümer.

Wallace, P. F. 2016. *Viking Dublin: The Wood Quay Excavations*. Sallins: Irish Academic Press.

Walton Rogers, P. 1997. *Textile Production at 16–22 Coppergate*. The Archaeology of York The Small Finds 17/11. York: York Archaeological Trust.

Weidemann, M. 1982. *Kulturgeschichte der Merowingerzeit nach den Werken Gregors von Tours*, Vol. 1. Römisch-Germanisches Zentralmuseum. Forschungsinstitut für Vor- und Frühgeschichte. Monographien 3:1. Mainz: Habelt.

Weinmann, C. 1994. *Der Hausbau in Skandinavien vom Neolithikum bis zum Mittelalter: mit einem Beitrag zur interdisziplinären Sachkulturforschung für das mittelalterliche Island*. Berlin: De Gruyter.

Weise, S. 2000. Mikrostratigraphische Ausgrabung und Analyse des Grabbefundes Bischof Rudolf von Schleswig: Methode und Erkenntnisse. Master's thesis, Hamburg University.

Wendt, A. 2012. Wikingerzeitliche Goldringe: Eine Fundgruppe ohne Kontext? In P. Gammeltoft & V. Hilberg (eds.), *Beretning fra Niogtyvende Tvaerfaglige Vikingesymposium*: 50–68. Højbjerg: Forlaget Wormianum.

Wessén, E. 1923. Birca och bjärköarätt. *Namn och Bygd* 11: 135–78.

Wessén, E. 1940. *Upplands Runinskrifter* 1. Sveriges Runinskrifter 6. Kungl. Vitterhets Historie och Antikvitets Akademien. Uppsala: Almqvist & Wiksell.

Westerdahl, C. 1986. Die maritime Kulturlandschaft. *Deutsches Schiffahrtsarchiv* 9: 7–58.

Westerdahl, C. 1992. The Maritime Cultural Landscape. *The International Journal of Nautical Archaeology* 21(1): 5–14.

Westphal, F. 2006. *Die Holzfunde von Haithabu. Ausgrabungen in Haithabu 11*. Neumünster: Wachholtz.

Westphal, F. 2013. Eine Wassermühle am Bach von Haithabu? In S. Kleingärtner, U. Müller & J. Scheschkewitz (eds.), *Kulturwandel im Spannungsfeld von Tradition und Innovation: Festschrift für Michael Müller-Wille*: 139–43. Neumünster: Wachholtz.

White, J. 2010. Building Innovative Sites. In The World Bank (ed.), *Innovation Policy: A Guide for Development Countries*: 303–34. Washington, DC: The World Bank.

White, J. 2011. Fostering Innovation in Developing Economies through SEZs. In T. Farole & G. Akinci (eds.), *Special Economic Zones: Progress, Emerging Challenges, and Future Directions*. Directions in Development – Trade: 183–205. Washington, DC: The World Bank.

Wickham, C. 2005. *Framing the Early Middle Ages: Europe and the Mediterranean, 400–800*. Oxford: Oxford University Press.

Wiechmann, R. 2007a. Haithabu und sein Hinterland – ein lokaler numismatischer Raum? Münzen und Münzfunde aus Haithabu (bis zum Jahr 2002). Das archäologische Fundmaterial 8. *Berichte über die Ausgrabungen in Haithabu* 36: 182–278. Neumünster: Wachholtz.

Wiechmann, R. 2007b. Hedeby and Its Hinterland: A Local Numismatic Region. In J. Graham-Campbell & G. Williams (eds.), *Silver Economy in the Viking Age*: 29–48. Walnut Creek, CA: Left Coast Press.

Wiechmann, R. 2021. Advancing into Unknown Lands: The Numismatic Material of Groß Strömkendorf Near Wismar during the Early Viking Age (ca. 8th–9th Centuries). In H. Nol (ed.), *Riches beyond the Horizon: Long-Distance Trade in Early Medieval Landscapes (ca. 6th–12th Centuries)*. Medieval and Post-Medieval Mediterranean Archaeology Series 4: 269–98. Turnhout: Brepols.

Wikborg, J. 2017. Stolpmonumented. In L. Beronius Jörpeland, H. GöthBerg, A. Seiler & J. Wikborg (eds.), *At Upsalum – mäniskor och landskapande. Utbyggnad av Ostkustbanan genom Gamla Uppsala*. Arkeologisk undersökning. Report No. 2017: 1.1: 258–336. Stockholm: Arkeologerna.

Wikström, A. 2011. *Fem stadsgårdar – arkeologisk undersökning i kv. Trädgårdsmästaren 9 & 10 i Sigtuna 1988–90*. Meddelanden och Rapporter från Sigtuna Museum 52. Sigtuna: Sigtuna Museum.

Williams, A. 2009. A Metallurgical Study of some Viking Swords. *Gladius* 29: 121–84.

Willroth, K.-H. 1992. *Untersuchungen zur Besiedlungsgeschichte der Landschaften Angeln und Schwansen von der älteren Bronzezeit bis zum frühen Mittelalter. Eine Studie zur Chronologie, Chorologie und Siedlungskunde*. Siedlungsarchäolgische Untersuchungen in Angeln und Schwansen 1. Offa-Bücher 72. Neumünster: Wachholtz.

Wimmer, L. F. A. 1892. *Sønderjyllands Historiske Runemindesmærker*. Copenhagen: Thieles bogtrykkeri.

Windler, R. 2008. Mittelalterliche Webstühle und Weberwerkstätten – Archäologische Befunde und Funde. In W. Melzer (ed.), *Archäologie und mittelalterliches Handwerk – Eine Standortbestimmung*. Soester Beiträge zur Archäologie 9: 201–15. Soest: Westfälische Verlagsbuchhandlung Mocker & Jahn.

Wiséhn, E. 1989. *Myntfynd från Uppland*. Sveriges mynthistoria. Landskapsinventeringen 4. Stockholm: Kungl. myntkabinettet.

Wouters, B. 2020. A Biographical Approach to Urban Communities from a Geoarchaeological Perspective: High-Definition Applications and Case Studies. *Journal of Urban Archaeology* 2: 85–101.

Wührer, K. 1981. s.v. 'Bryte'. In H. Beck, D. Geuenich & H. Steuer (eds.), *Reallexikon der Germanischen Altertumskunde* 4: 25–6. Berlin: De Gruyter.

Zachrisson, T. 1992. Silver and Gold Hoards from the Black Earth. In B. Ambrosiani & H. Clarke (eds.), *Early Investigations and Future Plans*. Birka Studies 1: 52–63. Stockholm: Riksantikvarieämbetet & Statens Historiska Museer.

Zachrisson, T. 1994. The Odal and Its Manifestation in the Landscape. *Current Swedish Archaeology* 2: 219–38.

Zachrisson, T. 1998. *Gård, gräns, gravfält. Sammanhang kring ädelmetalldepåer och runstenar från vikingatid och tidigmedeltid i Uppland och Gästrikland*. Stockholm Studies in Archaeology 15. Stockholm: Stockholm University.

Zachrisson, T. 2017. The Background of the Odal Rights: An Archaeological Discussion. *Danish Journal of Archaeology* 6: 118–32.

Zagal-Mach Wolfe, U. I. 2013. *Grasping Technology, Assessing Craft: Developing a Research Method for the Study of Craft-Tradition*. Acta archaeologica Lundensia, Series in 8°, Vol. 63. Stockholm: Almqvist & Wiksell International.

Index

Aachen, 49
Aarhus, 45, 162, 171, 172, 181, 195
abandonment, 9, 11, 12, 13, 47, 78, 121, 148, 154, 156, 157, 160, 165, 179, 182, 187, 193, 203, 204
Abu Salih Mansur, 160
Adalbert of Hamburg-Bremen, 182, 183, 184, 194, 195
Adalbrand Becelin, 183, 184
Adaldag, 181
Adam of Bremen, 4, 30, 31, 33, 111, 158, 168, 181, 184
Adelsö. *See* Hovgården
administration, 10, 11, 12, 34, 36, 43, 46, 54, 90, 93, 95, 98, 99, 100, 101, 103, 105, 117, 123, 124, 132, 135, 136, 147, 162, 187, 189, 191, 192, 195, 197, 198, 199, 200, 206
Ælfwald of East Anglia, 79
Æthelbald of Mercia, 94
Æthelstan, 191
agency, 19, 43, 82, 91, 92, 93, 110, 113, 126, 142
agriculture, 21, 28, 50, 68, 124, 127, 131, 140, 169, 198
 crop rotation, 139, 140
Åhus, 14, 18, 149
Åland, 128
Alcuin, 76
Aldeigjuborg. *See* Staraja Ladoga
Alfred the Great, 119
al-Masisah, 160
Alps, 106, 144, 178
Anglia, 54, 125, 126
Anglo-Saxons, 3, 5, 10, 61, 65, 85, 86, 93, 94, 101, 105, 110, 132, 152, 153, 200, 201, 206
Ansfrid, 156
Ansgar, 4, 37, 51, 99, 108, 110, 154, 156, 177, 189
antiquity, 88, 101, 145, 199, 200
Anund, 119
Anund 'the Land Clearer', 38, 43

apprenticeship, 129, 130, 202
architecture, 18, 28, 45, 46, 172, 177, 181, 185, 197
aristocracy, 19, 26, 28, 45, 46, 55, 139
Arkona, 150
Arnulf I of Flanders, 176
Aros. *See* Aarhus
artefacts, 1, 2, 4, 21, 28, 48, 55, 63, 72, 73, 97, 127, 145, 156, 159, 173
assemblies, 28, 29, 33, 34, 35, 36, 37, 38, 39, 40, 41, 42, 48, 50, 51, 53, 61, 65, 78, 95, 96, 100, 107, 119, 123, 131, 132, 137, 197
 assembly mound, 31
 disaþing, 38
Auður and Gunnhildr, 183
Austrasia, 68
authorities, 10, 61, 65, 76, 77, 78, 80, 92, 94, 100, 115, 126, 191, 199
autonomy, 10, 27, 61, 76, 100, 154, 155, 156, 160, 204
Avars, 106
axis mundi, 33

Baltic Sea, 2, 7, 9, 13, 17, 26, 28, 59, 60, 64, 88, 96, 110, 118, 129, 138, 147, 149, 150, 151, 168, 198, 203
Balts, 61
Bannbezirk. *See* market peace
Barva, 130
Bath, 103
beads, 16, 150, 160, 161, 162
Beaduheard, 65, 98
bells, 119, 178, 181, 185, 205
Belobereg, 110
Benedict of Nursia, 93
Beorhtric of Wessex, 65, 98
Berezan, 110
Bergen, 144
Bergslagen, 60, 128
Bernhar, 101
Bernhard, 183

266

Bernhard II of Saxony, 168, 169, 184
Birger Magnusson, 52
Birka, 1, 4, 7, 8, 16, 18, 19, 21, 25, 34, 37, 38,
    43, 48, 50, 51, 53, 60, 61, 66, 72, 73, 75, 90,
    95, 98, 99, 100, 103, 108, 111, 114, 119,
    121, 122, 124, 126, 128, 129, 130, 131,
    142, 147, 150, 151, 153, 154, 156, 157,
    159, 160, 162, 163, 164, 165, 201, 203,
    204, 207, 208
bishops, 37, 103, 181, 182, 183, 184, 194, 195
    archbishops, 4, 156, 181, 183
Björkö. *See* Birka
Björn at Haugi, 37, 51, 99, 108
Björn Ironside, 53
Blekinge, 27
Blusso, 188
Bodmin, 103
Boernwulf, 102
border, 4, 7, 8, 10, 11, 14, 28, 59, 61, 68, 82, 91,
    101, 106, 107, 118, 142, 166, 167, 168,
    169, 182, 198, 200, 205
Borgarfjörður, 65
Bornholm, 27
boundaries, 28, 33, 35, 41, 50, 59, 61, 84, 85,
    87, 88, 90, 95, 105, 114, 115, 118, 123,
    130, 132, 135, 166, 167, 169, 175, 177,
    194, 198, 199, 201
    legal boundaries, 84, 86
Bremen, 8, 157
buildings, 1, 13, 21, 22, 28, 31, 32, 33, 43, 46,
    47, 49, 52, 71, 73, 141, 142, 143, 155, 157,
    158, 159, 172, 173, 175, 176, 193,
    197, 205
    booth, 35, 48
    dwelling, 11, 22, 70, 74, 80, 90, 142, 173,
        174, 180, 189
    hall, 28, 31, 32, 33, 45, 46, 47, 49, 54, 158,
        159, 173, 177, 205
    Hedeby house, 141
    house platform, 31, 32, 33, 54, 72,
        157, 159
    longhouse, 22, 23, 55, 72, 73, 142
    outbuilding, 22, 23, 32, 174
    pit house, 22, 23, 29, 33, 36, 48, 55, 70, 74,
        165, 176
    Trelleborg house, 45, 46, 142
    Warendorf house, 142, 203
burhs, 191
burials, 4, 28, 30, 31, 44, 52, 72, 119, 120, 121,
    122, 156, 158, 160, 178, 180, 204

burial grounds, 22, 26, 27, 33, 37, 53, 56,
    73, 78, 79, 80, 86, 120, 121, 122, 133,
    151, 178, 179, 180, 181, 185, 193, 201
cemeteries, Christian, 32, 164, 172, 177,
    178, 179, 180, 181, 185, 190, 205
Byzantium, 3, 5, 89, 90, 91, 94, 101, 108, 109,
    112, 114, 115, 116, 117, 132, 140, 151, 200

Caliphate, xv, 150, 151, 165
Canterbury, 94, 103, 182, 183, 194
Canute the Great, 182, 183, 184, 194
capitalism, 14, 135
cargo, 62, 63, 96
    cargo capacity, 94
    cargo vessels, 62, 152
Carolingian Empire, 3, 28, 50, 59, 105, 112,
    114, 138, 141, 149, 151, 166, 167, 200,
    202, 203, 244
Carolingians, 14, 41, 49, 92, 106, 107, 133,
    141, 176, 200
catchment area, 24, 48, 125
central place, 9, 10, 13, 14, 15, 17, 19, 20, 28,
    29, 53, 56, 76, 140, 192, 196, 197
    central place theory, 17
characteristics, 17, 19, 59, 64, 121, 123, 135,
    136, 142, 174, 177, 178, 180, 184, 197,
    202, 208
Charlemagne, 14, 41, 59, 80, 105
Charles the Bald, 102
Charles the Fat, 149
Chernigov, 108
chieftains, 20, 43, 75, 156
Christianisation, 1, 8, 14, 26, 27, 30, 37, 39,
    97, 108, 111, 121, 154, 155, 156, 157, 158,
    177, 204
churches, 29, 31, 32, 35, 42, 44, 45, 46, 51, 53,
    67, 86, 100, 132, 164, 172, 177, 178, 180,
    181, 182, 183, 184, 185, 186, 189, 191,
    194, 195, 205, 206
    abbey, 41, 94, 141
    archdiocese, 30, 194, 195
    cathedral, 31, 157, 164, 171, 172, 177,
        184, 190, 195, 206
    diocese, 30, 41, 94, 158, 163, 171, 178,
        181, 182, 183, 195, 205, 206
    minster, 86, 164, 171
    stave church, 172, 177
civitas, 7, 12, 20, 102, 103, 158, 166, 177, 182,
    186, 188, 191, 193, 205, 206
coexistence, 50, 198

INDEX

coinage, 16, 67, 68, 70, 126, 133, 149, 150, 151, 152, 158, 165, 193, 203, 207
   dirhams, 128, 148, 150, 151, 158, 160, 203
   Hauberg types, 193
   Hedeby coins, 126
   Otto-Adelheid-pennies, 180
   sceattas, 70, 74, 82, 151
   Sigtuna coins, 159
   Slesvig coins, 189
collapse, 13, 91, 94, 149
Cologne, 126, 182
Comacchio, 91, 101
commerce, 3, 15, 42, 59, 63, 70, 82, 83, 92, 101, 106, 107, 108, 109, 114, 118, 119, 132, 156, 189, 192, 193, 196, 200, 204
   commercial policy, 81, 105, 106, 107, 135, 136, 199, 201, 204, 208
commodities, 19, 39, 62, 63, 114, 127, 139, 141, 198, 203
communication, 2, 8, 19, 35, 77, 134
communities, 4, 12, 19, 28, 35, 42, 50, 62, 82, 115, 118, 127, 131, 133, 147, 153, 154, 156, 163, 196, 198
concepts, 6, 9, 10, 17, 19, 23, 35, 58, 64, 131, 166, 196, 202
conflicts, 96, 154, 156, 158, 159, 172, 204, 206
Conrad II, 168, 182, 184, 194
consolidation, 13, 125, 138, 155, 156, 204
Constantinople, 62, 89, 108, 113, 115, 150, 201
consumables, 23, 41, 64, 118, 125, 128, 133
contacts, 5, 139, 147, 150, 156, 171, 192
Continental Europe, 4, 7, 59, 67, 78, 83, 95, 101, 121, 124, 139, 140, 142, 162, 165, 175, 192, 197, 199, 202, 205
continuity, 17, 24, 175, 177
control, 7, 13, 33, 43, 54, 59, 61, 67, 69, 77, 78, 79, 81, 83, 84, 91, 105, 106, 115, 123, 133, 134, 155, 158, 160, 165, 189, 198, 199, 202
conversion, 14, 121, 162
convoys, 110, 111, 153
Córdoba, 165
cosmopolitanism, 115, 147, 177, 185, 201
Courland, 110
craft, 1, 2, 13, 16, 17, 19, 36, 74, 78, 124, 125, 139, 191, 202
crafters, 12, 25, 76, 129, 133, 163, 202, 207
   itinerant crafters, 119, 129, 130
crisis, 18, 148, 150, 152, 154, 163, 165, 203, 204
   silver crisis, 150, 151, 203

cult, 17, 33, 34, 38, 47, 48, 49, 131, 158, 177, 197
cultivation, 21, 22, 139
custom duties. *See* taxes

Dagobert I, 41
Dalarna, 128
Danelaw, 137
Danes, 8, 107, 155, 167, 168, 181, 187, 194, 205
Danevirke, 59, 155, 165, 166, 168, 169, 205
Dankirke, 70
debate, 2, 4, 13, 14, 20, 58, 75, 130, 141, 166, 196
decline, 148, 164, 187, 193, 203, 204
definitions, 2, 9, 10, 11, 14, 15, 20, 63, 90, 136, 196
delegations, 5, 107, 108, 109, 112, 200
demand, 41, 139, 140
demise, 68, 73, 99, 154, 163, 165, 171, 204, 206
Denmark, 1, 5, 7, 14, 21, 25, 27, 28, 29, 36, 44, 59, 61, 65, 76, 77, 80, 82, 107, 108, 110, 111, 113, 115, 119, 121, 122, 152, 153, 155, 167, 168, 169, 176, 181, 182, 183, 184, 189, 194, 195, 205, 206, 208
desirables, 118, 129, 133, 134, 138, 200
diaspora, 3
Diedenhofen. *See* Thionville
discontinuity, 2, 5, 20, 154, 155
disruptions, 150, 203
distribution, 2, 19, 25, 26, 70, 77, 120, 125, 128, 136, 140, 161
Domburg, 68
Dorchester, 66
Dorestad, 8, 14, 67, 68, 72, 101, 106, 124, 126, 139, 148, 151, 200
Douai, 176
downfall, 12, 149, 160, 161, 203, 204, 206
dualism, 50, 163, 187, 188
Dublin, 98
dues. *See* taxes
dynamics, 3, 147, 163, 167, 203, 208
dynasties, 20, 29, 31, 45, 46, 197
   Dankirke, 70
   Jelling, 44, 45, 55, 153, 155
   Olof, 152
   Rurikids, 108, 151, 203
   Skjǫldungar, 29
   Ynglinga, 30, 76

INDEX 269

Eadberht II of Kent, 94
East Anglia, 137
Eastern Europe, 101, 150, 159, 224
ecclesiastic, 39, 67, 92, 138, 162, 163, 172, 177, 178, 181, 183, 185, 187, 189, 191, 194, 195, 205, 206
economy, 1, 2, 3, 8, 10, 12, 13, 14, 15, 23, 50, 63, 67, 79, 81, 82, 123, 124, 126, 131, 133, 135, 136, 137, 138, 139, 140, 148, 152, 162, 163, 164, 165, 166, 187, 191, 193, 196, 202, 204, 206, 207, 208
edibles. *See* consumables
Egill Skallagrímsson, 65
Ekkehard, 182, 194
elites, 13, 49, 55, 68, 77, 78, 79, 80
Ellingstedt, 125
emergence, 5, 8, 13, 21, 35, 68, 70, 76, 77, 80, 127
emporium, 7, 11, 12, 13, 14, 15, 19, 20, 40, 48, 63, 67, 68, 70, 78, 85, 94, 103, 106, 118, 124, 138, 141, 147, 148, 150, 162, 163, 187, 191, 200, 201, 203, 204
    type-A emporia, 11, 12, 63, 67, 80, 83, 137, 147
    type-B emporia, 11, 12, 83, 84
    type-C emporia, 12, 147
enclosure, 23, 33, 35, 45, 46, 47, 49, 55, 85, 86, 87, 88, 90, 164, 180
    special fenced area, 47
England, 41, 42, 77, 80, 85, 102, 103, 106, 110, 117, 159, 171, 182, 184, 185, 191, 192, 194
English Channel, 78, 101, 148, 200
entrepreneurship, 19, 58
envoys, 107, 109, 111, 112, 113, 165
Eorforwic. *See* York
Erik Refilsson, 51
Erik Segersäll, 108, 113, 158, 160
Eriksgata, 43
Erimbert, 156
Esesfelth, 167
estates, 17, 43, 44, 45, 46, 48, 49, 50, 52, 53, 79, 98, 99, 177, 184, 197, 198
Estonia, 110
excavations, 1, 4, 18, 21, 31, 33, 42, 44, 45, 48, 54, 55, 62, 64, 71, 72, 73, 74, 75, 82, 86, 130, 143, 145, 164, 166, 171, 173, 175, 177, 189, 193
exchange, 10, 18, 29, 40, 42, 65, 77, 78, 88, 90, 93, 124, 125, 126, 139, 197, 207
expeditions, 24, 25, 128, 153, 181, 197, 201

exports, 19, 101, 106, 139, 200
exterritorial, 98, 133, 165

fairs, 11, 29, 34, 39, 41, 42, 48, 50, 114, 131, 197
    annual fairs, 41, 42
    disting, 38, 39, 40, 41
    seasonal fairs, 41, 42, 131, 197, 198
    St. Dionysius's fair, 41
    St. Mathias fair, 41
festivals, religious, 29, 30, 41, 42, 197
    dísablót, 30, 38
feudalisation, 41, 155, 163
Finnveden, 27
Flanders, 176, 205
Folkbert, 182, 183
food. *See* consumables
Fordwich, 94
foreigners, 8, 10, 12, 26, 42, 78, 96, 101, 108, 111, 112, 114, 115, 116, 117, 118, 119, 120, 122, 123, 126, 129, 130, 133, 142, 200, 201, 202, 207
fortification, 12, 59, 60, 155, 165, 166, 168, 191, 205
Fos-sur-Mer, 92
framework, 5, 84, 105, 109, 114, 136, 175, 189, 198, 199, 200, 207
France, 176
Francia, 43, 67, 68, 77, 78, 90, 92, 94, 107, 111, 117, 132, 138, 152, 171, 199
Franconia, 145
Frisians, 8, 28, 59, 61, 66, 68, 69, 77, 78, 114, 121, 139, 141, 142, 151, 153
frontiers. *See* border
Fulda, 107, 141, 145, 152
Funen, 64, 183
Füsing, 54, 56

Gamla Uppsala, 7, 29, 30, 31, 33, 38, 40, 46, 48, 54, 60, 128, 143, 158, 197
Gandersheim, 182
Gascony, 117
gateways, 10, 14, 22, 106, 142, 151, 207
    gateway communities, 11
Gauzbert, 37
Gerbrand, 183
Germany, 1, 5, 17, 28, 188
Gervold of Fontanelle/Saint Wandrille, 102, 103
gift-giving, 63, 96, 97, 111, 134, 138

Gipeswic. *See* Ipswich
glass vessels, 139, 141, 203
Gluomi, 167
Gnupa, 152
Godfred, 7, 56, 76, 80, 167
Golden Circle, 3, 20, 207
Gorm the Old, 44
Gotland, 34, 40, 64
Gottschalk, 188
graves. *See* burials
  boat graves, 30, 121, 122
  chamber graves, 120, 122
  coffin graves, 120, 122
  cremation graves, 26, 30, 31, 52, 120, 121, 122, 201
  equestrian graves, 25, 125
  grave mounds, 26, 31, 54, 179
  graves without coffins, 120
  inhumation graves, 26, 120, 121, 122, 178, 179, 180, 181, 185, 193, 201
  mass graves, 162
  wagon-body graves, 122
  weapon graves, 25
Great Belt, 28, 48
Gredelby, 129
Grippo, 102, 103
Grobin, 149
Groß Strömkendorf. *See* Reric
Großhöbing, 145
guests, 96, 117, 120, 129, 130
guilds, 153
Gulf of Finland, 203
Gunnarr Hámundarson, 96, 97
Gästrikland, 128
Gävle, 128

Hærvejen, 59
Halland, 27, 155
Hamburg, 8, 59, 101, 181
Hamburg-Bremen, 4, 156, 182, 183, 194, 195, 206
Hamwic, 14, 77, 79, 85, 138, 148
Harald Bluetooth, 44, 96, 108, 155, 169, 172, 181, 182, 185
Harald Fairhair, 108
Harald Hardrada, 89, 110, 171, 172, 188, 189
harbours, 53, 56, 62, 63, 64, 66, 68, 74, 80, 87, 88, 90, 91, 92, 93, 94, 95, 96, 97, 98, 103, 122, 132, 152, 165, 178, 181, 185, 193, 198, 199, 203, 205

custom harbours, 92, 93, 98
harbour chains, 88, 89, 90, 199
harbour facilities, 15, 63, 69, 92, 98, 152, 185
jetties, 130, 157, 192
Harthacnut, 193, 194
Hārūn al-Rashīd, 150
Hastings, 1
Hedeby, 1, 3, 7, 8, 14, 16, 18, 19, 21, 34, 35, 48, 54, 55, 59, 61, 62, 66, 73, 76, 80, 87, 89, 95, 96, 97, 100, 103, 107, 110, 114, 121, 125, 126, 129, 134, 141, 143, 145, 147, 149, 151, 152, 153, 163, 164, 165, 167, 168, 169, 171, 172, 173, 174, 175, 176, 177, 178, 181, 182, 183, 184, 187, 188, 189, 191, 193, 194, 195, 199, 203, 204, 206, 207, 208
Helgö, 159
Henry the Fowler, 168, 171
hereditary, 22, 24
Herigar, 37, 98, 100
Herrmann of Jever, 193
heyday, 13, 82, 138, 162
hiatus, 126, 152, 203
Hildesheim, 182
hillforts, 56, 73, 120, 121, 159
hinterland, 10, 36, 55, 60, 67, 78, 79, 118, 123, 124, 125, 126, 129, 133, 137, 138, 142, 154, 201, 203, 207
Hlothhere and Eadric, 102, 118
Hollingstedt, 59
Holmgård. *See* Rjurikovo Gorodišče
Holstein, 59, 126
Holy Roman Empire, 182, 194
Hored, 181, 183
Horik the Elder, 100, 108, 111
Horik the Younger, 100
hostels, commercial, 116, 117, 201
Hovgården, 51, 52, 53, 55, 56, 58, 61, 99
Hovi, 100
hubs, 2, 10, 18, 129, 139, 207
Håkan the Red, 52, 98
Håkon Sigurdsson, 113

Ibrâhîm ibn Ya`qûb al-Ṭurṭûshî, 164
Iceland, 38, 65, 95
identity, 14, 26, 154
ideology, 154, 155, 156, 158, 159, 204
Igor of Kiev, 109
implementation, 6, 81, 132, 137, 176

INDEX

imports, 16, 17, 19, 28, 77, 79, 129, 140, 150, 152, 171, 202, 207
industrial manufacture, 139, 163, 202
Ingelheim, 112
Ingvar Emundsson. *See* Yngvar the Fartraveller
innovations, 123, 129, 133, 136, 137, 138, 140, 141, 142, 143, 145, 146, 176, 202, 203, 207
    diffusion of innovations, 127, 133, 137, 140, 146, 202
instability, 13, 149
institutions, 34, 74, 92, 132, 136, 197, 203
interconnectivity, 1, 2, 3, 9, 196, 207
interment. *See* burials
Ipswich, 77, 78, 79, 137, 138
Ireland, 114
Iron Age, 25, 26, 196, 197
    Early Iron Age, 36
    Late Iron Age, 8, 65, 131
    pre–Roman Iron Age, 167
    Roman Iron Age, 13, 17, 24, 29, 30, 72, 131, 167
isostatic rebound, 4
itinerant kingship, 43, 56, 131, 197
    veizla, 44
    visthus, 43, 44

Jańow Pomorski. *See* Truso
Jelling, 44, 45, 46, 155
Jerusalem, 20
jurisdiction, 10, 11, 26, 29, 31, 35, 40, 49, 84, 87, 88, 90, 95, 97, 98, 100, 101, 103, 105, 119, 123, 132, 197, 199, 201
Jutland, 21, 23, 28, 44, 61, 70, 145, 164, 168, 171, 181, 188, 195
Jämtland, 39
Järrestad, 47

Kaupang, 1, 3, 16, 18, 21, 36, 48, 53, 61, 66, 73, 76, 121, 122, 163, 164, 165, 201, 204, 207, 208
Kent, 77, 94, 102, 118
Kiev, 108, 109, 153
kingdoms, 1, 38, 43, 61, 80, 107, 111, 167, 168, 197
kings, 7, 14, 30, 33, 37, 38, 39, 43, 52, 58, 61, 75, 76, 77, 80, 83, 87, 96, 97, 98, 99, 100, 102, 103, 105, 107, 111, 113, 114, 119, 133, 134, 137, 152, 154, 156, 160, 165, 167, 184, 200, 204
knowledge transfer, 129, 130, 136, 141, 203
Knut Lavard, 89
Knut the Saint, 108
Kosel, 125
Kurburg, 169
Könugård. *See* Kiev

Lake Mälaren, 7, 39, 60, 124, 128, 159
    Mälar valley, 21, 24, 54, 60
landing places. *See* landing sites
landing sites, 14, 48, 63, 64, 70, 72, 73, 74, 78, 82, 93, 198, 203, 207
landnám, 3
language, 25, 166, 187, 197
law, 5, 11, 22, 26, 34, 36, 38, 41, 48, 66, 84, 87, 90, 95, 96, 105, 109, 111, 114, 117, 118, 129, 131, 132, 133, 136, 191, 197, 199, 200, 201, 202
    legal customs, 28, 34
    legal traditions, 34
    provincial laws, 26, 34, 105
ledung, 24, 61
Lejre, 29, 45, 46
Leo VI the Wise, 108, 115
Liafdag, 181
limes Saxoniae, 59
Lincoln, 137
Lincolnshire, 119
Lindisfarne, 1, 65
Lisbjerg, 45, 47
Liutprand of the Lombards, 91
Ljørring, 145
Lombardy, 92, 94, 101
London, 77, 79, 94, 102, 117, 138, 148, 185, 192
Lorraine, 117
Lorsch, 141
Louis the Child, 105
Louis the German, 107
Louis the Pious, 93, 102, 106, 107, 112, 113
Lund, 19, 144, 162, 191, 195
Lundenwic. *See* London
Lürschau. *See* Lyrskov
Lyrskov, 188

Magnus Eriksson, 117
Magnus Håkonsson, 96
Magnus Ladulås, 52

Magnus the Good, 183, 184, 188
manor, 14, 17, 32, 33, 35, 46, 47, 48, 50, 51, 52, 55, 56, 57, 58, 60, 70, 131, 132, 139, 163, 177, 184, 189, 197, 198, 202
manorial system, 41, 138, 163
Marco, 182, 183
markets, 10, 14, 17, 38, 39, 40, 41, 42, 43, 48, 49, 65, 66, 70, 77, 78, 79, 82, 83, 84, 87, 90, 92, 93, 95, 100, 105, 117, 123, 131, 133, 191, 197, 198, 200
   beach markets, 53, 64, 65, 66, 70, 73, 74, 93, 132, 147, 148, 199, 203
   border markets, 64
   harbour markets, 93, 94, 192
   legal markets, 83
   local markets, 18, 42
   market cycles, 41, 42
   marketplaces, 4, 14, 70, 71, 72, 76, 86, 192
   market tithe, 90, 96, 106, 200
   market trade, 29, 207
   weekly markets, 42
   winter markets, 39, 43
Marseille, 92
material culture, 25, 28, 133, 207
Mayen, 126, 139
Mecklenburg, 59
Mediterranean, 19, 91, 115, 118, 143
Menzlin, 149
merchants, 7, 8, 10, 12, 25, 39, 42, 56, 66, 68, 76, 78, 80, 87, 88, 90, 93, 96, 106, 107, 109, 111, 113, 114, 115, 116, 117, 118, 123, 126, 129, 133, 147, 153, 156, 160, 199, 200, 203, 207
   long-distance merchants, 41, 42, 77, 82, 111, 114, 118, 119, 133, 199, 200
Merovingian period, 14, 29, 31, 32, 41, 46, 53, 56, 69, 72, 75, 159, 198
Merovingians, 67, 73, 78, 92, 103, 200
Metz, 107
Middle Ages, 10, 14, 19, 140, 145
Migration period, 13, 17, 30, 37, 56, 72, 125, 131, 159
Miklagård. *See* Constantinople
military, 14, 19, 28, 58, 81, 103, 156
mints, 10, 68, 126, 134, 150, 151, 152, 160, 189, 191, 193, 194, 203
mission, Christian. *See* Christianisation
models, 2, 3, 5, 13, 17, 19, 20, 86, 94, 137, 175, 191, 200, 207
monopolisation, 77, 78

monuments, 15, 27, 45, 166
monumental architecture, 15
monumental mounds, 30, 32, 33, 35, 37, 44, 45, 52, 53, 72
monumentality, 19, 31, 58
Mýrkjartan, 114
Möre, 27

Nantes, 93
negotiations, 102, 108, 183, 184, 195
networks, 2, 3, 8, 9, 11, 17, 18, 20, 28, 44, 61, 118, 124, 140, 148, 150, 151, 156, 191, 196, 198, 202, 203, 207
   network theory, 2, 9, 17, 20, 196
Neustria, 67
neutrality, 50, 131, 198
Nidaros. *See* Trondheim
no man's land, 60, 119, 123, 165, 169, 198, 205
non-places, 14, 15
Nordalbingia, 59, 167, 188
Normans, 192
Norrtälje, 128
North Atlantic, 25, 35
North Sea, 7, 13, 28, 59, 61, 64, 70, 86, 106, 118, 121, 138, 148, 150, 151, 163, 199, 203
North Sea Empire, 192, 206
Northern Arc, 8
Northern Europe, 6, 7, 8, 12, 19, 25, 62, 66, 133, 139, 144, 162, 176, 197
Northumbria, 1, 86, 137
Norway, 1, 8, 21, 25, 30, 34, 38, 44, 54, 75, 76, 113, 114, 115, 126, 130, 155, 171, 183, 184, 188, 190, 195, 206
Norwich, 137
novelties, 53, 142, 169, 176, 196, 200
Novgorod, 89, 101, 153, 160
Nyköping, 128
Närke, 128

obligations, 110, 118, 138, 139
Obotrites, 7, 56, 59, 80, 167, 188, 189
Ochsenweg. *See* Hærvejen
óðal. *See* hereditary
Odense, 162
Offa of Mercia, 94, 102, 105
officials, royal, 91, 93, 98, 100, 101, 102, 103, 105, 115, 132, 200
   bailiff, 52, 98, 198, 200
   bryte, 99

INDEX 273

comes, 92, 100, 101, 103, 114, 117, 132, 185, 200
portgerefa, 102, 103
praefectus, 37, 100, 102, 103, 114, 117, 132, 200
procurator, 90, 93, 101, 102, 103
reeve, 65, 98, 102, 105, 119, 134, 201
wicgerefa, 102
Ohthere, 27
Okholm, 70, 141
Olaf Hǫskuldsson, 114
Olaf II of Norway, 39, 95, 113
Olaf Tryggvason, 95, 110
Öland, 27
Olaus Magnus, 39
Oleg of Novgorod, 89, 108, 109, 153
Olof I of Sweden, 37, 51
Olof Skötkonung, 158
Omgård, 145
Ongedus, 76
oppidum, 7
Örebro, 128
Öresund, 28
Orléans, 67, 93
Oslo, 162
Östergötland, 24
Östra Aros, 30, 39
otherness, 5, 131, 196, 200
Otto II, 165, 168
Otto the Great, 181
Ottonian, 14, 87, 169, 176, 177, 186, 189, 205, 206
oval brooches, 128, 130
Oviken, 39

paganism, 1, 20, 37, 44, 97, 100, 156, 157, 158, 177, 179, 180, 197, 198, 204
palace, 41, 49, 51, 52, 56, 86, 133, 184, 197
palisade. *See* enclosure
Paris, 67
patronage, 1, 148, 157, 207
Paulinus of York, 86
peace, 39, 66, 107, 111, 113, 134, 182, 184, 194
  market peace, 39, 87, 114, 133, 134, 200
  municipal peace, 11
  peace of the town, 87, 199, 200
  thing peace, 35
  trading peace, 109, 114, 152, 200, 207
Pepin II of Herstal, 67
Pereyaslavl', 108

permanency, 12, 13, 33, 42, 43, 49, 70, 71, 72, 73, 74, 76, 77, 78, 79, 80, 90, 120, 129, 131, 134
persistence, 4, 121, 164, 165, 187, 188, 204, 208
Pfalz. *See* palace
pilgrims, 67, 111, 183
pirates, 108, 110, 132, 153, 159, 200, 204
place names, 35, 36, 37, 53, 55
Poland, 151
politics, 10, 13, 14, 19, 20, 29, 30, 31, 33, 36, 40, 57, 59, 67, 105, 106, 108, 123, 131, 134, 136, 140, 149, 154, 158, 159, 165, 166, 169, 184, 194, 195, 197, 198, 205, 206, 208
Pollista, 129, 142
polyfocal, 80, 85
Pomerania, 110
Poppo, 182, 183
port, 7, 9, 19, 63, 64, 67, 85, 88, 90, 92, 94, 101, 110, 114, 117, 132, 192, 196, 200
  port of trade, 9, 131
portage, 7, 35, 59
Portland, 65
portus, 7, 12, 93, 94, 137
pottery, 28, 129, 139, 141
  Badorf ware, 28, 141
  Muschelgrus ware, 28, 141
  Tating ware, 126
  wheel-turned pottery, 141, 203
privileges, 11, 41, 67, 75, 92, 94, 95, 96, 114, 136, 202
production, 3, 9, 12, 13, 16, 19, 20, 22, 48, 58, 124, 125, 127, 130, 136, 139, 140, 141, 150, 163, 196, 202
  agricultural production, 19, 139, 202
productive sites, 41
protection, legal, 17, 26, 79, 80, 88, 90, 96, 109, 111, 112, 113, 114, 118, 133, 200, 201, 207
provinces, 7, 14, 26, 27, 36, 39, 60, 61, 68, 89, 155, 166, 195
Pskov, 150
purpose, 3, 5, 20, 31, 42, 50, 64, 117, 129, 136, 145, 173, 194, 196, 207

Quentovic, 14, 67, 101, 103, 106, 139, 200
quern stones, 28, 126, 141

274 INDEX

Raffelstetten customs, 105
raids, 1, 55, 65, 68, 84, 87, 96, 101, 108, 111, 119, 134, 148, 150, 159, 167, 168, 171, 172, 178, 188, 190, 191, 195, 197, 199, 204, 206
Ralswiek, 149
Rammelsberg, 178
ramparts, 4, 56, 60, 72, 73, 74, 85, 87, 88, 121, 142, 157, 159, 166, 168, 169, 171, 176, 177, 178, 180, 181
Ratibor, 188
Ratolf, 182, 195
Ravning Enge, 155
realignment, 151, 195, 203
realms, 14, 38, 43, 57, 105, 108, 140, 154, 166, 167, 169, 200, 202, 205
   Danish realm, 14, 60, 166, 175, 176, 191
regalia rights, 80, 84, 199
Reginbert, 183
Reginbrund, 181
regionality, 8, 12, 17, 25, 26, 28, 34, 35, 36, 38, 41, 55, 64, 124, 125, 131, 139, 147, 162, 192
regulation, 13, 66, 94, 96, 105, 106, 117, 132, 201
Reisekönigtum. *See* itinerant kingship
religion, 10, 19, 20, 23, 29, 30, 34, 36, 38, 48, 58, 100, 107, 131, 158, 166, 183, 191, 196, 197, 198
relocation, 7, 46, 82, 154, 162, 165, 167, 172, 187, 188, 189, 190, 191, 194, 195, 199, 206
reorganisation, 13, 79, 154, 174, 175, 176, 185, 191, 195, 202, 205
Reric, 7, 18, 56, 80, 82, 96, 106, 163, 199
resources, 17, 23, 156
restrictions, 66, 88, 101, 105, 108, 109, 115, 117, 120, 121, 123, 130, 152, 202
retinue, 43, 49, 134, 183, 197, 207
Rhineland, 41, 69, 77, 138, 140, 141
Rhos. *See* Rus'
Ribe, 1, 3, 14, 16, 18, 21, 48, 61, 63, 66, 70, 76, 78, 82, 86, 126, 129, 141, 151, 152, 163, 171, 172, 177, 180, 181, 189, 191, 194, 195, 204, 207, 208
Rimbert, 4, 37, 39, 107, 119, 156
ring fortress, 45, 155, 169, 172
rituals, 15, 26, 27, 35, 48, 197
Rjurikovo Gorodišče, 150
Rodulf, 182, 194
Roma, 40

Roman Empire, 1, 41, 90, 101, 140
Roman World, 8
Romanos I Lekapenos, 109
Rome, 183, 194, 195, 206
Roskilde, 64, 162
Rostock-Dierkow, 149
Rouen, 67
royal, 13, 14, 19, 30, 35, 42, 43, 44, 45, 48, 49, 50, 51, 54, 55, 57, 60, 66, 75, 76, 78, 79, 86, 91, 93, 94, 96, 98, 101, 106, 111, 113, 114, 118, 126, 131, 132, 133, 138, 148, 153, 154, 156, 158, 162, 163, 165, 169, 177, 184, 189, 193, 197, 198, 199, 202, 204, 205, 206, 207
rune stones, 22, 24, 26
   Berezan stone, 110
   Haddeby stones, 59, 152, 188, 190
   Hovgård stone, 52, 98, 99
   Ingvar stones, 24
   Jelling stones, 44, 155, 182
   Sigtuna stones, 153
   Slesvig stone, 59, 189, 190, 195, 206
rural, 5, 13, 20, 21, 23, 24, 25, 29, 35, 41, 48, 50, 53, 74, 78, 82, 105, 122, 123, 125, 130, 131, 133, 137, 139, 145, 154, 162, 177, 196, 198, 202
Rus', 108, 109, 112, 115, 150, 151, 153, 159, 203

sagas, 30, 89, 96, 97, 110, 113, 132, 134, 183, 200
Saint Denis, 41
Sambians, 8, 115
Sanda, 129
Sarre-on-Thanet, 94
Saxons, 8, 59, 79, 107, 167, 187
   Saxon Wars, 13, 59, 167
Sayf al-Dawla, 160
Scandinavia, 1, 3, 4, 7, 14, 16, 24, 26, 34, 35, 38, 42, 46, 50, 59, 72, 80, 106, 112, 124, 131, 132, 134, 138, 139, 142, 144, 145, 149, 150, 151, 162, 165, 176, 191, 196, 197, 200, 201, 202, 204
   Scandinavian homelands, 3, 21
   Scandinavian periphery, 3
Scania, 21, 27, 28, 47, 110, 153, 155, 183
Schlei fjord, 54, 59, 64, 88, 89, 125, 167, 187, 188, 195, 206
Schleswig-Holstein, 5, 126
Schuby, 125

Schwansen, 125
Scythians, 8, 115
seasonality, 11, 12, 29, 36, 41, 48, 50, 55, 62, 63, 66, 67, 70, 71, 73, 74, 76, 77, 80, 83, 137, 147, 197, 198, 199, 207
seclusion, 26, 129, 197
security, legal, 96, 114, 154
Seehandelsplätze, 9
seigniorage, 126, 134, 207
Serkland, 24
settlement, 3, 4, 11, 12, 17, 20, 21, 23, 26, 28, 33, 53, 54, 59, 67, 69, 71, 72, 73, 74, 78, 85, 86, 120, 121, 122, 130, 137, 143, 145, 151, 160, 162, 165, 167, 171, 172, 173, 175, 178, 183, 191, 193
  agricultural settlement, 45
  farmstead, 22, 23, 24, 33, 35, 44, 72, 128, 131, 197
  hamlet, 22, 55, 131, 169
  urban settlement, 12, 15, 54, 137, 163
  village, 21, 23, 24, 28, 55, 100, 125, 128, 197
shifts, 3, 28, 80, 151, 156, 162, 164, 171, 175, 187, 188, 190, 191, 193, 195, 196
ships, 44, 52, 63, 64, 65, 89, 90, 93, 94, 96, 97, 109, 111, 153, 185, 193, 205
  shipbuilding, 62, 152, 154
Sigfrid and Halfdan, 107
Sigtrygg, 152, 190
Sigtuna, 4, 30, 50, 60, 98, 144, 153, 158, 160, 162, 172, 174, 175, 176, 177, 178, 181, 184, 205
Skiringssal, 36, 53, 55, 56, 76
Skäggesta, 143
Slavs, 8, 59, 61, 110, 115, 121, 126, 153, 154, 167, 191
  Great Slavic Revolt, 169
Slesvig, 4, 50, 61, 88, 89, 96, 98, 162, 164, 165, 168, 169, 178, 181, 183, 184, 187, 189, 191, 193, 195, 206, 208
Sliaswig. *See* Hedeby
Snorri Sturluson, 30, 39, 43, 75, 89, 110
society, 1, 5, 6, 15, 20, 21, 24, 25, 28, 29, 34, 42, 50, 53, 58, 74, 84, 114, 118, 119, 122, 123, 127, 129, 131, 132, 133, 154, 196, 197, 198, 199, 201, 207
Southampton. *See Hamwic*
special economic zones, 6, 135, 136, 137, 140, 169, 184, 186, 202, 203, 204, 205, 208

specialisation, 13, 16, 32, 90, 124, 128, 129, 152
Stamford, 137
Stamford Bridge, 1
standardisation, 13, 45, 165
Staraja Ladoga, 150
state formation, 1, 149, 155, 203
Stenkil, 52
Storebælt. *See* Great Belt
strangers. *See* foreigners
Strängnäs, 39
surplus, 19, 41, 42, 78, 79, 124, 127, 139, 202
Svealand, 30, 38, 60, 128, 158
Sven Forkbeard, 185, 194
Svend Estridsen, 165, 172, 182, 183, 184, 188, 189, 193, 194, 195, 206, 208
Svíþjóð. *See* Svealand
Sweden, 1, 11, 21, 24, 25, 26, 27, 29, 34, 38, 40, 43, 44, 60, 107, 108, 111, 113, 117, 120, 126, 127, 130, 151, 152, 155, 158, 162
swords, 25, 107, 140, 158, 159
  Ulfberht swords, 140
symbolism, 33, 35, 85, 87, 132, 166, 199
Syria, 115, 116
Säby, 129
Södermanland, 7, 24, 60, 128, 130
Södertälje, 7, 60

tariffs. *See* taxes
Tattershall Thorpe, 119
taxes, 7, 29, 34, 41, 43, 52, 66, 67, 78, 80, 83, 84, 87, 88, 89, 90, 92, 93, 94, 95, 96, 97, 99, 100, 101, 102, 103, 105, 106, 107, 108, 114, 117, 132, 133, 134, 135, 136, 192, 199, 200, 207
technology, 62, 129, 137, 138, 141, 202, 207
temple, pagan, 30, 31, 33, 49, 68
terminology, 9, 10, 13, 15, 20, 196
territories, 10, 108, 109, 135, 166, 167, 169
Theodoros of Tarsos, 67
Theophilus, 112
theory, 9, 11, 166
  systems theory, 147
Thietmar of Merseburg, 165
things. *See* assemblies
Thionville, 105
Þórður Kolbeinsson, 113
Thyra, 44
Tilleda, 49
time slices, 3, 147, 203

Tissø, 44, 45, 46, 48, 54, 56, 197
Toftegård, 28
Tolir, 52, 98, 99
tolls. *See* taxes
topography, 11, 22, 53, 59, 60, 61, 70, 82, 123, 129, 132, 172, 187, 198
towns, 1, 2, 3, 4, 8, 9, 10, 11, 12, 13, 15, 17, 19, 20, 25, 35, 36, 38, 50, 53, 54, 57, 59, 60, 63, 64, 66, 72, 74, 75, 76, 77, 80, 84, 87, 88, 93, 94, 95, 96, 98, 99, 101, 105, 108, 114, 115, 117, 120, 121, 122, 123, 124, 125, 126, 128, 129, 130, 132, 133, 137, 138, 141, 148, 152, 154, 158, 159, 160, 163, 164, 166, 168, 169, 171, 172, 175, 176, 177, 178, 179, 181, 182, 184, 185, 186, 187, 188, 189, 191, 193, 198, 199, 201, 203, 204, 205, 207, 208
  Christian towns, 20, 158, 165, 176
  church towns, 29
  early towns, 11, 13, 14, 50, 53, 58, 124, 140, 148, 155
  medieval towns, 2, 5, 9, 10, 11, 19, 20, 162, 196, 208
  mushroom towns, 15
  proto-towns, 11, 13, 14, 140
  town plots, 10, 69, 70, 71, 73, 74, 75, 76, 77, 80, 172, 173, 174, 176, 185, 205
  Viking-age towns, 1, 2, 3, 5, 6, 8, 15, 20, 21, 25, 29, 34, 43, 50, 51, 53, 57, 61, 63, 66, 74, 82, 95, 96, 97, 98, 103, 105, 114, 117, 119, 121, 123, 129, 130, 131, 132, 133, 134, 136, 140, 142, 146, 147, 148, 152, 154, 155, 163, 165, 169, 171, 177, 196, 198, 199, 200, 201, 202, 203, 204, 207, 208
trade, 1, 2, 3, 7, 8, 12, 13, 16, 17, 19, 20, 34, 36, 40, 42, 58, 60, 65, 69, 74, 77, 79, 80, 83, 93, 94, 101, 105, 118, 124, 128, 131, 132, 133, 134, 136, 138, 140, 147, 148, 150, 151, 153, 154, 160, 162, 163, 175, 177, 191, 192, 198, 202, 203, 207
  barter trade, 14
  down-the-line trade, 128
  international trade, 42, 105, 118, 135, 142, 163, 207
  long-distance trade, 2, 9, 11, 16, 17, 18, 50, 63, 65, 69, 84, 94, 108, 114, 124, 126, 138, 139, 141, 163, 165, 171, 198, 199, 202, 207
  maritime trade, 9, 20, 196

  market trade, 39, 41, 43, 50, 126, 131
traders. *See* merchants
trading places, 9, 10, 12, 13, 17, 20, 61, 62, 63, 64, 75, 76, 78, 80, 81, 82, 84, 87, 95, 96, 113, 114, 118, 132, 148, 163, 171, 199, 200, 203
  second-level trading places, 13, 149, 150, 154, 203
traditions, 26, 28, 34, 92, 111, 120, 196
traffic, 17, 63, 89, 92, 156
transformation, 3, 4, 15, 20, 75, 84, 148, 175, 176, 185, 187, 189, 199, 205, 206, 208
transport, 39, 59, 60, 62, 92, 94, 132
  transport geography, 7
  transport zones, 19, 59, 198
treadle looms, 143, 144, 203
treaties, 91, 92, 109, 115, 149, 182, 194, 195
Trelleborg, 149
Trondheim, 95, 162
Truso, 18, 61, 87, 110, 149, 150, 153
typology, 12, 145

Ukraine, 110
underdevelopment, 137, 138
Unni of Hamburg-Bremen, 156, 157
Uppland, 7, 24, 29, 38, 60, 128, 129, 142
Uppsala. *See* Östra Aros
Uppåkra, 33, 150
urbanisation, 1, 3, 6, 8, 12, 13, 19, 62, 75, 82, 87, 140, 147, 193, 196, 198, 207
  second wave of urbanisation, 162, 187, 189, 191, 204, 206
urbanism, 2, 9, 15, 17, 18, 140, 148, 196
urbanity, 9, 19, 193, 196
urbs, 7, 168, 169

Valdemar II of Denmark, 36
Valsta, 129
Varangians, 89, 109, 112, 113, 115, 153
Vendel, 7, 60
Vendel period. *See* Merovingian period
Verdun, 149
Vestfold, 36, 53, 61
via regia, 43
Viborg, 59, 162, 194, 195
vicus, 7, 9, 37, 99, 117, 199
Viken, 36, 155
Viking world, 3, 20, 21, 25, 29, 62, 123, 131, 146, 196, 197, 202
violence, 108, 158, 159, 160, 162

Visby, 66
Vitruvius, 88
Vladimir the Great, 101, 160
Vorbasse, 23, 28, 45
Värend, 27
Västmanland, 24, 60, 128

Wadi El Natrun, 141
Walcheren, 68
water level, changes, 4
water mills, 145, 146, 203
waterways, 7, 18, 35, 64, 133, 138, 153, 198
  Fyrisleden, 7, 60
wealth, 8, 39, 128, 134, 156, 160, 207
Wends. *See* Slavs
Wessex, 65, 118

Western Europe, 8, 14, 129, 151
Westphalia, 142
wiks, 12, 42, 67, 84, 117
Wilfrid of York, 67
Winanceastre. *See Winchester*
Winchester, 102, 192
workshops, 22, 32, 48, 130, 140, 173, 174, 175, 202, 205
Worms, 107
Wulfhere of Mercia, 80
Wulfhild of Norway, 184
Wulfstan, 27, 61, 110, 153, 203

Yngvar the Fartraveller, 24
York, 85, 98, 137, 144, 148

Zealand, 28, 29, 44, 183